Centenary Essays on Alfred Marshall

Centenary Essays
on Alfred Marshall

edited by
JOHN K. WHITAKER

A Royal Economic Society Publication

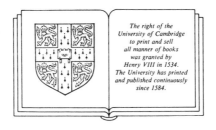

The right of the
University of Cambridge
to print and sell
all manner of books
was granted by
Henry VIII in 1534.
The University has printed
and published continuously
since 1584.

CAMBRIDGE UNIVERSITY PRESS
Cambridge
New York   Port Chester   Melbourne   Sydney

Published by the Press Syndicate of the University of Cambridge
The Pitt Building, Trumpington Street, Cambridge CB2 1RP
40 West 20th Street, New York, NY 10011, USA
10 Stamford Road, Oakleigh, Melbourne 3166, Australia

First published 1990

Printed in the United States of America

Library of Congress Cataloging-in-Publication Data
Centenary essays on Alfred Marshall / edited by John K. Whitaker.
p. cm.
"A Royal Economic Society publication."
ISBN 0–521–38133–9 HB
1. Marshall, Alfred, 1842–1924. 2. Neoclassical school of
economics. I. Whitaker, John K. (John King) II. Royal Economic
Society (Great Britain)
HB103.M3C44 1990
650.1'4–dc20   89–48879
                                                     CIP

British Library Cataloguing in Publication Data
Centenary essays on Alfred Marshall. – (A Royal Economic
Society publication)
1. Economics. Theories of Marshall, Alfred, 1842–1924
I. Whitaker, John K. II. Series
330.1

ISBN 0–521–38133–9 hardback

Contents

Notes on Contributors

CHRISTOPHER BLISS is Nuffield Reader in International Economics at the University of Oxford and a Fellow of Nuffield College, Oxford. He previously taught at Cambridge and Essex Universities, and has written widely on capital and growth theory, economic development, and international economics.

JOHN S. CHIPMAN is Regents' Professor of Economics at the University of Minnesota, Minneapolis–St. Paul. He is a specialist in international economics and microeconomic theory, noted for his command of the history of economic theory.

DAVID A. COLLARD is Professor of Economics at the University of Bath, having previously taught at University College Cardiff and the University of Bristol. His writings have centred on public economics and the history of economics.

JOHN CREEDY is Professor of Economics at the University of Melbourne, Australia, and has previously taught at the Universities of Reading and Durham, England. He has written extensively on questions of income distribution and the history of economic theory.

A. K. DASGUPTA was formerly Professor of Economics at the Jawaharlal Nehru University, New Delhi. One of India's leading economists, he has written widely on Indian economic problems and the history of economics.

DAVID E. W. LAIDLER is Professor of Economics at the University of Western Ontario, London, Canada, and taught previously at the Universities of Essex and Manchester, England. He is a leading authority on monetary economics and its history.

BRIAN J. LOASBY is Emeritus and Honorary Professor of Management Economics at the University of Stirling and has also taught at the University of Bristol. His writings have focussed on the economics of organisations.

ROBIN C. O. MATTHEWS is Professor of Political Economy at the University of Cambridge and Master of Clare College, Cambridge. He has also held the Drummond Professorship in Oxford University and headed Britain's Social Science Research Council. His wide-ranging writings have covered economic history, economic growth, and the economics of institutions.

PETER NEWMAN is Professor of Economics at the Johns Hopkins University, Baltimore, Maryland. He taught previously at the University of the West Indies and the University of Michigan. His wide-ranging interests in economic theory and its history are revealed in both his writings and his recent editorial work for *The New Palgrave*. He has also written on problems of economic development.

DENIS P. O'BRIEN is Professor of Economics at the University of Durham and taught previously at the Queen's University, Belfast, Northern Ireland. An expert on Classical economics, he has written extensively on the history of economics and on industrial organisation.

GEORGE J. STIGLER is director of the Center for the Study of the Economy and the State at the University of Chicago, where he was formerly Walgreen Professor of American Institutions. He has also taught at Iowa State University, the University of Minnesota, and Brown and Columbia Universities. Recipient of the Nobel Memorial Prize in Economics for 1982, he is a leading scholar in the areas of industrial organisation, regulation, and the history of economics.

JOHN K. WHITAKER is McIntire Professor of Economics at the University of Virginia, Charlottesville, and taught previously at the University of Bristol. He has written in the areas of economic theory and the history of economics, focussing in the latter on the work of Alfred Marshall.

Introduction

The year 1990 marks the centennial of one of the classics of economic literature: the *Principles of Economics* by Alfred Marshall (1842–1924), founder of the Cambridge School of Economics. The first edition of this work was published to immediate acclaim by Macmillan and Company in July 1890. It soon established itself as the bible of British economics, a role it monopolized until well into the present century. Marshall's *opus magnum* remains an apparently inexhaustible seam of insights and puzzles, still the focus of considerable, indeed increasing, scholarly enquiry and debate.

To mark this centennial, the Royal Economic Society has commissioned the present collection of original essays dealing with various aspects of Marshall's life and thought. With the hope of making the volume of interest to a wide audience of economists and other social scientists, and not just to historians of economics, the essays include broad evaluations of Marshall's work, its impact, and its lessons for today's economics as well as contributions of a more specialised interpretive or biographical character.

Three broad principles underlay the design.

1 The work should not be written entirely by Marshall specialists for Marshall specialists.

2 Consideration should not be restricted to the *Principles*, but should include other aspects of Marshall's thought, one reason for this being that the *Principles* was only the first part of

a never-completed larger work intended to cover additionally labour, money, international trade, industrial organisation, and so forth. (See Chapter 8.)

3   Authors should not have a particular topic or framework imposed upon them but should have free rein in refining and handling their topics, choose their own vantage points, and provide a personal reaction rather than a synthesis of others' views.

A consequence of this last goal is that the essays do not provide a comprehensive, impartial, and "definitive" coverage of the sort that might be looked for in a large-scale monograph. Nevertheless, the essays do cover collectively the salient features of Marshall's work and fall naturally into broad groupings. The general overview of Marshall's achievement provided by Stigler (Chapter 1) is supplemented by the assessments of Marshall's work in the fields of labour, money, international trade, and industrial organisation by Matthews, Laidler, Creedy, and Loasby, respectively (Chapters 2 through 5). The next two chapters place Marshall in relation to British economics. O'Brien (Chapter 6) considers Marshall's ties to the antecedent British Classical School of Economics, whereas Collard (Chapter 7) assesses the post-Marshallian Cambridge School. My own essay (Chapter 8) stands rather alone, taking up the essentially biographical question of Marshall's failure to complete the *Principles* along the lines he had originally envisaged. The final four chapters deal with various facets of the economics of the *Principles:* capital theory (Bliss, Chapter 9), the time-period analysis (Dasgupta, Chapter 10), barter (Newman, Chapter 11), and consumer's surplus (Chipman, Chapter 12). Collectively, the chapters provide many novel evaluations and fresh insights.

My most important debt is to my fellow authors for their thoughtful and stimulating contributions, provided efficiently and enthusiastically. I also owe an important debt of thanks to Professor Donald Winch, who has acted for the Royal Economic Society and been both instigator and invaluable advisor.

                                                        John K. Whitaker

List of Abbreviated Titles

To facilitate citations of Marshall's main works, the following abbreviated titles for them are adopted throughout this volume. These works are consequently omitted from the bibliography appended to each chapter.

Principles   Alfred Marshall, *Principles of Economics*. London: Macmillan. Unless the contrary is expressly indicated, reference is to the 8th edition, 1920. (Earlier editions appeared in 1890, 1891, 1895, 1898, 1907, 1910, 1916. The first five bore the subtitle *Volume One,* replaced by *An Introductory Volume* in the 6th, 7th, and 8th editions.)

Variorum   Volume 2 of Claude W. Guillebaud (editor), *Alfred Marshall's Principles of Economics: Ninth (Variorum) Edition*. London: Macmillan, 1961, for the Royal Economic Society. This reproduces notes, variant passages, and supplementary material for the various editions of *Principles*. (Volume 1 of Guillebaud's work is a reprint of the 8th edition of *Principles*.)

IT   Alfred Marshall, *Industry and Trade*. London: Macmillan. The four editions appeared in 1919, 1919, 1920, 1923; variations between editions were slight.

MCC   Alfred Marshall, *Money Credit and Commerce*. London: Macmillan, 1923.

Memorials Arthur C. Pigou (editor), *Memorials of Alfred Marshall.* London: Macmillan, 1925, for the Royal Economic Society. Reproduces many of Marshall's occasional pieces, as well as selected letters and memoirs by students and colleagues.

OP John M. Keynes (editor), *Official Papers by Alfred Marshall.* London: Macmillan, 1926, for the Royal Economic Society. Reproduces Marshall's contributions to governmental enquiries.

EEW John K. Whitaker (editor), *Early Economic Writings of Alfred Marshall, 1867–1890.* London: Macmillan, 1975, for the Royal Economic Society. Reproduces Marshall's early manuscripts. The two volumes are cited as *EEW* 1 and *EEW* 2, respectively.

1

The Place of Marshall's Principles *in the Development of Economics*

GEORGE J. STIGLER

Let us begin by reflecting upon the task of this essay: the determination of how Alfred Marshall influenced the course of economics. The task is not simply to ascertain which theories Marshall invented, for others may have invented them first or have been more successful in their development and dissemination. Thus, although Marshall did not contribute utility theory to economics, he was not prepared to acknowledge his heavy indebtedness in this area to Jevons or Walras.[1] The task is to determine how the prevailing science of economics in the first quarter of the twentieth century was different because of his work.

That is an extraordinarily exacting criterion of scientific importance. No doubt every significant economist has had (perhaps by definition) some influence upon the direction and pace of the profession's prevailing beliefs. We owe to Mill such specific doctrines as the theory of the value of joint products produced in fixed proportions. We owe to Böhm-Bawerk – among other things – an extra decade or so of the currency of the idea that utility is the sole or dominant source or determinant of the value of goods. We owe to Henry Sidgwick a sketch of market failures that influenced Pigou's calculus of social welfare. But of Marshall we are asking more: Not how did he influence this disciple or that adversary, but how did he change the course of economics? To ask this question seri-

I wish to thank David Laidler and John Whitaker for helpful comments.

1. See the discussion in *EEW*, 1, pp. 37–52. Whitaker gives what I would describe as the minimum defensible estimate of the possibility of Marshall's independent discovery of utility theory.

ously of a scientist is already a compliment to him; to answer it with an enumeration of major changes in the science due to him is to admit him to the pantheon.

I Some Common, Mistaken Claims

I shall begin, perhaps perversely, by analyzing some claims often made in Marshall's behalf which I believe to be mistaken. A consideration of these mistaken attributions serves to clarify the nature of genuine contributions. I begin with three items in the list of Marshall's contributions that Keynes presented in his famous obituary essay (1924),[2] and then turn to claims made by Schumpeter and Marshall himself.

(1)   Marshall is held to have resolved the dispute between the Austrians and Jevons, who urged the primacy of utility in setting values, and the Classical economists, who had asserted the primacy of cost of production. He is credited with the famous resolution that the two forces were coordinate and indispensable, and in the process employed the influential metaphor about the two blades of a scissor: "We might as reasonably dispute whether it is the upper or the under blade of a pair of scissors that cuts a piece of paper, as whether value is governed by utility or cost of production."[3]

Böhm-Bawerk in his defense of utility as the ultimate source of value dismissed money costs of production because they owe their value to the value of the goods and services which production provides. He allowed a role to disutility in the few services produced and directly sold by a labourer and proposed that "the ten parts of that blade which represents demand consisted entirely of *utility*, while of the blade which represents the 'costs,' nine parts are utility and only one part disutility" (Böhm-Bawerk, 1894, p. 52; italics in original). Böhm-Bawerk asserted that the determination of values by a system of simultaneous equations "has nothing to do" with causality (1959, pp. 190–1).

2. The assistance of Edgeworth in completing the list was acknowledged: *Memorials*, p. 41.
3. *Principles*, p. 348; differently phrased in the first edition (p. 535). Rather more explicit than a metaphor is Marshall's comment: "while they [Ricardo and Mill] admitted that cost of production could have no effect upon exchange value, if it could have none upon the amount which producers brought forward for sale; their doctrines imply . . . that the utility of a commodity could have no effect upon its exchange value, if it could have none on the amount which purchasers took off the market" (*Principles*, ed. 1, p. 533).

The Austrian thesis was, of course, mistaken; the proper resolution of the dispute had already been made in Walras' equations of 1877. The essential point is that there could be no longevity to a doctrine of unilateral determination of the prices of goods. If Marshall had never lived, the roles of supply and demand (or rather wants, resources and technology) in the mutual determination of values would have been generally acknowledged in early-twentieth-century economics.

(2)   The concept of elasticity was, Keynes asserted, a great service to "terminology and apparatus to aid thought" (1924, p. 45). It is true that Marshall invented the concept (probably with assistance from Cournot and conceivably even from Whewell), but it is simply devoid of substantive economic significance. Elasticities sometimes offer elegant formulations of relationships and have provided an unlimited number of examination questions in elementary economics. That is all.

(3)   The theory of monopoly is also on Keynes's list. The theory does not go far in Marshall's hands and it is not assisted by the use of curves of average revenue and average cost with the ancillary apparatus of rectangular hyperbolas. Surely Edgeworth and Walras and Bowley and rediscovered Cournot were doing more than Marshall with the formal theory of monopoly.

(4)   Schumpeter presented a curious and even elusive appraisal of Marshall. He referred to some of Marshall's fundamental contributions as "handy tools" (1941, p. 241) and then turned around and made extravagant claims for Marshall as the father of econometrics:

> Marshall's was one of the strongest influences in the emergence of modern econometrics. Many as are the points in which the *Principles* resemble the *Wealth of Nations*, there is one in which the former is definitely superior to the latter, if, eliminating time, we reduce both to the common denominator of subjective, time-conditioned performance. Adam Smith judiciously assembled and developed whatever he thought most worth while in the thought of his own and of the preceding epoch. But he did nothing to develop one of the most significant of the achievements within his reach, the "Political Arithmetick" of the seventeenth century, whereas Marshall who, proportions guarded, had really less to go upon firmly led the way toward, and prepared the ground for, an economic science that would be not

only quantitative but numerical. The importance of this cannot be overestimated. Economics will never either have or merit any prestige until it can figure out results.

How clearly Marshall realized this can be seen from his address on "The Old Generation of Economists and the New" (1897). But we owe him much more than a program; we owe him a definite approach. All we have to do in order to satisfy ourselves of this, is to glance once more at what I have described as his "handy tools." They are all of them eminently operational in the statistical sense. . . . we do not appreciate them fully until we realize that, whatever else they may be, they are first of all methods of measurement – *devices to facilitate numerical measurement* – and parts of a general apparatus that aims at statistical measurement. . . .

For instance, it is obviously no coincidence that those endeavors were, on a large scale, first directed toward the derivation of statistical demand curves: Marshall's theory of demand had provided an acceptable basis.[4]

A showing that Marshall was the parent of the quantification of economic relationships would be enough to make him the author of the most important single development in economics in the twentieth century. It is difficult to believe that the claim is justified. Certainly the pioneer econometricians such as Marcel Lenoir and Henry Moore neither displayed nor acknowledged any debt to Marshall's work, and it is difficult to find a reason why they should have.[5] The demand curves they calculated – price-quantity relationships for one commodity – were far removed from the complex discussions of Marshall or, for that matter, Walras.

(5)   Marshall himself placed immense emphasis upon his formulation of the theory of general equilibrium: "My whole life has been and will be

---

4. Schumpeter, 1941, p. 247.
5. See my "The Early History of Empirical Studies of Consumer Behavior", reprinted in Stigler, 1965. Marshall's treatment of Moore's *Laws of Wages* in a letter (dated June 6, 1912) to Moore revealed hostility to econometric studies (ibid., pp. 352–3): "I will be frank. I have had your book on Laws of Wages in a prominent place near my writing chair ever since it arrived, intending to read it when opportunity came. It has not come: and I fear it never will come. For what dips I have made into the book made me believe that it proceeds on lines which I deliberately decided not to follow many years ago; even before mathematics had ceased to be a familiar language to me. My reasons for it are mainly two. (1) No important economic chain of events seems to [*sic*] likely to be associated with any one cause so predominantly that a study of the concomitant variation of the two can be made as well by mathematics, as by a comparison of a curve representing those two elements with a large number of other curves representing other operative causes: the "caeteris paribus" clause – though formally adequate seems to me impracticable. (2) Nearly a half of the whole operative economic causes have refused as yet to be tabulated statistically."

given to presenting in a realistic form as much as I can of my [mathematical] Note XXI".[6] There is no reason to question his claim to independent discovery of the general equilibrium framework, but there is also no reason to credit him with a realistic development of the equations of general equilibrium. Realism and general equilibrium theory have never joined hands, and Marshall could not bring himself to make extensive elaborations of the theory of general equilibrium as purely formal exercises. However, the members of the Lausanne School (in particular Walras and Pareto) considered Marshall the premier partial equilibrium economist of the world, and they were right.

II Marshall's Major Influences on Economic Analysis

We consider now the basic influences that Marshall exerted upon the evolution of economic analysis. In each case he introduced a subject which otherwise would probably have come considerably later and in a different form.

(1) First and foremost, Marshall made time itself a major factor in the theory of value. Where there had previously been scraps of recognition of the roles of time in price determination, it now became a central force and a fundamental basis for classification.

More important, the roles of time were made manageable and instructive by a set of empirical hypotheses:

(*a*) Demand curves were held to be little changed by the passage of time: "those demands which show high elasticity in the long run, show a high elasticity almost at once" (*Principles*, p. 456). Modern economists will argue that this proposition is dubious, but it was accepted fully for a long time and is often accepted today.

(*b*) When Marshall partitions operational time into (i) market periods (when supply is given), (ii) periods when some productive factors are fixed in supply and (iii) periods in which all production factors are variable in supply, he makes the following assumption: In any period, price is determined by the forces primarily operative in that period. Thus in the short run normal period, the determinants of price in the market period (that is, demand fluctuations and the allocation of fixed supplies over a

---

6. *Memorials*, p. 417. Note XXI (XX in the first edition) ended with the Walrasian incantation: "Thus however complex the problem may become, we can see that it is theoretically determinate because the number of unknowns is always exactly equal to the number of the equations we obtain" *Principles* (1st ed., p. 746).

crop year) cancel out or become negligible. The determinants of long run normal price (plant construction or replacement, entry and exit of firms) operate so slowly that they also leave little imprint upon short-run normal price. Similarly, in long run normal periods the effects of short-run normal fluctuations in prices and outputs are negligible, and in the market period investment and production play no significant role.

This assumption of separability of periods made the role of time a manageable component of the theory of value. An elementary dynamics became a part of the standard theory without requiring the complex methodology necessary to deal with interdependent periods. The great Viner article indicates by its date (1931) that this apparatus continued to be a dominant paradigm well into the twentieth century, and of course it is still recognizably present. The separability, we should note, was possible only under conditions of competition: A monopolist could not sensibly ignore the effect of present decisions upon future demands.

Marshall developed the doctrine of quasi-rents as the distributive complement of the short run inelasticity of supply of some factors of production. The fertility of time in economic theory was increased by this extension, which eventually contributed to the theory of investment.

Keynes was much influenced by Marshall's period analysis in the *General Theory*. We may quote Leijonhufvud: "This device [short and long run period analysis] was not Keynes' invention. Marshall had made much use of it, and in this aspect of his method as in many others, Keynes was very Marshallian".[7]

(2)   The doctrine of external and internal economies was a major Marshallian contribution. The classification permitted an analytical reconciliation of competition and increasing returns, and thus repaired a major gap in classical price theory. Besides enriching the theories of production and price, the distinction played a major role in welfare economics: for example, it was absolutely central to Pigou's *Wealth and Welfare* (1912) and *The Economics of Welfare* (1920 and later).

Because the point is often overlooked,[8] it is desirable to point out that Marshall did not make Pigou's famous mistake of proposing a tax on increasing cost industries.[9] Consider the following passage:

7. Leijonhufvud, 1968, p. 50 et seq.
8. See, for example, Samuelson: 1967, pp. 112–13.
9. Pigou himself presents a puzzle. Although *Wealth and Welfare* (1912) was dedicated to Marshall, and the work is strewn with deferential references to his teacher, Pigou never mentioned Marshall in the critical chapter, "Divergences of Marginal Social Net Product and Marginal Private Net Product" (especially pp. 176–7), where the calculus of externalities is deployed.

§6. One simple plan would be the levying of a tax by the community on their own incomes, or on the production of goods which obey the law of diminishing return, and devoting the tax to a bounty on the production of those goods with regard to which the law of increasing return acts sharply. But before deciding on such a course they would have to take account of considerations, which are not within the scope of the general theory now before us, but are yet of great practical importance. They would have to reckon up the direct and indirect costs of collecting a tax and administering a bounty; the difficulty of securing that the burdens of the tax and the benefits of the bounty were equitably distributed; the openings for fraud and corruption; and the danger that in the trade which had got a bounty and in other trades which hoped to get one, people would divert their energies from managing their own businesses to managing those persons who control the bounties.

Besides these semi-ethical questions there will arise others of a strictly economic nature, relating to the effects which any particular tax or bounty may exert on the interests of landlords, urban or agricultural, who own land adapted for the production of the commodity in question. These are questions which must not be overlooked; but they differ so much in their detail that they cannot fitly be discussed here.[10]

In a footnote attached to this passage Marshall analyses the effects of a tax on agricultural produce and shows that once producers' rents are included, the tax yields less than the sum of the losses of producer and consumer surplus.

Schumpeter listed the doctrine of external economies as one of Marshall's handy tools. Indeed it is, like such handy tools as adverbs and logarithms.

(3)   G. F. Shove credits Marshall with the prominence he gave to the theory of the firm (Shove, 1942, pp. 304–5). This is a valid claim but it deserves some interpretation. Marshall was not interested in the *individual* firm, and his concept of the representative firm was explicitly designed to get away from the complications which arise when one studies a variety (in fact a frequency distribution) of individual firms. The representative firm, to recall, was an average of the individual firms in an industry, average in size, in age, in shares of external and internal economies, in skill of management. Clearly such a firm is studied because it is the very prototype of the industry and its behaviour will be that of the industry.

The introduction of the representative firm, then, is directed not to the

10.   Marshall, *Principles,* pp. 472–3 (1st ed., p. 452).

firm's individual differentia but to the role it plays as a decision unit in decentralized industries. It is at the level of the firm that resources are engaged and combined subject to "the principle of substitution." The very purpose of the study of the firm is to deduce from its behaviour the properties of industry demands for inputs and supplies of outputs. It cannot be doubted that Marshall was the first economist to make the analysis of the individual firm an integral part of his theory of production and pricing. He had useful predecessors such as Cournot, but recall that Cournot did not address problems such as the entry or exit of firms from an industry or the implications of falling marginal costs.[11]

This may be a suitable point at which to enter a dissent from a central theme of Shove's brilliant paper – the theme that the *Principles* is largely explicable as the outcome of Marshall's early translation of "Mill's version of Ricardo's or Smith's doctrines into mathematics". Marshall's contributions to economics were in no sense natural consequences of emending Mill's work, and that is best shown by comparing him with Henry Sidgwick.

Sidgwick was indeed primarily a commentator upon Mill in his *Principles of Political Economy* (1883). This intelligent, wide-ranging work was strictly backward-looking. Its task was to make minor improvements upon Mill's *Principles*. A telling evidence of its orientation is that Sidgwick (1883, pp. 325–6) shared Mill's lurking fear of a contemporary Malthusian population threat.

(4)   Marshall's introduction of and emphasis upon consumer surplus was a significant step in the development of welfare economics. The introduction (I do not say discovery, since he knew Dupuit's work) was greeted with a good deal of controversy, and treated thereafter with a good deal of neglect. His nephew, Claude W. Guillebaud, has recounted Marshall's later feelings:

> He [Marshall] told me on one occasion that a major disappointment
> in his life was the recognition, which gradually forced itself on him,
> that his concept of consumer's surplus was devoid of important prac-

---

11.   It should be said in Cournot's defence, however, that he never made the blunder of which Marshall accused him, of believing that falling marginal costs were compatible with competition. Compare *Principles*, p. 459n (1st ed., pp. 485n–6n), with Cournot's explicit recognition of the problem, "It is, moreover, plain under the hypothesis of unlimited competition, and where, at the same time, the function [marginal cost] should be a decreasing one, that nothing would limit the production of the article" (Cournot, 1927, p. 91).

tical application, because it was not capable of being quantified in a meaningful way.[12]

The major credit for the revival of the concept belongs to J. R. Hicks, with his famous articles on the subject (1941, 1944).

Consumer surplus is now widely used, for example in environmental and recreational studies. In the litigation over the Cadiz oil spill in 1978, France based vast claims on the loss of consumer surplus of tourists (but without success). Marshall's role in this literature is surely prominent though long delayed in fruition.

(5) Finally, Marshall contributed a variety of other advances which had a lasting effect upon economic doctrine. These advances are perhaps minor in scope but add up to a significant part of Marshall's legacy.

Consider the chapters (Book VI, Chapters 4–5) in which he analyses the differences in compensation of labourers and the content of the proposition that it is the "net advantages" of different occupations that are equalized by competition. In reviewing the first edition of the *Principles,* Edgeworth (1890, p. 165) offered the following challenge:

> We recommend the economist who wishes to test this judgment [on Marshall's performance] to write out, before reading the latter part of the *Principles of Economics,* what he himself has to say in answer to questions like the following: What are the peculiarities in the action of demand and supply which determine the wages of the labourer, or the profits of the employer? Then let him compare the suggestions of his own memory and meditation with our author's original and exhaustive treatment of the subject. He must be a very great, or a very small, man who, in making this comparison, does not recognize his superior.

The correct inference is that Marshall contributed significantly to what has become the theory of human capital.

Marshall's development of the Cambridge theory of monetary economics, including the demand for money, was presented primarily in testimony before Royal Commissions and in an oral tradition. Keynes discussed this work in some detail (1924, pp. 27–33) and concluded:

> There is no part of Economics where Marshall's originality and priority of thought are more marked than here, or where his superiority of insight and knowledge over his contemporaries was greater. There is

12. Guillebaud, 1971, p. 6.

Table 1.1. Cambridge Economists Graduated
from 1908 to 1930

E. H. Dalton	F. W. Paish
H. D. Dickinson	D. H. Robertson
M. H. Dobb	H. M. Robertson
R. F. Kahn	E. A. G. Robinson
H. D. Henderson	J. Robinson
F. Lavington	G. F. Shove
J. E. Meade	

Chief source: Mark Blaug. *Who's Who in Economics*
(2d ed.). Cambridge: MIT Press, 1986.

hardly any leading feature in the modern Theory of Money which
was not known to Marshall forty years ago.[13]

We would not credit this work with great influence if it had not strongly
influenced his disciples.

III The Teacher

When Marshall came back to Cambridge in 1885, he transformed Fawcett's trickle of popularization into the premier fountain of economics in
the English-speaking world. Indeed, judged by the next half-century, he
turned Cambridge into the premier fountain of economics in the entire
world.

Marshall's direct students at Cambridge include A. C. Pigou, his successor to the chair; J. M. Keynes, A. L. Bowley, S. J. Chapman, J. H. Clapham, H. H. Cunynghame, C. R. Fay, and D. H. Macgregor. Then followed a second generation of whom the more prominent are listed in
Table 1.1.

The names of Dobb and Dalton are enough to demonstrate that all
products of Cambridge economics did not share Marshall's views on
public policy. In general, however, Marshallian value theory was accepted by these Cambridge economists even when they eventually followed different paths in monetary and macroeconomic theory. One could
add some Cambridge noneconomists who came under Marshall's influ-

13. Keynes, 1924, p. 27.

ence, such as A. W. Flux and C. P. Sanger, both of whom wrote on mathematical economics.

For several decades, moreover, no other influential school of economists emerged in Great Britain. Oxford, under Edgeworth, was explicitly Marshallian in its economics after the abortive efforts to form a rival economic school (see Kadish, 1982, and Koot, 1987). Oxford produced some major economists in the 1920s (notably Harrod and Hicks) but no school comparable to that in Cambridge.

The London School of Economics gradually became the second major centre of economics in England. Edwin Cannan was the premier economist at the School until his retirement in 1926. In the area of economic theory he was primarily an historian, and he never developed a system which could serve as an alternative to Marshall's. He found Marshall as enjoyable a target for his acerbity as Ricardo and Malthus, but he had no influence on prevailing economic thought. In the years that followed, first Lionel Robbins and then F. Hayek created the exciting intellectual centre that the London School became in the nineteen-thirties (see O'Brien, 1988). At first Austrian economics, and then increasingly the general equilibrium theory, came to dominate at the School. One can find clear traces of Marshall in various works of J. R. Hicks (for example, in *The Theory of Wages* and the articles on consumer surplus), but it is evident from Hicks's own accounts that he owed little to Marshall,[14] and much the same could be said of Kaldor and Lerner.

Marshall was so clearly the dominant as to be almost the exclusive influence on British economics in the first quarter of this century, and only the London School was an important independent centre in the second quarter of the century. Great Britain did not yield up the leadership in economics until after World War II. Then the American economists seized the leadership, perhaps inevitably because of their relatively great numbers but also because they were much more receptive towards the major new development, the quantification of economics. Leading American economists of the first third of this century (Knight, Viner, and Taussig are examples), however, continued to be essentially Marshallian in their microeconomics.

IV Conclusion

Although I have not even touched upon many of Marshall's contributions to international trade and money (discussed in other essays in this vol-

14. See accounts in Hicks, 1982, pp. 3–10 and Hicks, 1983, pp. 355–64, as well as the addendum to Hicks, 1963, pp. 305–15.

ume), I hope that a strong case has been made for Marshall's preeminence in the history of our science. His influence on the development of value theory was wide and lasting.

One should reckon among a scholar's achievements not only what he wrought but also what he prevented. I believe that Marshall by his towering prestige delayed the coming of age of abstract formalism of the Lausanne tradition by at least a generation, and with the aid of his premier student, Keynes, by possibly two generations. Marshall insisted that the primary task of economics was the explanation of observable economic phenomena, and displayed impatience with theorizing which was not closely oriented to that task. Although a majority of later economic theorists would deny the wisdom of Marshall's position, and attribute to it the disappearance of his *Principles* from contemporary literature, the fact of his influence cannot be denied.

At the time of Marshall's death, Keynes wrote that "As a scientist he was, within his own field, the greatest in the world for a hundred years" (Keynes, 1924, p. 12). Viewing Marshall with the increased objectivity that comes from the passage of 65 years and the absence of filial obligations, I find this judgment as valid today as it was in 1924.

References

Böhm-Bawerk, E. von (1894). "The Ultimate Standard of Value", *Annals of the American Academy* 5:149–208.

(1959). *Capital and Interest,* III. South Holland, Ill.: Libertarian Press. First published in German 1889.

Cournot, A.-A. (1927). *Mathematical Principles of the Theory of Wealth.* N. T. Bacon, trans. New York: Macmillan. First published in French 1838.

Edgeworth, F. Y. (1890). "Review of Marshall's *Principles*", *Academy* (August 30):165–6.

Guillebaud, C. W. (1971). "Some Personal Reminiscences of Alfred Marshall", *History of Political Economy* 3:1–8.

Hicks, J. R. (1941). "The Rehabilitation of Consumers' Surplus", *Review of Economic Studies* 8:108–16.

(1943). "The Four Consumer's Surpluses", *Review of Economic Studies* 11:31–41.

(1963). *Theory of Wages,* 2d ed. London: Macmillan. First published in 1932.

(1982). *Money, Interest and Wages.* Cambridge, Mass.: Harvard University Press.

(1983). *Classics and Moderns.* Cambridge, Mass.: Harvard University Press.

Kadish, A. (1982). *The Oxford Economists in the Late Nineteenth Century.* Oxford: Clarendon.

Keynes, J. M. (1924). "Alfred Marshall, 1842–1924," *Economic Journal* 34:311–72. Reprinted in *Memorials,* pp. 1–65. Page references are to the latter version.

Koot, J. M. (1987). *English Historical Economics, 1870–1926.* Cambridge: Cambridge University Press.

Leijonhufvud, A. (1968). *On Keynesian Economics and the Economics of Keynes.* New York: Oxford University Press.

O'Brien, D. P. (1988). *Lionel Robbins.* New York: St. Martins.

Pigou, A. C. (1912). *Wealth and Welfare.* London: Macmillan.

  (1920). *The Economics of Welfare.* London: Macmillan.

Samuelson, P. A. (1967). "The Monopolistic Competition Revolution". In R. E. Kuenne (ed.), *Monopolistic Competition Theory: Studies in Impact.* New York: Wiley.

Schumpeter, J. A. (1941). "Alfred Marshall's *Principles:* A Semi-Centennial Appraisal," *American Economic Review* 31:236–48.

Shove, G. F. (1942). "The Place of Marshall's *Principles* in the Development of Economic Theory", *Economic Journal* 52:294–329.

Sidgwick, H. (1883). *Principles of Political Economy.* London: Macmillan.

Stigler, G. J. (1965). *Essays in the History of Economics.* Chicago: University of Chicago Press.

Viner, J. (1931). "Cost Curves and Supply Curves", *Zeitschrift für National-ökonomie* 3:23–46.

2

Marshall and the Labour Market

ROBIN C. O. MATTHEWS

I Introduction

The range of labour-market issues that were addressed by Marshall was
not much narrower than the range that exists today. It was not much
different either: unemployment, low wages, methods of wage determination, government regulation of hours and pay, social security, education
and training – even inflation is not entirely absent. But he discussed these
issues in the context of conditions that have greatly changed. This stands
in the way of appreciating his rather subtle treatment. Nor is this the only
difficulty.

In the first place, the parts of Marshall's works that deal with labour
contain more than their share of the moralising that has irritated Marshall's readers ever since the end of the Victorian era.

In the second place, there is no canonical exposition by Marshall of his
views on the labour market after the publication of the first edition of the
Principles, notwithstanding the important developments taking place in
the British labour market during the period that elapsed between the first
edition and the eighth (Phelps Brown, 1965) and notwithstanding Marshall's increasing first-hand knowledge of the subject. In 1891, very soon
after the publication of the first edition, Marshall became a member of
the Royal Commission on Labour. He is said to have been active in the
work of the Commission and to have played a large part in drafting its

I am greatly indebted for helpful comments on a first draft from Henry Phelps Brown, John
Whitaker, Donald Winch, William Brown and Geoff Harcourt.

14

final report, published in 1894.[1] He described his service on it as "the most valuable education of my life" (*IT*, p. vii). But changes in Marshall's treatment of the labour market between successive editions of the *Principles* were by no means as great as this remark might lead one to expect. Apart from certain shifts in emphasis, the main change came in the fifth edition (1907), with the addition of the very general concluding chapter "Progress in relation to the standard of life". Nor is there a systematic treatment in *Industry and Trade* or his other later writings.

The present paper refers chiefly to the treatment of the labour market in the eighth edition of the *Principles*. The main relevant passages are the chapters on the supply of labour (IV, 4–6), on the effects of industrial organisation on labour (IV, 8–11), on derived demand (V, 6), on the earnings of labour (VI, 3–5), and the two concluding chapters (VI, 12–13); various other pertinent passages are scattered throughout the book. I also make quite frequent references to Marshall's other writings, insofar as they are not incorporated in the *Principles*.[2] In addition, I quote on occasion from the report of the Royal Commission on Labour, as representing views from which Marshall at least did not dissent, whether he drafted them or not.

In sections 2 and 3 I focus on two general themes which are central to Marshall's own treatment of the labour market and are also of interest to the present-day economist. In sections 4 and 5 I consider in relation to them Marshall's treatment of two particular labour-market topics, trade unions and unemployment. Concluding remarks are offered in section 6.

II Asset-Specificity and Bargaining Power in the Short Period and the Long Period

The interaction of long-period and short-period supply and demand in the determination of price and quantity in the goods market is the central

1. Keynes (1924), p. 52. Keynes there says (presumably on the basis of information from Mrs. Marshall) that the parts of the Commission's report dealing with trade unions, minimum wage, and irregularity of employment were especially Marshall's work. (By "minimum wage" Keynes presumably meant the discussion in the report of the so-called Common Rule – the negotiated occupational minimum for a district. The report does not say much about a *national* minimum wage, because it was not a proposal that anyone was seriously putting forward.) Marshall's role in the work of the Royal Commission has not been much studied, as far as I know. Not much can be learned from the shelfful of supporting documents published by the Commission. In these, Marshall appears by name only in his questioning of witnesses (especially on dock labour) in four of the volumes.
2. Marshall had a habit of using the same passage almost verbatim in different writings. It is therefore not easy to be sure where a given statement first appeared or what is the most considered version of it.

theme of Book V of the *Principles*. The central theme of Book VI is that, in the broadest terms, the same approach is valid for factor markets, including the labour market.[3]

However, says Marshall, there are important differences between goods markets and the labour market. In consequence, the marginal productivity principle, though correct and important in itself as a description of the underlying basis of the demand for labour, "covers only a very small part of the real difficulties of the wages problem" (letter to J. B. Clark, 1900, p. 413). As will be seen presently, the logic of this statement is unaffected by the fact that Marshall's long struggle to free himself from the wages-fund doctrine caused him in Book VI to make what seems to the modern reader unnecessarily heavy weather of the marginal productivity principle and its relation to the production function.[4]

The concept of quasi-rent, the main theoretical novelty emerging from the distinction between the short period and the long period in Book V, is itself a concept that relates to factor rewards. The concept developed out of Marshall's study of the Classical economists, with their preoccupation with the rent of land. Land-rent has ceased to play such a central part in modern economics. I shall suggest, however, that Marshall's application of the concept to the labour market had much in common with present-day theories about asset-specificity and the internal labour market.

In the goods market, Marshall distinguished three periods and correspondingly three types of equilibrium: the market period, in which the supply of goods is fixed, yielding "temporary market equilibrium"; the short period, in which prime inputs are variable; and the long period, in which fixed capital inputs are also variable.[5]

In the labour market, things are more complicated. On the one hand, the demand for labour, being a derived demand, is affected by short-period/long-period responses in the goods market. In the market period, a rise in demand will not increase the demand for labour at all; it will only increase prices and profits. In the short period, there will be a rise in the demand for labour, and sensible employers will not wait too long before passing on some of their gains to their workers in wage increases (1887*b*,

3. This state of affairs is held to mark a point of difference from earlier times, when immobility permitted factor rewards to be determined more largely by custom (*Principles*, Appendix A).
4. Throughout his life, Marshall continued to struggle against wrong inferences drawn from the wages-fund doctrine. The struggle was on two fronts: against right-wingers, who took it to imply that increases in real wages were impossible, and against left-wingers, who thought that the earnings of labour were immune from the effects of restrictive practices or reductions in hours.
5. As Whitaker has shown, the exact basis of the distinction between the various periods underwent some changes before assuming its final form (*EEW*, I, pp. 71, 179; Whitaker, 1982).

p. 217). In the long period, the variability of fixed capital inputs provides scope for both complementarity and substitution between labour and capital (*Principles*, pp. 541–2).

On the other hand, there are also short-period/long-period distinctions in the *supply* of labour. In the shortest period, the employer has a given work force; there is scope for variation only in hours of work. In a longer period, workers may be attracted from other firms or other occupations. Marshall noted that such a movement into an occupation, once made, may take time to go into reverse, as happened after the great rise in wages in the coal industry in 1872–3, when the presence of large numbers of men who had been attracted to the industry contributed to the unusual depression of wages that ensued when demand fell off (*Principles*, p. 575). In the longest period, parents will bring their children up to one trade rather than another in response to their perception of labour market conditions and prospects. The very long lags involved in this create a danger of overshooting (*Principles*, pp. 571–2). Alternatively, parents' choices of occupations for their children may be over-conservative, their own background restricting their knowledge or their contacts. This can cause earnings in an occupation to remain for many years below earnings elsewhere, as happened with the hand-loom weavers (*IT*, pp. 212–3). For these reasons the rate of wages in an industry or occupation may depart significantly from its long-period equilibrium.

There is one important feature of the labour market, in Marshall's treatment, that has the effect of making permanent certain of the characteristics of the very short period in which the supply of labour to the firm is fixed.

This is the tendency for particular workers to be attached to particular firms. For a number of reasons, "Practical permanence of engagements is common in many industries" (Royal Commission on Labour, 1894, p. 15). They amount to asset-specificity (Williamson, 1985),[6] that is a situation where the net value of a worker's services is higher in his present job than it would be elsewhere. This may come about because of frictions—transaction costs for workers in moving to new jobs and for employers in hiring new hands. Geographical considerations may also be responsible. A different source of asset-specificity is illustrated by the example of the head clerk whose skill is "of a kind to be of no value save to the business in which he already is . . . his departure would perhaps injure it by several times the value of his salary, while probably he would not get half that

---

6. Williamson notes Marshall's use of the concept (1985, pp. 52–3). The "fundamental transformation" in Williamson that occurs between the periods before and after the contract has been agreed on also has much in common with Marshall's distinction between short and long period.

salary elsewhere" (*Principles*, p. 626). More generally, continuity of association makes a contribution to good industrial relations and hence is in the interest of both parties. This is asset-specificity through mutual familiarity. While asset-specificity is the ultimate cause of continuity of association, it gives rise to an implicit *contract* of continuity which then acquires independent force in strengthening the continuity.

Marshall does not use the term asset-specificity, of course. Moreover, he takes the example of the head clerk as an extreme case. But the assumption of continuity of association, and *hence* of some kind of asset-specificity, pervades his treatment of the labour market. We may note in passing that asset-specificity in the labour market is implied by Marshall's favourite anecdote about his rich sheep-farming uncle in Australia, who was alleged to have made a fortune because of his penchant for hiring the disabled (Keynes, 1924, p. 4, Coase, 1984). This enabled him to retain his labour force at a time when other farmers' men were all going off to the diggings. If Charles Marshall's men were not in some way asset-specific, why did the other farmers not bid them away from him when their own employees left and they became short-handed?

Methods of production that involve asset-specificity and continuity of association are likely to be efficient from the cost point of view. Indeed the Royal Commission on Labour suggested that where continuity of association did not exist, one should welcome the introduction of arrangements that would encourage it, such as nonportable pension schemes.[7]

There is another less welcome consequence, however. Wages like profits, become quasi-rents in the short period. Insofar as the worker and the employer are literally inseparable in the short period, their rewards acquire the character of *composite quasi-rents* (*Principles*, p. 626) – a notion that brings together two of the theoretical concepts of Book V. The distribution of income between labour and capital is then indeterminate and must be determined by bargaining. This points to another reason why, even in less extreme cases, the actual rate of wages observed at any time may diverge from the long-period equilibrium. This short-term bilateral monopoly can be a source of inconvenience for both parties, by potentially putting them at each other's mercy. There are thus serious disadvantages in the more

7. The system of joint benevolent funds "does much to give men an interest in working permanently in the same establishments. This is particularly desirable in the case of unskilled labour, seeing that the unsettled and roving habits of this class of workmen appear to be an evil, both to themselves and to society. It is clear from the history of institutions that permanency and regularity of work is a condition precedent to anything like good organisation and the rise in prosperity and the standard of life of any labouring class" (Royal Commission on Labour, 1894, pp. 47–8). There is perhaps some inconsistency here with the description in Marshall (1875) of the economic *benefits* that flowed from the restless disposition of American workers. Perhaps he intended a distinction between skilled and unskilled.

extreme forms of asset-specificity, such as exist in company towns, where workers have no alternative employment. This may limit the extent to which such arrangements occur (*Principles*, p. 272).

There is a further important point. In the bargaining process between an employer and an individual worker, said Marshall, the worker was normally at a disadvantage for a number of reasons (*Principles*, pp. 566–9). His labour was perishable; he had only one unit to sell while his employer was buying many; his needs were urgent and he lacked financial reserves. This was so even in the absence of the grosser forms of inequality in bargaining power, such as had been suffered by the parish apprentices in the early days of the Industrial Revolution. Moreover, employers' short-period monopsony, conferred by genuine asset-specificity, might be magnified artificially by collusion. Hence the bargaining situation created by asset-specificity was much more likely to work to the disadvantage of the worker than to his advantage. This applied both to *ex ante* bargaining about the terms of the labour contract and to disputes about the implementation of an existing contract.

In the context of asset-specificity, the notion of a "fair" rate of wages was not a meaningless one, Marshall held. It meant the long-period equilibrium rate for the job, paid without cavilling in normal times, and adjusted by no more than a moderate amount in times when the trade itself was experiencing rapid change and so was not in long-period equilibrium. Some unscrupulous employers might abuse their bargaining strength by failing to pay the fair rate. "It is this unfairness of bad masters which makes trade unions necessary and gives them their chief force" (1887*b*, p. 214).

Marshall's general picture of the labour market, as I have been describing it so far, can be summed up as one in which broad trends are determined by long-period forces of supply and demand but in which the actual situation at any time may depart from what those forces would dictate because of nonstationary conditions in the relevant product market, slow supply responses, asset-specificity, opportunism, or the exercise of monopoly power in the labour market. The outcome is not one that would result from the working of unrestrained competition in the short period, but something between that and the long-period normal. Long-period and short-period forces are interwoven. Despite the apparent arbitrarinesses introduced by bilateral monopoly or by custom, Marshall believed that this interweaving could adequately explain most of the observed phenomena (*IT*, p. vii). The disturbing effects of collective bargaining tended to be little more than eddies in the tide. It was noteworthy that wage rates had actually risen more in non-unionised occupations than in unionised ones (1899, p. 389).

The long-run forces were affected by changes in human nature. This brings us to the topic of the next section.

III   The Endogeneity of Human Nature

> The fact that highly paid labour is generally efficient and therefore not dear labour . . . though it is more full of hope for the future of the human race than any other that is known to us, will be found to exercise a very complicating influence on the theory of distribution.   (*Principles*, p. 510)

The economy-of-high-wages argument is prominent in Marshall from his earliest writings on.[8] It is part of a more general Marshallian theme.

That theme is the nonconstancy of human nature. It is the subject of the innumerable "moralising" passages which later economists, such as Schumpeter (1941), found so repugnant. Even such an ultra-loyal Marshallian as Guillebaud was apparently willing to jettison them (Guillebaud, 1952, p. 114). But it is a poor tribute to Marshall to suppose that he persistently muddled up scientific analysis with Victorian prejudices, especially since he himself went out of his way to criticise Ricardo's opposite assumption (of unchanging human nature) as a scientific limitation (*Principles*, pp. 762–4). I do not think that Marshall can be acquitted altogether of the charge of importing his own prejudices. But his development of the theme was an important element in his system, particularly in regard to the labour market.[9] I shall argue that what he said involved some quite sophisticated ideas about human capital and was also an attempt, at least, to resolve some problems that standard neo-classical economics has until recently swept under the carpet because of its assumption of utility-maximisation with an unchanging utility function.

Let me first state in simplified outline what seems to be Marshall's argument, translated into modern language. (The translation inevitably means some departures from Marshall's own conceptual framework.)

1   Human nature is not a constant. Changes take place not only in physique and skills, but also in utility functions and in standards of morality; hence description of the changes in terms of human capital accumulation is not adequate, though

---

8. See (1877a), 2, pp. 24–26 and (1893), p. 225, Q. 10,272.
9. For a variety of views on this aspect of Marshall's thinking and its origins see Parsons (1931, 1932), Shove (1942), Whitaker (1977), Collini et al. (1983, Chapter 10), Chasse (1984), Collini (1985); and on the relation between Marshall's "activities" and Keynes's "animal spirits" Matthews (1984). The normative implications are further discussed below.

that is an important element. Changes in human nature occur both within a given generation and between generations.

2 Economic growth systematically alters people's nature and the nurture they give to their children, through the effects that growth has on real wages, hours of work, and the nature of work.[10] Human nature is also affected by variables that are not determined by economic growth, especially climate, the ultimate source of most differences in national character.[11]

3 The changes in human nature that are brought about by growth are, on balance, themselves conducive to economic growth. They are labour-augmenting, though not necessarily to an equal degree for all classes of labour.

4 There is therefore a cumulative process. The process, however, is a gradual one. *Natura non facit saltum.*

5 For purposes of positive economics, the cumulative process is relevant (*a*) to growth itself and (*b*) to the distribution of income, both the distribution between labour and other factors and the distribution between different classes of labour.

6 For purposes of normative economics, the systematic tendency for people's utility functions to shift over time is a fatal objection to relying exclusively on revealed preferences as a criterion of the social optimum. States of affairs that people prefer now are not necessarily the ones that they will prefer in the future, let alone the ones that their children and grandchildren will prefer. The *ceteris paribus* assumption regarding tastes is systematically wrong.

7 Since revealed preferences are no guide, the policy-maker has no choice but to seize the bull by the horns and apply his own view of what constitutes progress.

Let us now look more closely at this argument.

The underlying ideas in Marshall about the nonconstancy of human nature are a mixture, not always successfully blended, of two elements.

10. For the effect of the nature of work, see the idealistic "The Future of the Working Classes" (1873), not wholly repudiated by him in later life, in which this effect is taken as the point of difference between the working classes and the rest of society. In the course of his career Marshall seems to have come to attach rather more weight to the inter-generational effect relative to the intra-generational effect [compare the above passage with (1893), pp. 24–6].

11. National character features prominently in the *Principles*, especially in Appendix A (Book I, ii–iii, in earlier editions). It is quite an important element in Marshall's thinking about human nature and about the origins of economic change, but I shall not discuss it further here.

The first is an almost formalised model about the interaction of wants and activities, contained in Book III of the *Principles* (pp. 86–91). The second consists of much more general notions, relatively commonplace among Victorian writers, about character formation. Marshall's own contribution to this brew was probably not very great. His originality lay in combining it with partial-equilibrium analysis of economic behaviour at any given state of human nature. His notion of the agenda is plainly announced in the definition of economics on page 1 of the *Principles:* "It is on the one side a study of wealth; and on the other, and more important side, a part of the study of man".

The empirical conclusions that he drew about the implications for economic performance were quite strong. Marshall wrote with remarkable enthusiasm, at least in some passages, about the extent to which human nature had improved in his own lifetime, both in its capacity to create economic efficiency and by absolute standards. "Human nature ... has progressed very fast in this country during the last fifty years" (*IT*, p. 650). "The working class intelligence that we want to utilise [in the administration of poor relief] is almost entirely a creation of the last sixty years, and in great measure of the last twenty years" (1893, p. 245, Q. 10,363). The assessment in the *Principles* (pp. 203, 680, 752), though rather more cagey, is in the same general direction. Improvements in the working classes are singled out for comment, but the improvements have not been confined to them. Not all the changes, it is true, had been for the better. Some of the changes which in themselves were to be regretted, such as increased proneness to ostentatious consumption, might have been necessarily associated with the development of more important traits of a beneficial kind. To that extent they were a price that had been worth paying (*Principles*, p. 245).

The changes in human nature that were conducive to economic growth were seen by Marshall as having taken a number of forms. Those included better educational standards, greater "deliberateness", an improved "telescopic" faculty, better allocation of expenditure between different types of consumer goods, better allocation of time, and improvements in morality.[12] In modern language, some of these amount to human capital accumulation, some to greater rationality, and some to changes in preferences or moral standards. Marshall does not make distinctions in those terms.

The economic significance of changes in educational standards or rationality is obvious. The economic significance of morality requires more

---

12. *Principles*, pp. 6, 680. For Marshall's personal interest in the allocation of time, see *EEW*, 1, p. 11 (his popular lectures to women on the subject) and Keynes (1924), p. 2 ("we are not at liberty to play chess games").

comment. One application has already been mentioned, in connection with "bad" employers who exploit short-period monopoly advantage in the context of asset-specificity. Marshall was also much concerned with the avoidance of immoral or guileful behaviour generally, that is, "opportunism", including opportunism on the part of the employee in the form of "shirking". Compared with modern writers on the principal-agent problem, Marshall attached more importance to morality and less to cunningly designed schemes of incentives and monitoring. Opportunism by one party led to opportunism by the other. Morality was therefore not only an internalised sanction against opportunism; it also elicited trust, which was a requirement for the successful working of the system. This is a major Marshallian theme. It appears, for example, as an advantage of the small firm. The small firm was, admittedly, well placed to police opportunism by its workers because "the master's eye is everywhere" (*Principles*, p. 284) – monitoring rather than morality. But at the same time, the employer in such firms had better opportunities and also more incentive to elicit the "trust, affection, and esteem" of his workforce, valuable business assets. Hired managers and foremen were likely to be less successful in doing this. They were, moreover, subject to some principal-agent distortions themselves in relation to their employers (*IT*, p. 353), notwithstanding some improvement in commercial morality that had taken place and had historically been a prerequisite of the growth of the joint-stock company (*Principles*, p. 303). Reputation, which can be regarded as partly a moral sanction on opportunistic behaviour and partly a form of monitoring, is also recognised as important; great geographical mobility weakens the sanction of reputation, a drawback to be set against the advantages of mobility (*Principles*, p. 198, n. to p. 197; cf. 1875, 2, p. 364, "money is a more portable commodity than a high moral reputation").

On the empirical side, Marshall makes an attempt to document some of his conclusions, while others remain essentially impressionistic. The nature of work, as well as the level of wages, was important as a source of improvement (1873). Less than a sixth of the industrial classes now did work of the degrading kind measurable by the degree of physical exertion (*Principles*, p. 194, n. to p. 193 – wherever did he get that statistic?). It might have been thought that deskilling brought about by mechanisation was bad for people's nature, but the danger was exaggerated, because new skills came to be needed (*Principles*, pp. 254–8). In regard to morality, an increase in altruism had taken place, and more was to be hoped for in the future. But in the meanwhile it would be a mistake to suppose that institutions would flourish if they depended on altruism being universal (1897, pp. 310–11). This is the famous passage about the need to use the strongest, and not merely the highest, forces of human nature for the increase of social good.[13]

Is the cumulative interaction between economic growth and change in human nature convergent or divergent? Mathematical Note XI of the *Principles* indicates that it is nonconvergent, within a certain range. That Note takes an evolutionary analogy. A bird develops some webbing on its feet, the webbing facilitates water-going habits, and these new habits increase the usefulness of further development of the web. The aquatic bird appeared for the first time in the third edition. Previously, the analogy used was the giraffe's neck (*Variorum*, p. 834). In view of the obvious tendency to diminishing returns from the length of the giraffe's neck, Marshall's decision to alter his text in this way surely shows that he intended the process to be seen as nonconvergent within a certain range (even in the absence of a concomitant increase in physical capital). However, this cumulative process was seen by him as only one of a number of forces producing a tendency to increasing returns.[14] It would have been un-Marshallian to have been too specific about the stability properties of one element in the system taken in isolation.

Let us now consider the implications of the nonconstancy of human nature, as seen by Marshall, first on the positive side (step 5 in the outline argument above), then on the normative side (steps 6 and 7).

On the positive side, changes in human nature created a distinction between labour measured in physical units (L_p) and labour measured in efficiency units (L_E). The trend of wages per worker would be affected by the rate of increase of L_E/L_P. Moreover, an upward trend in the capital–labour ratio K/L_P did not necessarily imply an upward trend in K/L_E, hence did not necessarily imply diminishing returns to K. Quite complicated questions might also arise about the relationship in the production function between nonhuman capital, human capital, and labour. Thus Marshall suggests that the general rise in the standard of education had at the same time lowered the *marginal* product of education and reduced the employability of those with *very* poor education (1885a, pp. 611–13).

These macro considerations had counterparts at the interpersonal level. Marshall gave a good deal of emphasis to the importance of personal qualities of workers in the interpretation of differences in wages

13. A still gloomier view of the potential of the working classes *on the moral side* is taken in the concluding pages of "Some Possibilities of Economic Chivalry" (1907), written when Marshall was 65, in which he says that jealousy is a more potent force than chivalry in the breast of the common man, and conjectures that the business classes are more promising agents for advance on the moral front than the working classes.

14. Verdoorn's Law or Marshall's Law? "An increase in the aggregate volume of production of anything . . . will enable it [the representative firm] to manufacture at a less proportionate cost of labour and sacrifice than before" (*Principles*, p. 318).

between regions and occupations, as well as between individuals. Thus, workers in the North of England (in his day) were stronger and more energetic than workers in the South, partly explaining their higher average earnings (*Principles*, p. 547). Similarly if the wage in a particular occupation fell relative to wages elsewhere, this might be because it was now being pursued by less qualified people than formerly, for example, by recent immigrants (*Principles*, p. 264, n. to p. 263). The environment had a significant effect on human nature: frontier conditions made people more self-reliant, urban conditions were bad for their health, and both had to be taken into account in interpreting wage-differentials (*Principles*, pp. 197–201). The "Residuum" of people unable to earn a decent living because of their personal weaknesses featured prominently in all Marshall's discussions of the problem of poverty. The children of those classes of the population who were ill-equipped, whether for genetic or environmental reasons, would suffer in their upbringing and would become the deprived class in their generation (*Principles*, pp. 562–4) – the problem of transmitted deprivation in modern social science terminology. They might also have a more widespread corrupting effect.[15] The genetic aspect was somewhat toned down after the earliest editions of the *Principles*.[16] Even in the first edition Marshall did not see fit to repeat his rash conjecture (in 1885*a*) that "probably half of all the lives of extreme misery and want in this country" were due to the dysgenic effects of the pre-1834 Poor Law. But inter-generational transmission remained a central element in Marshall's treatment of the problem of poverty.

What was the theoretical significance of these considerations? Non-homogeneity of labour is not in itself a particularly striking idea theoretically, however much neglected in practice. Nor would mere dependence of efficiency on wages introduce great complications. After all, said Marshall, the farmer knew he had to feed his horses properly, and the slave-owner did likewise for his slaves [the wise slave-owner would also provide them with some "rough musical or other entertainment", to keep their spirits up (*Principles*, p. 691)].[17] It would make matters a degree more complicated if the effect of the wage on efficiency were durable, but

15. "The incursion of the offscourings of low-paid labour, largely agricultural, from the South of England and Ireland into the best hives of high-class industry, brought with it a degradation of the quality of life, from which the chief manufacturing district of England has not wholly freed itself". (*IT*, pp. 76–7)

16. For the toning down see *Variorum*, notes to *Principles* pp. 200b, 200c, 201b, 217a, 263a.

17. It is easy enough to accommodate the economy-of-high-wages argument by writing the marginal productivity equation (w = wage, N = employment) as

$$w = f(N, w) \qquad f'_N < 0, f'_w > 0, f''_w < 0$$

just as one might for a horse or a slave.

the analogy of the horse and the slave would still apply. The real complications arose precisely because workers were not slaves (*Principles*, p. 504). Thus:

1   The effect of a rise in wages on efficiency depended on how the extra money was spent. This depended on workers' attitudes, and hence on their natures. Moreover, the effects of rises and falls of wages might not be symmetrical in this regard (cf. Whitaker, 1988, p. 114).

2   The consequences of changes in hours and conditions of work likewise depended on attitudes and would not necessarily always be the same.

3   Externalities existed, especially through intergenerational effects. The extent to which employers, on the one hand, and parents, on the other, chose to internalise these externalities depended, again, on attitudes. The outcome could not, therefore, be predicted by simple partial-equilibrium methods.

On the positive side, the foregoing implications of the nonconstancy of human nature can be adequately expressed in terms of human capital theory, provided that human capital is understood, in a broad sense, to include not only skills but also habits of rationality and honesty and assiduity (cf. North 1984). This is not the case with the implications on the normative side, to which we now turn.

Marshall's innumerable references to higher or nobler satisfactions make it abundantly clear that he was not a utilitarian, in the Benthamite sense of seeking to maximise the satisfaction of human preferences as they stand.[18] I dare say Marshall would have been temperamentally inclined to reject Benthamism in any case, but the doctrine of endogenous change in human nature provided an intellectual justification, in the negative sense that it invalidated Benthamite reliance on currently revealed preferences. If change in people's nature is endogenous to the process of economic growth, then we can be sure that changes in people's nature *will* take place. A change in someone's nature, whether exogenous or endogenous, causes him or her to become a different person, with different preferences. If revealed preferences were to be taken as the criterion, there would be in effect a problem of the distribution of income: the distribution between Mr Hyde and Dr Jekyll. It is no way out to postulate that Mr Hyde understands all this and fully internalises the utility of Dr Jekyll; if he did, he would not be Mr Hyde. How is one to judge whether

18.   Marshall's attempt (fragment in *EEW*, 2, pp. 316–9) at a mathematical expression of utilitarianism is notable for its tentative tone.

behaviour that transmutes Mr Hyde into Dr. Jekyll represents an increase in the sum of utilities or not?

This is close to the area of "multiple persons" explored in modern times by such writers as Elster (1979) and Schelling (1984).

To intrapersonal changes in human nature is to be added the more familiar intergenerational aspect. Here we are dealing with people who have a different identity in a literal sense. There arise not only the familiar conundrums about the weight to be given to the utility of people not yet born (and who may never be born), but also questions about what sort of people they should be.

One possible way for the economist to meet the dilemma is to decline to make any normative statements, except in the (rare) contexts when unchanging preferences can safely be assumed. Marshall paid periodical lip-service to such agnosticism – but most unconvincingly. How could he accept it, if he regarded changes in preferences as part and parcel of the process of economic growth and at the same time thought economic science was important?

The terms of one of his avowals of agnosticism is revealing. "[The economist] does not attempt to weigh the real value of the *higher* affections of our nature against those of our *lower*" (*Principles*, p. 16, italics added). Hardly neutral language! The underlying idea of a hierarchy of motives, with strong normative connotations, is directly related, in Book III of the *Principles* (pp. 86–91), to the theory of *activities* as the source of the highest satisfactions. He summarised it elsewhere as follows:

> There are some doubts as to what social good really is; but . . . there has always been a substratum of agreement that social good lies mainly in that healthful exercise and development of faculties which yields happiness without pall, because it sustains self-respect and is sustained by hope.   (1897, p. 310, repeated in *IT*, p. 664)

This could be interpreted in a paternalistic sense. Alternatively, it could be taken as a conjecture about what ultimately maximises satisfaction (implying, of course, a cardinal measure of utility). This was the line taken by Mill in his discussion of higher and lower pleasures (1861, pp. 8–9), though Mill's concept of what constitute the higher pleasures would no doubt have been less entrepreneurial than Marshall's. And Marshall certainly went beyond Mill when he said that "poverty and pain, disease *and death* are evils of greatly less importance than they appear, except insofar as they lead to weakness of life and character"![19]

---

19. Letter to Mrs. Bosanquet, 1902, quoted in Collini (1985, p. 29), italics added. Marshall's notion of a hierarchy of activities and wants derived in part from his reading of Herbert Spencer and Hegel, to whom he expressed his indebtedness in the preface of

Be that as it may, the general philosophy that some states of human nature are in themselves better than others underlies Marshall's policy prescriptions for the labour market, as for many other problems. What confuses the modern reader is that he does not draw any sharp distinction between the policy implications of this philosophy and the policy implications of those aspects of the endogeneity of human nature that can be ranked as straightforward human capital accumulation.

The policy conclusions drawn by Marshall do not follow any set formula. Generally speaking, policy should avoid standing in the way of the macro-cumulative process and if possible should make its own contribution towards it. At the same time it should alleviate the ill-effects of the micro-cumulative process at the bottom of the socio-economic ladder. Let us now refer briefly to policy implications as seen by Marshall in a few specific areas.

Does the endogeneity caused by the economy of high wages call for policy action to raise wages? If the favourable effect of high wages on productivity were felt fully and immediately, it would be irrational for employers to fail to pay them — like failing to feed your horse properly. There would be no case then for policy intervention, provided employers were rational.[20] Marshall did not rule out the possibility that, in a limited number of cases, low wages might be attributable simply to employers' irrationality (1877, p. 24; *IT*, p. 354), but he did not regard that as typical. In general, therefore, he saw the case as one of external economies. Was there, then, some way for public policy to internalise the externality — just as Marshall recommended subsidies for industries sub-

---

the *Principles* (p. ix), though similar ideas were also to be found in earlier and less philosophical writers whom Marshall quoted (cf. the quotation from McCulloch in *Principles*, p. 90). Included in the hierarchy notion was Hegel's concept of subjective freedom (*Variorum*, p. 299; Whitaker, 1977; Chasse, 1984). As applied in practical policy, it was desirable for this freedom to be restricted to those who would use it in the right way. "It would be better for them [the 'Residuum'] and much better for the nation that they should come under a paternal discipline like that which prevails in Germany" (*Principles*, p. 714). "Partly through the suppression of the gipsy encampments, there has got into the large towns a quantity of unstable excitable blood, for whom the privileges of absolute freedom are not well adapted" (1893, p. 244). See also the curious passage in "Where to House the London Poor" (1884, p. 147), in which he endorses the proposal that young women, other than those entering domestic service, should be deterred from migrating to London by "insisting on strict regulation as to their manner of living there".

20. This argument could be taken a step further, in Coasian manner: Even if part of the benefit accrued irretrievably to the employee (as postulated in *Principles*, pp. 565–6), there would still be clearly defined property rights and the employee could if necessary borrow and repay out of his later enhanced earnings; so there would be no necessary departure from efficiency. Such an extension of the argument, however, would disregard endogenous changes in rationality and tastes (as well as disregarding imperfections in the capital market).

ject to increasing returns? The objection was seen to lie mainly in possible disincentives to capital accumulation, especially in view of the scope for capital export, rather an ad hoc argument (*Principles*, pp. 699–700). Marshall was conscious of the dilemma and he did favour redistributive taxation, in a general way.

Similar considerations applied to reductions in hours of work but with some distinctive twists. Long hours of back-breaking toil were harmful to human nature. Man would not attain his higest form, however, if he were idle, because of the primacy of "activities". Thus, reductions in hours ought to be welcomed only up to a certain point. Moreover, reductions in hours, unless accompanied by the introduction of shift-working,[21] reduced the utilisation of capital and were therefore liable to discourage embodied technical progress. Indeed, they were sometimes sought precisely for that restrictive purpose. Finally – a curious argument – leisure is by its nature a consumer good, not capable of being saved.[22]

Marshall's view of the endogeneity of human nature is relevant to his attitude about the employment of women. His personal prejudices on this subject are blatant.[23] The emphasis that he placed on intergenerational effects and nurture, however, at least gave some logical coherence to his hostility to women working. It made it logical, for example, for him to support restrictions on hours of work under the Factory Acts for women but not for men. It provided a basis for his ambivalent attitude even to rises in women's wages, insofar as they were liable to encourage greater female labour-force participation (*Principles*, p. 685).

An area where the compulsory powers of the state should most emphatically be called upon to assist the cumulative process was education and training. An important part of the cumulative process consisted of voluntary increases by many parents in expenditure on their children's education, as those parents became better off and hence better able or more willing to provide for their offspring. Since not all parents would do this the state should take a part. Education, with public health and town planning, was preeminently the field to which Marshall applied his memorable dictum: "I cry '*Laissez-faire:* – Let the State be up and doing' " (1907, p. 336).

21. Marshall was enthusiastic about the potentialities of double-shift working as a way of encouraging employers to invest in expensive equipment. His particular proposals were not very practical. They required a worker to do a five-hour shift and a three-hour shift each day, with a break of three and a half hours between the two – rather as Cambridge College servants did in his time (*Principles*, pp. 695–6 n.).
22. This appears to be implicit in *Principles*, p. 681.
23. More unbuttoned expression of Marshall's prejudices is sometimes to be found in his letters than in his publications. On the employment of women, see his letter to Dumur, 1909, pp. 459–60. The psychological sources of Marshall's hostility to female employment are discussed by Coase (1984).

Finally, the endogeneity of human nature, as seen by Marshall, had one other implication of a rather different kind. It concerns the meaning of "policy" and policy recommendations, whether in regard to the labour market or to anything else. "Policy" in present-day economics is usually taken to mean government policy. We are accustomed to draw a sharp distinction between governments, supposedly amenable to the advice of economists, and private economic agents, whose preference functions and behaviour patterns are taken as given. Marshall did not think in this way. Since human nature is variable, both in its cognitive aspects and in preference functions, there is no reason why the behaviour of private economic agents should not be influenced by what economists can tell them. In fact, their position in this respect may not be all that different from that of governments, because human nature is to be found in government, as elsewhere (1885a, p. 174). Consequently, Marshall's policy recommendations are fired off in all directions – to employers and workers and consumers, as much as to governments. Some examples of this will be found in the following sections.

I have so far discussed two theoretical themes underlying Marshall's treatment of the labour market, with summary indication of some applications to particular problems. I shall now consider more fully his treatment of two problem areas, trade unions and unemployment. Both theoretical themes were important elements (though not the only elements) in his treatment of both these problem areas.

IV   Trade Unions

Both asset-specificity in the labour market and the progressive potential of human nature suggested to Marshall that there were merits in trade unionism. These had to be weighed against rather more obvious possible ill-effects.

In the first place, one should welcome trade unionism for the purpose already touched on, that of providing countervailing power against the advantage that employers would otherwise have in the bargaining situation. There was substance in the claim of the unions that they were making the force of friction operate in favour of the workman, instead of against him, as it would have done in their absence. Trade unions thus had great potential in previously unorganised industries, like the "sweated trades" and the docks (1899, pp. 367, 385). The principle of the Common Rule – the agreed minimum wage for an occupation within a district – had merit in preventing opportunism by bad employers. It was often welcomed by employers as a whole (*Principles*, pp. 704–6; cf.

letter to Bishop of Durham, 1900, p. 389). In trades where wages were determined by collective bargaining between a strong trade union and a strong employers' association, the situation was analogous to diplomacy. Like diplomacy, it offered scope for strategic plays, which could occasionally lead to outright conflict.[24] The system did not always work well, but it could work adequately, given the important proviso that the parties acted moderately and were governed by "ethico-prudential" motives (*Principles*, p. 628).

In the second place, trade unions in their capacity as friendly societies fostered independence and self-respect (c. 1893, p. 3); trade unions had, moreover, educational effects on their members, and they encouraged unselfishness (1899, pp. 385–6). They called for qualities of sagacity in their leaders. These leaders had in general been "able and far-seeing men who have a grave sense of responsibility" (1899, p. 381; cf. p. 360). It was, perhaps, the emergence of these working-class eminent Victorians in the 30 years or so before the publication of the *Principles* that aroused Marshall's greatest enthusiasm.[25]

Considerations about character did not all pull one way, however. There was a danger that trade unions might foster new discords and substitute class selfishness for individual selfishness (letter to Caird, 1901, pp. 396–7). This was something to be added on the debit side to the more obvious dangers: first, the tendency to monopolistic practices, possibly in collusion with employers, especially in cases where a trade union was sufficiently encompassing to be relatively unconcerned about competition in the product market; and, second, obstruction to technical progress, a tendency not necessarily peculiar to unionised industries, but capable of being strengthened by unions. Marshall identified it as the main source, on the employee side, of Britain's low productivity by comparison with the United States – what he called her "Achilles' heel". He put forward the interesting suggestion that the reason for this British disease was that for a long time British industry had had no serious foreign competition; in other words it had not mattered that the restrictive writ of British labour did not run abroad, because the foreigner was

24. The analogy between industrial relations and international relations was a favourite of Marshall's, though he did not develop it in any detail (1877*b*, 2, p. 124; 1899, pp. 364, 375n). The analogy was used, *a propos* of infrequent major strikes under collective bargaining, by the Royal Commission on Labour in 1894, in a passage with a strongly Marshallian stamp: "Just as a modern war between two great European States, costly though it is, seems to represent a higher state of civilisation than the incessant local fights and border raids which occur in times and places where Governments are less strong and centralised, so . . ." (p. 36).
25. The moral benefits of trade unionism were emphasised by numbers of Marshall's contemporaries also (Phelps Brown, 1983, pp. 23–4).

so far behind (*IT*, pp. 641–2, 650).[26] For the time being, it had to be accepted as a fact of life that the sectional spirit among British workers was strong and that, as a result, the principles of "scientific management" were less readily applicable than in America (*IT*, p. 393).

In view of these opposing considerations, Marshall's attitude towards trade unions was naturally ambivalent.[27] At one extreme is the remarkable statement "I have often said that T.U.'s are a greater glory to England than her wealth" (letter to Caird, 1897, p. 400). More often, the assessment offered is a guarded one:

> Combinations as to employment . . . bring in no economies that could not be obtained by an improvement in moral attitude: and they necessarily involve waste. At the same time the evils against which they are directed are *some of them* so vital that, so long as the moral improvement route is not practicable, the combination route may be worth, and indeed is worth, what it costs in many cases: and, in some cases, more.
>
> (Undated fragment, *Memorials,* p. 362, italics in original)

Sometimes the assessment is made to depend on the strength of trade unions:

> though the growing strength of a Trade Union up to certain limits is almost sure to benefit the community at large, no sure conclusion can yet be reached as to whether it is for the public interest that its strength should grow without limit.   (c. 1893, p. 21)

In other passages the assessment depends on the purposes for which unions use their strength:

> If [unions] do what they can to make labour honest and hearty, they can reply that an addition to the wages of their trade is as likely to

26. For Marshall's views on the the totality of sources of the productivity gap (in one particular industry), see letter to Caird, 1900, p. 401: "The balance against us, allowing for the superior weight of American locomotives, comes out at about 3:1 . . . I should put (say) a quarter of this to account of our employers, a half to account of new-unionism, and the remaining quarter to no account at all. I mean that, when a man works in a leisurely way and for relatively short hours, he does get some gain which may be set off against the loss in his efficiency."

27. The fullest statement of Marshall's views on trade unions is in *The Elements of the Economics of Industry*, Book VI, Chapter 13, first published in 1892; it incorporates much material from the earlier *Economics of Industry* (1879). The subject was not dealt with comprehensively in the *Principles,* because Marshall thought it was too closely related to themes that were being postponed to the never-written Volume 2, that is, international trade and business cycles (*Principles,* p. 702). Another treatment is in the unpublished paper (c. 1893), originally written for inclusion in the report of the Royal Commission (whether the decision not to include it was Marshall's or someone else's is unclear – its rather theoretical style would not have fitted too well with the pragmatic tone of the rest of the published report).

be invested in the Personal Capital of themselves and their children, as an increase in profits is to be invested in Material Capital: that from the national point of view persons are at least as remunerative a field of investment as things: and that investments in persons are cumulative in their effects from year to year and from generation to generation. But this answer is not open to those Unions, or branches of Unions, that in effect foster dull and unenergetic habits of work. (1899, p. 387)

Marshall feared that some deterioration was taking place in this regard. Hence his hostility to the labour side in the great industrial dispute in the engineering industry in 1897–8, in which he considered the real issue to be the power of labour to prevent innovation.[28]

In 1890 barely a tenth of the British labour force was unionised. It may therefore seem rather surprising that Marshall gave as much prominence as he did to unions and to collective bargaining. One reason was that the degree of unionisation was much higher than average among the more highly skilled and educated workers, whom Marshall took to be the model for the working classes as a whole in the future. Another reason was that he was well aware that the proportion of wage-earners who were members of trade unions and whose wages were settled by collective bargaining was rising rapidly. He expected it to go on rising, though he was sceptical about how far the rise would go, because he thought it was liable to stand in the way of mutually advantageous deals between individual employees and their employers (1897, p. 306).

V Unemployment

Marshall's views on unemployment are related in a variety of ways both to the theme of asset-specificity and short-period/long-period interactions and to the theme of changes in human nature.

Unemployment, particularly in combination with inflation, has made the functioning of the labour market a central topic in present-day economics. Unemployment has been judged as both intellectually anomalous and a social challenge. This emphasis is absent in Marshall. The social problem that disturbed *his* conscience was poverty;[29] and poverty might have a number of causes, of which unemployment was only one.

28. The hardening of Marshall's attitude towards trade unions in the course of his life is emphasised, with some exaggeration, by Petridis (1973).
29. "I should perhaps say that I have devoted myself for the last twenty-five years to the problem of poverty, and that very little of my work has been devoted to any inquiry which does not bear on that" (1893, p. 205).

Marshall usually discusses unemployment under the designation "inconstancy of employment", implying that the people affected do have work some of the time. This was realistic. The social security system that prevailed at the time the *Principles* was written scarcely allowed an able-bodied man to stay wholly without earnings for years at a stretch. Marshall therefore had no need to address himself to the problem of persistent long-term unemployment. But even a limited spell of unemployment could be a serious source of poverty for a working class family, given its low financial reserves, and it could cause a "nasty notch" in the nurture of its children (1885a).

Nonetheless, Marshall was inclined to think that the problem was exaggerated or at least that it was a mistake to suppose that it had got worse over time, or that it was worse than it had been for many workers in preindustrial times. The comparison with preindustrial times derived from his observation of underemployment in medieval Palermo. This evidently made quite an impression on Marshall; he referred to it on several occasions (*Principles*, p. 688 n.; 1887–8, Q.9816, pp. 92–3; *MCC*, pp. 242–3; cf. 1885a, p. 175). It suggested to him that the history of hiring practices had gone in a circle, with three phases: 1. the worker permanently attached to a feudal patron, but chronically underemployed and also lacking in personal freedom; 2. labour hired and fired on a casual basis; 3. a reversion to a more or less permanent attachment of the worker to one employer, but now because of asset-specificity rather than patronage, and with a full whole-time wage being paid, and without loss of personal freedom. The transition from phase 2 to phase 3 had served to reduce the inconstancy of employment.

More specifically, a beneficial effect had resulted from the increasing prevalence of *de facto* hiring by the year, that is, the treatment of labour as an overhead cost. "This is for instance the general rule in many of those trades connected with transport which are growing fastest; and which are, in some respects, the representative industries of the second half of the nineteenth century, as the manufacturing trades were of the first half" (*Principles*, p. 688). He does not say why those industries chose to adopt such employment practices. Was it that asset-specificity was especially great in transport, for example, because the railways had to rely on their employees' skill and reliability for safety reasons? Was it because they had a high ratio of fixed to variable costs? Or had there been a general increase in asset-specificity and hence in hiring-and-firing costs everywhere?

In common with many of his contemporaries (Jha 1973, Ch. 5), Marshall was inclined to view the problem of unemployment as consisting of several distinct problems, according to its cause.

One cause was low human capital. He attributed the persistent excess supply of labour in the London docks to this cause, as well as to the irregular nature of the work to be done. It had a self-perpetuating nature, because of transmitted deprivation. The poor quality of the workers concerned took the form, in some cases, of a preference for working only occasionally (letter to Alden, 1903, pp. 446–7). Lax and undiscriminating systems of poor relief were therefore undesirable. The grant of relief should always be accompanied by what he described as "personal care and sympathy", that is, by attempts to improve if necessary the human nature of the recipients.[30]

Quite different was "transitional" (structural) unemployment, caused by a decline in the fortunes of a particular industry. The problem here arose not from lack of human capital, but from human capital being specific to one occupation (not necessarily to one employer). Marshall noted that the more rapid tempo of industrial change had tended to increase the incidence of this kind of unemployment. He noted also that, with increased specialisation, a man who had lost his job would naturally first look for a similar one, very likely without success, even though he might be readily employable in some quite different occupation, a bias in "search" due to incomplete information (*Principles*, p. 260).

Another major category of unemployment, cyclical unemployment, was *par excellence* a "Vol. II" subject, along with business cycles generally. It does get some treatment in the *Principles*, but to a large extent Marshall's views have to be pieced together from his various writings (Wolfe 1956, Eshag 1963). Those are often fragmentary or aphoristic. They lack the rigour imposed by the Mathematical Appendix in the *Principles* and by its diagrammatic footnotes. The trouble is rather more than just a matter of exposition. I do not think he had it entirely clear in his own head. Nor is he entirely consistent in the importance he assigns to the question.[31] However, there are some persistent themes.

30. 1893, p. 199. This reference – Marshall's memorandum and evidence to the Royal Commission on the Aged Poor in 1893 – is among Marshall's most vigorous official papers. In it he expresses general agreement with the hard line on poor relief favoured by the then-dominant Charity Organisation Society; but at the same time he completely recognises the justice of the complaint of the working classes that the charity officials called on to sit in judgement on the poor belonged themselves entirely to the middle class.

31. In speaking of the damage done by fluctuations in prices, he refers to "fluctuations . . . ever either flurrying up business activity into unwholesome fever, or else closing factories and workshops by the thousand" (1887a, p. 192; cf. 1877a, 2, p. 35). Elsewhere, in quite numerous passages, he says that severe recessions in the real economy are exceptional, as, correspondingly, are the occasions when public works would be a useful response (e.g., *Principles*, p. 524; 1887–8, Q.9876, p. 91; undated fragment, *Memorials*, p. 363).

There is no suggestion in Marshall that events in the labour market are the *initiating* cause of cycles. That was to be found in credit markets, especially in "reckless inflations of credit – the chief cause of all economic malaise" (*Principles*, p. 710). However, events in the labour market, particularly with regard to wages, did have a bearing on the severity of the cycle.

There are several strands about this in Marshall's writings and they are not altogether easy to weave together. They are all closely connected with the long-run/short-run question and the asset-specificity that goes with it.

One is strongly "new classical". Nominal wages are stickier than prices, both in the upswing and in the downswing. Hence real wages move perversely over the cycle. This accentuates fluctuations in profits and in employment. Multiplier repercussions ensue. This line of argument was put forward in (1887*a*) not as a criticism of workers or their representatives but as part of the case for trying to avoid violent price fluctuations. It was not altogether unreasonable for workers to resist wage cuts in cyclical contractions and accept ("voluntary") unemployment instead, because the two-way stickiness in wage rates gave them genuine grounds to fear that a new low level of pay might become permanent.

A variant of the argument appears in *Principles* (pp. 709–10), with reference to downward stickiness only. In this passage it is suggested that workers should not try during a cyclical contraction to hold on to all the gains they may have made during a preceding upswing. In contrast to the two-way stickiness hypothesis, these gains are now seen as having possibly been considerable. The difference in emphasis is carried further in "A fair rate of wages" (1887*b*). The description there of what *ought* to happen to nominal wages over the cycle leaves the reader in some doubt whether *actual* changes in wages tend to be too small or too large, either in booms or in slumps (see also *Principles*, p. 575).

A strand in the argument that is different in a more fundamental way arises from Book V of the *Principles*. This concerns the short-period downward stickiness of prices of goods, created by fear of "spoiling the market". Rather than cut prices to the bone, producers prefer to cut output. This plays an important part in Marshall's theory of the long period and the short period. It is seen as preventing prices from departing too much from the long-period normal, even in times of excess supply. Marshall regarded this not only as a fact of life but also as one that was not to be regarded as wholly undesirable, even though it did mean some departure from competition. In its absence there would be large variations in prices which "are in the long run beneficial neither to producers nor to consumers" (*Principles*, p. 375), because they lead to overshooting. In anticipation of a familiar modern theme, he regarded fluctuations in prices as more harmful than steady movements in prices in one direction or another (1886, p. 9).

If employers' output policy is as just described, there would be little point in trying to clear the labour market by wage cuts. As it is, says Marshall, labour is not too unhappy with this aspect of business behaviour, and one of the motives for resisting wage cuts in recessions is to prevent the occasional producer from trying to break ranks in the product market (*Variorum*, p. 391). We may note in this connection that restriction of output in the nineteenth century was often achieved by concerted short-time working, thereby giving employees a minimum livelihood and at the same time sustaining their attachment to their respective firms.

What, then, were the policy implications regarding the cycle, as seen by Marshall?[32] The prime desideratum was to prevent the credit fluctuations that lie at the root of the trouble. As far as the labour market was concerned, matters were complicated by there being several objectives. It was important to prevent fluctuations not only in employment but also in prices. Both were harmful, in their different ways. It is not entirely clear which Marshall thought was worse in its ultimate effect, and this must be regarded as something of a weakness in his treatment. An important third objective was to maintain harmonious industrial relations.

One recommendation, originally put forward by Marshall in his paper to the Industrial Remuneration Conference in 1885 and energetically pressed in his memorandum to the Royal Commission on the Depression of Trade and Industry in the following year, was the publication of official price indices, in order to prevent false perceptions and to facilitate indexed contracts. The first of these purposes appears Lucasian, but as far as the labour market is concerned it had reference in Marshall's mind more to the conduct of bargaining than to substitution over time between income and leisure.[33] The indexation proposal was originally put forward for all contracts, including the wage contract. It was toned down in *Money Credit and Commerce* (pp. 36–7) to refer mainly to long-term loans.

Another recommendation was that both sides should exercise modera-

32. The question of policy to reduce unemployment was directly addressed by Marshall in his paper to the Industrial Remuneration Conference (1885*a*). Some references will be made to this below. Unfortunately it is not one of his better papers. The more diffuse coverage of the question in the *Principles* is more impressive.

33. However, he did think that fluctuations influenced *habits* in undesirable ways, discouraging steady work and wise patterns of consumption (that is, making it difficult to distinguish permanent from transitory income?). See *Principles*, p. 190; 1877*a*, 2, pp. 36–7; 1886, p. 9.

tion in the bargaining process, aided by conciliation and arbitration. Harmony in industrial relations was an important objective in this, as well as being a prerequisite. There were good reasons why employers should bear the main risks that stemmed from their own conduct of their businesses. Moreover, it was difficult to separate firm-specific from industry-specific causes of bad trade, except in a few industries like coal mining where the forces affecting the industry as a whole could easily be summed up in a single publicly ascertainable price. Accordingly, employers should not exploit the asset-specificity of their employees so as to make them bear in wage cuts too much of the cost of the recession. The workers, for their part, should not over-exploit *their* position in booms, and they should be realistic about making *some* concessions (in real terms) in recessions, especially if they were very asset-specific by virtue of their skills or their location or if the demand for the product were very price-elastic [unions in exporting industries had been reasonable about this (1899, p. 379)]. Formal profit-sharing schemes were fine if they could be agreed on in advance, but that was likely to be exceptional. There were problems even with sliding scales based on product prices. The proposal therefore amounted to this. There should be some limited amount of real-wage flexibility over the cycle, and a perverse movement should certainly be avoided, but there should not be any attempt to maintain wages always at a "market-clearing" level over the cycle. This reflects Marshall's more general rejection of the idea that short-period forces wholly determine, or ought to determine, short-period price movements, whether of goods or of factors.

Thus, apart from monetary stabilisation, the recommended policies in face of the cycle amounted to better information (through the availability of price indices) and a kind of voluntary incomes policy. These, it was claimed, would limit the magnitude of fluctuations in employment, though they would not eliminate them altogether.[34] Better information might also help to reduce transitional employment in declining industries. As for chronic underemployment among the lowest class of worker, human capital accumulation and improvements in character promised the best, if not the only, answer.

34. Improvements in information could go beyond the mere publication of price-indices. "As far as pure theory goes, I see no reason why a body of able and disinterested men . . . should not be able to issue predictions of trade storm and trade weather generally, that would have an appreciable effect in rendering the employment of industry more steady and continuous . . . though the time has not yet come for putting it into practice" (1885a, p. 181). The "able and disinterested men" would be businessmen. Marshall did not consider the possibility that they might be economists.

VI Concluding Comments

Textbook Neo-classical economics distinguishes labour markets from goods markets in respect of certain forces operating on the demand side and certain other forces operating on the supply side. The demand for labour, as for other factors, is a derived demand. The supply of labour is affected in the long run by demographic forces; there may also be complications about backward-rising supply curves. The theory can, in addition, take account of human capital accumulation. Otherwise, different markets are treated much on a par.

I have suggested that Marshall, as well as covering that ground (including much of the ground of human capital theory), did better in two main respects.

(1) He recognised that continuity of association between employer and employee was characteristic of many occupations. This did not mean, of course, that the employee had absolute tenure. But it meant he could expect to keep his job as long as he performed reasonably well and as long as there was work to do (or likely to be work soon). In particular, it meant that he was not competing on a par with the outsiders "at the gate".

Continuity of association was ultimately due to asset-specificity, to use modern parlance. For Marshall it created a link with his theory of the short period and the long period. Continuity of association created bilateral monopoly in the short period. Hence the "temporary market equilibrium" of the Marshallian very short period was inapplicable. Bargaining became important, and with it the concept of fair practice (one aspect of non-opportunism). One consequence was that wages in any occupation would keep not too far from their long-period normal, though they should show some sensitivity to excess demand or supply. A further consequence was that employment would be to some extent stabilised over the cycle, so long as employers stayed in business at all. The other side of the coin, of course, was that things might be made more difficult for the workers who failed to get permanent attachments, but Marshall does not make much of that point. He often says that outsiders are hurt by craft exclusiveness, but that is not the same thing.

Marshall admitted that the "normal" wage was difficult to identify in times of rapid change. Since World War I, changes affecting the British labour market have been more rapid than anything he experienced in his day. Technical change has speeded up; international competition has increased and has come from more numerous countries, to say nothing of changes in the institutional and legal framework of the labour market itself. This does not invalidate the general point about continuity of association and its importance, but it has to be admitted that the speed-up of change has made Marshall's concept of the long-period normal wage less useful now than it was in the nineteenth century.

(2)   Marshall recognised that human capital, in the broad sense of the quality of labour, depended on people's attitudes as well as on their skills. Changes in attitudes reflected changes in human nature. Changes in human nature brought about changes in preferences and in standards of morality. He held that economic change affected both attitudes and skills. He identified internalised moral standards as one possible solution for the principal-agent problem that pervades industrial relations (another aspect of non-opportunism). He made clear the difficulties involved in defining the social optimum when preferences are endogenous to the process of economic change, so that economic change causes an individual to become in effect a different person. He offered his own way of cutting the knot by his postulate that the *summum bonum* lay in activities rather than in the satisfaction of wants.

The theme of the endogenous nonconstancy of human nature in Marshall has consequences that range much more widely than the labour market. But it is particularly important in regard to the labour market, because of the effects on human nature of change in pay, hours, and conditions of work.

Marshall may be praised for raising these issues and thereby going beyond many economists. He may also be criticized for the way he handled them. The activities hypothesis is an interesting one, but is not fully worked out, nor is it by any means the only possible one. Parsons (1932) criticised Marshall for confining himself to an individualistic framework.[35] Even within the individualistic framework, there are plenty of other hypotheses that could be pursued more systematically than he did. Marshall does touch on them, for example in his discussion of relative income as an objective (the "craving for distinction"). He is less dogmatic about what actually happens than about what it would be desirable to have happen. As with so much else, one can wish that he had spent more

---

35. Parsons also criticises him for being too Anglo-centric. This criticism is not altogether just, in view of the amount of attention that Marshall gave to other countries, especially the United States, going back to his early paper of 1875. It would be more accurate to say that he lacked insight on countries peopled by non-Europeans. But he was not purporting to write about them, save incidentally.

of his later years in developing his earlier ideas instead of rearranging them.

One final question. Marshall was anxious for his writings to have an influence for the good. This is why he wanted the *Principles* to be read by the general reader, not just by other economists. How successful was his treatment of the labour market by that criterion? The answer is mixed.

As far as government policy towards the labour market was concerned, the major influence in Britain of Marshall's thinking was possibly through the report of the Royal Commission. That report has not commonly been considered a landmark. But it *was* important, in a negative sense.[36] It reaffirmed that no major change was needed in the legislative framework. In this way it entrenched a situation that persisted, in essentials, until after World War II. Had it reported otherwise, events might have unfolded very differently. On the executive side of government, the Royal Commission made some contribution to the establishment of the important Labour Department of the Board of Trade, though the relation between the two was complicated.[37] Marshall's views on conciliation and arbitration may also have had some influence on the able civil servants in the Department who were active in those areas.

As earlier noted, Marshall sought to influence businessmen and labour leaders at least as much as to influence government. Here it is more difficult to discern, in the labour field, any evidence that he succeeded. The main developments in British labour market arrangements after 1890 had altogether different origins.

References

Brown, E. H. P. (1965). *The Growth of British Industrial Relations*. London: Macmillan.

(1983). *The Origins of Trade Union Power*. Oxford: Clarendon.

Chasse, J. D. (1984). "Marshall, the Human Agent and Economic Growth: Wants and Activities Revisited", *History of Political Economy* 16:381–404.

Coase, R. H. (1984). "Alfred Marshall's Father and Mother," *History of Political Economy* 16:519–28.

Collini, S. (1985). "The Idea of 'Character' in Victorian Political Thought", *Transactions of the Royal Historical Society* 35:29–50.

36. I am indebted to Sir Henry Phelps Brown for this idea.
37. Davidson (1971). The energetic first head of the Department, Hubert Llewellyn Smith, was, moreover, well known to Marshall. He was one of those involved in the foundation of the Royal Economic Society in 1890. Marshall thought sufficiently well of him to advise him to be a candidate for the Chair of Political Economy in Oxford (Davidson, p. 243). Intellectually, however, Llewellyn Smith seems to have owed rather more to Charles Booth than to Marshall.

Collini, S., Winch, D., and Burrow, J. (1985). *The Noble Science of Politics.* Cambridge: Cambridge University Press.

Davidson, R. (1972). "Llewellyn Smith, the Labour Department and Government Growth 1886–1909". In Gillian Sutherland (ed.), *Studies in the Growth of Nineteenth Century Government.* London: Routledge.

Elster, J. (1979). *Ulysses and the Sirens.* Cambridge: Cambridge University Press.

Eshag, E. (1963). *From Marshall to Keynes.* Oxford: Blackwell.

Guillebaud, C. W. (1952). "Marshall's *Principles of Economics* in the Light of Contemporary Economic Thought", *Economica* N.S. 19:111–30.

Jha, N. (1973). *The Age of Marshall,* 2d ed. London: Cass.

Keynes, J. M. (1924). "Alfred Marshall, 1842–1924". In *Memorials,* pp. 1–65.

Marshall, A. (1873). "The Future of the Working Classes". In *Memorials,* pp. 101–18.

(1875). "Some Features of American Industry". In *EEW,* 2, pp. 355–77.

(1877a). "Foreign Trade in its Bearing on Industrial and Social Progress". In *EEW,* 2, pp. 14–61.

(1877b). "The Pure Theory of Foreign Trade". In *EEW,* 2, pp. 117–81.

(1884). "Where to House the London Poor". In *Memorials,* pp. 142–51.

(1885a). "Theories and Facts about Wages". In *Variorum,* pp. 598–614.

(1885b). "How Far do Remediable Causes Influence Prejudicially (a) the Continuity of Employment, (b) the Rate of Wages?" In *Industrial Remuneration Conference; the Report of the Proceedings and Papers Read in Prince's Hall, Piccadilly, under the Presidency of Sir Charles W. Dilke* (on spine: *The Remuneration of Capital and Labour*). London: Cassell.

(1886). Memorandum to the Royal Commission on the Depression of Trade and Industry. In *OP,* pp. 1–16.

(1887a). "Remedies for Fluctuations of General Prices". In *Memorials,* pp. 188–211.

(1887b). "A Fair Rate of Wages". In *Memorials,* pp. 212–26.

(1887–8). Memoranda and Evidence to the Royal Commission on Gold and Silver. In *OP,* pp. 17–195.

(1893). Memorandum and Evidence to the Royal Commission on the Aged Poor. In *OP,* pp. 197–262.

(c. 1893). "Memorandum on Disputes and Associations within Particular Trades Considered in Relation to the Interests of the Working Classes in Other Trades". Unpublished manuscript in Marshall Library, Cambridge.

(1897). "The Old Generation of Economists and the New". In *Memorials,* pp. 295–311.

(1899). *Elements of Economics of Industry,* 3d ed. London: Macmillan.

(1907). "Social Possibilities of Economic Chivalry". In *Memorials,* pp. 323–46.

Fragments, undated. In *Memorials,* pp. 358–68.

Letters, various dates. In *Memorials,* pp. 371–496.

Marshall, A., and Marshall, M. P. (1879). *Economics of Industry.* London: Macmillan.

Matthews, R. C. O. (1984). "Animal Spirits", *Proceedings of the British Academy* 70:209–30.

Mill, J. S. (1861). *Utilitarianism*. Everyman edition, London: Dent, 1910.

North, D. C. (1984). "Transaction Costs, Institutions, and Economic History", *Zeitschrift fur die gesamte Staatswissenschaft* 140:7–17.

Parsons, T. (1931). "Wants and Activities in Marshall", *Quarterly Journal of Economics* 46:101–40.

   (1932). "Economics and Sociology: Marshall in Relation to the Thought of his Time", *Quarterly Journal of Economics* 46:316–47.

Petridis, A. (1973). "Alfred Marshall's Attitude to the Economic Analysis of Trade Unions", *History of Political Economy* 5:165–98.

Royal Commission on Labour (1894). Fifth and Final Report. *Parliamentary Papers* XXXV.

Schelling, T. C. (1984). "Self-command in Practice, in Policy, and in a Theory of Rational Behavior", *American Economic Review* 74:1–11.

Schumpeter, J. A. (1941). "Alfred Marshall's *Principles*: a Semi-Centennial Appraisal", *American Economic Review* 31:236–48.

Shove, G. F. (1942). "The Place of Marshall's *Principles* in the Development of Economic Theory", *Economic Journal* 52:294–329.

Whitaker, J. K. (1977). "Some Neglected Aspects of Alfred Marshall's Economic and Social Thought", *History of Political Economy* 9:161–97.

   (1982). "The Emergence of Marshall's Period Analysis", *Eastern Economic Journal* 8:15–29.

   (1988). "The Distribution Theory of Marshall's *Principles*". In A. Asimakopulos (ed.), *Theories of Income Distribution*. Dordrecht: Kluwer.

Williamson, O. E. (1985). *The Economic Institutions of Capitalism*. New York: Free Press.

Wolfe, J. N. (1956). "Marshall and the Trade Cycle", *Oxford Economic Papers* N.S. 8:90–101.

3

Alfred Marshall and the Development of Monetary Economics

DAVID E. W. LAIDLER

I Introduction

Alfred Marshall's status as a contributor to the development of the theories of value and distribution is completely secure. His standing as a monetary economist is more problematic. The "Cambridge cash-balance approach" to monetary theory is well known, but it *is* usually called the "Cambridge" not the "Marshallian" approach after all, and the student eager to learn about it is more often referred to Pigou (1917) or Keynes (1923) than to any of Marshall's writings. *Money Credit and Commerce* (1923) is interesting, but cannot stand comparison with the *Principles*. It gathers together, in an orderly enough way, Marshall's thoughts on monetary topics; but almost all of those thoughts, and sometimes the very words in which they are expressed, date from the last three decades of the nineteenth century and had, by 1923, "nearly all . . . found expression in the works of others" (Keynes, 1924, p. 28). *Money Credit and Commerce* is, in the main, an old man's record of past contributions, not an account of new ones.

Nevertheless, if *Money Credit and Commerce* is of little historical significance, the ideas it contains, considered as the product of the

I am grateful to Milton Friedman, Peter Howitt, Tom Kompas, Don Patinkin, George Stigler, and John Whitaker for helpful comments on earlier drafts of this paper, to Tony Bernardo for research assistance; to Jane McAndrew for bibliographic help; to the SSHRCC for financial support; and to the University of Western Ontario for an appointment in 1988–89 as Research Professor which has enabled me to devote myself full time to the research project of which this essay forms a part.

1870s and 1880s, certainly are; and they had been disseminated much earlier, albeit unsystematically, in lectures and occasional articles, evidence to committees of enquiry and royal commissions, not to mention passages in *The Economics of Industry* (Marshall and Marshall, 1879) and the *Principles* itself.[1] Their importance for the development of monetary economics at Cambridge is attested to by Keynes (1924) and more recently by Eshag (1963), and the fact that they were known to others outside of Marshall's immediate circle is easily documented, for example: Fisher (1896, p. 71, and 1911, pp. 71–2) quotes the *Principles* (3d ed. 1895 and 5th ed. 1907 respectively) on the distinction between real and nominal interest rates, and was aware (evidently through Edgeworth (1895; see 1911, p. 328), of Marshall's "symmetallism" proposals which I shall discuss below. Wicksell (1898, pp. 76–7, 158) was familiar with Marshall's evidence to the Gold and Silver Commission of 1887–88. Marshall's is thus not the case of a monetary economist whose original contributions remained hidden from view until the time at which they would have been important had passed. He was read and understood by other contributors to the field early enough to matter; I shall discuss later how much he did, in fact, matter.

The lack of a systematic and timely monograph is not the only obstacle faced by the modern reader who seeks to appreciate Marshall's monetary economics. Much of it was first published in the form of responses to contemporary policy problems, and those problems were very different from those which currently concern us. Inflation and real fluctuations in a world of flexible exchange rates are today's issues. That is why Henry Thornton (1802) and David Ricardo (1809), or the Keynes of the *Tract* (1923), who wrote about the same questions, can command an interested audience among modern monetary economists not otherwise interested in the history of their discipline. The last three decades of the nineteenth century were dominated by secularly falling prices associated with the spread of the gold standard, and cyclical fluctuations were relatively

---

1. The materials not conventionally published during Marshall's lifetime are to be found in three posthumous volumes: *Memorials of Alfred Marshall* (ed. A. C. Pigou), 1925, *Official Papers by Alfred Marshall* (ed. J. M. Keynes), 1926, and *The Early Economic Writings of Alfred Marshall* (2 vols., ed. J. K. Whitaker), 1975, referred to below respectively as *Memorials*, *OP*, and *EEW*. Some of Marshall's most important contributions to Monetary Economics turn up in *OP* in the form of transcripts of oral evidence given to the Gold and Silver Commission in 1887–88 and the Indian Currency Committee in 1899. Readers should note that such committees habitually granted considerable leeway to their witnesses in correcting their comments prior to publication, and Marshall appears to have availed himself of it. His recorded responses are inevitably carefully punctuated and well organised, in at least one place (cf. fn 18 below) contain an extensive and essentially verbatim quotation from the *Principles*, and sometimes contain carefully organised statistical material. This evidence of careful editing gives one confidence that the transcripts in question faithfully reflect Marshall's views.

mild. The major policy issue of Marshall's day was the desirability of giving a role to silver in the domestic and international monetary systems in order to relieve deflationary pressures. It is easy to be misled by the apparent irrelevance of such problems to our own immediate concerns into underestimating the durability and originality of the analytic tools Marshall brought to bear on them.

In this essay, I shall stress this last point, and argue that Marshall's monetary theory is of much more general importance than the problems to which he applied it. There was, by the 1870s, a well established orthodoxy in British monetary economics, but an orthodoxy whose central doctrines were not logically complete. Marshall's contributions to monetary economics built upon the doctrines he inherited, and are much better understood as efforts to eliminate their internal inadequacies than as ad hoc responses to current policy issues. Monetary (or macro-) economics is sometimes said to lack that essential characteristic of a mature science, namely an internal dynamic whereby the problems which engage its practitioners are generated by anomalies within the existing corpus of ideas that make up the discipline, rather than by external circumstances.[2] That charge is only too well formulated in some instances, but not always, as the case of Marshall shows. He claimed continuity for his economics with that of his Classical predecessors in general and John Stuart Mill in particular. Provided we allow continuity to amount to more than mere repetition, he was right to make this claim, at least about his monetary economics.

In the following pages, I shall first of all sketch out the Classical Monetary Economics on which Marshall built. I shall then discuss in turn the Classical elements in his own thought, his innovations as a monetary theorist, and his views on policy. I shall then say something about his influence on others, and the unresolved problems which he bequeathed to Neoclassical Monetary Economics.

II   The Classical Inheritance

The Classical monetary economics of the 1870s which Marshall inherited dealt with a number of interrelated issues: the purchasing power of money, the cycle, the balance of payments, the choice of a monetary standard, and within the constraints imposed by the standard selected, the conduct of discretionary monetary policy.[3] In the case of a commodity

2. Stigler (1983, p. 534) is one of those who criticises macroeconomics for being overly responsive to current policy problems.
3. The evolution of this orthodoxy over the preceding century is the topic of Fetter's (1965) classic study. Laidler (1988) surveys its principal features and the following four paragraphs are based on that account. Note that, in the terminology of this paper, Jevons and Bagehot are exponents of "Classical" monetary economics.

standard, a much elaborated version of the Hume price-specie flow mechanism formed the basis of balance of payments theory, and the price level was, in the long run, said to be determined by the cost of production of the money commodity. This straightforward application of the classical theory of natural value was supplemented by a "productivity and thrift" theory of the long run equilibrium value of the rate of interest which had that variable determined, like any other relative price, independently of monetary factors. In Classical economics, money was neutral in the long run and monetary theory had to do only with the determination of the price level.

In the short run, matters were more complex, and money was not neutral. Here the Classical economists took a Quantity Theory approach to explaining price level behaviour, and shifts in velocity, particularly those associated with the activities of the banking system, played at least as important a role as variations in the supply of money. Just as the price level could deviate from its natural value in the short run, so too could the rate of interest in response to monetary disturbances, though the short run was, in the case of the interest rate, understood to be a good deal shorter than in the case of the price level. Monetary expansion was associated with the market interest rate falling below its natural level, and vice versa. Closely related, the "credit cycle" was treated as mainly a matter of price fluctuations in financial and commodity markets. The task of discretionary monetary policy was not so much to stabilise this cycle, as it was to ensure that its upper turning point did not precipitate a financial panic and a collapse of the banking system. As to a purely paper currency system, this lacked an anchor for the price level in the form of the natural price of gold (or silver), and though its mechanisms both domestic and international were understood to be technically viable, this lack was regarded as a fatal drawback by Classical orthodoxy.

Coherent though the above sketch may make it seem, there were crucial gaps and tensions in Classical monetary theory. To begin with, the cost of production theory of value and the Quantity Theory co-existed uneasily as explanations of price level behaviour within its framework. Earlier in the nineteenth century some Banking School economists, notably Tooke (1844), had gone so far as to treat them, under gold convertibility at least, as alternatives, and in opting for the former had ended up denying any role in determining prices to the quantity of money and its velocity of circulation.[4] Later Classical writers treated them as complementary hypotheses for the long and short run respectively. For these

---

4. The Banking School had opposed the passage of the 1844 Bank Charter Act. On the debate between the Banking School and their Currency School opponents, see Fetter (1965, Ch. 6) or Anna J. Schwartz (1987).

writers, the proximate influence on prices of variations in the quantity of money and its velocity was the crucial mechanism whereby changes in the cost of production of the precious metals were translated into changes in the purchasing power of money. Even so, the details of this mechanism were left obscure, both because the roles of bank credit and the circulating liabilities it generated in affecting the velocity of what we nowadays call currency were not properly understood, and because, being a transactions velocity concept, it was extremely difficult to apply in an economy where goods passed through many hands on their way from producers to ultimate consumers.

Classical analysis of interest rate behaviour was also often unclear. Its exponents usually took a constant price level for granted as a characteristic of the long run, and hence treated the "natural value" of the market rate of interest as what we would now call a "real" variable. They did not have a sharp notion of the distinction between real and nominal interest rates and so their discussions of the behaviour of interest rates within the credit cycle, when credit expansion tended to push rates one way and associated price level effects the other, often lacked sharpness. Nor was the treatment of interest rate behaviour the only weak point in Classical analysis of the cycle. That analysis also displayed a certain tension between theory and empirical evidence. By the 1870s it was clear that the cycle involved not just price level and interest rate fluctuations, but also systematic variations in real output and employment too. Though these had been noted and discussed long before the 1870s, the theory of the "credit cycle" had not been expanded to deal with them in any systematic way.[5] Marshall, as we shall now see, made major contributions to the clarification of all these issues.

III The Classical Element in Marshall's Thought

Nothing could illustrate the Classical basis of Marshall's monetary economics more vividly than his unequivocal endorsement of the Classical dichotomy between the real and monetary economy in response to the following enquiry from Mr. D. M. Barbour, a member of the Gold and Silver Commission of 1887–88.

> I do not know whether you go so far as some of the older economists, who say that all trade tends to be conducted as a system of barter, and that money is only a mechanism by which that gigantic system of

5. Notable here is the work of John Mills of Ashton-under-Lyne, a banker and member of the Manchester Statistical Society, cited by Jevons in his textbook *Money and the Mechanism of Exchange* (1875).

barter is carried out? . . . "So far as permanent effects go I accept that
doctrine without any qualification.   (*OP*, p. 115)

Marshall was equally Classical in the views he expressed to the Commission about the determination of the rate of interest. He told them that, in the long run, "the supply of gold exercises no permanent influence over the rate of discount" (*OP*, p. 41). But he also told them that, in the short run, monetary factors could affect the interest rate, arguing specifically that, in an open economy, an influx of gold from abroad would "make a sort of ripple on the surface of the water" (*OP*, p. 41).

Marshall's account of the role of this "ripple" as an integral part of the transmission mechanism whereby a gold inflow would ultimately raise the price level while leaving interest rates to be determined "by the extent and the richness of the field for the investment of capital on the one hand, and on the other by the amount of capital seeking investment" (*OP*, p. 51) is essentially the same as that given by Mill in the 1865 and subsequent editions of his *Principles of Political Economy* (1871). There, writing under the influence of Cairnes, who had made a careful study of the mechanisms whereby the price level effects of the 1851 Australian gold discoveries had been transmitted through the world economy, Mill had discussed the consequences of a gold inflow into Britain.[6] Marshall followed Cairnes and Mill in noting that the gold inflow would initially be concentrated in the City. Like them, he argued that though

> This does not increase the amount of capital, in the strictest sense of
> the word . . . it does increase the amount of command over capital
> which is in the hands of those whose business it is to lend to specula-
> tive enterprise. . . . [L]enders lower . . . the rate which they charge
> for loans . . . till a point is reached at which the demand will carry off
> the larger supply. When this has been done there is more capital in
> the hands of speculative investors, who come to the market for goods
> as buyers and so raise prices.   (*OP*, p. 52)

Just as Mill had allowed for an upward influence on the discount rate arising from expectations of rising prices to influence this process, so too did Marshall. "[I]t must be remembered that the influx of bullion would have caused people to expect a rise of prices, and therefore, to be more

---

6. For an accessible account of Cairnes's work on this issue, see Bordo (1975), and see
    Hollander (1985, Vol. 2, pp. 540–1) for a discussion of Cairnes's influence on Mill.
    Note that Keynes (1924, p. 30) quite erroneously credits Marshall with having origi-
    nated the analysis of the role of the interest rate in the transmission mechanism.
    Marshall's work here differed marginally from Classical orthodoxy in granting a bigger
    role to inflation expectations prompted by a fall in the production costs of gold than
    did his predecessors, and, as I shall show below, more significantly in incorporating
    into it an essentially correct account of the bank-credit multiplier.

inclined to borrow for speculative investments" so that "it might not be necessary to lower the rate of discount very much" (*OP*, p. 52). Even so, the process would come to an end with a higher equilibrium level of prices being "held up by the fact that there was currency to sustain [them]" (*OP*, p. 50).[7]

The origins of this analysis of interest rate behaviour can be traced all the way back to David Hume's (1752) essay "Of Interest", and the thoroughly Classical analysis of exchange rates and the balance of payments which Marshall presented to the Gold and Silver Commission of 1887–88 also has Humean roots, this time in the essay "Of the Balance of Trade". Marshall dealt with international monetary issues in two written memoranda submitted to the Commission, the first of which was partially reprinted as a section of Appendix G to *Money Credit and Commerce*. These memoranda, particularly the second, are far more notable for their succinctness than for their originality [except perhaps for some discussion of the consequences of money wage stickiness for the international adjustment mechanism (cf. *OP*, pp. 193–4)]; nor did Marshall claim any originality for them. The first of them begins by invoking the authority of Ricardo, Mill, Goschen, Giffen, and Bastable (cf. *OP*, p. 170) and refers to the analysis upon which it is based as "old, and I had thought well established" (*OP*, p. 177).[8] Indeed, the main purpose of the memorandum in question was, according to Marshall, to defend Classical theory against "the new doctrine which has been put forward in opposition to it" (*OP*, p. 178), a doctrine which he characterized as arguing that a fall in silver prices gave Indian manufacturers a long run advantage over their British competitors because of their willingness to accept unvarying silver prices for their own output, both at home and abroad, regardless of silver's purchasing power.

The essential characteristics of Marshall's version of Classical doctrine

7. See Mill's (1871, p. 656) comment that monetary expansion "[c]onsidered as an addition to loans tends to lower interest, more than in its character of depreciation it tends to raise it". Henry Thornton had discussed inflation expectations in a speech on the Bullion Report in 1811 [printed in the (1939) Hayek edition of Thornton's *Paper Credit*] and Irving Fisher (1896, p. 4) quotes an anonymous tract published in Boston in 1740 as providing an early discussion of what we now term the "Fisher effect". Even so, this effect was never a central part of Classical Monetary Economics.

8. It is worth noting that Goschen, to whose *Foreign Exchanges* (1861) Marshall is presumably here referring, was the Chancellor of the Exchequer who set up the Gold and Silver Commission, and that Giffen also gave evidence to the Commission, though he was not a member as Milgate (1987) asserts. Charles Bastable, a rather younger contemporary of Marshall, for a long time occupied a chair at Trinity College Dublin, and is now remembered mainly as an expositor of international economics "firmly in the English classical tradition" (Bristow, 1987, p. 203). His *Theory of International Trade* which was to go through four editions, first appeared in 1887.

may be set out in the words with which he began the second of his two memoranda:

> Let two countries *A* and *B* trade with one another. Let *A* have throughout a gold currency.
>
> I. Let *B* also have a gold currency. Then trade tends so to adjust the supplies of gold relatively to the demands for gold in the two countries as to bring gold prices at the sea-boards of the two countries to equality (allowance being made for the carriage). . . .
>
> II. Let *B* have an inconvertible paper currency (say roubles). . . . The gold price of the rouble will be fixed by the course of trade just at the ratio which gold prices in *A* bear to rouble prices in *B* (allowing for cost of carriage). . . .
>
> III. Let *B* have a silver currency. This case differs from the preceding one only in consequence of the fact that silver is, and roubles are not, an exportable commodity. Trade tends so to adjust the supplies of gold and silver in the two countries relatively to the demands, as to bring gold prices in *A* to bear to silver prices in *B* (after allowing for carriage) a ratio equal to the gold price of silver.
>
> (*OP*, pp. 191–2)

The mechanisms which will bring about these equilibria are described with similarly concise vigour, and are equally conventionally Classical in character. Net trade imbalances generate pressures on the commercial bill market which, in turn, lead to gold (and/or silver) flows, or exchange rate changes, till the imbalance is removed. There is nothing here that would have puzzled Mill, unless it be that the version of the purchasing-power–parity doctrine (as we would now call it) employed by Marshall is less subtle than Mill's, which makes careful and explicit allowance for the influence of taste and technology changes on the equilibrium "real exchange rate" (to use a modern phrase).[9] Productivity changes are discussed by Marshall, but in the context of how a depreciation of the home currency due to monetary factors might mislead exporters who have simultaneously obtained some cost advantage in production into believing that their greater success in foreign markets is due to that depreciation (cf. *OP*, pp. 192–3). The potential independent influence of productivity

9. Cf. Mill's discussion of these issues in his *Principles of Political Economy* (1871, pp. 604 et seq. and particularly p. 621) for the qualification to simple purchasing power parity ideas referred to in the text. Keynes (1924, pp. 30–1) attributes far more originality to Marshall's treatment of purchasing power parity than is justified. In addition to Mill, Goschen (1861) had much to say about this doctrine.

changes on the real (and hence *ceteris paribus* nominal) exchange rate is not discussed.

The long run independence of the real economy from the monetary sector, of which a productivity and thrift theory of the long run value of the interest rate is an important corollary, and the Humean anlaysis of the international distribution of the precious metals, not to mention its extension to the determination of exchange rates between inconvertible currencies and currencies convertible into different metals, are doctrines utterly central to the Classical tradition. Marshall upheld them, and in so doing demonstrated how deeply the roots of his monetary theory were embedded in that tradition. Nevertheless, as we shall see, that same monetary theory bore fruit which his Classical predecessors would have had difficulty recognising.

IV Innovations in Monetary Theory

I have already noted the uneasy relationship which existed within Classical theory between the cost of production theory of the "natural" value of a commodity-based money and the Quantity Theory. Later Classical writers, notably Mill, treated the former as relevant to the long run and the latter as relevant to the short run, but this approach was not altogether satisfactory, not least because they treated mining as an activity, like agriculture, subject to diminishing returns. Given diminishing returns, marginal production cost could not be determined until the scale of output was also determined, and hence could not, as Classical writers claimed, be the "ultimate regulator" (Mill, 1871, p. 517) of the purchasing power of money. Moreover, the Classical short run theory of the price level relied on a transactions velocity of circulation concept, which, as its exponents were well aware, was hopelessly complex when applied in an economy in which much trading took place on credit, and in which there were many intermediate transactions involved in moving goods between their producers and ultimate consumers.

Marshall's earliest known writings on monetary economics, his notes on "Money" and their complementary mathematical fragments, which date from about 1871, address just these problems (*EEW*, 1, pp. 165–77; 2, pp. 277–8). The writings in question clearly establish that the "Cambridge cash-balance approach" was indeed Marshall's creation, and though they remained unpublished until 1975, they were not unknown. Keynes (1924, pp. 29–30) quotes extensively from them, and remarks that "When I attended [Marshall's] lectures in 1906 he used to illustrate this theory with some very elegant diagrams" (p. 29 n. 1). It is perhaps not stretching the probabilities too far to suppose that the diagram from 1871 (see *EEW*, 2, p. 278) which includes the rectangular hyperbola demand for nominal balances function more often associated, albeit in an algebraic formulation, with Pigou (1917), is representative of these.[10] Though the supply and demand theory of the value of money, applied to both the short and long run, which these writings expound occurs in various forms throughout Marshall's published work, this, his first account of it, is a piece of purely theoretical exposition which clearly represents a response to a problem posed by the internal logic of the body of economic analysis he had inherited, rather than to some contemporary policy issue. Thus, though applications to policy issues abound in Marshall's later writings, they are applications of analysis whose essential properties had been worked out before the policy problems in question presented themselves.

I have quite deliberately referred here to Marshall's theory of the *value* of money, rather than to his theory of the *demand* for money. The problem he inherited from Mill, to provide a general theory of the price level, was the problem he sought to solve. To lose sight of this is to lose sight of the essential element in the continuity between Marshall's thought and that of his Classical predecessors. Marshall did, to be sure, jettison a key component of their monetary theory, namely the concept of the transactions velocity of circulation. He did so because "The fact that in general goods pass through a great but varying number of hands on their way from the producer to the consumer . . . introduces grave complications" into any attempt to "establish a connection between 'the rapidity of circulation' and the value of money". As he notes, "Mr. Mill is aware of the evil, but he has not pointed out the remedy" (*EEW*, 1, p. 169). Marshall did not find in Classical monetary theory, and therefore sought to provide, "a clear statement of the balancing of advantages which in the ultimate analysis must be found to determine the magnitude of every quantity that rests upon the will of man". In the case of money the "quantity" to be determined was "its [money's] value" (*EEW*, 1, p. 165).

For Marshall, the place to look for the relevant "balancing of advan-

10. Patinkin (1965) has argued that this rectangular hyperbola would be better termed a "market equilibrium curve". Certainly it is a curve compensated for variations in real wealth induced by price level changes, a qualification which Marshall never explicitly discussed. This curve also appears in the "Diagrammatic Note on a Metallic Currency" printed as Appendix C to *Money Credit and Commerce*. This appendix deals with the determination of prices under a metallic currency when there is an alternative nonmonetary demand for the metal, essentially the most general case of the analysis developed in the 1871 unpublished note (see below). Its style is terse and rigourous, and in it Marshall is very careful about the stock-flow distinction. These characteristics lead me to presume that its composition long antedated its 1923 publication.

tages" was in the individual's decision "to retain in his possession a supply of money" (*EEW*, 1, p. 167). The advantage gained by so doing lay "in being able readily to satisfy such of his wants as he cannot easily make provision for a long time beforehand", but it was gained at the cost of the income forgone by applying his wealth to some other use – the alternative asset actually cited as an example is a horse – so that, in general

> If he retains but a very small ready command over commodities he is likely to be put occasionally to a considerable inconvenience; if he retains a very large one he receives no adequate compensation for the inaction to which his wealth is doomed. He has then to settle what is the exact amount which on the average it will answer his purpose to keep in this ready form.   (*EEW*, 1, pp. 167–8)

Note that Marshall here explicitly treats the decision about how much cash to hold as involving the allocation of a stock of *wealth*. However, he went on to express the amount of cash chosen in units of *real income* (thus creating the basis for a stock-flow confusion that was to plague monetary economics till the early 1930s).[11] He took this extra step because, as I have already emphasised, he was interested in the theory of portfolio choice in general, and the theory of the demand for money in particular, not for their own sakes, but as components of a theory of the price level. Thus, the model economy in which he develops his analysis uses as its means of exchange "the shells of a certain extinct fish" and produces corn. The decision to hold money is characterised as a decision to hold purchasing power over corn in the form of shells, and Marshall shows that "If . . . there be a million such shells, and the income of the country be sixty million bushels of corn" then, if the average individual wishes to hold purchasing power equal to one tenth of income in the form of money, "a shell will be worth . . . six bushels", and that if desired money holdings then fall to one twentieth of income "the value of each shell will diminish . . . until [it] is only worth three bushels" (*EEW*, 1, p. 168).

Here we have a special exogenous nominal money stock case of a general supply and demand theory of the purchasing power of money over current output. Marshall, however, immediately and successively generalised it, first to the case in which the stock of shells, rather than being given, can be increased by dredging, second to the case in which the shells "are used for ornament and for other purposes" (*EEW*, 1, p. 172) and finally to the case in which "other things beside shells are used as money, paper or whatnot" (*EEW*, 1, p. 173), in the process bringing his

11. On the failure of later Cambridge economics to be careful about the income–wealth distinction and the implications of this fact for our interpretation of the significance of Liquidity Preference theory in the development of Monetary Economics, see Patinkin (1974) and Laidler (1986).

model closer and closer to the complex commodity-based monetary system of the late nineteenth-century world. In the first case he notes that a downward shift in the economy's demand for money might leave the value of shells "permanently below their cost of production" but that an upward shift would make it "profitable to dredge in deeper and deeper water" (*EEW*, 1, p. 171); in the second he remarks that the influence of the demand for shells as a commodity would break (except in a very special case) the proportionality relationship between the quantity of shells and their value; and in the third he notes that

> the effect of these contrivances [paper money and whatnot] is to cause other modes of exchange to be substituted for those into which money enters . . . They cause the amount of commodities over which persons choose to keep a command in the form of money to diminish: they thus diminish the value of shells or (as we may now say) of gold and silver: thereby setting free more of them to be used as commodities and at the same time diminishing the labour spent in working mines to obtain the means of doing what can in many cases be better done by the avoidance of than by the use of gold and silver.   (*EEW*, 1, pp. 173–4)

Now the idea that paper money economised on real resources had been understood and taken seriously by Classical economists since Adam Smith, but before Marshall, their analyses had emphasised the alternative uses to which an existing stock of specie could be devoted.[12] They had paid little attention to the possibility that its introduction, or extension, might influence the amount of "labour spent working in the mines". If they had, perhaps they would have realised, as did Marshall, that the marginal production cost of specie, which they treated as exogenously determining the long run value of the price level, was in fact an endogenous variable whose value depended upon the nature of monetary institutions. Only in a stationary economy in which the purchasing power of money was just equal to the cost ruling on the margin of production in the most fruitful mines, and hence in which output was equal to zero, could the price level be thought of as determined solely by technical factors. Marshall derived precisely this latter result in his mathematical notes with the aid of both a differential equation and a discrete time diagrammatic approximation to the model yielding that equation.[13]

---

12. The most notable discussions of this issue occur in the *Wealth of Nations* (Smith 1776, Book 2, Ch. 2) and Ricardo's (1816) *Proposals for an Economical and Secure Currency* of which Marshall was a careful reader.
13. In discussing these mathematical fragments, Whitaker (*EEW*, 2, p. 177) explicitly draws attention to the way in which "the quantity-theory and cost-of-production approaches are synthesised" in the analysis they present.

The full implications of this analysis were not lost on Marshall. In 1887 he told readers of the *Contemporary Review,* in an essay which he also submitted as part of his evidence to the Gold and Silver Commission (*Memorials,* pp. 188–211), that

> as things are, gold and silver have no natural value. They are so durable that the year's supply is never more than a small part of the total stock. And therefore their values do not conform closely to their costs of production. and, insofar as their values are regulated by the relations between the demands for them and existing stocks of them, their value is artificial, because the demand for them as currency is itself artificial.   (*Memorials,* p. 200)

He returned to this same theme in his 1899 evidence to the Indian Currency Committee, telling the Committee that

> I think it is also agreed that there is something fiduciary in the value of gold and silver; that is, that part of their value depends upon the confidence with which people generally look forward to the maintenance and extension of the monetary demand for them. Of course, their value is, in the long run, controlled by cost of production; but that influence is remote, and new supplies are always small relatively to the existing stock. And so fluctuations of their value are mainly governed at any time by currency legislation, actual and prospective.   (*OP,* p. 269)

Indeed, as late as 1923, in a letter quoted by Keynes (1924, p. 33, fn. 2), he referred to "the – in itself foolish – superstition that gold is the 'natural' representative of value".

Thus, as with his general approach to value theory, so in his specific application of it to the value of money, which appears to be the first case for which he worked it out, Marshall's "correction" of Classical economics' overemphasis on costs of production resulted in a radical revision of doctrine.[14] Even so, as I have remarked above, so long as continuity is not confused with mere repetition, Marshall's own view of his work as growing out of Classical economics rather than standing in opposition to it is easily sustained in this instance.

Marshall claimed that, by basing monetary analysis on the notion of a demand for money, he rendered it more practically useful than the alternative transactions velocity approach. Certainly, as I have pointed out elsewhere (Laidler, 1988), this latter way of going about things led Mill into

---

14. Marshall did not, of course, mean that the cost of production had no influence on the value of a commodity money, as should be clear from reading the preceding quotation, but only denied that it ever was, for practical purposes, its sole or even predominant determinant.

considerable confusion about the role of credit and credit instruments as influences on the price level. Sometimes he argued that, because transactions financed by credit could affect prices, it was the existence of credit itself, rather than any instruments to which it might give rise, that undermined the simplicity of the Quantity Theory; sometimes he attributed a causative influence on prices to the fact that credit instruments themselves formed part of the "circulating medium". Marshall's supply and demand analysis enabled him to be much more sure footed in dealing with these matters in the course of his evidence to the Gold and Silver Commission. Mill thought, as an empirical matter, that changes in velocity were at least as important as changes in the quantity of money in affecting the price level, and Marshall's view was similar. In his "Preliminary Memorandum" to the Commission he stated:

> While accepting the doctrine that, "*other things being equal*, prices rise or fall proportionately to every increase or diminution in the metal or metals which are used as the standard of value," I consider that the conditioning clause, "other things being equal," is of overwhelming importance and requires careful attention.
>
> (*OP*, p. 21; Marshall's italics)

He clarified his concerns here, both in that memorandum and in the subsequent oral evidence from which the following quotations are drawn, demonstrating in the process the capacity of his supply and demand apparatus to cut through many complexities. Marshall's reasons for taking the "other things equal" clause seriously may be summarised, in his own words, as follows:

> without any change in the amount of currency the average level of prices might be altered, not only by a change in the proportion of credit to other means of purchasing, but also by any other change in the methods of business.   (*OP*, p. 38)

He did not regard the question of where to draw the line between other assets and "currency" as crucial here, provided that consistency was observed, and used the term himself (as we nowadays would) to include coin and banknotes. That being the case, the role of what he called "bank money" – deposits – in the monetary system was of crucial importance, and Marshall presented to the Commission a sketch of what we would now call money multiplier analysis to show how their quantity was linked to the banking system's reserves. This sketch was not quite the first of this process to appear in the history of monetary economics – the essential point is to be found, for example, in Pennington (1829) – but it did, as Humphrey (1986) has noted, represent an important step forward in the development of the doctrine. Marshall put things as follows:

> I should consider what part of its deposits a bank could lend, and then I should consider what part of its loans would be redeposited with it and with other banks and, *vice versa,* what part of the loans made by other banks would be received by it as deposits. Thus I should get a geometrical progression; the effect being that if each bank could lend two-thirds of its deposits, the total amount of loaning power got by the banks would amount to three times what it otherwise would be. If it could lend four-fifths, it will then be five times; and so on.   (*OP,* p. 37)

An influx of gold reserves to the banking system would thus "enable people to increase their speculation on borrowed capital; it would therefore, increase the demand for commodities and so raise prices" (*OP,* p. 38).[15] However,

> it would have the ultimate effect of adding to the volume of the currency required for circulation . . . because, prices having risen, a person who had found it answer his purpose to have on the average 17 *l.* in currency in his pocket would now require 18 *l.*, or 19 *l.*; and so on for others.   (*OP,* p. 38)

Now the notion of a demand for a stock of money was not completely absent from Classical economics. References to agents keeping a certain amount of cash on hand "to meet occasional demands" occur frequently from Adam Smith onwards, while Marshall himself (*MCC,* p. 47) gave credit to Sir William Petty as an originator of the idea. Even so, with one important exception, the notion played no essential role in Classical analysis, the exception in question concerning the crisis phase of the credit cycle, particularly as it appears in the work of Mill, not only in his *Principles of Political Economy,* but also, and indeed more conspicuously, in his "Of the Influence of Consumption upon Production" (1844). For Mill, a crucial factor in precipitating and amplifying the downturn of a speculative boom was a loss of confidence on the part of agents which drove them to attempt to build up cash balances at the expense of their demand for inventories of goods.

The Classical theory of the cycle was, to modern eyes, incomplete in at least two respects. First, its account of speculative activity during the upswing of the cycle was more descriptive than analytic; second, as I have already noted above, fluctuations in real variables such as output and employment were not integrated into it. Marshall made important advances in cycle theory, once again responding to inadequacies of Classical

---

15. Eshag (1963, pp. 9–10) records that the geometric progression referred to in the above quotation is explicitly worked out in a marginal note found in Marshall's personal copy of Giffen's 1877 *Stock Exchange Securities.*

analysis. That this was his starting point is easily confirmed by inspecting pages 152 through 154 of *The Economics of Industry* (Marshall and Marshall 1879, hereafter *EI*). The account of the characteristics of the cycle which appears there is, in essence, a paraphrase of Mill's analysis as it appears on pages 542 and following of his *Principles of Political Economy* (1871), and is aptly summarised in what the Marshalls refer to as "the famous words of Lord Overstone": "First we find . . . a state of quiescence,—next, improvement,—growing confidence,—prosperity,—excitement,—over-trading,—convulsion,—pressure,—stagnation,—distress,—ending again in quiescence" (*EI*, p. 153).[16] Quoting Mill to the effect that "What constitutes the means of payment for commodities is simply commodities", the Marshalls take pains to deny that the crisis and downswing phases of the cycle are marked by general over-production. Nevertheless, they concede, as once again had Mill, that "though men have the power to purchase they may not choose to use it", attributing this "evil" to "a want of confidence". The result is a "state of commercial disorganisation" for which the remedy is "a restoration of confidence" (*EI*, p. 154).

All this is conventional Classical analysis, but what comes next sets the Marshalls' analysis of the cycle apart from that of Mill: namely their realisation that "The connexion [*sic*] between a fall of prices and a *suspension of industry* requires to be further worked out" (*EI*, p. 155; my italics) and their explanation of that connection.

> It . . . very seldom happens . . . that the expenses which a manufacturer has to pay out fall as much in proportion as the price which he gets for his goods. For when prices are rising, the rise in the price of the finished commodity is *generally* more rapid than that in the price of the raw material, *always* more rapid than that in the price of labour; and when prices are falling, the fall in the price of the finished commodity is *generally* more rapid than that in the price of the raw material, *always* more rapid than that in the price of labour.
>
> (*EI*, p. 156; my italics)

Here, we have an explanation of fluctuations in real income and employment based on the postulate of money wage stickiness.[17] This postulate

---

16. Parts of this 1879 account of the cycle were incorporated verbatim into Marshall's 1887 *Contemporary Review* paper, and later still into *Money Credit and Commerce* (pp. 249 et seq.). The quotation from Overstone is also repeated in *Money Credit and Commerce* (p. 246).

17. Henry Thornton discussed money wage stickiness in *Paper Credit* (1802), but this idea did not enter the mainstream of Classical Economics. Thornton's work was almost completely forgotten by the 1870s, and seems to have been quite unknown to Marshall, at least until much later in his life. Jacob Hollander (1911) discussed *Paper Credit* in an essay cited in *Money Credit and Commerce*, but followed McCulloch's (1845) example of confusing Henry with his brother Samuel Thornton, a one-time

was, of course, to become the mainstay of attempts to explain unemployment before the publication of the *General Theory* (Keynes, 1936), and, Keynes's denials of its importance notwithstanding, of "Keynesian economics" too.

This extension of Classical theory to encompass real variables is not Marshall's only contribution to cycle theory. The *Economics of Industry* does not refer explicitly to the behaviour of the demand for money over the course of the cycle, but Marshall's already cited *Contemporary Review* essay of eight years later does take up this other element of Mill's analysis. In this essay Marshall first notes that

> We often talk of borrowing or lending on good security at, say, 5 per cent . . . [but] Suppose, for instance, a man borrows £100 under contract to pay back £105 at the end of the year. If the purchasing power of money has meanwhile risen 10 per cent . . . he cannot get the £105 which he has to pay back without selling one-tenth more commodities than would have been sufficient for the purpose at the beginning of the year . . . while *nominally* paying 5 per cent . . . he has *really* been paying at $15\frac{1}{2}$ per cent. . . . if prices had risen so much that the purchasing power of money had fallen 10 per cent . . . he would *really* be paid $5\frac{1}{2}$ per cent.   (*Memorials*, p. 190, my italics)

He then goes on to argue that

> when prices are likely to rise, people rush to borrow money and buy goods, and thus help the prices to rise . . . those working on borrowed capital pay back less real value than they borrowed, and enrich themselves at the expense of the community

and that "[w]hen afterwards credit is shaken and prices begin to fall, everyone wants to get rid of commodities and get hold of money which is rapidly rising in value" (*Memorials*, p. 191).

The mechanism driving what we would now call aggregate demand here is a real balance effect, caused by changes in the quantity of money demanded which themselves arise from perceived changes in the relative returns to be had from holding cash and goods, supplemented by the credit-market effects of a lag in the real interest rate behind the nominal rate. The latter factor receives more explicit emphasis in Marshall's brief discussion of the cycle in his *Principles,* where the passages just quoted, and which originally appeared in the 1887 *Contemporary Review,* are repeated essentially verbatim, but with the following addition:

> Governor of the Bank of England. Hence he downgraded *Paper Credit* as a piece of special pleading on the part of the Bank. I suspect that a careless reading of this paper of Hollander's is the source of Marshall's extraordinary error (*MCC*, pp. 41–2) of numbering Ricardo among the authors of the *Bullion Report*.

When we come to discuss the causes of alternating periods of inflation and depression of commercial activity, we shall find that they are
intimately connected with those variations in the real rate of interest
which are caused by changes in the purchasing power of money.
(*Principles*, 1st ed., Book VII, Chapter 7, p. 627; all other eds.,
Book VI, Chapter 6, various pages)

By 1890 then, Marshall had clarified the analysis of the behaviour of demand over the course of the cycle with which, in 1887 he had supplemented
that of wage stickiness developed in the *Economics of Industry*, and had
produced what amounts to a prototype for any number of pre-Keynesian
analyses of the business cycle, not least that of Irving Fisher (1911).[18]

Now I am not here suggesting (as did Keynes, 1924, p. 30, fn. 3) that
Marshall has priority over Fisher in all aspects of the analysis of nominal
and real interest rates. Fisher (1896) used the distinction in an elaborate
statistical analysis intended to show that the paradoxical empirical association between high prices and high interest rates, and low prices and
low interest rates could be explained in terms of the lagged effect of
previous rates of change of prices on inflation expectations, and hence on
nominal interest rates. Marshall cited this work of Fisher's in considerable detail in his evidence to the 1899 Indian Currency Committee (*OP*,
pp. 270–4), and there is no sign in his earlier work of his having seen this
particular implication of the real–nominal interest rate distinction. Finally, it should be noted explicitly that though his analysis of monetary
mechanisms has much in common with that of Fisher, one should not
attribute to Marshall a "monetary" theory of the cycle in the sense of
treating exogenous fluctuations in the quantity of money as key impulses
initiating cyclical fluctuations. He analysed monetary fluctuations as
propagation mechanisms, but followed the predominant Classical tradition in not attempting to single out any one factor as a dominant impulse
initiating the cycle.

V   Monetary Policy Proposals

The account which I have given so far of Marshall's monetary economics
has concentrated on the relationship of his theoretical work to the ideas
which he inherited from the Classical tradition. That it has been possible
to get so far without mentioning the policy concerns of his own day is

18. The numerical example of the effects of inflation on real interest quoted earlier also
appears in the *Principles*, as it does (with Pounds changed to Rupees and Annas) in
Marshall's oral evidence to the Indian Currency Committee (*OP*, p. 271) not to
mention in *Money Credit and Commerce* (p. 74).

surely in and of itself convincing evidence that, in Marshall's hands, monetary economics took on the characteristics of a mature branch of economic science. Even so, no account of his monetary thought would be complete without some discussion of his responses to current policy problems. Here too, we shall find that combination of respect for inherited wisdom and great originality which marks his more abstract innovations. In particular, Marshall took for granted the Classical view that monetary policy was best directed to a price level goal. Nothing illustrates this better than his choice of title for the 1887 *Contemporary Review* article in which he set out his major monetary policy proposals. It is "Remedies for Fluctuations of General Prices".

Marshall's reasons for thinking price level fluctuations to be socially important reflect Classical concerns too, particularly those of Mill, about the welfare of the working classes.[19] To be sure, one would have to look far and wide in Classical economics to find any systematic discussion of a connection between price level behaviour and working class welfare, but for Marshall, the connection arose from his belief in the stickiness of money wages even as a secular phenomenon. This belief led him to make redistributive consequences the acid test of the importance of any long run pattern of price level behaviour. The first substantive passage of his "Preliminary Memorandum" to the Gold and Silver Commission (dated November 9, 1887) begins as follows:

> I think that the general interests of the country are best promoted by stationary prices; but that the benefits resulting from a rise in prices and the evils resulting from a fall of prices are commonly over-rated; and I think that it is not clearly established that a rise of prices is . . . to be preferred to a fall. . . . I doubt whether the influence exerted in this direction [i.e., irregularities of employment and discouragement of enterprise] by a slow and gradual fall is very great. On the other hand, during such a fall a powerful friction tends to prevent money wages in most trades falling as fast as prices; and this tends almost imperceptibly to establish a higher standard of living among the working classes, and to diminish the inequalities of wealth.
>
> (OP, pp. 19–20)

In his oral evidence he returned to this theme:

> Supposing that it [a falling price level] does not diminish considerably the total productiveness of industry, then its effect is . . . on the

19. In particular I have in mind here Mill's discussion of the problem of low wages in the *Principles of Political Economy*. Note also that Marshall's early (1873) essay on "The Future of the Working Classes" (*Memorials*, Ch. 2) begins with a reference to Mill's *Autobiography*.

whole good; because it tends to cause a distribution of wealth better than that which we should otherwise have. . . . some rich lenders of money . . . get their incomes increased . . . which I regret; but the greater part of the redistribution is in the direction of . . . employees, and that, I think, is a gain.   (*OP*, p. 91)

In 1899, Marshall was still arguing in the same vein before the Indian Currency Committee:

> [F]or ten or fifteen years after I began to study political economy, I held the common doctrine, that a rise of prices was generally benefi- cial to businessmen directly, and indirectly to the working classes. But after that time I changed my views. . . . The assertions that a rise of prices increased the real wages of the worker were so consonant with the common opinion of people who had not specially studied the matter, that it was accepted almost as an axiom; but within the last ten years, the statistics of wages have been carried so far in certain countries . . . that we are able to bring it to the test . . . the rise of real wages after 1873 when prices were falling was greater than before 1873 when prices were rising.   (*OP*, p. 286)

Marshall thus read a cause and effect relationship into the association between falling prices and rising real wages, but his judgement that rising real wages had a negligible influence on employment was confined to secular effects. We have already seen that a key mechanism in his positive analysis of the business cycle involved the effects on employment of the interaction of short run variations of the price level with more slowly moving money wages. As one would expect in light of the criteria by which Marshall judged the desirability of secular price level movements, the consequences of those fluctuations of employment for the welfare of their victims made stabilising the cycle an important policy goal for him.[20]

> The fluctuations in the value of what we use as our standard are ever either flurrying up business activity into unwholesome fever, or else closing factories and workshops by the thousand in businesses that

---

20. There is considerable discussion of unemployment and related issues in the *Official Papers*, some of the themes of which found their way into *Money Credit and Com- merce*. Marshall's views on the topic may be summarised as follows: cyclical unem- ployment was no more serious a problem in the late nineteenth century than it had been earlier, but was more visible as a result of industrialisation (*OP*, pp. 92–3); technical change and its associated structural disruption of the economy was a particu- larly important source of unemployment in the 1880s (*OP*, pp. 100–1); minimum wages negotiated by trade unions might contribute to unemployment among the aged (*OP*, pp. 97–8); and secularly falling prices, even though they increased real wages, made no significant contribution to unemployment (*OP*, pp. 91, 98).

have nothing radically wrong with them. . . . Perhaps the bad habits
of mind and temper engendered by periods of business fever do more
real harm than periods of idleness; but it is less conspicuous. . . . In
time of stagnation he who runs may read in waste and gaunt faces a
degradation of physique and a weakening of energy, which often tells
its tale throughout the whole of the rest of the lives of the men,
women, and children who have suffered from it.

(*Memorials*, p. 192)

Stabilising the price level in the short run, or failing that, preventing price
level fluctuations from having real consequences, provided, in Marshall's
eyes, two means whereby the stability of real variables could be attained.

The 1887 *Contemporary Review* article from which the foregoing quotation is taken contained a proposal for what Marshall termed a "Stable
Bimetallism", [but which has come to be called, following Edgeworth
(1895), symmetallism]. This was conceived at least as much with an eye
to promoting short term price level stability as it was to pursuing any
longer term goals. Marshall shared the belief of most of his contemporaries that, in the circumstances of the 1880s, increasing industrial use of
gold along with its growing adoption as an international currency was
causing, and was likely to continue to cause, secular deflation of gold
prices, but, as we have seen, he did not share the fear of many of them
that this deflation would have serious real consequences. Nor did he find
very attractive the most widely touted cure for this problem, namely the
monetisation of silver alongside gold at a fixed relative price set by the
monetary authorities. Such a scheme could only be implemented by international agreement, and was likely to degenerate quickly into silver
monometallism as a result of the well understood operation of Gresham's
Law, particularly if the fixed relative mint price of the metals overvalued
silver, as Marshall feared it would.[21]

Instead of conventional bimetallism, Marshall proposed a scheme
which, as he said, differed from Ricardo's 1816 *Proposals for an Economical and Secure Currency*

> only by being bimetallic instead of monometallic. I propose that
> currency should be exchangeable at the Mint or Issue Department
> not for gold, but for gold and silver, at the rate of . . . £1 for $56\frac{1}{2}$
> grains of gold, together with, say, twenty times as many grains of
> silver. . . . There would, as now, be token coins of silver and bronze,
> but none of gold.   (*Memorials*, pp. 204–5)

21. There is no space here to go into either the analytic details of bimetallism, or the
historical and political details of attempts to establish it in the late nineteenth century.
Bordo (1987) provides a brief and readable account of the essentials of the matter.

So that, although

> [t]o insure convertibility the currency would not be allowed to exceed, say, three times the bullion in the Issue Department[, t]he country would save so much on the cost of its currency that it could well afford to keep, as a normal reserve, bullion worth, say £30,000,000 in excess of this limit.   (*Memorials*, p. 205)

Marshall listed a number of advantages for this scheme, which, as Bordo and Schwartz (1987) have pointed out, amounted to making sterling convertible into a basket of two international currencies: "(1) It would be economical and secure; (2) Though economical, the largeness of its reserve would obviate the sharp twinges that now frequently occur in the money market" (*OP*, p. 206). He also claimed that it would tend to stabilise sterling by making its purchasing power vary with the mean value of gold and silver, rather than with one of them alone; that it did not require any attempt to peg the relative price of the metals; that it could be adopted by one country in isolation; that it could constitute the basis of an international monetary system if and as other countries adopted it; and that it represented a step towards adopting a "tabular standard" for deferred payments (surely this claim is rather forced). The first two reasons he listed and particularly the second of them were the really important ones, if we may judge by the attention he paid to the general issue of the size of the Bank of England's specie reserves in his oral evidence to the Gold and Silver Commission.[22]

In that oral evidence, starting from "the arguments at the end of Bagehot's *Lombard Street* [(1873)], and pushing them rather further than it does" (*OP*, p. 111), Marshall expressed concern about the slenderness of the Bank of England's gold reserve and the "extreme sensitiveness" (*OP*, p. 110) which that created for the banking system as a whole. Without referring explicitly to his "stable bimetallism" scheme, he argued the desirability of introducing a fiduciary issue of one pound notes (five pounds was the smallest note then in circulation) and of using the bulk of the gold thus released from the coinage to strengthen the Bank of England's specie reserve so that "the bank could afford to lose 5,000,000 *l*, or 6,000,000 *l*, or more gold without feeling bound to act at all violently on the money market" (*OP*, p. 110). Moreover, to give the Bank extra room for manoeuvre, he suggested a merging of its Issue and Banking Departments, and hence an abandonment of the organisational principles laid down in the 1844 Bank Charter Act (*OP*, pp. 112, 164). The avowed

---

22. It will be recalled that the 1887 *Contemporary Review* piece was submitted by Marshall to the Commission as part of his written evidence.

purpose of all this was to give to the directors of the Bank more room to exercise "their discretion, . . . acting on their knowledge of the special circumstances of each case" (*OP*, p. 112) in insulating the domestic monetary sector from balance of payment shocks.

Marshall did not propose relying on increased discretionary powers vested in the Bank of England, whether under gold or gold-and-silver convertibility, as the sole means of ensuring greater cyclical stability in the British economy. Central to the "Remedies for Fluctuations of General Prices" which he proposed in 1887, was indexation, or, as Jevons (1875) had earlier called it, a "tabular standard of value" (see *Memorials*, pp. 197–9). Once an index number measuring a "suitable standard of purchasing power" to be called "the unit" had been chosen, information about variations in its value in terms of cash should be published regularly by the government. The use of the unit to denominate credit transactions, and, "where not determined by special sliding scales", wages and salaries too, was to be encouraged, though not legally required. Marshall clearly thought that the scheme was sufficiently attractive that nothing more would be needed to get it widely adopted. Its advantages were, of course, twofold. The real rate of interest on indexed loan contracts would not vary with the rate of inflation, nor would the real value of indexed money wages. Hence the main mechanism driving speculative activity over the course of the cycle would be disconnected, as would the link between price level variations and fluctuations in output and employment.

Keynes (1924, p. 33) tells us that "The *Economist* mocked at Symmetallism and the optional Tabular Standard; and Marshall, always a little over-afraid of being thought unpractical or above the head of the 'business man' (that legendary monster), did not persevere". Symmetallism (or rather bimetallism) receives but one passing reference in Marshall's 1899 evidence to the Indian Currency Committee, indexation none at all, and it was left to others, notably Edgeworth (1895), to keep Marshall's ideas on monetary reform alive.[23]

23. The *Economist* had ridiculed Jevons's proposal for a "tabular standard" in an 1875 review of *Money and the Mechanism of Exchange*, unsigned, but written by Bagehot. In the second (1892) volume of the *Economic Journal*, Aneurin Williams, then a director of Linthorpe Iron Works Middlesborough, a leading figure in the cooperative movement, later a Labour Member of Parliament, and to whom Leon Walras (1886, p. v) referred as "un de mes correspondents anglais", published a proposal for an indexed currency very much along the lines of Fisher's later "compensated dollar" scheme (Williams, 1892). This article referred to Marshall's *Contemporary Review* essay (though not to the footnote in which Marshall had himself described, though not endorsed, a similar scheme). Williams's proposal, surely impractical to the extent that it envisaged the daily adjustment of the rate at which the pound was convertible into specie, prompted a scornful reply from no less a person-

Marshall's 1899 evidence is strongly marked by a general concern with smoothing out short term price level fluctuations in order to mitigate the cycle, and by a belief that the key to curing the ills of the downswing is to be found in avoiding the preceding speculative boom. In the last respect, Marshall's ideas harked back to those of Overstone and other members of the Currency School, but only to a degree. The latter had hoped to avoid inflationary booms by the automatic device of subjecting the Bank of England's note issue to a 100 percent marginal specie reserve requirement. This mechanism, embodied in the 1844 Bank Charter Act, had of course failed to achieve its desired end, and in proposing that it be pursued by discetionary policy, Marshall moved beyond orthodox Classical views on this issue. Bagehot's principles of activist central banking were aimed not so much at eliminating the cycle as they were at ensuring that its crisis phase did not degenerate into a financial panic. For Marshall, addressing the Indian Currency Committee in 1899, the "sudden fall of prices" which accompanies the downswing

> is an almost unmixed injury to the employé [*sic*] as it is to the employer, but a fall of prices of this kind is seldom or never the product of natural causes. It is nearly always, if not always, the result of a previous inflation of prices and launching of frail enterprises by fraudulent or incompetent people who have floated into prosperity at the cost of others on the top of a wave of rising prices. To attribute this social *malaise* to the fall of prices, instead of to the previous morbid inflation which caused it, is as reasonable as to attribute the headaches which follow a night of feasting and rioting to want of a sufficiently nourishing breakfast, instead of to the bad condition of the digestive organs that took away the appetite for the breakfast. This is perhaps, the chief centre of difference between those bimetallists who, like myself, wish for bimetallism only as a means of diminishing fluctuations; and those who wish for it also, and, perhaps, mainly, as a means of raising prices.   (*OP*, pp. 285–6)

This 1899 evidence of Marshall's leaves the impression that he had, by then, become rather satisfied with the resilience of the British monetary system, and perhaps it is this fact, as much as any fear of being thought

age than Robert Giffen, who also prevailed upon the editors of the *Economic Journal* to reprint Bagehot's 1875 review of Jevons (Giffen, 1892; Bagehot, 1892). Giffen, who had been assistant editor of the *Economist* under Bagehot in 1875, was vehemently opposed to any sort of indexation, not just Williams's proposal, though his attack on Jevons and Williams avoided explicit mention of Marshall. In his attack, Giffen's famous common sense and practicality dominated his skills as an economic analyst; Marshall, whose paper defending his treatment of economic history in the *Principles* appeared in the same issue of the *Economic Journal* as Giffen's and Bagehot's critiques of indexation, did not, to the best of my knowledge, ever take public issue with Giffen on this matter.

impractical, that accounts for the absence from the evidence in question of radical reform proposals. The Baring crisis of 1890 had occurred since Marshall's previous pronouncements on monetary policy, and this crisis, unlike its many predecessors, had been managed without any major failures in the financial community. It had also, in Presnell's (1968, p. 168) words,

> accelerated the amalgamation and strengthening of banks and . . . encouraged the keeping of higher and more stable cash ratios; . . . emphasised . . . the primacy of the Bank of England, and encouraged grudging bankers to recognise their own and the national interest in co-operation with the Bank.

Marshall noted these same developments with satisfaction, and indeed gave them as reasons for his opinion that the British model was not a good one to adopt in reforming the less sophisticated Indian monetary system whose operations were the main subject of the 1899 Committee's enquiries. In India, banking, and particularly branch banking, was less developed, and currency played a much bigger role. In Marshall's view, the main threat to financial stability there came not from external drains of bullion, but from internal drains of currency. Moreover, India was poor, and could not afford the luxury of a large bullion reserve, so that, for her case "it seems better to adopt the more economic provision of a moderate reserve stock of bullion and coin, combined with a limited and automatic elasticity of fiduciary paper currency" (*OP*, p. 324).

Marshall recommended that any reform of India's monetary system should "go on the lines of the 1844 [Bank Charter] Act, somewhat modified as in the Reichsbank Act" (*OP*, p. 284). The particular provisions of this latter document that attracted him were those "enabling the Reichsbank to increase its issues to meet any emergency, whether due to variations from one part of the year to another, or to a variation in one particular year of the general course of business" (*OP*, p. 283), provisions which, he thought, did not in fact violate the spirit of the Bank Charter Act itself, and which certainly had been *de facto* adopted before the 1870s.[24] Thus, though Marshall had, by 1899, abandoned his 1887 pro-

24. Marshall's conception of the "spirit" of the Bank Charter Act derived from his reading of then recently published evidence about the views of Sir Robert Peel, to the effect that he had "not supposed that the Act could be maintained under all circumstances" (*OP*, p. 283). Since the evidence in question stemmed from Parliamentary hearings held in the wake of the Act's suspension during the financial crisis of 1847, a consequence which the Act's opponents had foreseen and predicted before its enactment, Marshall was probably rather ingenuous to accept it at face value. Note that Marshall's concern with providing an "elastic" currency for India has many parallels with arguments advanced in the subsequent decade in the United States in the course of the debates that led to the founding of the Federal Reserve System.

posals for monetary reform, the underlying thrust of his views on the conduct of monetary policy was nevertheless the same as it had been in 1887. In particular he still stressed the desirability of avoiding rapid short term oscillations in prices and he still attached great importance to designing monetary institutions so as to grant to a central bank (or some similar entity) scope for discretionary action to forestall or iron out such fluctuations. This latter concern underlay both his approval of the way in which the British monetary system had evolved by 1899, and his proposals for improving the operation of an Indian system that was at a different, earlier, stage of evolution.

As will be apparent from the foregoing discussion, this 1899 evidence of Marshall's shows that his monetary thought had changed only a little on the policy front, and not at all on theoretical issues, over the previous decade. Nothing more was to appear from him in this area till *Money Credit and Commerce*. His important monetary ideas were thus products of the 1870s and 1880s, even though they did not become readily accessible until 1923. It remains now to assess the influence of those ideas and their significance for the development of monetary economics. The next two sections of this essay are devoted to these questions.

VI Marshall's Influence

In the introduction to this essay, I claimed that Marshall's contributions to monetary economics were both original and important, and I noted that, his unusual publication practices notwithstanding, his work from the 1880s was read and cited by other important contributors to monetary economics. That the work was cited, however, does not automatically establish that it was also influential, and so something needs to be said explicitly about this matter.[25] To begin with, it hardly needs arguing that Marshall was influential in Cambridge. Pigou's classic (1917) paper on "The Value of Money" is thoroughly Marshallian, as is the monetary theory underlying Lavington's *English Capital Market* (1921) and Keynes's *Tract* (1923). Moreover, though as Patinkin (1974) and Laidler (1986) have both stressed, the Keynesian theory of liquidity preference is much more than a mere repetition of Marshall's ideas about the demand for money, there can be no denying Eshag's (1963) view that the latter doctrine grew out of the Marshallian tradition. Even so, it is worth remarking that Cambridge Monetary Economics was not synonymous with Marshallian Economics. Thus Dennis Robertson's cycle theories (1926) owe little to

25. I am grateful to George Stigler for drawing my attention to this all important point.

Marshall and his celebrated discussion of "money on the wing" and "money sitting" as two approaches (Quantity Theory and cash-balance) to the same problem of price level determination does not appear in the first edition of his *Money* (1922). It is only with the revised (1928) edition of this influential textbook that the cash-balance approach makes an explicit appearance. Furthermore, though Ralph Hawtrey's (1913) business cycle theory looks very Marshallian, not least in the critical role played therein by the "unspent margin" (firms' cash balance holdings), Hawtrey himself is on record as denying a direct influence of Marshall on his work.[26]

Cambridge was not, in any event, the only centre in which important advances were made in monetary economics at the turn of the nineteenth century, and the transformation of Classical into Neoclassical Monetary Theory was the work of many others besides Alfred Marshall. *Interest and Prices* (Wicksell 1898) and *The Purchasing Power of Money* (Fisher 1911) are two key works here and though both contain references to Marshall, they are far from being essays in Marshallian economics. There is nothing in Marshall's work on monetary problems to match Wicksell's careful analysis of the microeconomic factors determining the "natural" rate of interest and no anticipation of anything resembling his explicitly dynamic analysis of inflation as a "cumulative process"; Fisher's exposition of the Quantity Theory is remarkable precisely because it is based on the older transactions velocity tradition which Marshall discarded. Marshall's work did antedate that of Wicksell and Fisher, however, they had read some of it, and in each instance, a case may be made for a Marshallian influence on the details of their analysis.

As Patinkin (1965 Supplementary Note E) has noted, key elements in Wicksell's cumulative process are the influence of gold inflows on the interest rates at which banks are willing to lend and the subsequent influence of an internal drain of currency from the banks brought about by rising prices on those same interest rates. We have seen that Marshall dealt with just these points in his evidence to the Gold and Silver Commission, and Wicksell (1898, p. 76) referred to this evidence as "[b]y far the most valuable contribution towards a solution of this question . . ." namely "how it was possible for the quantity of gold in the banks . . . to exert an influence on prices". Wicksell, then, whose analysis of inflation

26. Rather he claimed to have built on the then prevailing conventional wisdom of the City. This does not rule out an indirect Marshallian influence by way of that conventional wisdom, though Hawtrey claimed Bagehot as its true originator. I am grateful to John Whitaker for providing me with a copy of the letter from Hawtrey to Claude Guillebaud dated October 22, 1963, in which Hawtrey makes these points. Note that Hawtrey was educated at Cambridge, but learned his economics from Sir John Clapham and G. P. Moriarty. On this see Bigg (1987).

was far richer than anything Marshall offered, nevertheless acknowledged Marshall's contribution in a context and manner that at least suggest an influence on his own thought. A similar point may be made with regard to Fisher. Marshall's discussion of the role of real and nominal interest rates in the mechanics of the business cycle is a mere sketch compared to Fisher's (1911, Chapter 4) treatment of "transition periods", but Fisher quoted the passage from the *Principles* dealing with this very issue not only here, but also in the much earlier *Appreciation and Interest* (1896, p. 79), when his monetary approach to cycle theory was still in an embryonic state. Once again it appears that Marshall did perhaps influence the work of one of his younger contemporaries.

VII   Unresolved Problems in Marshall's Monetary Economics

Be all this as it may, Marshall's indisputable influence on Pigou and Keynes is quite enough in itself to make him a figure of the first importance in the development of Monetary Economics, but it would be to miss the significance of his contribution to regard him as having simply participated in the completion of an edifice known as Classical monetary economics. Rather, in the process of coping with some of the logical difficulties that Classical economics had left open, he helped transform it into something else – namely Neoclassical monetary economics, a body of doctrine which was replete with tensions and unresolved problems of its own to which a later generation of monetary economists, not least at Cambridge, could and did respond.

Nowhere are these tensions more evident than in the policy positions which Marshall espoused in relation to the theory which informed them. His supply and demand theory of the price level undermined, once and for all, the powerful idea that, in the long run, a commodity based currency would provide the means of determining the price level independently of the human arrangements involved in the operation of the monetary system. Moreover, he did not believe that a commodity based currency could, or would, provide the price stability which he regarded as so important to economic and social welfare, and he understood perfectly the principles upon which a managed currency might be made to perform better than any commodity based system could. A footnote in his 1887 *Remedies* paper, quoted with great approval by Keynes (1924, pp. 32–3), who was then engaged in a campaign to put Britain once and for all on a managed paper currency and an adjustable exchange rate, read in part as follows:

> I will indicate briefly two such plans, though I do not advocate either of them. On the first plan the currency would be inconvertible. An automatic Government Department would buy Consols for currency whenever £1 was worth more than a unit, and would sell Consols for currency whenever it was worth less. . . . Those who had to pay balances to foreign countries would buy gold or silver in the open market; they would be certain of getting in exchange for this money gold and silver that had a fixed purchasing power in England. . . . The other plan is that of a convertible currency, each £1 note giving the right to demand at a Government Office as much gold as at that time had the value of half a unit, together with as much silver as had the value of half a unit. (*Memorials*, pp. 206–7n.)

The first of these plans is a scheme for fine tuning the price level by managing the quantity of a paper currency in circulation, and was essentially the same as that advocated by Wicksell (1898, p. 189). The second amounts to a blend of Irving Fisher's "compensated dollar" idea [see Fisher (1911, pp. 337 et seq.)] with Marshall's symmetallism.[27] Either of these plans seemed to offer a better chance of achieving Marshall's own stated policy goals than the measures he actually did suggest. He stopped short of advocating these alternatives, however, because "Every plan for regulating the supply of the currency, so that its value shall be constant, must, I think, be national and not international", and the adoption of either of them "would hinder rather than help the adoption of an international currency" (*Memorials*, pp. 206–7n.), something which Marshall hoped would eventually evolve.

In Classical Economics, there had been no tension between a commitment to price stability and an international money, since specie convertibility was regarded as a *sine qua non* for both goals. Advocates of inconvertible national monetary systems were regarded, usually with good reason, as inflationists. It was because Marshall did not believe that specie convertibility would guarantee price stability, a belief stemming from his theoretical doubts about the relevance of the idea of a "natural" value for gold and/or silver, that he was unable to embrace the Classical position. This tension between the desirability of price stability, something that could only be achieved with a managed, and hence (in the absence of supranational institutions which Marshall did not envisage) national currency, and the attractions of an international money, which first appeared in Marshall's work more than a century ago, ran through Keynes's work, both academic and practical, and still remains unresolved in modern policy debates on these issues.

Marshall's most obviously enduring contribution to monetary econom-

---

27. Neither Wicksell nor Fisher cites Marshall as having anticipated them.

ics was, as I have already argued, his modelling of the demand for money decision, but his work here left some important loose ends for his successors to take up. The 1871 notes, upon which my own account of Marshall's treatment of this relationship is based, were in fact more carefully put together than any of his later expositions of it. In particular, the notion that money holding involves a wealth allocation decision, which is utterly clear in 1871, was not explicitly developed in later accounts. This ambiguity found its way into Pigou's (1917) definitive account of the "Cambridge" theory of the price level, which followed Marshall's own later practice of using the imprecise word "resources" in contexts where it could only mean "wealth", where it could only mean "income", and where it could mean either. It took Keynes (1930, 1936) and Hicks (1935) finally to clarify this matter in the course of their development of liquidity preference theory.

Even in his 1871 account, however, Marshall stopped far short of developing a complete portfolio choice theory of the demand for money. Like the Classical economists before him Marshall believed that "The chief functions of money fall under two heads. Money is, first of all a *medium of exchange*. . . . The second function of money is to act as a *standard of value* or *standard of deferred payments*" (*Memorials*, p. 189, Marshall's italics). He did not think of money as a store of value *per se*, and hence did not analyse with any care the relationship between holding money as an asset and the forgone return on alternative assets. The closest that Marshall ever came to treating the money holding decision as one involving a demand for a store of value is in *Money Credit and Commerce* (p. 44), when he speaks of "The inhabitants of a country . . . keep[ing] by them on the average ready purchasing power to the extent of a tenth part of their annual income, *together with a fiftieth part of their property*" (my italics), and (p. 38) when he includes "stock exchange securities" among the alternatives to money.[28] By then, though, Lavington (1921) had already progressed much further in the direction of anticipating liquidity preference theory.

28.   Marshall's examples of alternative assets to money were typically highly indivisible durables, including a horse (*EEW*, 1, p. 167), a coat or a piano (*MCC*, p. 38), furniture, machinery, or cattle (*OP*, p. 267; *MCC*, p. 44). It might be noted that Walras, whose 1886 *Théorie de la Monnaie* gives him an undoubted claim to be regarded as one of the originators of the "cash balance approach", came no closer than did Marshall to formulating the money holding decision as one involving a portfolio choice in which rates of return on alternative assets might have a systematic influence on money holding. Indeed, Walras's algebraic formulation relating the demand for cash to money income is distinctly inferior to Marshall's 1871 equation relating it to wealth. It might further be noted that there is essentially no evidence of Walras's work on this topic influencing any important monetary economist before Marget (1931) drew attention to it.

Furthermore, Marshall never formulated the demand for money as involving a smooth functional relationship between desired cash holdings and either the rate of interest or the expected inflation rate. He told the Indian Currency Committee that

> it seems specially important, with reference to the Indian currency problem, to note that the level of prices which a given volume of currency will sustain, is liable to be affected by any lack of trust and confidence in the currency itself. . . . The lower is the credit of the currency, the lower will be the share of their resources which people keep in the form of currency; . . . I think it is agreed that, if the credit of the currency falls, its value falls relatively to commodities, even when there is no change in its volume.   (*OP*, p. 269)

This argument recurs in Pigou's (1917) paper, underlies Cannan's (1921) argument that repeated increases in the supply of money will raise prices more than proportionally, and also informs Keynes's (1923, pp. 42 et seq.) treatment of inflation as a tax on cash balances. It was not until the publication of Friedman's *Studies in the Quantity Theory of Money* (1956), however, that the inflation rate was formally and explicitly incorporated as an argument into the type of equation which Marshall first wrote down in 1871.[29]

Marshall's analysis of the cycle also left his successors with work to do. His treatment of the upswing was, as we have seen, centred on the postulate that the rate of profit expected by businessmen ran ahead of the real rate of interest at which they could borrow. Marshall could have considered the possibility that systematic changes in the composition of output might stem from this relative price distortion, and hence have been led into an Austrian style analysis of "forced saving" and its destructive consequences.[30] However, he did not. Instead he treated the cycle's upswing, or at least its later stages after previously unemployed resources had been put to work, as predominantly a matter of rising prices with no real consequences stemming from relative price distortions. It was left to the followers of Wicksell (1898) to take up this line of enquiry. During

---

29. On all this, see Patinkin (1974).
30. The forced saving idea, which underlies Austrian analysis, was well understood by Classical economists, as Hayek (1932) showed. Moreover, in a popular textbook of the late nineteenth century, Francis Walker (1878, pp. 472 et seq.) attributes an important, though not unique, causative role in panics to a distortion in the ratio of fixed to circulating capital in the economy brought about by speculative activity; Walker hence anticipates to a degree the Austrian idea of a distorted time structure of production. This general line of enquiry was thus available for Marshall to develop had he wished. As it was, among Cambridge economists, it was Dennis Robertson (1926) who took up the forced saving idea as an important building block of cycle theory.

the downswing and slump, Marshall argued, as we have seen, that sticky wages would cause unemployment. Moreover, because "a stoppage of work in any one trade diminishes the demand for the work of others" (*Memorials*, p. 191), Marshall believed that spillover effects would spread unemployment throughout the economy, particularly to investment goods industries. However, he offered no guide as to what factors would actually determine the level of output and its time path in "the resulting state of commercial disorganisation" (*EI*, p. 155). Formal treatments of the potentially equilibrating role of output changes, and associated analyses of multiplier and accelerator processes were not to come until after 1936.

VIII   Concluding Comment

I have not drawn attention to the fact that economists other than Marshall also contributed to the development of monetary economics during his lifetime, nor to the fact that his work has its shortcomings, to denigrate his achievements; quite the contrary. As I noted earlier, it is sometimes claimed that Monetary Economics lacks that strong internal dynamic which is the hallmark of a well defined discipline. The development of the area in the first seven decades of the nineteenth century was, as Fetter (1965) has shown, intimately linked to the challenges offered by the period's monetary history. Britain's suspension of gold convertibility between 1797 and 1821, the cyclical instability of her monetary system in subsequent decades, and the monetary consequences of the gold discoveries of 1849–51, all had a profound influence on the evolution of Classical monetary economics. On the other hand, Marshall's major contributions to the area were not, by and large, prompted by the policy problems of his time. He discussed policy issues, but used a theoretical apparatus created in response to the analytic problems which his forerunners, and Mill in particular, had left unsolved. So too did his younger contemporaries, notably (but not only) Fisher and Wicksell, address questions left open by their predecessors; and like Marshall, they too left behind unsolved theoretical problems of their own, and helped ensure that monetary economics would continue to grow independently of the accidents of the monetary history of the early twentieth century. As I have tried to document in this essay, Alfred Marshall thus made a crucial and early contribution to the transformation of monetary economics into a mature branch of Economic Science. One could hardly pay him a greater compliment than that.

References

Bagehot, W. (1873). *Lombard Street – A Description of the Money Market.* London: King.

(1892). "A New Standard of Value" *Economic Journal* 2: 427–77. Reprinted from *The Economist, 1875.*

Bastable, C. F. (1887). *Theory of International Trade.* Dublin: Hodges Figgis.

Bigg, R. J. (1987). "Hawtrey, Ralph George (1879–1975)". In J. Eatwell, M. Milgate, and P. Newman (eds.), *The New Palgrave: A Dictionary of Economics.* London: Macmillan.

Bordo, M. D. (1975). "John Cairnes on the Effects of the Australian Gold Discoveries, 1851–1872: an Early Application of the Methodology of Positive Economics," *History of Political Economy* 7:337–59.

(1987). "Bimetallism". In J. Eatwell, M. Milgate, and P. Newman (eds.), *The New Palgrave: A Dictionary of Economics.* London: Macmillan.

Bordo, M. D., and Schwartz, A. J. (1987). "The ECU – an Imaginary or Embryonic Form of Money: What Can We Learn From History". Paper presented at a Conference on "The ECU and European Monetary Integration". Leuven, June 1987, mimeo.

Bristow, J. A. (1987). "Bastable, Charles Francis (1855–1945)". In J. Eatwell, M. Milgate, and P. Newman (eds.), *The New Palgrave: A Dictionary of Economics.* London: Macmillan.

Cannan, E. (1921). "The Application of the Theoretical Apparatus of Supply and Demand to Units of Currency", *Economic Journal* 31:453–61.

Edgeworth, F. Y. (1895). "Thoughts on Monetary Reform", *Economic Journal* 5:434–51.

Eshag, E. (1963). *From Marshall to Keynes: an Essay on the Monetary Theory of the Cambridge School.* Oxford: Blackwell.

Fetter, F. W. (1965). *Development of British Monetary Orthodoxy 1797–1873.* Cambridge, Mass.: Harvard University Press.

Fisher, I. (1896). "Appreciation and Interest", *AEA Publications, Series Three* 2:331–442.

(1911). *The Purchasing Power of Money.* New York: Macmillan.

Friedman, M. (ed.) (1956). *Studies in the Quantity Theory of Money.* Chicago: University of Chicago Press.

Giffen, R. (1877). *Stock Exchange Securities.* London: Bell.

(1892). "Fancy Monetary Standards", *Economic Journal* 2:463–71.

Goschen, G. J. (1861). *The Theory of Foreign Exchanges.* London: Effingham Wilson.

Hawtrey, R. G. (1913). *Good and Bad Trade.* London: Constable.

Hayek, F. A. von (1932). "A Note on the Development of the Doctrine of Forced Saving", *Quarterly Journal of Economics* 47:123–33.

Hicks, J. R. (1935). "A Suggestion for Simplifying the Theory of Money", *Economica* N.S. 2:1–14.

Hollander, J. (1911). "The Development of the Theory of Money from Adam Smith to Ricardo", *Quarterly Journal of Economics* 25:429–70.

Hollander, S. (1985). *The Economics of J. S. Mill*. Toronto: University of Toronto Press.

Hume, D. (1752). "Of Interest" and "Of the Balance of Trade" in *Essays Moral Political and Literary*. Reprinted, London: Oxford University Press, 1963.

Humphrey, T. M. (1986). "The Theory of Multiple Expansion of Deposits – What it is and Whence it Came," *Federal Reserve Bank of Richmond Annual Report*, Richmond, Virginia.

Jevons, W. S. (1875). *Money and the Mechanism of Exchange*. London: King.

Keynes, J. M. (1923). *A Tract on Monetary Reform*. London: Macmillan.

(1924). "Alfred Marshall 1842–1924", *Economic Journal* 34:311–72. Reprinted in *Memorials:* 1–61. All page references are to the reprint.

(1930). *A Treatise on Money*. London: Macmillan.

(1936). *The General Theory of Employment Interest and Money*. London: Macmillan.

Laidler, D. (1986). "What Was New about Liquidity Preference Theory?" University of Western Ontario, mimeo.

(1988). "British Monetary Orthodoxy in the 1870s", *Oxford Economic Papers* 40:74–109.

Lavington, F. (1921). *The English Capital Market*. London: Methuen.

Marget, A. (1931). "Leon Walras and the 'Cash-Balance Approach' to the Value of Money", *Journal of Political Economy* 39:569–600.

Marshall, A., and Marshall, M. P. (1879). *Economics of Industry*. London: Macmillan.

McCulloch, J. R. (1845). *The Literature of Political Economy*. London: Longmans Green Brown and Longmans.

Milgate, M. (1987). "Giffen, Robert (1837–1910)". In J. Eatwell, M. Milgate, and P. Newman (eds.), *The New Palgrave: A Dictionary of Economics*. London: Macmillan.

Mill, J. S. (1844). "On the Influence of Consumption on Production", in *Some Unsettled Questions of Political Economy*. London 1844. 2d ed. (1874) reprinted, Clifton, N. J.: Kelley, 1974.

(1871). *Principles of Political Economy with Some of Their Applications to Social Philosophy*, 7th edition. Reprinted in 2 vols., ed. J. M. Robson. Toronto: University of Toronto Press, 1965.

Patinkin, D. (1965). *Money Interest and Prices*, 2d ed. New York: Harper and Row.

(1974). "Keynesian Monetary Theory and the Cambridge School", in H. G. Johnson and A. R. Nobay (eds.), *Issues in Monetary Economics*. London: Oxford University Press.

Pennington, J. (1829). "Paper Communicated by Mr. Pennington". Appendix No. 1 (pp. 117–27) to T. Tooke, *Letter to Lord Grenville on the Effects Ascribed to the Resumption of Cash Payments on the Value of the Currency*. London: Murray.

Pigou, A. C. (1917). "The Value of Money", *Quarterly Journal of Economics* 32:38–65.

Presnell, L. S. (1968). "Gold Reserves, Banking Reserves, and the Baring Crisis of 1890". In C. R. Whittlesey and J. S. G. Wilson (eds.), *Essays in Money and Banking in Honour of R. S. Sayers*. Oxford: Clarendon.

Ricardo, D. (1809). "Contributions to the *Morning Chronicle*". Reprinted in P. Sraffa (ed.), *Works and Correspondence of David Ricardo*, Vol. 3. Cambridge: Cambridge University Press, 1951.

(1816). *Proposals for an Economical and Secure Currency*. Reprinted in P. Sraffa (ed.), *Works and Correspondence of David Ricardo*, Vol. 4. Cambridge: Cambridge University Press, 1951.

Robertson, D. H. (1922). *Money*. Cambridge: Cambridge University Press. Revised ed., 1928.

(1926). *Banking Policy and the Price Level*. London: King.

Schwartz, A. J. (1987). "Currency School, Banking School, Free Banking School". In J. Eatwell, M. Milgate, and P. Newman (eds.), *The New Palgrave: A Dictionary of Economics*. London: Macmillan.

Smith, A. (1776). *An Enquiry into the Nature and Causes of the Wealth of Nations*. Reprinted, R. H. Campbell, A. S. Skinner, and W. B. Todd (eds.), Oxford: Clarendon, 1976.

Stigler, G. J. (1983). "Nobel Lecture: The Process and Progress of Economics", *Journal of Political Economy* 91:529–45.

Thornton, H. (1802). *An Enquiry into the Nature and Causes of the Paper Credit of Great Britain*. Reprinted, with two speeches on the Bullion Report 1811, ed., with an introduction, by F. A. von Hayek. London: Allen and Unwin, 1939.

Tooke, T. (1844). *An Inquiry into the Currency Principle*. Reprinted, London: London School of Economics, *Scarce Works on Political Economy No. 15*, 1959.

Walker, F. A. (1878). *Money*. New York: Holt.

Walras, L. (1886). *La Théorie de la Monnaie*. Lausanne: Corbaz.

Wicksell, K. (1898). *Interest and Prices*. Trans. R. F. Kahn, 1936. Reprinted, New York: Kelley, 1962.

Williams, A. (1892). "A 'Fixed Value of Bullion' Standard: a Proposal for Preventing General Fluctuations of Trade", *Economic Journal* 2:280–9.

4

Marshall and International Trade

JOHN CREEDY

I Introduction

The importance for Marshall's early work of the stimulus provided by Cournot and J. S. Mill is well documented. When writing to J. B. Clark in 1908, Marshall himself stated that during the four years after 1870, "I worked a good deal at the mathematical theory of monopolies, and at the diagrammatic treatment of Mill's problem of international values" (*Memorials*, pp. 416–8).[1] Historians of economic thought have generally suggested that, despite the acknowledged elegance and usefulness of Marshall's international trade diagrams, his contribution amounted largely to clarifying the less transparent analyses of Mill and other writers such as Torrens and Pennington. For example, although Schumpeter was known to be less sympathetic towards Marshall than other commentators, his judgement in this context is not atypical:

> Let us note at once that in this field Marshall did not do more than to polish and develop Mill's meaning. He cast it into an elegant geometrical model . . . that clarified the theory. But he was well aware . . . that his curves "were set to a definite tune, that called by Mill." This applies even to the geometrical apparatus; Mill's reads almost like a

I should like to thank Professor Denis O'Brien for comments on an earlier draft.
1. See also Marshall's letter to J. B. Clark of July 1900 (*Memorials*, pp. 412–13).

somewhat clumsy instruction for choosing these curves rather than
others.   (1954, p. 609)[2]

Viner, the major historian of international trade theory, also remarked
that Marshall's treatment "is in the main an exposition and elaboration
in geometrical form of Mill's analysis" (1955, p. 541).[3]

A major purpose of the present chapter is to assay the value of these
judgements by examining in some detail the genesis of Marshall's trade
diagrams. Any assessment of Marshall's contribution and its originality is
necessarily complicated by the need to have a clear view of the precise
nature of Mill's analysis. This itself is far from being a straightforward
matter; it has been all too easy for later writers to make exaggerated
claims for Mill. Furthermore, with the insight provided by Marshall's
analysis, there has been a temptation to read deeper meanings into Mill
than actually exist. Mill's "model" is therefore the subject of Section II. It
should be stressed that these comments are in no way intended to dis-
agree with Edgeworth's description of Mill's famous chapter 18 (Book
III) as being "stupendous" (1925, 2, p. 20), or with O'Brien's judgement
that it is "one of the greatest performances in the history of economics"
(1975, p. 183).

Section III goes on to show how the offer curve can be derived from the
basic diagrammatic form of Mill's model, produced in Section II. Marshall's early treatments of trade are then compared. In assessing Marshall's originality it is also necessary to consider the rather neglected
contribution of Whewell (1850). It will be argued that while Whewell
probably had a significant influence on Mill's "supplementary sections"
(added to the third edition of his *Principles*), no direct influence on Marshall can be traced.

The influence of Cournot is usually associated only with Marshall's
work on monopoly. However, Marshall's brief analysis of Cournot's
trade model is examined in Section IV.[4] The fundamental difference
between Cournot's and Mill's models of international trade is that the
former is a partial equilibrium treatment involving a single good, whereas the latter is a general equilibrium model. Marshall produced, at an
early stage, a "surplus" analysis of the gains from trade in the Cournot
model, but had more difficulty in dealing with the two-good general

2. Schumpeter is here quoting from Marshall's letter to Cunynghame of 28 June 1904
    (*Memorials*, p. 451). This is discussed in Section IV below.
3. See also O'Brien (1981, p. 57). The two book-length treatments of Marshall's econom-
    ics, by Davenport (1935) and Reisman (1987), ignore his contributions to international
    trade theory.
4. It will be seen that there is a technical connection between the analysis of monopoly
    developed by Marshall and the diagrammatic treatment of trade. The link involves the
    use of rectangular hyperbolas.

case. This is also examined in Section IV. Before turning to details, some broad comments on Marshall's use of diagrams are made in the following subsection.

Marshall and the Graphical Method

Marshall's facility with graphs contrasts sharply with his attitude towards their publication: the word ambivalent is too weak here. The obvious example is the *Principles*, where all diagrams are "relegated" to footnotes.[5] His international trade diagrams were given an even more extreme treatment. Indeed, in the modern atmosphere of "publish or perish" it is astonishing to realise that Marshall developed his diagrams in the early 1870s, but did not publish them until fifty years later when they were included in an appendix to *Money Credit and Commerce* (1923), compiled just before his death. It is true that parts of an early draft were printed for private circulation by Sidgwick in 1879 under the heading of *The Pure Theory of Foreign Trade*, but Marshall, being ill at the time, played no part in their selection.[6] Just as in his treatment of monopolies, Marshall wanted to treat the "realistic side" extensively before publishing anything.

Despite Marshall's extreme diffidence concerning publication, there seems no reason to dispute Keynes's claim that his diagrammatic exercises

> were of such a character in their grasp, comprehensiveness, and scientific accuracy, and went so far beyond the "bright ideas" of his predecessors, that we may justly claim him as the founder of modern diagrammatic economics.   (1972, p. 185)[7]

Marshall's reluctance to give his diagrams more prominence has been associated with his "puritanical views." For example, Viner has suggested that "Mathematics, and especially graphs, were Marshall's fleshpots, and if he frequently succumbed to their lure it was not without struggle with his conscience" (1958, p. 256).[8]

There is, however, no doubt that Marshall's diagrams have had a firm

5. Marshall used diagrams extensively in his teaching, however; see Keynes (1972, p. 118, n.2).
6. See (*EEW*, 2, p. 4), where in correspondence with Seligman, Marshall refers to some of the work as belonging "to the economic toy shop rather than practical work shop." The diagrams became better known through their use by Pantaleoni (1898) and Edgeworth (1894).
7. Although Cournot (1838) and Jenkin (1870), for example, had used diagrams earlier, they did not use geometric methods of analysis in the way exemplified by Marshall's trade and monopoly diagrams.
8. A similar point was made by Keynes (1972, p. 200).

place in the literature for many years. In the hands of economists such as Edgeworth, and later Meade (1952), they have become extremely powerful techniques of analysis. It therefore seems worthwhile to consider their genesis in some detail, not simply to establish priorities but also to appreciate their nature.

II The Mill/Whewell Model

Mill's "Great Chapter"

In order to place Marshall's contribution in proper perspective it is necessary to have a clear view of Mill's analysis. What is without dispute here is that in considering the determination of the terms of trade, between the comparative cost ratios of the two countries, Mill was able to indicate the importance of "reciprocal demand" much more clearly than previous writers because of his conception of demand as a schedule.[9] But Mill did not use mathematical notation, preferring to give numerical examples. The crucial element of the analysis is the idea that demand depends on relative prices. Hence England, assumed to have a comparative advantage over Germany in the production of cloth (while Germany has a comparative advantage in linen production), has a demand for linen that depends on its price relative to that of cloth. This relative price can be expressed in terms of an amount of cloth per unit of linen. This is the basis of Mill's argument that "all trade is in reality barter, money being a mere instrument for exchanging things" (1920, p. 583).

If England demands a certain quantity of linen, then there is an associated, or reciprocal, supply of cloth equal to the amount of linen multiplied by the relative price. The quantity of linen multiplied by the amount of cloth per unit of linen obviously gives an amount of cloth.[10] Neglecting transport costs, equilibrium requires that the post-trade relative price is the same in each country and that the price is such that Germany's import demand for cloth precisely matches England's export supply (associated with its demand for linen at the corresponding relative price). After giving a numerical example, Mill added, "As the inclinations and circumstances

9. See, for example, Mill (1920, p. 585). Mill's conception of demand in terms of a schedule is stressed by Robbins (1958, p. 242) when comparing his trade analysis with that of Torrens, and by O'Brien (1975, p. 183).

10. Despite the importance of Torrens's and Pennington's work, Viner (1955, p. 447) stresses the pivotal role of Mill's analysis for subsequent work. Although Pennington refers to the strength of demand when examining the gains from trade, he suggests (1840, pp. 36, 39, 40–41) that the exchange rate will fluctuate between extremes, rather than tend to some determinate value.

of consumers cannot be reduced to any rule, so neither can the proportions in which the two commodities will be interchanged" (1920, p. 587).

He then went on, when considering the gains from trade, to add that "the circumstances on which the proportionate share of each country more remotely depends, admit only of a very general indication" (1920, p. 587). It is in Mill's subsequent discussion of the "general indications" that he used the concept of demand elasticity – although he described it with the term "susceptibility." Mill effectively argued (1920, pp. 587–8) that if the German demand for cloth is completely inelastic, then all the gains from trade go to Germany. In general, Mill was able to demonstrate that

> If, therefore, it be asked what country draws to itself the greatest
> share of the advantage of any trade it carries on, the answer is, the
> country for whose production there is in other countries the greatest
> demand, and a demand the most susceptible of increase from additional cheapness. (1920, p. 591)[11]

The direct translation of Mill's analysis into diagrammatic form requires the two demand schedules (German and English demand for cloth and linen respectively) expressed in terms of the relative price of cloth and linen. Before developing such a diagram it is first useful to examine the much neglected contribution of Whewell (1850). Twenty years before Marshall, Whewell had produced a mathematical model based on Mill's chapter. This model is not only useful for its own sake, but helps to throw some light on the "supplementary sections" to the chapter that Mill added in 1852 in the third edition of the *Principles*. It is this supplementary material that has received a variety of interpretations.

Whewell's Mathematical Model

Whewell, Mill's long time adversary on the subjects of scientific method and moral philosophy, produced in 1850 a mathematical version of Mill's analysis. Whewell argued that the use of numerical examples led to the neglect of several important factors.

Whewell denoted the English demand for linen and its relative price before trade as q and p respectively, with the German demand for cloth and its pre-trade relative price as Q and P respectively. After-trade prices and quantities are distinguished by the use of a dash, so that the equality of prices means that:

$$p'P' = 1 \tag{4.1}$$

11. Mill also introduced additional countries, transport costs, and additional goods, as well as examining the effects of technological change and shifts in demand.

(since, for example, P' is the reciprocal of the price of linen relative to that of cloth in Germany). The reciprocal supply of cloth implied by England's demand for linen is, from the earlier argument, simply $p'q'$. Hence trade balance is achieved when:

$$p'q' = Q' \qquad (4.2)$$

As a result of trade, the relative price of linen in England and that of cloth in Germany would fall by proportions x and X respectively, so that:

$$p' = p(1 - x) \qquad \text{and} \qquad P' = P(1 - X) \qquad (4.3)$$

If, in addition, the relative price of linen in Germany before trade is a proportion k lower than in England, then $1/P = p(1 - k)$ and combining this with equations (4.3) and (4.1) gives

$$X = \frac{k - x}{1 - x} \qquad (4.4)$$

A novel feature of Whewell's model concerns his treatment of demand. Whewell supposed that, for the English linen demand, the proportionate fall in the relative price of x would lead to a proportionate fall in "revenue" (which in this context is the reciprocal supply of cloth) of mx. The coefficient m was referred to as the "specific rate of change" of the commodity, which Whewell supposed would vary over the demand curve. In fact it is possible to show that m is simply one plus the elasticity of demand.[12] Similarly M is the "specific rate of change" of the German demand for cloth. Hence:

$$p'q' = pq(1 - mx) \qquad \text{and} \qquad P'Q' = PQ(1 - MX) \qquad (4.5)$$

Substituting equations (4.4) and (4.5) into equation (4.2) gives, after rearranging, Whewell's result

$$x = \frac{n(1 - Mk) - 1}{n(1 - M) - m} \qquad (4.6)$$

where $n = PQ/q$ and is the value of cloth demanded in Germany before trade divided by the value of linen consumed in England before trade, measured in German prices. Alternatively n can be interpreted as the German pre-trade opportunity cost of cloth in terms of linen forgone, divided by the English demand for linen before trade. Whewell argued that when $x = 0$, England gains all the advantage from trade, and when $x = k$ (that is, when $X = 0$), Germany obtains all the advantage. It is

12.   For further analysis see Creedy (1989).

therefore possible to obtain the limiting values of n under which trade takes place. Whewell's result gives a precise expression from which the terms of trade can be obtained in terms of the two demand elasticities and the relative "sizes" of the two countries as measured by their demand. He also indicated that a country which receives no advantage from trade may well not specialise; that is, part of its relatively large demand for the imported good will be met from domestic production.

Whewell therefore made a significant advance over Mill's analysis. The main limitation of his approach is the highly restrictive specification of demand, which is strictly limited to small price changes. This examination of Whewell's neglected contribution is warranted because it is argued that Whewell's results provided the major impetus for Mill's supplementary sections. Although Mill (1920, p. 586) only mentioned William Thornton, it is clear that he had other "intelligent criticism" in mind. Thornton may well have argued that the type of "equilibrium" indicated by Mill might not be unique, a point Mill acknowledged at the beginning of the supplementary sections,[13] but this might have been reinforced by the recognition, indicated by Whewell, that m and M would generally vary along the respective demand curves. Mill's attempt to deal with non-uniqueness is of interest, and will be discussed below in the context of Marshall's later criticism. However, there is much stronger contextual evidence that Mill's discussion of the limits within which his "equation" applied, his recognition of partial specialisation and emphasis on the domestic transfer of resources came directly from Whewell.[14] Mill's discussion of inelastic, unitary, and elastic demands can easily be generated by appropriate substitution into equation (4.6) above.[15]

Diagrammatic Form of the Model

It has been shown that the main elements of what may now be called the Mill/Whewell model are the two demand curves, specified in terms of relative prices, and the equilibrium condition that trade must "balance." Denote the (English) demand for linen as L_d and the (German) demand for cloth as C_d, with prices P_L and P_C respectively. The two demand curves can be illustrated as in Figure 4.1. Since C_d is assumed to fall as P_C/P_L rises, the German demand curve in the right hand side of Figure 4.1 must be upward sloping. Suppose that $(P_L/P_C)^*$ denotes the equilibrium relative

13. Thornton's emphasis on indeterminacy in barter was also noted by Jevons and Edgeworth; see Creedy (1986, p. 48).
14. For further analysis of Whewell's contribution, see Creedy (1989).
15. See in particular Mill (1920, p. 598).

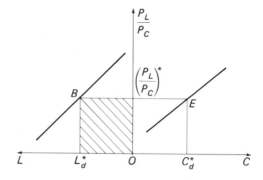

Figure 4.1. J. S. Mill's model.

price of linen after trade takes place. From the left hand side of Figure 4.1, the corresponding demand for linen is L_d^*, which carries with it an associated (reciprocal) supply of cotton of $L_d^*(P_L/P_C)^*$. This must be equal to the demand for cotton at the same relative price, C_d^*.

The equilibrium condition therefore requires the area of the shaded rectangle to be equal to the length OC_d^*. (This is equivalent to Whewell's condition $p'q' = Q'$.) This is extremely simple to state algebraically, but the question arises of how the equilibrium can be found using only graphical methods. A complete diagrammatic treatment of the model should be able to find the equilibrium, given two arbitrarily drawn demand curves.

Extensions of the Model

A natural way to proceed would be to derive the English supply curve of cloth from the demand curve for linen. The supply curve, to be placed on the right hand side of Figure 4.1, has the property that the abscissa is equal to the corresponding area of the rectangle beneath the demand curve; it would cut the German demand curve at E. Similarly, the German supply curve of linen would cut the English demand curve at B.

A geometric method of producing the English supply curve of cloth from the demand curve of linen is shown in Figure 4.2. This technique requires the use of a set of rectangular hyperbolas, two of which are shown as H_1 and H_2. The curve H_1 is tangential to the demand curve at E; hence it is known that the elasticity of demand at E is unity and the corresponding supply of cloth is a maximum.[16] If a 45° line is drawn through the origin it is clear that the square with sides $FG = GO$ has the

16. For further discussion of the geometrical aspects, and the method of drawing rectangular hyperbolas, see Creedy and McDonald (1989).

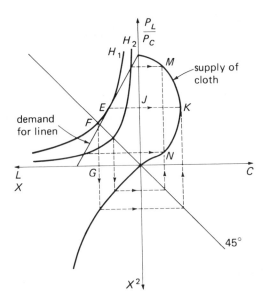

Figure 4.2. Derivation of supply from demand curve.

same area as the rectangle with sides *EJ* and *JO*. Hence *OG* is the square root of the required length. The bottom left hand quadrant of Figure 4.2 has a graph of X^2 plotted against X, so that, combined with the $45°$ line in the bottom right hand quadrant, the appropriate abscissa *JK* can be traced. The diagram also illustrates how the rectangular hyperbola H_2 can be used to plot the points *M* and *N* on the "reciprocal supply" curve. The latter, the locus of such points, can be seen to be backward bending.

All that is necessary to trace the supply curve corresponding to a demand curve (and vice versa) is a set of rectangular hyperbolas drawn on transparent paper, along with a graph of X against X^2, as in the two quadrants in the left hand side of Figure 4.2. What is interesting about this method, in the present context, is that Marshall made a great deal of use of a set of rectangular hyperbolas in his analysis of monopoly. He recommended using a set of these "constant outlay" curves and Henry Cunynghame produced a machine to enable Marshall to draw the curves on the blackboard.[17] The question of Marshall's own derivation of his trade curves will be taken up in the next section; the present discussion aims simply to produce a diagrammatic version of Mill's model from

17. For Marshall's use of rectangular hyperbolas, see (*Principles*, Book V, chapter 14) and (*EEW*, 2, pp. 242–4).

basic principles and to see how it can be manipulated. Only after carrying out such an exercise is it possible to judge Marshall's contribution.

A Special Case

Further insight into the diagrams may be obtained by considering the special case where the two demand curves are linear. Hence, suppose that

$$L_d = a - b\frac{P_L}{P_C} \tag{4.7}$$

and

$$C_d = \alpha - \beta\frac{P_C}{P_L} \tag{4.8}$$

The English supply of cloth C_s is thus given by

$$C_s = L_d\frac{P_L}{P_C} = a\frac{P_L}{P_C} - b\left(\frac{P_L}{P_C}\right)^2 \tag{4.9}$$

while the German supply of linen L_s is given by:

$$L_s = C_d\frac{P_C}{P_L} = \alpha\left(\frac{P_L}{P_C}\right)^{-1} - \beta\left(\frac{P_L}{P_C}\right)^{-2} \tag{4.10}$$

The relevant curves are shown in Figure 4.3. The German supply of linen is also backward bending, having a maximum when the relative price of linen is $2\beta/\alpha$, and a point of inflexion where the relative price is $3\beta/\alpha$. The points F and G of unit elasticity of demand for cloth and linen occur respectively when the relative price of linen is $2\beta/\alpha$ and $a/2b$. The corresponding supply elasticities at those prices are thus zero, and the supply curves are vertical.[18] Equilibrium occurs at point E on the left hand side, corresponding to point E' on the right hand side of Figure 4.3. This example shows a single equilibrium value of the relative price of linen, between the two "extremes" a/b and β/α. However, it can easily be seen that an English demand curve for linen could intersect the German supply curve three times; the same is true of the cotton supply and demand curves. Thus linear demand curves do not necessarily generate a unique (feasible) equilibrium.

Equilibrium requires $C_s = C_d$, so that combining equations (4.8) and (4.9) gives

$$\beta - \alpha\left(\frac{P_L}{P_C}\right) + a\left(\frac{P_L}{P_C}\right)^2 - b\left(\frac{P_L}{P_C}\right)^3 = 0 \tag{4.11}$$

18. The relationship between supply and demand elasticities is dealt with algebraically by Viner (1955, pp. 539–40, n. 11).

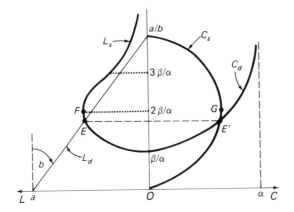

Figure 4.3. J. S. Mill's model with linear demands.

The equilibrium price ratio is therefore the root of the cubic in equation (4.11), which will in general have three roots though they need not necessarily be real or distinct, as Figure 4.3 shows.

III   From Mill to Marshall

Having clarified Mill's "trade model," the previous section began to explore its geometrical properties. The generation of the reciprocal supply curves from the demand curves was not entirely straightforward, but could be carried out using a set of rectangular hyperbolas similar to that used by Marshall in his analyses of monopoly. This exercise is itself quite revealing, since it shows the possibility, for quite simple demand curves, of multiple equilibria. It also illustrates the useful point that so long as the demand curves are elastic (having elasticities numerically not less than unity), the corresponding supply curves cannot be backward bending and so only one equilibrium will be possible. While Whewell was found to extend Mill's results by the use of particular demand functions, the diagrammatic approach is seen to be capable of avoiding the constraints imposed by the use of specific functional forms. A large variety of comparative static exercises can be carried out, showing the implicit assumptions required for some of Mill's statements to hold. However, the investigation has not yet produced curves corresponding to Marshall's offer curves.[19]

19.   The term "offer curve" is not Marshall's. Its first appearance seems to have been in Johnson (1913), but it became more widely used as a result of Bowley (1924).

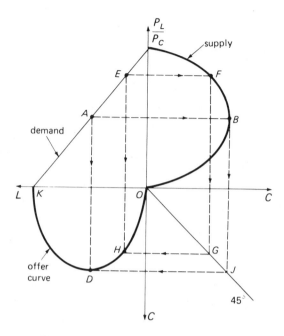

Figure 4.4. Derivation of the offer curve.

A Derivation of the Offer Curve

Given a demand curve specified in terms of relative prices, the corresponding (reciprocal) supply curve can be plotted using the method shown in Figure 4.2. These two curves can then be combined to form an offer curve. The procedure is illustrated in Figure 4.4, for England's demand for linen in terms of the offer of cloth. The top two quadrants of Figure 4.4 show England's supply of cloth and demand for linen. The diagram shows how two points H and D on the offer curve may be plotted, using a 45° line in the bottom right hand quadrant. As seen earlier, point A corresponds to the point of unit elasticity of demand, where the elasticity of supply is zero at B. Starting from any point on the demand curve, it is only necessary to move around the quadrants in the direction of the arrows. Using this technique it is obvious that the point D represents both a turning point of the offer curve and a point where the elasticity of demand for linen is unity. Between O and point D the elasticity of demand is numerically greater than unity, while between K and D the demand is inelastic.

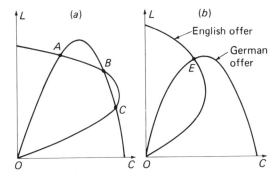

Figure 4.5. Multiple equilibria.

For a linear demand curve, the offer curve of England is obtained algebraically as follows. From equation (4.7), solve for the price ratio to get

$$\frac{P_L}{P_C} = \frac{-(L_d - a)}{b} \tag{4.12}$$

Then substitute for P_L/P_C in equation (4.9) to give the equation of the offer curve as:

$$C_s = \frac{aL_d - L_d^2}{b} \tag{4.13}$$

The offer curve in this case is thus quadratic in L_d. On the assumption that both demand curves are linear, both offer curves (of Germany and England) are quadratic, so that as before it is quite possible to have more than one equilibrium. Examples are shown in Figure 4.5, where part (a) shows that A, B, and C can all be equilibrium points. In part (b) the curves are such that they intersect only once, at E (other than at the origin, of course). This part of Figure 4.5 also shows that at E England has an inelastic demand for linen while Germany has an elastic demand for cloth. The result (also clear from Figure 4.3) is that the relative price of linen is much lower than before trade. Thus the terms of trade are in England's favour.

It only remains to show that the slope of a ray from the origin to any point on the offer curve represents the relative price. Consider the English offer curve in Figure 4.5. The ordinate represents L_d while the abscissa measures $C_s = L_d(P_L/P_C)$; hence the slope of the ray equals $L_d/C_s = P_C/P_L$.

Marshall and Offer Curves

It has been shown how offer curves can be derived graphically from the type of demand curve, expressed in terms of relative prices, that is implicit in Mill's model; the starting point is the recognition of the concept of reciprocal supply. In view of the insights provided by the derivation and use of offer curves, particularly concerning the role of demand elasticities and the possibility of multiple solutions, combined with their great potential for comparative static exercises, it seems rather hard on Marshall to describe the development of such valuable "analytical tools" as merely "polishing" Mill's meaning. Certainly his starting point was "Mill's problem," although Marshall's solution is really a significant advance over that offered by Mill.

To provide a diagrammatic route leading from Mill to Marshall does not demonstrate that it was necessarily the path taken by Marshall himself. Even though the above method uses Marshall's familiar rectangular hyperbolas, there is no evidence that they were used in any context other than the treatment of monopoly. It is certainly of interest to compare Marshall's first "Essay on International Trade" (*EEW* 1, pp. 260–80) with the "Pure Theory of Foreign Trade" (*EEW*, 2, pp. 117–81), and finally with the published material in *Money Credit and Commerce* (*MCC*, pp. 330–60). He begins in each case with basic offer curves for each country (that are elastic over the whole length shown) and then discusses their possible shapes in terms of elasticities. The earliest essay finds Marshall using the rather clumsy expression "guidance by the rate" for "elasticity." By 1923, however, the analysis is clearly stated in terms of elasticities and includes a footnote giving the now standard geometrical method of finding the elasticity (*MCC*, p. 337, n.1).[20]

Marshall's recognition of the circumstances under which multiple equilibria would occur led him to devote much energy to dynamic adjustment problems and the question of which of several equilibria will be stable. Instead of presenting the mathematics of differential equations, Marshall applied, for the first time in economics, the now standard phase-diagram method. As usual, and after what must have been a great deal of thought on the question, Marshall was very sceptical about the use of mathematics to examine dynamic problems. Even if the equations of the offer curves were known precisely, he argued that

---

20. Consider England's offer curve in which cloth and linen are on horizontal and vertical axes respectively. If T and M are, respectively, the points where the tangent to the offer curve and a vertical line dropped from the point of tangency cut the horizontal axis, then the elasticity is OM/OT. The two points obviously correspond when the elasticity is unity.

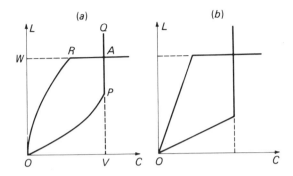

Figure 4.6. Offer curves with unit elasticities.

the methods of mathematical analysis will not be able to afford any considerable assistance in the task of determining the motion of the exchange-index. For a large amount of additional work will have to be done before we can obtain approximate laws for representing the magnitude of the horizontal and vertical forces which will act upon the exchange-index in any position.   (*EEW*, 2, p. 163)[21]

It is obviously not possible to examine the details of Marshall's dynamic and comparative static exercises here; they have fortunately been well rehearsed elsewhere.[22] But it may be worth while to look briefly at his note on Mill's discusssion of the possibility of multiple solutions. Marshall argued (*EEW*, 2, pp. 148–9; *MCC*, pp. 354–5, n. 3) that Mill (1920, pp. 596–7, para. 6) made the special assumption of unit elasticities of demand for cloth and linen. Marshall argued that this would lead the offer curves to "degenerate" into straight lines, as shown in Figure 4.6(*a*). It is clear that on this assumption the offer curves cannot intersect more than once, so that "there is no problem to be solved" (*MCC*, p. 355 n.). Marshall made it clear that he was considering the situation where, after points *P* and *R* in Figure 4.6(*a*), the offer curves become straight lines. He stated, "Let *VP* be the amount of linen which England could make for herself with the expense to which she is put in order to make and export *OV* cloth, then *PQ* is a portion of England's demand [offer] curve" (*EEW*, 2, p. 148). The line *OP* therefore represents part of a "trade indifference curve" (using Edgeworth's terminology) which represents a situation of varying costs. The introduction of the "trade indifference curve" or curve of "constant advantage" is usually associated with Edgeworth (1925, p. 33), and was later derived from

21. Samuelson's treatment of dynamics is in (1948, pp. 266–9).
22. See especially Bhagwati and Johnson (1960) and Amano (1968). The latter concentrates on stability conditions.

production conditions by Meade (1952). It ties in beautifully with Edgeworth's analysis of exchange in *Mathematical Psychics,* but it is clearly in Marshall's note; Edgeworth himself made no claims to originality in his discussion of trade theory. In discussing the same issue, Edgeworth (1894, pp. 609–14; this six-page footnote was omitted from the 1925 version) also made it perfectly clear that in the extreme case of unit elasticities the offer curves would *not* start with a flat section, but would begin (when there are *constant* costs) with a straight line representing the domestic opportunity cost of producing the import. No country need accept a zero price for its export good; this is shown in Figure 4.6(*b*). At the end of the footnote, Edgeworth added, "I ought to repeat that I have had the advantage of reading Professor Marshall's unpublished papers" (1894, p. 614n.).

However, Marshall's criticism of Mill is curious because a close reading of Mill's section 6 shows that he did *not* in fact assume unit elasticities. His earlier numerical example involved an equilibrium relative price of 10 units of cloth for 17 units of linen, with Germany exchanging 17,000 yards of linen for 10,000 yards of cloth. Mill suggested that if the price of linen falls such that 10 units of cloth exchange for 18 units of linen, a new equilibrium would exist if England increases its demand for linen to 17,500 yards while Germany simultaneously reduces its demand for cloth to 9,722 yards (since the English demand for 17,500 at the new price involves a reciprocal supply or offer of 9,722 yards of cloth). A little calculation shows that Mill was assuming that the elasticity of the English demand for linen is 0.52 while that of Germany for cloth is 0.47. Hence, Mill actually showed that multiple equilibria can occur when the demands are inelastic; this is perfectly appropriate, as seen from the above discussion and Figure 4.5(*a*).

It is also worth noting Marshall's subsequent comment on the gains from trade, with reference to Figure 4.6(*a*):

> If *A* coincides with *P* England has to pay for her imported linen the full equivalent of what it would cost her to make it herself; and therefore she derives no benefit from the trade. (*EEW*, 2, p. 149)

This again supports the argument that *OP* in Figure 4.6(*a*) is part of England's "trade indifference curve" through the origin. Although Marshall is seen to do less than full justice to Mill's discussion of multiple equilibria, his own discussion is extremely valuable in its own right.[23]

Marshall came to regard his offer curve apparatus as capable of "being translated into terms of any sort of bargains between two bodies, neither

---

23. For strong comments on the use of constant elasticities, see (*MCC*, p. 388, n.; 355, n. 3).

of whom is subject to any external competition in regard to those particular bargains" (*MCC*, p. 351). A major context was, of course, bargaining between firms and trade unions, but it was left to Edgeworth to extend the analysis to those other areas.[24]

Triangular Barter

Although it is not known exactly how Marshall arrived at the concept of the offer curve, he can be seen at an early stage struggling with the problem of "triangular barter." In some "pages from a mathematical notebook" (*EEW*, 2, pp. 272–4), Marshall uses demand curves specified in terms of relative prices (similar to those considered in Section II above) to examine the situation in which Germany exchanges linen for cloth, England exchanges cloth for fur, while Russia exchanges fur for linen. Marshall's problem here is very similar to the three-country case considered by Mill, and the approach can be seen to follow Mill quite closely. As Mill suggested, "Everything will take place precisely as if the third country had bought German produce with her own goods, and offered that produce to England in exchange for hers" (1920, p. 592).

Marshall proceeds by drawing a German demand curve for cloth in terms of the relative price of cloth (the amount of linen that must be given per unit of cloth), followed by an English supply curve of cloth in terms of the price of cloth relative to fur (the amount of fur that will be obtained per unit of cloth). These two curves are then combined to produce a resulting demand curve for fur in terms of the price of fur relative to linen (the amount of linen that must be given per unit of fur). However, Marshall simply draws a demand curve and gives a numerical example of the properties of one point on the curve; he does not provide a mathematical argument or use a diagrammatic construction.

The essence of the problem can be seen as follows. Suppose the German demand for cloth from England is C_d. The corresponding supply of linen is, following the argument of Section II, $C_d(P_C/P_L)$. With that amount of linen, England can demand an amount of fur given by $C_d(P_C/P_L)(P_L/P_F)$. Here P_F is the price of fur, so that the last term is simply the amount of fur per unit of linen, or the relative price of linen in terms of fur. Then cancelling P_L, the English demand for fur, F_d, is $C_d(P_C/P_F)$. Now

---

24. In a letter to Edgeworth of March 1891, Marshall discusses the application to wage bargaining; see (*EEW*, 2, p. 112). Edgeworth's application came as early as 1881, and was directly stimulated by the Marshalls' *Economics of Industry* (1879) and the privately printed chapters from the *Pure Theory*; see Creedy (1986). Marshall also mentions such applications in his 1876 paper on Mill; see (*Memorials*, pp. 132–3).

C_d decreases as P_C/P_L increases, and from the result in the previous sentence, F_d decreases as P_C/P_F decreases. Hence F_d decreases as

$$\frac{P_L}{P_F} = \frac{P_C/P_F}{P_C/P_L} \qquad (4.14)$$

decreases. Therefore if the quantity of fur is measured on the vertical axis and the price of fur relative to linen, P_F/P_L, is measured on the horizontal axis, the demand curve is downward sloping to the right.

The final component of the model is the supply curve for fur in terms of the price of fur relative to that of linen, which Marshall draws as upward sloping. The equilibrium position is therefore the intersection of these last two curves. Without providing any discussion Marshall simply states that the conditions for the equilibrium to be stable are: (1) If England can get more furs she will sell in exchange more cloth. (2) If Germany can get more cloth she will sell in exchange more linen. (3) If Russia can get more linen she will sell in exchange more furs (*EEW*, 2, p. 275).

The above discussion might seem to suggest that the second condition should be expressed in terms of the German *demand* for cloth (increasing as the price of cloth relative to linen falls). But the problem is more complex, since Section II has shown that such a downward sloping demand curve can be associated with a backward bending reciprocal supply curve, which is then capable of generating multiple solutions. Indeed, the problem is more clearly examined using Marshall's offer curves – although he does not use them himself in this context. Consider Figure 4.7, which has the English, German, and Russian offer curves in quadrants 1, 2, and 3 respectively. Quadrant 4 simply has a 45° line. The diagram shows how, starting from arbitrarily chosen points A and B on England's offer curve, the points J and G on the "hybrid" offer curve OD can be plotted. The intersection of this offer curve with Russia's offer curve at E gives the relative prices of linen and fur, from which the other relative prices can easily be obtained by moving to quadrants 1 and 2.

The offer curves in Figure 4.7 have been drawn to reflect Marshall's three conditions given above. It is clear by the method of construction that there can be only one equilibrium. But if the offer curves were instead drawn to reflect inelastic demands beyond a certain point (that is, if they were "backward bending"), it can be seen by following the procedure of Figure 4.7 that the "hybrid" offer curve in quadrant 3 could have a rather unusual shape; viewed from above it would have two humps. Such offer curves that turn back several times are of course not uncommon in Marshall's *Pure Theory of Foreign Trade*.

It is most unfortunate that so little of Marshall's basic working is

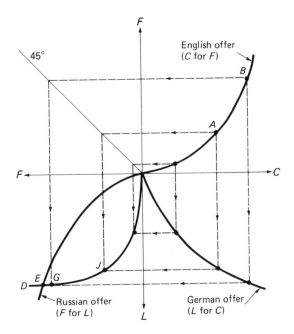

Figure 4.7. Triangular barter.

available.[25] What is clear from this example of triangular barter is that Marshall at some stage tried to make use of the types of curve that arise directly from Mill's framework. It has been shown that they are very awkward when compared with his own offer curves.[26]

Viner's Terms of Trade Diagrams

Mention may briefly be made of the diagrams used by Viner (1955, pp. 362, 468, 539, 544–5), which he refers to as "terms of trade diagrams." Viner says that his diagrams are simply "a modification of the Marshallian foreign-trade diagrams so as to make the vertical axis represent

25. Marshall clearly followed his own injunction to Bowley to destroy his basic working; see (*Memorials*, p. 427).

26. In introducing triangular barter Whitaker (*EEW*, 2, p. 272) says the notes are included to "illustrate to perfection the groping, intuitive way in which Marshall often tackled his problems – not at all what one would expect from an erstwhile Second Wrangler." However, it seems more likely that Marshall is trying to produce a more pedagogic discussion rather than work things out for himself. From Marshall's statement of the conditions for stability it is clear that his understanding extends beyond what is in the basic notes.

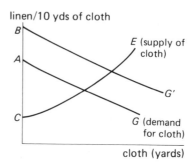

Figure 4.8. An increase in demand.

the linen-cloth terms of trade instead of the total quantity of linen"
(1955, p. 539). An example is shown in Figure 4.8, where Viner states
that *A* and *C* represent the German and English domestic costs of producing linen (in terms of cloth) respectively. The curve *AG* represents the
German demand for cloth while *CE* is the "English demand for linen in
terms of cloth" (1955, p. 540) or, more clearly, the English supply of
cloth. Viner uses the diagram to confirm Mill's suggestion that a reduction in the cost of producing linen in Germany, leading to a shift in the
German demand for cloth to *BG'*, implies a movement in the terms of
trade away from Germany. The extent of the change depends on the
shape of the English supply curve, *CE*.[27]

Since Viner has the relative price of cloth on the vertical axis, it can be
seen that Figure 4.8 compares directly with (the mirror image of) the left
hand side of Figure 4.3, which deals with the market for linen. But other
than pointing out the simple relationship between supply and (reciprocal)
demand elasticities, Viner does not explore the relationships between the
different sets of curves. Hence his presentation does not enable the full
taxonomy of different possibilities to be explored. It is certainly true,
however, as shown in Section II and the beginning of the present section,
that the "terms of trade" diagrams contain all the information that is
subsumed in the set of offer curves, so that the choice between the two is
"merely one of comparative convenience" (1955, p. 542). On the same
grounds Viner's criticism of Marshall, that "the unnecessary complexity
of Marshall's diagram seems to have concealed from him the fact that it
provided no answers to the questions which he was putting" (1955, p.
545) is misplaced. Viner's criticism concerns Marshall's analysis of the
effect of an increase in England's demand for linen and, not surprisingly,

27. For further analysis of this issue see Bhagwati and Johnson (1960).

the issue turns on the meaning attached to "increase in demand" rather than the logic of the two different writers.

Marshall and Whewell

In view of the quality of Whewell's work it is necessary to consider the possibility that Marshall was directly influenced by Whewell. There is no reference to Whewell in any of Marshall's writings on international trade; his only reference to Whewell seems to be to the latter's role as editor of Richard Jones's works (see *Memorials*, p. 296, and *EEW*, 2, p. 264). Some writers have nevertheless suggested that Marshall made use of Whewell's work; these include Henderson (1985, p. 422) and Cochrane (1975, p. 398). One argument to support this claim is that Marshall's signature has been found on other volumes of the *Transactions* in which Whewell's papers first appeared; see Collard (1968, p. xviii).

It does not seem possible, however, to attribute any particular analytical contributions of Marshall to the work of Whewell. Indeed, the fact that there are valuable aspects of Whewell's work not used by Marshall suggests the absence of any familiarity. A prime example is Whewell's development of an elasticity concept in his "specific rate of change." Furthermore, in a footnote to the 1850 paper, Whewell hinted that the famous King/Davenant "law of demand" follows a third-order polynomial precisely. Yet when Marshall discussed the "law" in the *Principles*, he simply reproduced some of Jevons's arguments about the shape of the demand curve.[28]

Surprising though it may seem that Marshall was not familiar with Whewell's work, it is worth recalling a query raised by Hutchison (1955) in connection with Cournot's *Recherches*. The possible significance of Cournot's book was suggested to Jevons in 1875 by Todhunter, who added that "I never found any person who had read the book" (Hutchison, 1955, p. 8). Yet Todhunter was, like Marshall, a fellow of St. John's College, and Marshall stated that he read Cournot in 1868. The lack of communication between Todhunter and Marshall on the subject of Cournot must also have extended to Whewell, about whom Todhunter had considerable knowledge.[29] Reference to Cournot raises the question of his influence on Marshall's work in international trade, the subject of the following section.

---

28. The King/Davenant law is examined in detail in Creedy (1986). Further evidence suggesting that Marshall had not read Whewell is the fact, noted by Whitaker (*EEW*, 1, p. 45, n. 26), that Marshall made no reference to Whewell's criticisms of Ricardo.
29. See, for example, Todhunter (1876). Whewell's correspondence shows that he was aware of Cournot.

IV Marshall and Cournot

Despite the acknowledged importance of Cournot's work for Marshall, there is no reference to him in any of Marshall's published analyses of foreign trade. Yet it can be argued that an appreciation of Cournot's analysis of trade – or "the communication of markets" (1927, chapter 10) – provides further insights into the nature of Marshall's contribution.

The Back-to-Back Diagram

Cournot's basic framework of analysis, used mainly to examine the effects of various tariffs, was a relatively simple one in which a single good is initially produced in two countries that are isolated from each other. When communication between the markets occurs, the good is produced and exported by the country in which it is initially cheaper (allowing for transport costs); the equilibrium requirement being that the aggregate supply be equal, at the new price, to the aggregate demand of both countries combined.[30] Marshall published nothing on this analysis, but some early notes are reproduced in (*EEW*, 2, pp. 246–8). These notes show Marshall's translation of Cournot's model into diagrams, mainly for the purpose of examining the gains from trade using measures of producers' and consumers' surplus.

The diagrammatic analysis of Cournot's model was later refined by Marshall's former student Henry Cunynghame (1892, 1903),[31] who produced the machine used by Marshall for drawing his rectangular hyperbolas. After an unsatisfactory start (1892, p. 44), Cunynghame produced the now familiar "back-to-back" diagram without any reference to Cournot but virtually paraphrasing the latter's introduction to his model (1903, p. 317). It does not seem to be widely recognised that Cunynghame's treatment stems directly from Cournot.[32] Ignoring transport costs, the diagram is shown in Figure 4.9 where the equilibrium price is such that $CT = EF$. The essential feature of the model is that it involves only one good and the demand and supply schedules are specified in terms of the absolute price of the good (in terms of units of a common currency).[33]

The use of simple partial equilibrium schedules involving money prices

30. For further examination of Cournot's analysis of trade, see Creedy (1988).
31. This work culminated in Cunynghame's book (1904), reviewed at length by Edgeworth (1905).
32. Viner (1955, p. 589) refers to Barone and Cunynghame (1904) without mentioning that the diagram represents Cournot's model, though Viner had just completed a section on Cournot's analysis of the gains from trade.
33. Allowing for transport costs is achieved simply by displacing the horizontal axes by their amount per unit of the good.

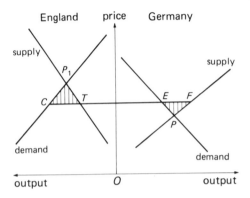

Figure 4.9. Cournot's model.

is precisely what Marshall rejected when it came to the analysis of foreign trade. The model cannot be generalised simply by adding further demand and supply schedules for another good and imposing a balance of payments constraint.[34] The interdependences between the various schedules are far from straightforward. The recognition that the "ordinary" demand and supply curves are inadequate for international trade contexts led Marshall to develop his "offer curves" capturing the reciprocal nature of supply and demand stressed by Mill. He argued that

> Students frequently fall into errors which they may easily avoid if they will resolve that when discussing the pure theory [of foreign trade] they will not speak of the imports or exports of a country as measured in terms of money. (*EEW*, 2, p. 131)

Although this is possible, the complexities can become "wholly unmanageable" (*EEW*, 2, p. 132). When comparing his "terms of trade" diagrams with Marshall's offer curves, Viner (1955, p. 542) quotes Marshall to the effect that ordinary demand curves would lead to "unmanageable complications." But it is argued that Viner missed the point here, since the two types of diagrams used by Viner and Marshall are (as seen earlier) essentially complementary. Marshall was actually stressing the need for a barter model rather than a model along the lines of Cournot. Further support for this interpretation is given in the brief but illuminating remarks on the contrast between Mill's and Cournot's analyses of exchange values in domestic and international contexts made by Marshall in "Mr. Mill's Theory of Value" (*Memorials*, p. 129), his first major paper in economics.

34. For further discussion and references see Creedy (1988).

The precise nature of Marshall's offer curves was misunderstood by Cunynghame, who went so far as to criticise Marshall's analysis on the grounds that it should deal explicitly with more demand and supply curves (1903, p. 317). Marshall, who had other reasons for disliking Cunynghame's later work,[35] commented rather tersely in a letter to Cunynghame, "As to international trade curves – mine were set to a definite tune, that called by Mill" (*Memorials*, p. 451).

This is the statement referred to by Schumpeter, in the quotation given earlier, and by other writers in suggesting that Marshall merely translated Mill into diagrams. But when this quotation is seen in its proper perspective, rather than being read in isolation, it can be seen that the standard interpretation is not really accurate. Marshall is saying that he had good reasons for following the path of Mill rather than Cournot when considering international values, not that his diagrams do little more than restate Mill in another language.

The Gains from Trade

Marshall's notes on Cournot (reproduced in *EEW*, 2, pp. 246–9) show clearly the influence of Cournot on Marshall's analysis of consumers' and producers' surplus. Marshall produces a diagrammatic version of Cournot's model and translates the surplus analysis (of Cournot's chapter 12) into the now familiar triangles.[36] Using the back-to-back version of Figure 4.9, the left hand side shows that the gain to English consumers arising from the price reduction outweighs the loss to producers, so that the net gain is equal to the shaded area P_1CT. The price increase in Germany produces a net gain equal to the shaded area EPF in the right hand side of the figure. Marshall adds that if in each country the cost of production is independent of output, then the exporting country gains nothing from trade (*EEW*, 2, pp. 247–8). Although these notes are not dated, there seems little doubt that Cournot was the sole influence and that Jenkin's brilliant analysis (1870) was quite independent, as Marshall himself insisted.[37]

Having rejected Cournot's partial equilibrium trade model in terms of money prices, Marshall nevertheless wished to apply the "surplus" analysis to his own diagrams. But this presented a difficult task. Marshall later told Cunynghame that he "found all methods of representing the 'total

35. See (*Variorum*, pp. 808–11) where Marshall complains to Edgeworth about Cunynghame, especially the latter's interpretation of "successive cost curves."
36. Marshall accepted Jevons's criticism of Mill's measure of the gain – the change in the terms of trade – as confusing marginal with total utility; see (*EEW*, 1, p. 280).
37. On Jenkin and Marshall see (*EEW*, 1, p. 45; 2, p. 241 n. 7). Also relevant are (*Variorum*, p. 534) and Marshall's letter to J. B. Clark of 1908 (*Memorials*, p. 416).

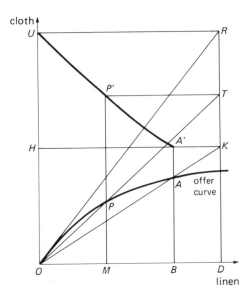

Figure 4.10. The gains from trade (Marshall).

benefit' of foreign trade by their special curves very cumbersome" (*Memorials*, p. 449). Reference to Figure 4.4 above shows that it is possible to move from any point on the offer curve in the bottom left hand quadrant to the associated point on the demand curve, shown in the top left hand quadrant. The area between the demand curve and the horizontal price line would give the appropriate value of the surplus, measured in terms of cloth (the export good).

Whether or not Marshall was aware of the kind of derivation involved in Figures 4.3 and 4.4, he nevertheless started directly from the offer curve. His method, involving "considerable geometrical ingenuity" (Bhagwati and Johnson, 1960, p. 84), is shown in Figure 4.10, which is based on Marshall (*MCC*, p. 339).[38] The vertical line *DR* is placed arbitrarily at point *D* on the horizontal axis. Consider point *A* on the English offer curve and draw a ray from *O* through *A*, extending to *K* on *DR*. The ratio of *KD* to *OD* represents the price of linen at *A*; that is, it is the amount of cloth per unit of linen (when all units are purchased at the same price). The vertical line through *A* intersects the horizontal through *K* at *A'*. Now consider point *P* on the offer curve, and draw the ray *OPT*.

38.   Marshall's earlier attempt is reproduced in (*EEW*, 1, pp. 280–1) where the diagram is drawn on its side; that is, it has cloth and linen on the horizontal and vertical axes, respectively.

The intersection of the vertical line through P with the horizontal line through T is shown as point P'. The locus of points such as P' traces out a quasi-demand curve for linen, since vertical distances are proportional to prices in terms of the number of units of cloth that must be given per unit of linen. The absolute vertical distances depend on the arbitrary position of the line DR. The ray OR is tangential to the offer curve at the origin; hence P' moves from A' to U.

The price DK/OD is paid for OB units of linen whereas, for example, consumers would have been willing to pay the higher price of TD/OD for the smaller quantity OM. Since $TD/OD = DK/OD + TK/OD$, the surplus on the OMth unit of linen is represented by an ODth part of TK units of cloth. The aggregate surplus, when consuming at A, is thus an ODth part of the area UHA'; that is, the area is divided by OD and is measured in terms of cloth. Unlike the standard context where the surplus is measured in money terms, the appropriate area between the "demand curve" and a price line has to be normalised because of the arbitrary choice of the point D that affects the relative price scale. It is hardly necessary to add that Marshall's measure here is open to all the usual objections against the concept of consumers' surplus.[39]

V   Conclusion

This chapter has examined Marshall's diagrammatic analysis of international trade, involving some of his earliest work in economics, ironically not published for almost fifty years until it was included in his last book. To place his contribution in perspective it was found necessary to consider in some detail the precise nature of J. S. Mill's analysis of trade, along with the neglected mathematical treatment of Whewell. Marshall chose, following Mill, to consider international trade as a type of barter in which the demand for imports carries with it a reciprocal supply of exports, rather than follow Cournot in using demand schedules specified in terms of money. The general view emerges that it seems an injustice to Marshall to suggest, with Schumpeter and others, that he, "did not do more than to polish and develop Mill's meaning."

It is not possible to discover precisely how Marshall arrived at his results, although early notes published in *EEW* have been found to throw

---

39. For further analysis of the gains from trade see Viner (1955, pp. 570–5), and Bhagwati and Johnson (1960, Section 3). Marshall himself suggested that in the context of barter it is not really appropriate to assume constancy of the marginal utility of one of the goods (which is Marshall's assumption in the usual context where one of the goods is money); see (*Principles*, p. 793; *Variorum*, p. 790).

valuable light on some of his preliminary work. It must be added that Marshall became "rather tired" of his curves. As he explained to Cunynghame,

> I had followed Mill in taking a yard of cloth as *representative* of England's exports and Germany's imports: which I still think is right. But then I had glided, as he had done, unconsciously into regarding the demand for imports in general as having a similar character to that for a single commodity. And I now think that is illegitimate, and vitiates a great part of my curves.
>
> (*Memorials*, pp. 449–50; italics in original)[40]

Nevertheless, a close analysis of Marshall's early work in trade theory confirms without doubt the accuracy of Edgeworth's response to Cunynghame's misunderstanding (mentioned above) of the nature of the offer curves. Edgeworth observed calmly that "there is more than meets the eye in Professor Marshall's foreign trade curves" (1905, p. 70).[41] This comment could just as appropriately be applied to the vast majority of Marshall's published work, and goes some way towards explaining why he will continue to be studied with profit by many generations of economists.

References

Amano, A. (1968). "Stability Conditions in the Pure Theory of International Trade: a Rehabilitation of the Marshallian Approach", *Quarterly Journal of Economics* 82:326–39.

Bhagwati, J., and Johnson, H. G. (1960). "Notes on Some Controversies in the Theory of International Trade", *Economic Journal* 70:74–93.

Bowley, A. L. (1924). *The Mathematical Groundwork of Economics*. Oxford: Clarendon.

Chipman, J. S. (1965). "A Survey of the Theory of International Trade. Part I: The Classical Theory", *Econometrica* 33:477–519.

Cochrane, J. L. (1975). "William Whewell's Mathematical Statements", *Manchester School* 43:396–400.

Collard, D. (1968). Introduction to J. E. Tozer, *Mathematical Investigations of the Effect of Machinery* (1838). Reprinted, New York: Kelley.

Cournot, A. A. (1927). *Researches into the Mathematical Principles of the Theory of Wealth*. Trans. N. T. Bacon, introduced by I. Fisher. New York: Macmillan; London: Stechert-Hafner. First published in French, 1838.

40. It seems likely that Marshall would have agreed with O'Brien's judgment that "concentration upon the results of static reasoning, upon theorems which lend themselves to neat geometrical exposition, has led to the neglect of much that was valuable in the Classical literature" (1975, p. 200).
41. This aspect of Marshall's work has been well described by Pigou in (*Memorials*, p. 86).

Creedy, J. (1986). "On the King–Davenant 'Law' of Demand", *Scottish Journal of Political Economy* 33:193–212.

(1986). *Edgeworth and the Development of Neoclassical Economics*. Oxford: Blackwell.

(1988). "Cournot on the Communication of Markets", University of Melbourne, Department of Economics, Research Paper no. 202.

(1989). "Whewell's Translation of J. S. Mill", *Scottish Journal of Political Economy* 36: 266–81.

Creedy, J., and McDonald, I. M. (1989). "Marshall's Rectangular Hyperbolas Once More", University of Melbourne, Department of Economics, Research Paper.

Cunynghame, H. (1892). "Some Improvements in Simple Geometrical Methods of Treating Exchange Value, Monopoly and Rent", *Economic Journal* 2:35–52.

(1903). "The Effect of Export and Import Duties on Price and Production Examined by the Graphic Method", *Economic Journal* 13:313–23.

(1904). *A Geometrical Political Economy*. Oxford: Clarendon.

Davenport, H. J. (1935). *The Economics of Alfred Marshall*. Reprinted, New York: Kelley, 1965.

Edgeworth, F. Y. (1881). *Mathematical Psychics*. London: Kegan Paul.

(1894). "The Pure Theory of International Values", *Economic Journal* 4:35–50, 424–43, 606–38.

(1905). Review of Cunynghame's *Geometrical Political Economy*. *Economic Journal*. 15:62–71.

(1925). *Papers Relating to Political Economy*, Vol. 2. London: Macmillan.

Henderson, J. P. (1985). "The Whewell Group of Mathematical Economists", *Manchester School* 53:404–31.

Hutchison, T. W. (1955). "Insularity and Cosmopolitanism in Economic Ideas 1870–1914", *American Economic Association Papers and Proceedings* 45:1–16.

Jenkin, F. (1870). "The Graphic Representation of the Laws of Supply and Demand". Reprinted, LSE Reprints of Scarce Tracts, no. 9, London: Longmans Green, 1931.

Johnson, W. E. (1913). "The Pure Theory of Utility Curves", *Economic Journal* 23:483–513.

Keynes, J. M. (1972). "Alfred Marshall". In *Essays in Biography*. Vol. 10 of *The Collected Writings of John Maynard Keynes*. London: Macmillan. First published 1924. Also in *Memorials:* 1–65.

Marshall, A., and Marshall, M. P. (1879). *Economics of Industry*. London: Macmillan.

Meade, J. E. (1952). *A Geometry of International Trade*. London: Allen and Unwin.

Mill, J. S. (1920). *Principles of Political Economy*. Ed. W. J. Ashley. London: Longmans Green. First published 1848.

O'Brien, D. P. (1975). *The Classical Economists*. Oxford: Clarendon.

(1981). "A. Marshall 1842–1924". In D. P. O'Brien and J. R. Presley (eds.), *Pioneers of Modern Economics in Britain*. London: Macmillan.

Pantaleoni, M. (1889). *Pure Economics*. Trans. T. Boston Bruce. London: Macmillan.

Pennington, J. (1840). Letter to Kirkman Finlay, Esq. Reprinted in R. S. Sayers (ed.), *Economic Writings of James Pennington*. London: London School of Economics, 1963.

Reisman, D. A. (1987). *The Economics of Alfred Marshall*. London: Macmillan.

Robbins, L. C. (1958). *Robert Torrens and the Evolution of Classical Economics*. London: Macmillan.

Samuelson, P. A. (1948). *Foundations of Economic Analysis*. Cambridge, Mass.: Harvard University Press.

Schumpeter, J. A. (1954). *History of Economic Analysis*. London: Allen and Unwin.

Todhunter, I. (1876). *William Whewell. An Account of his Writings, with Selections from his Correspondence*. London: Macmillan.

Viner, J. (1955). *Studies in the Theory of International Trade*. London: Allen and Unwin.

(1958). *The Long View and the Short*. Glencoe: Free Press.

Whewell, W. (1850). "Mathematical Exposition of Some Doctrines of Political Economy – Second Memoir". Reprinted in W. Whewell, *On the Mathematical Exposition of Some Doctrines of Political Economy*. Farnborough: Gregg International, 1968; New York: Kelley, 1971.

5

Firms, Markets, and the Principle of Continuity

BRIAN J. LOASBY

I   Connecting Principles

In his *History of Astronomy*, Adam Smith sought to explain the development of scientific theory as a consequence of a general human desire for
some scheme of order which would comfortably accommodate experience. When objects or events fall into a familiar pattern,

> the thought glides easily along them, without effort and without
> interruption. They fall in with the natural career of the imagina-
> tion . . . . The ideas excited by so coherent a chain of things seem, as
> it were, to float through the mind of their own accord, without
> obliging it to exert itself, or to make any effort in order to pass from
> one of them to another.   (Smith, 1980, p. 41)

If this agreeable sequence is interrupted, our imagination is thrown into
disorder: we know that we do not understand, and have therefore lost the
means to predict, and perhaps to control future events. We therefore, says
Smith, urgently seek some new means of connecting the anomalous event
or object with what is already familiar. The search for such connections is
the motivation of science.

> Philosophy is the science of the connecting principles of nature. . . .
> [It] endeavours to introduce order into this chaos of jarring and
> discordant appearances, to allay the tumult of the imagination, and

to restore it . . . to that tone of tranquility and composure, which is
both most agreeable in itself, and most suitable to its nature.

(Smith, 1980, pp. 45–6)

After a brief consideration of the basic "connecting principle" of the
Wealth of Nations, which Marshall adopted and extended, we shall examine in this chapter some of the connecting principles of Marshall's work.

II Adam Smith: The Division of Labour

Adam Smith begins the first chapter of the *Wealth of Nations* by ascribing
improvements in productivity primarily to "the effects of the division of
labour" (Smith, 1976, p. 13). These effects are easiest to understand
when a whole process of production can be "placed at once under the
view of the spectator", as in a pin factory (Smith, p. 14). Having demonstrated the benefits of the division of labour within a trade, Smith extends
the argument to "the separation of different trades and employments
from one another" (Smith, 1976, p. 15), and traces the extent of the
specialisation both directly and indirectly entailed in the production of a
day labourer's woollen coat, an example which invokes not observation
but imagination (Smith, 1976, pp. 22–3). By such a rhetorically effective
sequence he establishes the division of labour as a connecting principle of
improvement which links such apparently diverse phenomena as the management of a single business and the complex patterns of national and
international trade.

In his second chapter Smith attributes this single principle to a single
cause. It is, he claims, the slowly maturing but unintended consequence of
"the propensity to truck, barter and exchange one thing for another"
(Smith, 1976, p. 25). Smith's central principle of economic progress thus
rests upon an "invisible hand" explanation, which he explicitly disclaims
any intention of pursuing further. Since he concluded the previous chapter by emphasizing the dependence of each person in a civilised country
on "the assistance and co-operation of many thousands" (Smith, 1976, p.
23) – a theme to which he very soon returns (Smith, 1976, p. 26) – the
association is easy and natural, well calculated to soothe the imagination.
But this easy association conceals a problem. If the division of labour is so
intimately associated with exchange, why are some of its manifestations
organised by master manufacturers? (It should not be forgotten that in
Smith's time the artisans in a single manufactory were not necessarily
employees; nevertheless the direction of labour was familiar enough.)
There are two ways of arranging the division of labour: by direction or

through voluntary exchange. How are we to explain when each method is used?

It was to be 161 years before a theoretical explanation was offered for this division of labour in the organisation of the division of labour (Coase, 1937). The question was not addressed by Alfred Marshall, although his analysis of progress was founded on an elaboration of Smith's principle. However, Marshall did attempt to deal with another issue which was hidden in Smith's treatment. If, as Smith maintains, the division of labour, every increase in which eventually leads to a fall in price, is always limited by the extent of the market (Smith, 1976, p. 31), why does not Smith's principle of progress lead inexorably to monopoly? The means by which Marshall attempted to answer that question may suggest why he failed to offer any theoretical explanation of the relative domains of firms and markets.

III Differentiation and Integration

Marshall begins his examination of industrial organisation by combining Adam Smith's doctrine of the division of labour with Darwinian theory (after noting Darwin's debt to Malthus) into a much grander connecting principle than Smith's. Marshall's own connecting principle embodied

> a fundamental unity of action between the laws of nature in the physical and in the moral world. This central unity is set forth in the general rule, to which there are not very many exceptions, that the development of the organism, whether social or physical, involves an increasing subdivision of functions between its separate parts on the one hand, and on the other a more intimate connection between them.   (*Principles*, p. 241)

This general rule not only suggests the importance of exploring the ways in which such intimate connections may be achieved, but also that the generation and selection of alternative patterns of subdivision and integration are the prime functions of a competitive economy. The second implication has been explored recently by Nelson and Winter, who argue that "the market system is (in part) a device for conducting and evaluating experiments in economic behavior and organization" (Nelson and Winter, 1982, p. 277). Marshall has a good deal to say about this process of experimentation, and about the ways in which it is supported by "intimate connections".

Before examining Marshall's treatment, it is important to recognise that, like Adam Smith, he drew attention to the incidental – and sometimes substantial – disadvantages of increased specialisation, and to the possibilities of modifying its operation. He also pointed out that the survival of those best able to benefit from their environment must not be identified with the survival of those who confer benefits upon it, and that characteristics which are important for survival may carry with them other characteristics which confer no advantage, or which may even be harmful (*Principles,* pp. 242–9).

Marshall also extended Smith's principle of progress through the division of labour to include the growth of knowledge. Indeed, in the introductory chapter of Book IV ("The Agents of Production"), after a brief definition of land, labour, and capital, he opens the second paragraph as follows:

> Capital consists in a great part of knowledge and organization; and of this some part is private property and other part is not. Knowledge is our most powerful engine of production; it enables us to subdue Nature and force her to satisfy our wants. Organization aids knowledge; it has many forms, e.g. that of a single business, that of various businesses in the same trade, that of various trades relatively to one another, and that of the State providing security for all and help for many.   (*Principles,* pp. 138–9)

It is to Marshall that we owe the suggestion that organisation might be identified as a distinct factor of production. That suggestion is now generally ignored, but what is not generally recognised is that it arises from the importance of organisation as an aid to knowledge and especially to the growth of knowledge. Thus theorists who exclude the growth of knowledge from microeconomics are right to ignore it.

The first section of Book IV, Chapter 1, with its emphasis on the importance of knowledge and organisation as forms of capital, was introduced into the third edition of the *Principles,* and the forms of organisation added in the fourth (*Variorum,* p. 268). Marshall did not, however, modify either the substance or the sequence of his five chapters (8–12) which bear the title "Industrial Organization" in order to reflect this change. These chapters do not, therefore, present a well structured treatment of the ways in which the various forms of organisation aid knowledge; indeed, many of the elements for such a structured treatment are to be found scattered through Book V, with a few in Book VI. The organisation of a single business is the last to be treated (in Chapter 12), after the discussion of production on a large scale (in Chapter 11), though much of that discussion relates to the opportunities and problems presented to management by increased size. The localisation of industry, which is sometimes an alternative to larger size for the individual enterprise, comes earlier still (Chapter 10). Moreover, Marshall's discussion of localisation cuts across his distinction between the organisation of businesses in the same trade and the organisation of various trades relatively to one another, being concerned sometimes with relations between similar firms and sometimes with firms whose activities are complementary.

Marshall unintentionally furnishes a good test of his own proposition that organisation aids knowledge in the obstacles to knowledge which he creates by this badly ordered exposition. In the following pages I will attempt to restructure Marshall's analysis of his first three forms of organisation, supplementing his treatment in the *Principles* with references from *Industry and Trade*. We should then be able to understand why it apparently did not occur to him that there was a need to explain why the coordination of economic activities was divided between two such sharply distinguished modes as markets and formal hierarchies.

Enterprise and Education

As a preliminary to this reconstruction, it may be helpful to remind ourselves that, in Marshall's view, the distinguishing feature of modern industrial life was not competition, but a set of characteristics which he summarised as "self-reliance, independence, deliberate choice and forethought" (*Principles*, p. 5). These characteristics, as usual with Marshall, are matters of degree, and the degree varies between individuals. In his discussion of the law of diminishing return, for example, he admits that much land in England could produce more than double its present yield "if all English farmers were as able, wise and energetic as the best" (*Principles*, p. 152), but he insists that this law should be applied to farmers as they are. He makes frequent references to the importance of increased "prospectiveness", or the "telescopic" faculty, in encouraging economic progress (*Principles*, pp. 217, 224–5, 233, 680). Self-reliance, deliberation, and forethought often promote competition, but they may also lead to "co-operation and combination of all kinds good and evil" (*Principles*, p. 5). Most of *Industry and Trade* is devoted to an examination and appraisal of various forms of cooperation and combination – especially if we include the cooperation that is essential within a single business. As we shall see, the process of competition itself often entails some form of cooperation.

Successful enterprise depends on education and training, and the British educational system was seriously deficient at all levels. "The absence of a careful general education for the children of the working classes, has been hardly less detrimental to industrial progress than the narrow range of the old grammar-school education of the middle classes" (*Principles*,

p. 208). The industrial leadership of Germany ("Science in the Service of Industry", *Industry and Trade,* Book I, Chapter 7) and of the United States ("Multiform Standardization", *Industry and Trade,* Book I, Chapter 8) were both enhanced by their superior systems of education (*Principles,* p. 211). If there was one way in which the State could most effectively and appropriately aid knowledge it was in the provision of an educational system which would develop both general and specialised ability, and above all eliminate "that wasteful negligence which allows genius that happens to be born of lowly parentage to expend itself in lowly work" (*Principles,* p. 212).

Increasing Return

Marshall gives particular expression to his connecting principle – that development entails increasing specialisation matched by more detailed interaction – in his law of increasing return, the almost unlimited scope of which was to give so much trouble to his equilibrium-minded successors:

> while the part which nature plays in production shows a tendency to diminishing return, the part which man plays shows a tendency to increasing return. The *law of increasing return* may be worded thus: – An increase of labour and capital leads generally to improved organization, which increases the efficiency of the work of labour and capital. (*Principles,* p. 318; italics in original)

Marshall's formulation differs from the standard definition of returns to scale in one crucial respect. Although greater efficiency is a consequence of increased scale, its direct cause is improved organisation. It is thus natural that whereas the part played by nature, which has no powers of conscious organisation, shows a general tendency to diminishing return, man should generally be expected to prove capable of devising better systems of organisation to exploit the opportunities accompanying larger size.

Note two consequences of identifying improved organisation as the direct cause of increasing return. One, which will be taken up later, is that since increasing return is typically displayed in both internal and external economies, we should expect a firm's relationships with other businesses to be a subject of conscious organisation. The other is that we are not to imagine firms selecting from readily available techniques of production. Though substantive new inventions are to be excluded, adaptations of existing ideas are not (*Principles,* p. 460), and Marshall clearly expected cost reductions to be achieved through changes in both techniques and factor proportions (*Principles,* pp. 319, 344).

Thus the measurement of the productivity gains which may follow increased scale is no simple matter of comparing proportional changes of inputs and output. It is made still more difficult by the need to allow time for full adjustment (*Principles,* p. 458), especially in building up trade connections to absorb the increased output; meanwhile the growth of knowledge continues, and in the absence of publicly available production functions it is very difficult to disentangle the effects of scale from those of new knowledge (*Variorum,* p. 362). It is made much more difficult, even in principle, by Marshall's broad conception of the normal activities of all firms.

Forms of Organisation: A Single Business

"Judicious, orderly and vigorous management of routine will often suffice to enable a business to prosper in an industry, the methods of which are for the time practically stereotyped. But such management, while useful in its generation, has contributed very little towards progress" (*IT,* p. 645). That view of routine is very similar to Schumpeter's; but instead of relying on the innovations of the hero-entrepreneur, Marshall looked for a continuous flow of incremental changes from ordinary enterprising businessmen, "who have been alert to invent or adopt new ideas; to put them into practice, bearing the risks of loss; to improve on them, and again to improve on them" (*IT,* p. 645). It is worth quoting at some length a passage which appears in every edition of the *Principles.*

> [T]he manufacturer who makes goods not to meet special orders but for the general market, must, in his first rôle as merchant and organizer of production, have a thorough knowledge of *things* in his own trade. He must have the power of forecasting the broad movements of production and consumption, of seeing where there is an opportunity for supplying a new commodity that will meet a real want or improving the plan of producing an old commodity. He must be able to judge cautiously and take risks boldly; and he must of course understand the materials and machinery used in his trade. But secondly in this rôle of employer he must be a natural leader of *men.* He must have a power of first choosing his assistants rightly and then trusting them fully; of interesting them in the business and of getting them to trust him, so as to bring out whatever enterprise and power of origination there is in them; while he himself exercises a general control over everything, and preserves order and unity in the main plan of the business.   (*Principles,* pp. 297–8; italics in original)

Thus a firm is a device for organising the knowledge of all who work in it, and for using that organised knowledge as a basis for new initiatives, which are not a matter for the head of the business alone. Because human ability and the strength of human motivation are not uniform, not every manufacturer will be equally successful in meeting all these requirements (*Principles*, p. 298). Nevertheless, in order to survive all manufacturers must meet them in some degree, and

> the advantages of economic freedom are never more strikingly manifest than when a business man endowed with genius is trying experiments, at his own risk, to see whether some new method, or combination of old methods, will be more efficient than the old.
>
> (*Principles*, p. 406)

A larger business can extend the division of labour by making greater use of specialised resources, primarily machinery and skills (*Principles*, p. 278), and can encompass a broader range of knowledge, including "information on trade and personal matters in distant places" (*Principles*, p. 282). Greater size and greater specialisation combine to make possible experiments which would be too expensive and thus too risky for a smaller firm. It is especially difficult for the small firm "to discharge, what Roscher calls a characteristic task of the modern manufacturer, that of creating new wants by showing people something which they had never thought of having before; but which they want to have as soon as the notion is suggested to them" (*Principles*, p. 280). The head of a large business can devise new systems of differentiation and integration which leave him free to seek further improvements both in his products and in his methods of production. Thus new knowledge is itself partly a consequence of improvements in organisation made possible by larger scale.

However, although "giant businesses alone are capable of some of the chief tasks of industry in the present age" (*IT*, p. 577), they have two disadvantages. They may grow beyond the ability of their owner to manage effectively – remembering that effective management includes the successful introduction of new products and processes. Marshall saw this as a recurrent problem because the ability and the incentive to run a progressive business were likely to vary over each individual's lifetime; thus the potential advantages of size were unlikely to be realised for long. The second disadvantage is that "the giant business does, as a rule, comparatively little to educate high creative faculty" (*IT*, p. 603).

In particular, the joint-stock companies, though offering opportunities to those with business talent but no capital (*Principles*, p. 302), were prone to develop bureaucratic methods which inhibited creative ideas and experiments (*Principles*, p. 304; *IT*, pp. 317–18). The temptations to an excessive enlargement of scope, which Marshall also ascribed to such businesses, made things worse, since such expansion was likely to be "at the expense of small businesses with greater elasticity and power of origination" (_IT_, p. 321–2). However skilfully managed are the routines, they do not contribute to progress, and they may crowd out innovation.

To understand why potentially superior products or methods may be inhibited, we must link two of Marshall's arguments: It takes time to create a new business capable of outperforming the old, and the process of selection favours that method of industrial organisation which

> offers a direct and immediate service at a lower price. The indirect and ultimate services . . . have, as a general rule, little or no weight in the balance; and as a result many businesses languish and die, which might in the long run have done good work for society if only they could have obtained a fair start. (_Principles_, p. 597)

This defect would be absent from a world of perfect capital markets, in which future benefits would be accurately known (if only as probability distributions) and correctly discounted; but that was not Marshall's world. Nor is it our own.

Forms of Organisation: Various Businesses in the Same Trade

The ways in which the organisation of businesses in the same trade aids knowledge can be most clearly seen when these businesses are gathered together in an industrial district. This local concentration gives rise to such external economies as the growth of subsidiary trades, easy access for small firms to expensive machinery which is operated by highly specialised businesses, and a localised labour market for the particular skills required (_Principles_, p. 271). Another consequence is the development of the attitudes conventionally assumed in modern formal analysis, but which Marshall realised were far from universal, for example, "a habit of responsibility, of carefulness and promptitude in handling expensive machinery" (_Principles_, p. 205). The "industrial atmosphere" also encouraged the rapid adoption of improved methods (_IT_, p. 287), though Marshall seems to have become increasingly concerned that it might impede change, because of trade union resistance or management inertia. Localisation was much more than a structure for diffusing new ideas, however. It facilitated their generation and development.

We have already seen that Marshall looked to each business as a source of improved products and improved methods. We have now to add that the firms in an industry were to be regarded not as competing to discover the same improvement (as in modern models of patent races) but as generators of different improvements. "The tendency to variation is a chief cause of progress; and the abler are the undertakers in any trade the greater will this tendency be ... Each man's actions are influenced by his special opportunities and resources, as well as by his temperament and his associations" (*Principles*, pp. 355–6). The prime advantage of an industry containing a large number of firms is that it provides a larger gene pool. We should never forget that any selection mechanism can work only with the material that is presented to it.

If we follow this analogy (which, we may recall, Marshall treated as much more than an analogy), we may be led to consider the advantages of out-breeding. Marshall considered them too. "Changes of work, of scene, and of personal associations bring new thoughts, call attention to the imperfections of old methods, stimulate a 'divine discontent', and in every way develop creative energy" (*Principles*, p. 197). A localised industry, by comparison, may promote too much uniformity.

Localisation, however, has special advantages. Improvements are not spontaneous mutations, but the result of human endeavour; they can be encouraged by human interaction. Where firms in the same trade are clustered together, "inventions and improvements in machinery, in processes and the general organization of the business have their merits promptly discussed: if one man starts a new idea, it is taken up by others and combined with suggestions of their own; and thus it becomes the source of further new ideas" (*Principles*, p. 271). Thus a localised industry behaves rather like a scientific community, advancing knowledge through a process of conjecture, criticism, and experimentation. The competitive process is made more effective through the creation of interdependence. The characteristics of modern life thus lead towards beneficial cooperation.

If firms are not near neighbours, the interplay of ideas is less intense, but still fostered by "public exhibitions, trade associations and congresses, and trade journals" (*Principles*, p. 210). In the first edition Marshall added that "those who cannot afford to venture on costly experiments themselves may, if they will, read the record of every new departure that is made in their businesses in any part of the world" (*Variorum*, p. 308). Thus the relationships between businesses in the same trade are actively, if often informally, organised – though the businesses continue to compete. This organisation is a powerful aid to progress.

Forms of Organisation: Various Trades Relatively to One Another

The division of labour between complementary trades has been touched on in considering the benefits of localisation, but since this part of Marshall's theory of progress has been so little noticed, it merits a fuller exposition. It provides a particularly striking application of his general rule that an increasing subdivision of functions requires a more intimate connection between them, because the task of developing this particular connection is clearly assigned to the businessman.

In his consideration of long run costs Marshall returns several times to the theme that capital consists in large part of knowledge and organisation. "A great part of the capital invested in a business is generally spent on building up its internal organization and its external trade connections" (*Principles*, p. 377). The trade connections may be particularly important. In the second edition of the *Principles* he writes of "firms whose business connections have been built up by a gradual investment of capital, and are worth nearly as much as, or possibly even more than, the whole of their material capital" (*Variorum*, p. 527). This sentence was removed from the third edition, but an equivalent statement may be found in *Industry and Trade* (p. 270). The capital includes not only "the heavy expenses, direct and indirect, which every business must incur in building up its connection" (*Principles*, p. 353), but also the appropriate allowance for compound interest over the lengthy period usually required; the valuation and depreciation of this capital causes practical difficulties and evokes differences of opinion (*Principles*, pp. 354–5). It is because "the returns expected on building up the external organization of his business" are a major item in supplementary costs that a manufacturer will try to hold prices in his own particular market (where this external organisation is strongest) when trade is slack (*Principles*, p. 458).

The development of a firm's external organisation receives more extensive treatment in *Industry and Trade*, especially in what is, in some respects, a modern treatment of marketing. "Production and marketing are parts of the single process of adjustment of supply to demand. . . . The term 'cost of production', as used in business and in economic literature, generally tacitly includes some portion of the costs of marketing" (*IT*, p. 181). Though in the long run the organisation of trade is no less vital to consumers than to producers, in the short run it is the producer who needs to seek out buyers (*IT*, pp. 271–4). The short run problems of building a market restrain the growth of an enterprising firm, and suggest the use of an individual demand curve which may be very steep (*Principles*, pp. 457–8). How much of the cost of sales promotion should be charged to building up a connection for the future may be little more than guesswork (*Principles*, p. 397). For marketing itself "is an integral process, and not a series of independent transactions" (*IT*, p. 270). Advertising is "seldom of much value, unless accompanied by capable and honourable dealing", but a reputation once gained extends across the firm's range of products (*IT*, p. 270). Some goods may be used to advertise others, and the allocation of marketing costs is then a matter of judgement (*Principles,* p. 396). Brand names allied to a reputation for quality provide "a good connection" (*IT,* p. 300), especially if price maintenance is used to keep the brands in favour with traders (*IT,* p. 302).

Industry and Trade contains much more material on large firms than the *Principles;* yet external as well as internal organisation is clearly seen as an essential task of management for all firms. The general setting is of free competition, but free competition is not anonymous. Because economics is concerned with "human beings who are impelled, for good or evil, to change and progress" (*Principles,* p. xv) – or perhaps because Marshall's own motivation in studying economics was to bring about change and progress in the condition of the people – business has to be analysed as a system which not only responds to opportunities but creates them. Each firm therefore requires a network of contacts through which it can test out its own ideas and learn of others. Prices do not convey all the information which is needed for this purpose.

This view of the relationships between firms has been restated by G. B. Richardson. Richardson argues that a pure market relationship is not the standard but a limiting case (1972, p. 886), from which extends a range of relationships which exhibit increasing degrees of cooperation until one reaches formal alliances and interlocking groups (1972, p. 887). The degree of inter-firm cooperation, he argues, depends upon the extent to which business success depends on managing the integration of different but complementary activities. Each business may be regarded as a pool of specialised resources, organised in an administrative framework (Penrose, 1959, p. 149). If one firm's skills are to be directed to the specialised needs of another business (rather than the fixed list of goods which populate formal models), then coordination by price is not enough, since what needs to be communicated is particular technical knowledge and trust. Formal specification of the terms of a continuing relationship could never be complete; it is made unnecessary by the gradual evolution of trade connections.

IV   Firms versus Markets

We can now suggest why Marshall did not address the question why the coordination of economic activities required to benefit from the division of labour is sometimes organised within firms and sometimes achieved by market contracts. For Marshall, both kinds of coordination required management. Coase's explanation of the firm as an institution which avoids the cost of market transactions uses marginal analysis to distinguish two very different kinds of arrangements. Alchian and Demsetz argued, however, that the apparent difference is illusory. "To speak of managing, directing, or assigning workers to various tasks is a deceptive way of noting that the employer continually is involved in renegotiation of contracts on terms that must be acceptable to both parties" (Alchian and Demsetz, 1972, p. 777). This line of argument has been extended to the analysis of the M-form firm as a more efficient form of capital market in the presence of transactions costs (Williamson, 1975, pp. 143–8), and to the general proposition (in which scant heed is paid to transactions costs) that the firm is simply a nexus of markets (Fama, 1980). On this view, there is no need to explain why firms are an exception to the general principle of coordination by markets: Firms are like markets.

Marshall's position is the mirror-image of this: His implicit claim is that markets are like firms. Both are structures for promoting the growth of knowledge and both require conscious organisation. As one might expect in a theory of economic progress which combines Adam Smith's principle of the division of labour with Darwinian evolution, conscious organisation is only part of the explanation; but the importance which Marshall ascribes to external organisation, its magnitude in relation to other components of a firm's capital, and its significance in determining normal value, in both the short and the long period, all suggest that conscious organisation should not be ignored. That it has nevertheless been ignored is primarily explained by its discordance with the dominant theory of market equilibrium, but some responsibility should be assigned to Marshall's own fragmented presentation.

V The Principle of Continuity

Since evolving patterns of contact and communication within and between firms represent various forms of organisation which aid knowledge, it is not surprising that Marshall apparently felt no need, in the *Principles,* to investigate the circumstances which would tend to favour one form rather than another. This was not a theme for a general theory which was based on a fundamental unity of action, but a question to be investigated in specific cases, some of which are examined in *Industry and Trade.* The reluctance to draw – let alone to explain – sharp distinctions is one of the most pervasive characteristics of Marshall's approach to economics. It was clearly advertised as such in his Preface to the first edition of the *Principles.*

Adam Smith, as we have seen, argued that the object of philosophy was to impose order (or rather, he seems to imply, the appearance of order) on a "chaos of jarring and discordant appearances" by "representing the invisible chains which bind together all these disjointed objects" (Smith, 1980, pp. 45–6). What better connecting principle could one invoke than the Principle of Continuity, the claim of continuous, perhaps universal, connection. In his original Preface, Marshall employs this principle very freely. It encompasses, in turn, "any motives, the action of which is regular", gradations of "sagacity, . . . energy and . . . enterprise", normal and market values, short and long periods, rent and interest [both of these latter pairs are governed by the element of (necessarily) continuous time], even labour and appliances (*Principles*, pp. vi–viii).

The most astonishing, if little remarked, use of the Principle of Continuity is to yoke together the "Fundamental Idea" of "the general theory of the equilibrium of demand and supply" (*Principles*, p. viii) and "continuity with regard to development" (p. ix), which came to be expressed in the sixth edition (*Variorum*, p. 58) as "the central idea of economics, even when its Foundations alone are under discussion, . . . that of living force and movement" (*Principles*, p. xv). Though the ideas of equilibrium and change are never starkly juxtaposed, the importance of progress was emphasised from the first. It was the explicit theme of the last two chapters and "we cannot guess where it will stop. On every side further openings are sure to offer themselves" (*Principles*, p. 223) (in a footnote Marshall sketches a brief scenario of future cities). Marshall tries to combine the "notion of continuity with regard to development," exemplified in modern ideas in biology, history, and philosophy, with "mathematical conceptions of continuity, as represented in Cournot's *Principes Mathématiques de la Théorie des Richesses*" by associating the substance of his thought with the former and its form with the latter (*Principles*, p. xi). He gives no hint that the mathematical principles of continuity were employed by Cournot to define the equilibria of a fully specified system, whereas continuity with regard to development is concerned with the emergence and adoption of novelty.

Marshall's juggling of incompatible notions under an ambiguous label is exemplified by his treatment of the Principle of Substitution. This is introduced as an optimising rule (*Principles*, p. 341), but next appears as a search for better methods (*Principles*, p. 355), explicitly related in the fourth and fifth editions to the businessman "watching the experiments of others and trying experiments himself" (*Variorum*, p. 370), and linked in all editions to the tendency to variation which results from individual opportunities, temperament, and associations. It quickly reverts, however, to a principle of resource allocation through equating returns at the margin, which "is closely connected with, and indeed partly based upon, that tendency to a diminishing rate of return from any excessive application of energies in any given direction, which is in accordance with general experience" (*Principles*, p. 356).

The static definition is restated in Book V, Chapter 8, entitled "Marginal Costs in Relation to Values". There it leads, appropriately enough, into a discussion of the margin of indifference, but into this discussion Marshall introduces the picture of "a business man trying experiments, at his own risk, to see whether some new method, or combination of old methods, will be more efficient than the old", before suggesting how the net product of an agent of production may be estimated, on the implicit assumption of an unchanging technology (*Principles*, pp. 404–7). On its next appearance, the law [not here changed, as it was elsewhere (*Variorum*, p. 370), to a principle of substitution] is described as "nothing more than a special and limited application of the law of survival of the fittest", which causes one method of industrial organisation to be supplanted by another which offers better value for money (*Principles*, p. 597). The two interpretations are finally combined in a single sentence.

> A chief function of business enterprise is to facilitate the free action of this great principle of substitution. Generally to the public benefit, but sometimes in opposition to it, business men are constantly comparing the services of machinery, and of labour, and again of unskilled and skilled labour, and of extra foremen and managers; they are constantly devising and experimenting with new arrangements which involve the use of different factors of production, and selecting those most profitable for themselves.   (*Principles*, p. 662)

The principle of substitution thus straddles the mathematical form, in which businessmen search along a continuous production function in search of the lowest-cost combination of inputs, and the substance of economic development, in which they discover, or invent, superior technologies by modifying some part of the existing function. To confuse optimisation within a given technology with a change of technology is nowadays regarded as a basic analytical blunder. Can Marshall's treatment be defended? A specific defence might be that since technologies are rarely fully specified, businessmen contemplating a somewhat different input combination within a given production function will often not know how that combination is to be deployed. If they do find an effective deployment, it may be impossible to say whether they have simply uncovered a previously hidden part of a production function which, in some sense, always existed, or whether they have hit upon one element in a new function. If the process of discovery is much the same, why make the distinction?

Progress and Equilibrium

At a fundamental level, however, this ambiguous principle of substitution is part of Marshall's design to use the form of equilibrium in order to present the substance of progress (which is examined in more detail in Loasby, 1989, Chapter 4). The crucial problem in this design is the analysis of long-period value. From the fourth edition onwards, Marshall began Book V by comparing "[b]iological and mechanical notions of the balancing of opposed forces", and introducing the simpler balancing of forces in static equilibrium as a preparation for more advanced study (*Principles*, p. 323). At the end of his analysis of long-period equilibrium, he contrasts the applicability of pure equilibrium theory in its elementary stages with the dangers of attempts at advanced applications:

> [W]hen pushed to its more remote and intricate logical consequences, it slips away from the conditions of real life. We are here verging on the high theme of economic progress; and . . . economic problems are imperfectly presented when they are treated as problems of static equilibrium, and not of organic growth.
>
> (*Principles*, p. 461)

As Marshall observes, the difficulties are most acute when dealing with industries which follow the law of increasing return, which, he noted in the second and third editions, is "a law that belongs essentially to an age of change and progress" (*Variorum*, p. 523). He attempts to circumvent these difficulties by combining the continuity of the evolution of firms with the continuity of stable functions into an equilibrium of the industry which relies crucially on the transience of every firm within it. The industry can be in equilibrium only because its member firms are not. But though the life cycle of the firm was invoked to extend (precariously, according to Marshall's own comments) the scope of mechanical equilibrium, it simultaneously helped to explain change. Darwinian evolution depends on mortality not only for selection but also to make room for new life, and therefore the chance of new characteristics. The creation and extinction of businesses were common enough to make plausible this extension of the evolutionary model.

Mortality also facilitated the theoretical conjunction of differentiated firms and free competition. "Every manufacturer, or other business man, has a plant, an organization, and a business connection, which put him in a position of advantage for his special work. He has no sort of permanent monopoly, because others can easily equip themselves in like manner" (*IT*, p. 196) – but not quickly, for internal and external organisations cannot be created quickly. While other firms are building up their own positions of advantage, advantages already created are liable to decay, because of the decline in the "energy, elasticity, and . . . liking for hard work" of those who built them (*Principles*, p. 457). Because the organisation of industry helps firms to learn from the experience of others, as well as their own, each firm will tend to reach a higher peak of performance (though not necessarily of profit) than predecessors which were equally well managed. Thus an industry may steadily progress, though its individual firms successively rise and decline.

"We cannot then regard the conditions of supply by an individual producer as typical of those which govern the general supply in a market" (*Principles*, p. 459). Yet this general supply is generated by the aggregate of these individual producers, each moving through his own life cycle. How are these continuing processes to be congealed into what may pass for a stable equilibrium? Marshall's answer is to represent all this bustle and movement by a still photograph of one carefully selected business. That the selected business must be representative is stated in the first edition (*Variorum*, p. 346); the term "representative firm" appears in the second edition (*Principles*, p. 317). The long-period supply price is then the cost of an increase in output by this representative firm. Marshall repeatedly emphasized that the relevant long run cost is the cost of "a whole process of production" (*Principles*, pp. 361, 376; *IT*, pp. 190, 424). From the second edition onwards he also pointed to the difficulties caused by relating supply price to output "without allowing for the length of time that is necessarily occupied by each individual business in extending its internal, and still more its external organization" (*Principles*, p. 500). The supply price which is to be used to construct an analysis of long-period equilibrium is derived from the study of a process. The firms which populate this process are not themselves in long run equilibrium, nor is the firm which represents them.

The representative firm is the device by which Marshall seeks to preserve the continuity between a process theory of the firm and an equilibrium analysis of price. Pigou's decision to replace it by an equilibrium firm – though it was still intended to be representative – destroyed the link (Pigou, 1928, p. 239). Marshall's achievement in having Pigou elected as his successor had consequences which he neither intended nor desired. With the link broken, the mathematical conceptions of continuity triumphed over the ideas of continuous evolution; the form of Marshall's ideas triumphed over their substance.

In the light of what was happening outside Cambridge, this was probably inevitable. That it was hardly noticed may be attributed to Marshall's use of his Principle of Continuity to produce a rounded globe of knowledge (*Memorials*, p. 48). He was so successful in apparently binding together disjointed objects that his readers' imaginations were not merely soothed but anaesthetized. Not only did they fail to enquire about a possible distinction between firms and markets, they did not even wonder about the difference between process and equilibrium. Effective concealment of problems is no doubt the way to build a coalition. It is perhaps not the best way to advance science. The discomfort produced by "jarring and discordant appearances" (Smith, 1980, pp. 45–6) provides the incentive to find a means of introducing order. If the imagination is prematurely soothed, the effort will not be made.

VI Conclusion

Sir Dennis Robertson once remarked on the propensity of proverbs to go around in contradictory pairs. "Look before you leap", but "he who hesitates is lost"; "many hands make light work" but "too many cooks spoil the broth". Economists (and perhaps other scientists, too) would do well to bear in mind a contradictory pair of guidelines. Sharp distinctions facilitate analysis, but sharp distinctions are rarely found in nature. By treating firms and markets as variations among the forms of organisations which aid knowledge, Marshall provided a better basis for understanding both firms and markets than many later economists. By not distinguishing between their contributions to coordination and to discovery – although these two roles overlap much more than do firms and markets – he helped to frustrate the development, or even the perception, of that basis.

References

Alchian, A. A., and Demsetz, H. (1972). "Production, Information Costs, and Economic Organization", *American Economic Review* 62:777–95.

Coase, R. W. (1937). "The Nature of the Firm", *Economica* N.S. 4:386–405.

Fama, E. F. (1980). "Agency Problems and the Theory of the Firm", *Journal of Political Economy* 88:288–307.

Loasby, B. J. (1989). *The Mind and Method of the Economist.* Aldershot: Edward Elgar.

Nelson, R. R., and Winter, S. G. (1982). *An Evolutionary Theory of Economic Change.* Cambridge, Mass.: Harvard University Press.

Penrose, E. T. (1959). *The Theory of the Growth of the Firm.* Oxford: Oxford University Press.

Pigou, A. C. (1928). "An Analysis of Supply", *Economic Journal* 38:238–57.

Richardson, G. B. (1972). "The Organisation of Industry", *Economic Journal* 82:883–96.

Smith, A. (1976). *An Inquiry into the Nature and Causes of the Wealth of Nations* (1776). Eds. R. H. Campbell, A. S. Skinner, and W. B. Todd, 2 vols. Oxford: Oxford University Press.

(1980). "The Principles which Lead and Direct Philosophical Enquiries: Illustrated by the History of Astronomy". In W. P. D. Wightman (ed.), *Essays on Philosophical Subjects*. Oxford: Oxford University Press. Originally published in 1795.

Williamson, O. E. (1975). *Markets and Hierarchies: Analysis and Anti-Trust Implications*. New York: Free Press.

6

Marshall's Work in Relation to Classical Economics

DENIS P. O'BRIEN

I Introduction

The question of Marshall's classical inheritance is a complex one, made more complex by both the extent and the peculiar nature of Marshall's claims in this respect. Following the introduction, the second section of this chapter will examine these claims – Marshall's own version of the achievements of Classical economics and thus, by implication, his claims about the differences between his own work and that of the Classical writers. Marshall made remarkable claims, both for the continuity of economics as a subject and for the prescience (indeed at times almost for the omniscience) of the Classical economists. Section III examines Marshall's own work, as distinct from his claims, in relation to Classical economics, and identifies what seems to be indisputably Classical at least in origin. Section IV shows that much of what is regarded as characteristically Marshallian is certainly not Classical. The conclusion which emerges is that Marshall's own acknowledgements, in their generosity of spirit towards his Classical predecessors, significantly distort the true distribution of the weight of his Classical inheritance. On the one hand, in those areas in which he was prone to make the most startling claims for Classical economics, he owed the least to the great Classical writers – the areas of value and distribution. On the other hand, in the areas of monetary and trade theory, and in his general habit of underpinning the analysis with a moving equilibrium of economic

I am extremely grateful to Professor John Creedy, Bob Black, John Whitaker and Roger Backhouse for constructive comments on an earlier draft of this paper.

growth, Marshall really did do what he claimed to have done in the areas
of value and distribution, that is, he worked out the implications of the
Classical analysis, restating it in terms which were more precise, and
which, in the case of trade and economic growth theory, contained a basic
mathematical skeleton (though not all of this was published).

We thus begin with an examination of Marshall's claims.

II Marshall's Claims

Marshall warned repeatedly of the dangers of misunderstanding Classical economics.[1] The Classical economists frequently failed to spell out
their assumptions and to make clear what they were doing, in order to
avoid unnecessary controversy. Because of their shortcomings in this
respect, they were easily misrepresented. Care was required to distinguish Classical economics from popular renderings of Classical ideas.[2]
The Classical economists themselves were not dogmatic: "[T]he dogma-
tism which seemed to pervade the chief English economic writings of the
first half of the nineteenth century was apparent, rather than real" (*IT*,
pp. 758–9). Adam Smith and Ricardo had developed the "main outline" of long run value theory,[3] the old wage theories were working
towards the modern one (*Principles*, p. 543, marginal note), and Smith's
distribution theory was grounded in an appreciation of demand for, and
supply of, factor services.[4] Ricardo was "well aware" of the marginal
character of rent analysis "though he did not emphasise it enough"
(*Principles*, p. 154), and he even, Marshall claimed at one stage (though
he later withdrew from such an exposed position), appreciated that
keystone of Marshallian analysis, the "principle of (factor) substitution".[5] Ricardo's inverse relationship between wages and profits was
interpreted by Marshall in purely proportionate terms[6] while Ricardo

1. *Principles*, pp. 37, 84, 97 n., 101 n., 763 n.; *Variorum*, p. 599; 1879a, p. 167.
2. *Principles*, p. 379; *Variorum*, p. 396; *IT*, p. 764. See also note 1.
3. *Variorum*, p. 407. See also 1879a, pp. 77–9.
4. Smith "goes a good way towards explaining how they [wages and profits] are deter-
    mined by the ever fluctuating conditions of demand and supply" (Marshall, *Principles*,
    p. 507).
5. *Variorum*, pp. 592, 593. Ricardo and his followers "were familiar with the action of the
    law of substitution, but they laid insufficient stress on the side of [factor] demand"
    (ibid., p. 593). Groenewegen correctly notes that the claim for Ricardo made in the first
    edition of the *Principles* was significantly reduced in the *text* of the third. However, the
    words quoted above come not from the first edition but from a *marginal note* to the
    third. Marshall, it would seem, was reluctant to recant.
6. *Principles*, p. 550 n. This turns it into a truism empty of its peculiarly Ricardian, and
    indeed of all, content.

and Smith were both held to have understood all the essentials of modern capital theory.[7]

Understanding of the essential modernity of the Classical position was hampered by carelessness in formulation of the wage-fund idea (*Principles*, p. 823; see also *Variorum*, p. 821) which, in its vulgar form, was actually inconsistent with Ricardo's and Smith's reasonings (*Variorum*, p. 817), while Mill's famous fourth proposition on capital (demand for commodities is not demand for labour) was held to express his meaning badly.[8] Indeed, the errors of the Classical economists on wages "when traced back to their origin are little more than careless modes of expression" (*Principles*, p. 763 n.).

Smith, Ricardo, and J. S. Mill

Three particular Classical economists attracted Marshall's attention and admiration, Smith, Ricardo, and J. S. Mill. Marshall appreciated Smith's "philosophic thoroughness" and "practical knowledge" (*Principles*, p. 240) and held that there was "scarcely any economic truth now known of which he did not get some glimpse" (*Principles*, p. 757). Where Ricardo was critical of Smith, Marshall, despite his intense admiration for Ricardo, was for the most part inclined to defend Smith.[9]

His expressed admiration for Ricardo's powers of analysis, however, was almost unlimited.

> Ricardo's power of threading his way without slip through intricate paths to new and unexpected results has never been surpassed. (*Principles*, p. 761)

> Ricardo himself had no mathematical training. But his instincts were unique; and very few trained mathematicians could tread as safely as he over the most perilous courses of reasoning. Even the acute logical mind of Mill was unequal to the task. (*Principles*, p. 836)

However, there was a real danger of misunderstanding Ricardo. His unfortunate literary style omitted many things which "statesmen and businessmen", as readers, "would regard as obvious".

7. *Principles*, p. 583. This claim was aimed at Böhm-Bawerk – see Gårdlund, 1958, pp. 339–43.
8. *Principles*, p. 828. See also 1879a, p. 16, on Mill's first proposition ("Industry is limited by capital").
9. See, for example, *Principles*, pp. 167 n., 439. See, however, *IT*, p. 734, where Marshall endorses Ricardo's rather than Smith's position on the colonial trade.

> If then we seek to understand him rightly, we must interpret him generously, more generously than he himself interpreted Adam Smith.   (*Principles*, p. 813)

> Unfortunately however he delighted in short phrases, and he thought that his readers would always supply for themselves the explanations of which he had given them a hint.
> (*Principles*, p. 816; see also *Variorum*, pp. 279, 396)

But we were getting to understand Ricardo better:

> [R]ecent progress has developed Ricardo's work; and has pruned away only the dogmas deduced from it by followers of a different stamp of mind from his.   (*Variorum*, p. 493, dating from 1893)

Ricardo's value theory did not need reconstructing (*Variorum*, p. 813), while his obsession with an Invariable Measure could be dismissed as concern with an index number problem (*MCC*, p. 22).

Particularly startling are Marshall's claims concerning Ricardo's "awareness" of demand. He and his associates were "aware that the conditions of demand played as important a part as those of supply in determining value, yet they did not express their meaning with sufficient clearness, and they have been misunderstood by all but the most careful readers" (*Principles*, p. 84; see also p. 503). Indeed, Mill and Ricardo "regarded the natural laws of variation of utility as too obvious to require detailed explanation" (*Principles*, p. 817; see also pp. 818–20). Ricardo was perfectly well aware that costs affect value only in relation to supply at the margin where it equals demand (*MCC*, p. 321; see also *IT*, p. 396).

Marshall's attitude to Ricardo led him, especially from 1890 onwards, to give insufficient credit to Mill, a point which will be discussed further below. If Mill presumed to criticise Ricardo's treatment, Marshall immediately came to the latter's defence (*Principles*, p. 510 n.). In the field of trade, Marshall, in discussing reciprocal demand, freely attributed the work of Torrens and Mill to Ricardo (*MCC*, Book III, Chapter 8). Marshall seems literally, in his later work, to have been unable to believe that Mill said anything on international trade which had not already been said (even if not fully explained) by Ricardo (*MCC*, pp. 225, 351; *OP*, pp. 170, 372).

His willingness to credit Ricardo with particular ideas can be disconcerting at times. At one point he even claims that Ricardo's "celebrated" chapter on sudden changes in the channels of trade "is in effect an argument that even a bad system of taxation should seldom be violently changed".[10] As Hutchison has remarked:

> There is, perhaps, something rather questionable in the sort of intellectual generosity which assumes that Ricardo's interests and purposes, rightly understood, must certainly have been the same as one's own, when, after all, Ricardo was as explicit as he could have been that they were distinctly different.
> (1952, p. 423; see also 1978, Chapter 8, especially pp. 234–6)

The somewhat embarrassing truth is that Marshall's treatment of Ricardo verges on what might be known in another context as "apologetics". This may stem in part from J. S. Mill, who hid his own brilliant originality behind reverential references to Ricardo just as Marshall, in the *Economics of Industry* (discussed below), hid the origins of his distribution theory and much else. Starting from the position that Ricardo had not written a formal treatise (he quotes Roscher with approval in support of this untenable opinion),[11] Marshall felt free to interpret Ricardo in a most imaginative way. Phrases such as "Assumptions such as these are made quietly by Ricardo: he took for granted that his readers would supply them" (*MCC*, p. 323 n.) do not inspire confidence.

When one considers the achievements of Classical economics in general, and of J. S. Mill in particular,[12] Jevons's excited claims to originality, and his denigrations of Ricardo (who shunted economics onto the wrong track)[13] and of Mill (whose authority exercised a noxious influence),[14] could hardly fail to produce a reaction, especially in someone like Marshall, who had already learned so very much from working at Mill before Jevons's claims appeared. But from the perspective of a later generation, and of later scholarship, the effects of Marshall's claims are unfortunate. He can be found attributing to Ricardo, for instance, a passage from the

10. *MCC*, p. 195; "in effect" is certainly a very necessary qualification because the issue referred to by Marshall is only a very subsidiary part of the argument of Ricardo's chapter which is mainly concerned with distinguishing economic dislocation from a state of stagnation.
11. *Principles*, pp. 163, 503; *Variorum*, p. 279. See also Groenewegen (pp. 10–12 and p. 36, n. 7), who points out that Sraffa decisively refuted such a claim.
12. "In terms of identifiable theories, he was one of the most original economists in the history of the science" (Stigler, 1955, p. 7).
13. "That able but wrong-headed man, David Ricardo, shunted the car of economic science on to a wrong line – a line, however, on which it was further urged towards confusion by his equally able and wrong-headed admirer, John Stuart Mill" (Jevons, 1879, p. 72).
14. "If, instead of welcoming inquiry and criticism, the admirers of a great author accept his writings as authoritative, both in their excellences and in their defects, the most serious injury is done to truth" (Jevons, 1879, p. 260).

Bullion Report, one almost certainly written by Thornton, which stressed variable velocity of circulation in a way Ricardo certainly did not (*MCC*, pp. 41–2). Moreover, while he was prepared to acknowledge the work of J. H. Hollander in showing that Ricardo's monetary theory was essentially unoriginal, Marshall still insists that "his masterly genius, like that of Adam Smith, was largely occupied with the supreme task of building up a number of fragmentary truths into coherent doctrine. Such a doctrine has constructive force, because it is an organic whole" (*MCC*, p. 41 n.). Perhaps most strikingly of all, when John Stuart Mill applied his theory of reciprocal demand in international trade to explain relative price levels, without any reference to Ricardo, Marshall promptly attributed the work to Ricardo (*MCC*, p. 231; Mill, 1848–71, p. 620).

As various commentators have noted, Marshall's attitude to Mill (who was, in truth, the starting point for virtually everything in Marshall's economics which could be called Classical) underwent something of a transformation (Whitaker, 1975, p. 50 n.; Groenewegen, pp. 7–8). In the 1870s, when his debt to Mill was most recent, he defended Mill. Many of the attacks on Mill were "due to their [his critics] not having perceived the full power, which is latent, if not patent, in Mill's work" (1876, p. 119). Mill's value theory was basically sound (1876, p. 121). There was little in Mill's treatment of value and distribution which was not true when properly interpreted.[15] Marshall's *Economics of Industry* of 1879 was presented to the public as simply an exercise in bringing Mill up to date in the light of recent writings while at the same time providing an introduction to Mill. In fact the "updating" went much further than acknowledged. It included the introduction, based on Jevons's work, of diminishing marginal utility, a demand curve, and the equality of price with marginal utility (1879a, Book II, Chapter 1, pp. 65–71). The only acknowledged departure from Mill was in the treatment of distribution. Mill had separated distribution from exchange whereas Marshall integrated the two treatments while implying quite clearly that he was merely bringing out what was "latent" in Mill's work (1879a, p. v). However, Marshall's symmetrical treatment of the earnings of skilled and unskilled labour, capital, and management, through (on the demand side) a discounted product approach, goes far beyond Mill (1879a, Book II, Chapters 6–12). Only the fact that the margin itself appeared intermittently and at times indistinctly prevents this treatment from being linked directly to Marshall's later work,[16] despite his

---

15. 1879a, p. v. See also 1898, p. 41, for strong claims about Mill's treatment of distribution.

16. For instances of marginal analysis see 1879a, pp. 122, 133, 142. See also 1898, p. 58, for a claim that "The general notion of distribution in the *Economics of Industry* . . . is the same as in my *Principles*."

claims to the contrary. Whitaker judges that in the book Marshall had broken free of the wage fund (as indeed he had) so that the misleadingly similar "earnings and interest fund" could easily be developed into a proper marginal productivity theory. But, as Whitaker correctly notes (1975, 1, pp. 77, 81), Marshall did not attempt this (cf. Marshall, 1879*a*, pp. 96, 203–5).

In this connection two points are of particular interest. First, Marshall gives only belated credit to other writers whose work pointed at least partially in the same direction (though he was later to acknowledge Thünen), while at the same time implying that the analysis is actually J. S. Mill's.[17] Second, it is apparent from Whitaker's researches in Marshall's papers that Marshall was still using a wage fund approach in the years 1870–74.[18] This leads inevitably to the conclusion that Marshall claimed J. S. Mill had a more modern theory only after he (Marshall) had abandoned what he clearly believed in the years 1870–4 to be both J. S. Mill's, and a correct, theory.

In defending Mill in 1876 he attributed to him a real cost theory of price, from which it was easy to attribute to him also a utility approach (1876, pp. 122–6). At the same time he argued that Mill regarded cost of production as variable with output, and thus dependent upon demand (1876, pp. 126–9).

It was not only Mill who benefited from such generosity of interpretation. Some of Marshall's defences go beyond what might politely be called "strained" interpretation to statements which it is hard to regard as anything but fiction. The most flagrant example is Marshall's repeated statement that Senior became a keen supporter of the Factory Acts.[19]

Critics of Classical Economics

Even after Marshall's ardour in defence of Mill had cooled somewhat, he still assailed the critics of the Classical economists along the lines already established. Thus, in the *Principles* he argued, just as he had done in the *Economics of Industry,* that demand and supply mutually determined value, and that, simply because the Classical economists had laid insufficient stress upon demand, there had been a reaction to an opposite extreme (*Principles,* pp. 85, 525, 817; 1879*a*, pp. 146–9). Jevons was no less misleading and one-sided than Ricardo. In fact, Marshall informed

17. 1879*a*, p. 205. On Marshall's acknowledgement of priorities see Whitaker, 1975, 1, pp. 39, 69.
18. Whitaker, 1975, 1, pp. 43, 48, 69. Marshall's early discussion of wages is in *EEW,* 1, pp. 184–201.
19. *Principles,* p. 763 n. (dating from the 5th edition); *IT,* pp. 763–4. See also Blaug, 1958*a*, p. 119; Bowley, 1937, pp. 256–7, 269–72.

his readers, Jevons's success was aided by his faults in misunderstanding and misrepresenting Ricardo:

> [H]e led many to think he was correcting great errors; whereas he was really only adding very important explanations.
>
> *(Principles,* p. 101)

Marshall felt similarly strongly about Böhm-Bawerk, despite apparently cordial personal relations with the Austrian economist.[20] His public comments were restrained, but he wrote to Wicksell:

> While he was still at school, I learnt from the men whom he reviles everything which he has vaunted as a great discovery: and especially in America, he has been taken at his own valuation by people *who have never studied the great men* on whose burial places he dances his war dance.[21]

But Jevons, like Böhm-Bawerk, in intellectual terms a self-proclaimed revolutionary, undoubtedly influenced Marshall, who borrowed from his work in "updating" Mill. Cairnes, by contrast a follower of Mill, had, in Marshall's opinion, done more harm, through his failure to interpret Mill "correctly", than the self-proclaimed intellectual revolutionaries (1876, p. 120; *Principles,* pp. 97, 218, 339 n.; *Variorum,* p. 796). This is not an entirely surprising attitude; Marshall, in seeking to stress both the intellectual coherence and the theoretical comprehensiveness of Mill, and the compatibility of his work with that of people like Jevons, could hardly accept as correct the writings of one (Cairnes) who sought to expound Mill while admitting to complete bafflement with regard to the work of Jevons (Cairnes, 1875, pp. vi–vii).

From 1890 onwards, as Marshall came to allot almost transcendental importance to the work of Ricardo, there was a corresponding down-playing of Mill's importance.[22] He claimed that work at the India Office must have lowered the quality of Mill's economics and compared Mill's analytical powers unfavourably with Ricardo's (*Principles,* pp. 252 n., 836).

It was not only Mill who suffered in this way. While continuing to maintain his curious version of Senior's views on the Factory Acts, Marshall showed a strange reluctance to recognise Senior's generalisa-

20. M. P. Marshall, 1947, p. 48. Mrs. Marshall relates that she had feared some friction if the subject of the rate of interest arose, as "he [Böhm-Bawerk] and Alfred had recently been corresponding warmly upon it" (ibid.).
21. Gårdlund, 1958, p. 342. See also *Memorials,* p. 417. For public comment on Böhm-Bawerk, see Marshall, *Principles,* pp. 235, 528 n., 532–3 n., 583–4 n., 790 n., 821; *Variorum,* pp. 215 n., 247, 368 n., 462 n., 552 n., 628 n., 631 n., 638 n., 643 n., 644 n., 783 n., 785. Some of these, though relatively restrained, are nonetheless distinctly tart by Marshall's self-denying standards.
22. On this see especially Groenewegen, pp. 7–9 and Whitaker, 1975, 1, p. 50 n.

tion of the rent concept, though he himself, in describing rent of land as the "leading species of a large genus" was almost echoing Senior's words.[23] Torrens also suffered to some extent. Though Marshall cites him only once, it is clear that he was familiar at first hand with some of Torrens's work,[24] which may have been more important to Marshall than he acknowledged.

These omissions are as unfortunate as the exaggerated claims. There seems no doubt that Mill's work was the origin of the basis of Marshall's economics, as Marshall's earlier accounts of his own development reveal clearly. This is particularly true when we look at the material on international trade and on growth found in his early papers.[25] Marshall also borrowed from Mill the latter's own particular version of the Law of Markets (*Principles*, pp. 710–12; 1879a, pp. 154–5; *IT*, p. 640). He even adopted Mill's ambiguity in this matter, both with respect to the likelihood of the arrival of the stationary state in the near future, and with respect to the reasons for a decline in profits. Endorsing Mill's statement of the Law of Markets, he also drew on Mill's use (in the context of Wakefield and colonisation) of Smithian ideas of possible exhaustion of investment opportunities (1879a, pp. 126–7). He followed Mill to some extent in matters of methodology (*Principles*, pp. 50, 771; 1879a, p. 211), of capital theory (*Principles*, p. 75; 1898, p. 56; see also Whitaker, 1975, 1, p. 220), on the equalisation of net advantage (1879a, pp. 103, 131, 139), and on noncompeting groups (1879a, p. 107). He was directed by Mill not only to matters of trade theory,[26] but also to problems like the valuation of joint products (*EEW*, 1, pp. 156–8; *Principles*, pp. 435–6 n.). His attitudes to such things as low wages (*Principles*, p. 509) and even investment in education[27] were influenced by Mill.

Of course Marshall drew on other Classical authors as well. He attrib-

---

23. *Principles*, p. 432; *Variorum*, p. 463. For land rent as "the leading species of a large genus" see *Principles*, pp. viii, 412, 421, 629; *Variorum*, pp. 51, 59, 495. For Senior see his Appendix to Whately, 1826. On his generalisation of the rent concept see O'Brien, 1975, p. 131, and Bowley, 1937, pp. 126–36.

24. *MCC*, p. 161. Although J. S. Mill refers to Torrens, none of his citations refers to the point on which Marshall refers to Torrens, viz. reciprocal demand. Marshall was already 22 when Torrens died, so his knowledge of a writer whose work rapidly disappeared into obscurity after his death in 1864 is less surprising than it might at first seem.

25. See Whitaker, 1975, 1, pp. 37–8, 260; 2, pp. 306–9; 1974; Marshall, *EEW*, 2, pp. 309–16; *MCC*, pp. 157, 160–1, 163, 168–9, 177; *Variorum*, pp. 8–9; *Memorials*, p. 412. See also Groenewegen, pp. 7–8.

26. *MCC*, pp. 157, 160–1, 163, 168–9, 177; *EEW*, 1, pp. 261–79, 280–9; 2, pp. 3–186; Whitaker, 1975, 1, pp. 260–1, 279–80.

27. 1879a, pp. 11, 105–7. See, however, note 49. In addition, the text for Marshall's Bristol lectures of 1879–80 on taxation was Book V of Mill (1848–71). See Whitaker, 1975, 2, p. 378.

uted his concept of long run normal value to Smith (*Principles*, p. 347),
he acknowledged his debt to Overstone on the trade cycle (1879*a*, p.
153), and his "Symmetalism" proposal was explicitly derived from Ricardo's *Economical and Secure Currency* (*MCC*, pp. 65–7; *Memorials*,
pp. 14, 28, 30, 102–3, 143–4, 165). (Indeed, one commentator has
argued that this is Marshall's only clear and unambiguous borrowing
from Ricardo; Groenewegen, p. 28). It is apparent from the Whitaker
volumes that Marshall's early lecture notes dealt with particular problems in Smith and Ricardo (rent, corn duties, bounties on production,
and demand and supply) – and here, in contrast to his later apologetics,
he is sometimes critical of Ricardo (*EEW*, 2, pp. 257–61). Moreover, he
had other sources than the English classics, especially Cournot and von
Thünen.[28] But again and again when one looks at Marshall's work,
especially in its formative years, the influence of Mill is writ large.

The balance of Marshall's indebtedness will be explored in much more
detail in the following two sections, but even at this stage it should be
clear that there is something wrong with Marshall's own account. He
made astonishing claims for continuity, and he persisted in these claims in
the face of contemporary criticism, despite his acute personal sensitivity
to criticism.[29] In so far as the aim was rhetorical, he seems to have had
some success – even Shove not only took Marshall at his word when
conflating Mill and Ricardo but also very largely accepted his claims
concerning continuity.[30] Moreover, it was the continuity of "truth"
which he claimed; to be referred to as a synthesiser irritated him intensely

28. *Variorum*, pp. 242–8, 250–2; Whitaker, 1975, 2, pp. 240–1, 248–50. There are also
     numerous citations of both writers in the *Principles*. Both Hutchison, 1956, pp. 64–6
     n. and Whitaker, 1975, 1, p. 45 n. express surprise that Marshall makes no reference
     to Whewell as a predecessor. In terms of the evidence now available about Whewell
     that is perfectly reasonable, but it would appear from Marshall's papers that he did
     not know of Whewell's work except in connection with the publication of Richard
     Jones's writings. Although Whewell undoubtedly developed a price elasticity concept
     it seems clear that Marshall arrived at his own elasticity concept independently, and
     some considerable time after his study of economics had developed. Mrs. Marshall
     dates it at 1881 (1947, p. 28). Had he known of Whewell's work he would hardly
     have spent time on the matter himself. But it is certainly puzzling that he did not know
     of it, particularly as it would appear, from a discovery by Professor Whitaker, that
     Marshall did know of the work of Tozer which was published in the same journal as
     that of Whewell; see Collard, 1968, p. xxi.
29. Ashley, 1891, correctly pointed out several misinterpretations of Ricardo by Marshall
     in the *Principles*, including the nature of Ricardo's value theory and a quotation, out
     of context, about a supposedly upwardly movable psychological subsistence level. See
     also Marshall, 1898, p. 44, on the broader question of continuity.
30. Shove, 1942, p. 295. This is all the more remarkable because, despite a small pub-
     lished output, Shove was an extremely able economist to whose lectures Joan Robin-
     son (1933) is apparently indebted. For a defence of Marshall's style of "personal
     exegesis", see S. Hollander, 1979, pp. 643–4 and for comment on this position see
     Groenewegen, pp. 13, 29.

(*Memorials*, p. 418). As we shall see, however, his own acknowledgements give a somewhat unbalanced picture – his claims in the fields of analysis of value and distribution are hard to accept, while his acknowledgements in the macroeconomic fields of money and trade, while less insistent (perhaps because more obviously correct), are actually much more consistent.

III   Marshall's Classical Inheritance

Marshall certainly owed a clear debt to his Classical predecessors. In this section we will examine that debt, and in the following the picture will be qualified by indicating those aspects of Marshall's work which cannot be called Classical. Undoubtedly, the most important debt was to J. S. Mill. Marshall's initial forays into economics involved mathematisation of Mill, his policy attitudes were influenced by Mill, and his first book, *The Economics of Industry*, is both an introduction to, and an updating of, Mill.

Value and Distribution

From classical economics, Marshall took the concept of "normal" values for economic variables as being competitive equilibrium values within a framework which limited the operation of competition.[31] These economic variables could be analysed by the economist as scientist. To go beyond this to policy and to particular situations it was necessary to move outside the science of economics. The influence of Senior and of Mill is apparent here.[32]

The whole economic system existed within a framework of continuing economic growth, for Marshall as for the Classical economists, and in such a framework a good deal of judgement was necessary to supplement analysis before arriving at practical conclusions.

Such an outlook influenced Marshall throughout his writings. In dealing with the supply of goods, he analysed the supply conditions affecting the goods-producing factors of land, labour, and capital (to which he added the fourth factor of "organisation") (*Principles*, pp. 138–9, 240–3). In dealing with the supply of labour he discussed the growth of population, its health and strength, industrial training and labour mobil-

31. *Principles*, pp. 34–6; 1879a, pp. vi–vii. On the operation of competition within a framework see Samuels, 1966, O'Brien, 1975, and above all Robbins, 1952.
32. 1879a, pp. 3–4, 211; 1874, pp. 423–30; *Memorials*, pp. 164–5; *Principles*, pp. 771, 774. On Senior see Bowley, 1937, Chapter 1. However, Marshall was arguing that practical decisions involved considerations from outside economics. He did not envisage capturing them within an "art" of economics (*Variorum*, p. 154).

ity, as well as that central classical labour market concept, equalisation of
net advantage (*Principles*, pp. 173–219, 547, 557, 661; see also *Variorum*, pp. 303–4). The discussion of the supply of capital reflects the work
of Mill in particular. It is held to depend on the size of the possible
sources of accumulation, and on the strength of the motives to save.
Positive time preference exists in the aggregate, so that meeting the cost of
this "waiting" is a necessary cost of production.[33]

Marshall's consideration of land naturally involves a very classical
emphasis on diminishing returns (and an equally classical recognition
that these might be offset by technical progress). It also exhibits a
tendency – widespread in the classical literature because of the historical
origins of the so-called "Ricardian" rent theory but perhaps surprising in
a writer as clear headed as Marshall – to confuse diminishing returns
with decreasing returns to scale and to relate these to increasing returns
to scale.[34] As will be seen in the next section, Marshall did not stop there,
but the Classical starting points are clear enough.

His demand theory really owed nothing to Classical origins, despite his
claims. His discussion of adjustments to equilibrium value, however,
though it went far beyond the classical analysis, betrays the initial influence of Smith (whom, as already noted, Marshall greatly admired)[35] in its
initial concentration on market and "normal" (that is, long run) values,
with price adjustment in the first case and quantity adjustment in the
second.[36] Moreover his reading of Mill, as already indicated, directed him
to some other value problems, especially those of joint demand and supply.[37] Though not the most distinguished part of his discussion of value
(Stigler, 1941, pp. 83–7) it is clearly classical in origin.

Not surprisingly, given his emphasis on conditions of factor supply, his
work on distribution exhibits classical elements. His discussion of labour
supply, while bowing in the direction of Jevons's disutility analysis, is
predominantly concerned with Classical issues such as population size,
and population quality – health, strength, and investment in education.

33. *Principles*, pp. 229–36, 353, 618–20; J. S. Mill, 1848–71, I, pp. 160–72, 400–15; II,
     pp. 733–46. Marshall was quite clear that his treatment of capital owed most to
     Classical economics and to Turgot. It is this which lies behind his comment to Wicksell
     on Böhm-Bawerk (note 21). Interestingly enough it may well have been Jevons who,
     on this issue at least, was closer to Ricardo; see Black, 1981, pp. 8–9.
34. *Principles*, pp. 149–70, 418–31, 436–9, 450, 499–500, 629–36; *Variorum*, pp.
     492–512; 1879a, pp. 21–6, 82–7.
35. See *Memorials*, p. 379, for a particular tribute by Marshall to Smith.
36. 1879a, pp. vii, 146–9, 158–67; *EEW*, 1, pp. 125–64; see also Whitaker, 1975, 1, pp.
     119–25, 160; Davies, 1963; Newman, 1960.
37. J. S. Mill, 1848–71, Book III, Chapter 16, pp. 582–6; Marshall, *Principles*, pp. 381–
     93, 852–6; *Variorum*, p. 400; *EEW*, 1, pp. 160–64. See also Whitaker, 1975, 1, p.
     160.

His discussion of noncompeting groups as a constraint on labour mobility[38] also shows the influence of Mill and Cairnes.

Like the classical economists, he was concerned with poverty and the interaction between poverty and low wages, though with more emphasis on labour *productivity* than on the problems associated with labour force increase in a situation in which a low "psychological subsistence" level is the key factor. Like Mill, he looked to education, family limitation, and capital accumulation, together with technical advance (and not to trades unions or socialism),[39] as the remedies for poverty.

His analysis of profit contained classical elements. Gross profit was a combination of interest and wages of management (as it had been for Smith) and of compensation for risk (as stressed by Tooke and McCulloch).[40] He went further than the classical analysis, however: in particular, earnings of management included rent of ability.[41]

Marshall's discussion of rent itself started from a Classical base, though it ultimately proceeded to a much higher level of generality. In dealing with land, Marshall attributed rent to the existence of diminishing returns (or decreasing returns to scale) and exhibited a Ricardo-like emphasis upon variable fertility. Moreover he managed to blur the role of transfer earnings and to avoid distinguishing rent from an individual and a social point of view, leaving a puzzle for twentieth century interpreters.[42] Indeed, he offered the Delphic remark, in rebuking Jevons, that it was "inexpedient to say that the rent of land does not enter into . . . price. But it is worse than inexpedient to say that the rent of land does enter into . . . price: that is false" (*Variorum*, p. 460; see also p. 439, and *Principles*, pp. 436–7 n.). Nonetheless he succeeded in developing rent analysis further. He made rent ultimately depend on the marginal productivity of land – it was the area under the marginal product curve after payments to cooperating factors – which was implicit in the Classical writers but not explicit. In

38. *Principles*, pp. 65, 138–43, 173–203, 217–19, 331, 525–30, 556–58, 567–74, 660–2, 716–19, 721, 843; 1879a, pp. 101–13, 173–5; *EEW*, 2, pp. 387–93; Whitaker, 1974, p. 7; Whitaker, 1975, 2, pp. 385–7. See also the discussion in Stigler, 1941, pp. 63–6. On the question of investment in education see also note 49.

39. *Principles*, pp. 509–10, 529–33, 559–63, 568, 684–5, 693–6, 702–8, 714–15; 1879a, pp. 102, 187–213; *Memorials*, pp. 227–53, 384–6, 396–9, 402–3; 1885a, p. 182; 1883, pp. 200–10; 1887a, pp. xi–xiii, xxv–xxvi; Whitaker, 1972, especially pp. 49–61; 1975, 1, pp. 79–80; Petridis, 1973.

40. Smith, 1776, 1, pp. 105–15, especially p. 113. For references to Tooke and McCulloch on this matter see O'Brien, 1970, p. 310.

41. *Principles*, pp. 71–82, 313, 505–10, 589–92, 598, 612–15, 618–20; *Variorum*, pp. 670–5 (from 1887b); 1879a, pp. 119–27, 135–45; *MCC*, pp. 285–94; *EEW*, 1, pp. 206–12; Whitaker, 1975, 1, pp. 204–6.

42. See Buchanan, 1929, and Robbins, 1930, pp. 209–11. See also Worcester, 1946, who, oddly, makes no reference to either Buchanan or Robbins. See also Stigler, 1941, pp. 92–4.

generalising the rent concept (as Senior and Bailey had done before him)[43] he was able to show the importance of the elasticity of factor supply in rent and, as noted, to introduce the concept of rent of ability.[44]

Economic Growth

The emphasis on the classical elements in the analysis of factor supply was an inevitable part of Marshall's treatment because his whole work is based entirely upon the concept of a moving economic system – a growing economy in which static equilibrium theorems (now particularly associated with Marshall) could only be explained in terms of all elements moving forward together at the same speed. Marshall explained this in terms of an analogy with a man packing parcels on the rack of a moving train; an equilibrium could be attained as long as everything was moving at the same relative speed, but it was likely to be disrupted if the onward motion was checked (*Memorials*, p. 312; see also 1898, p. 38). Understanding of economic growth was thus very important. Like Mill, Marshall was impressed by the premier position which England had attained through economic growth and was concerned with its preservation. Like Mill, he looked to economic growth to increase both material and nonmaterial wealth *and* aspirations so that wants increased with output.[45]

His formal analysis of growth – never published in his lifetime – was a differential equation version of J. S. Mill, with equations for the size of the working population, the standard of living, the efficiency of labour, the capital stock, total output, net annual product, piece wages, time wages, and the rate of interest.[46] But in his published work Marshall dealt with the growth of the economic system as a whole in more distinctly Classical terms, without recourse to such formality. Labour force increase in both quantity and (especially) quality was necessary for economic growth. In dealing with population he coupled a weak version of Malthus with eu-

43. For references see Bowley, 1937, pp. 126–36; O'Brien, 1975, pp. 130–1; Blaug, 1958*b*, pp. 55, 58, 155, 157, 158, 167, 171, 223.
44. *Principles*, pp. 149–70, 418–32, 436–9, 450, 499–500, 534–6, 577–9, 622–4, 629–36; *Variorum*, pp. 440–512, 670–8; 1879*a*, pp. 81–90, 110, 179; *EEW*, 1, pp. 239–60; 2, pp. 321–2; Whitaker, 1975, 2, pp. 319–21.
45. *Principles*, pp. 49, 56–7, 59, 80–1, 220–39, 675–8, 689–93, 749–52; 1879*a*, p. 6; *IT*, p. 697; 1883, pp. 184–91; *OP*, pp. 402–12. See also Parsons, 1931 and 1932; Whitaker, 1977. On the growth context of Marshall's work see also Walker, 1983. On the concept of endogenous tastes in Marshall's work see also Loasby, 1978, who correctly distinguishes this idea from the Galbraithian conception. On Parsons's critique, which economists may have cited a little too uncritically, see Wearne, 1981, and Chasse, 1984.
46. *EEW*, 2, p. 309–16. See also Whitaker, 1974, pp. 11–15; 1975, 2, pp. 305–9.

genic considerations[47] and maintained the Classical interest in investment in education,[48] extending this to the question of business education.[49]

Increase in the supply of capital was also necessary because it was required, as Smith had argued, to support increased division of labour. Marshall extended the meaning of "division of labour" enormously. His discussion of internal and external economies is the great source for all subsequent economists. Following Mill, accumulation depended on the size of the net product and the motives to save, including foresight, security, family affection, and the rate of interest (*Principles*, pp. 220–36, 353; Mill, 1848–73, 1, pp. 160–72, 400–15; 2, pp. 733–46). In the standard classical manner Marshall looked forward, in the *Economics of Industry*, to a "secular" (a corruption of the Latin *saecula*) decline in the rate of profit, as already noted.[50]

Government

Economic progress required, as Smith had recognised, a suitable institutional framework (Robbins, 1952; Samuels, 1956). Like the classical writers, Marshall emphasised security of property, human freedom, and the development of communications and financial institutions.[51] He was a little, but not very much, more enthusiastic about government involvement than the classical writers: Government involvement in enterprise was harmful to both managerial and innovative efficiency. He does, however, seem to have seen the role of government expanding in the areas of health, welfare, defence, and education. His concern with the link between poverty and low wages extended to the problem of urban overcrowding, and the lack of fresh air in towns, problems he proposed to

47. *Principles*, pp. 173–203, 219, 243–8, 740–5; *Variorum*, pp. 303–5; 1885*a*, p. 198; 1879*a*, pp. 27–37. See also Spengler, 1955.
48. For references to the Classical literature in this area, see O'Brien, 1975, pp. 282–5 and notes.
49. *Principles*, pp. 204–19, 229–30, 236, 560–6, 570–1, 619, 622, 660–1, 681–4, 858; 1879*a*, p. 39 (see also ibid., pp. 10–11, 32); *IT*, pp. 129–34, 356–7; *Memorials*, pp. 117–18; 1905*b*; 1905*c*; 1905*d*. See also 1905*a* and Blandy, 1967. It is both interesting and puzzling in the context of this chapter to note that Marshall apparently believed that he was going beyond the Classical economists in this respect. "The older economists took too little account of the fact that the human faculties are as important a means of production as any other kind of capital; and we may conclude, in opposition to them, that any change in the distribution of wealth which gives more to the wage receivers and less to the capitalists is likely, other things being equal, to hasten the increase of material production, and that it will not perceptibly retard the storing-up of material wealth" (*Principles*, pp. 229–30).
50. See *Principles*, p. 379 for "secular". For profit decline see 1879*a*, pp. 126–7.
51. *Principles*, pp. 197–8, 273–4, 301–4, 528, 678–9, 691, 726–33, 740–2, 744–7, 750–2; *IT*, pp. 32–85, 700–18; *MCC*, pp. 68–97.

tackle not only through taxation but also through a removal of some of the urban population to the country.

Much of this can be regarded for the most part as a development of the classical position with Sidgwickian overtones.[52] The only significant departure is that Marshall favoured increased *income* (and capital) taxation, with progression, to finance these excursions into welfare activities. He certainly did not favour government expansion financed by debt (1917, pp. 313–14, 317–22, 325–9, 345; *OP*, pp. 361–3). In the area of poor relief he showed no great hostility to the 1834 Poor Law – although, like Senior, condemning the Speenhamland system in particular, and widespread (though not small scale) "outdoor" relief in general – despite a very genuine concern with the alleviation of poverty and a strong interest in the work of the Charity Organisations Society.[53] Ultimately he believed, like Mill, that economic growth (together with the development of what he quaintly called "economic chivalry")[54] was the answer to poverty.

Whether in all this there are Utilitarian, as distinct from straightforward Classical, influences is a moot point. Marshall was probably not a wholehearted Utilitarian though not completely free of Utilitarian traits, many of them absorbed through J. S. Mill, others through Sidgwick. Utilitarianism influenced his economic psychology – thus he was able to absorb Jevons's Utilitarian-based approach to consumer maximisation – much more than his general stance on policy matters.[55] His aversion to ostentation and the influence of fashion more probably stemmed from his Calvinistic upbringing[56] – and possibly from the Classical distinction be-

---

52. *Principles*, pp. 199–200, 202–3, 304, 718, 803–4; 1879a, p. 113; *IT*, pp. 486, 494–7, 666–72; *Memorials*, pp. 118, 142–51; 1917, pp. 325–9, 345; 1885b; 1891a; 1891b; 1909; 1916; *OP*, pp. 197–262; 1885a, pp. 183–4; 1884; 1887c.

53. *OP*, pp. 199–262 especially pp. 199, 201, 211–25; 1879a, pp. 32–4; 1885a, pp. 187–8; *Memorials*, pp. 345, 373, 403; 1886; 1892a; 1892b. Marshall was tolerant, however, of localised and limited outdoor relief and did not favour its complete abolition.

54. *Memorials*, pp. 323–46 (from 1907). On the significance of economic chivalry, and the related question of Utilitarianism, see Birch, 1985.

55. See Birch, 1985; see also the contrary view in Jensen, 1985, which juxtaposes two misreferenced and very widely separated quotations from Marshall. Despite Jensen's contentions, Marshall's renunciation of a thoroughgoing Utilitarianism is clear enough (*Principles*, p. 17 n.), as was observed long ago by Schumpeter (1954, pp. 1056–7; Schumpeter also noted the point about Jevons made in the text of this chapter). Moreover, it is of interest that when Marshall transferred the chapter which originally included this note (*Principles*, p. 17 n.) to Appendix C in the 5th (1907) edition of the *Principles*, he retained the note itself in a prominent place in the main text of the book.

56. On this upbringing see Coase, 1984. On fashion and ostentation see, for example, Marshall, *Principles*, pp. 88 n., 288, 688, 720–1; *Memorials*, pp. 324–5, 443.

tween productive and unproductive labour – than from explicit adherence to Utilitarian ideals.[57]

Trade Theory and Policy

In the areas of trade and money, Marshall's classical inheritance is so clear as almost to require no comment. The treatment of international trade theory is undoubtedly the highest point of J. S. Mill's majestic *Principles;* and it seems to have been this area which, together with the material on economic growth (resulting in the equation system referred to above), first attracted Marshall's attention. A manuscript which Professor Whitaker dates at 1872–4 includes the now familiar offer curves, an investigation of the effects of tariffs, and an exploration of multiple equilibria (also explored by Mill). Indeed Marshall wrote (but did not publish) a book on international trade which was essentially complete by 1877 – and examination of this shows it to have been building almost completely on Mill (the other – unacknowledged – source is Torrens).[58] It is true that when Marshall used his famous apparatus – first published (with errors, some fairly obvious) by Sidgwick in 1879 on Marshall's behalf[59] – the discussion lacked the hallmarks of the Classical discussions, with their emphasis on balance of payments equilibrium being adjusted through specie flows, and the effects of these flows on relative income and price levels. But these considerations, it is apparent from *Money Credit and Commerce,* were present in the larger manuscript from which Sidgwick had extracted the Pure Theory (MCC, pp. 177–89, 338–40; Whitaker, 1975, 2, p. 6).

It should be emphasised that this was no mere regurgitation. The work was that of a properly trained mathematician; and Marshall, it is apparent from later work, considered many of the difficulties raised by the analysis while (as was his unfortunate habit) avoiding any indication to the reader that a number of difficult possible cases had been reviewed before the final version was presented (Chipman, 1965, pp. 689, 704, 722–4, 733, 734, 738, 739; Whitaker, 1975, 2, p. 115).

Beyond the formal technical discussion, Marshall followed the stan-

---

57. See also Chasse, 1984, for an informative discussion. The suggestion about productive and unproductive labour comes from this source (p. 393). The matter clearly requires further exploration.

58. *Principles,* pp. 261–79; *Variorum,* pp. 11–61, 63–89, 94–111, 116–81. See also Whitaker, 1975, 1, pp. 260–1; 2, pp. 3–11, 62–3, 89–94, 111–16. On Torrens see O'Brien, 1975, pp. 189–97 and O'Brien, 1977.

59. *EEW,* 2, p. 4 (Marshall to Seligman, April 1900). See also Whitaker, 1975, 1, pp. 20–1. Happily the errors have been corrected in the Whitaker edition of the material though they were preserved in the 1930 LSE reprint of the material; see Whitaker, 1975, 2, p. 7 n.

dard Smithian and Millian paths, with foreign trade originating in the supply of luxuries and then moving to more basic commodities. In this it benefitted all parties to trade. Trade facilitated technical advance and increased division of labour. It also enhanced the development of financial institutions in the form of money and capital markets. Perhaps Marshall was less optimistic than some of his predecessors; he also argued that the very process of expansion (and the increased capitalisation involved) separated employers and employees, and that the widening of financial markets increased fluctuations, though these could be offset by the demand-steadying effects of wider goods markets and better communications (*Principles*, pp. 672–5; *EEW*, 2, pp. 14–20, 33–61).

It was not just the trade analysis which was classical: it was the attitudes. Marshall's commitment to unilateral free trade as a concept had a fervour recalling the heated classical rejection of Torrens's *The Budget*.[60] Free trade was necessary, in Marshall's view, not only as a stimulus but also to avoid the conferring of sectional benefits at the cost of larger injury to the wider community. Protection not only distorted the distribution of income but reduced its level by interfering with the full realisation of scale economies.[61]

Marshall recognised that taxes on foreign trade could turn the terms of trade in favour of the country levying the duties, as Torrens had argued (though Marshall does not refer to him in this context) but he did not approve of such duties. They were limited in their effectiveness, in a many-country world, they involved a deadweight loss, product and factor market distortions, and regressive effects, as well as political corruption.[62]

Money

When we turn from the trade theory to the monetary theory, the roots in the Classical literature are clear enough. As Marshall himself said, the Classical economists "left very little to be added as regards fundamentals by their successors" (*MCC*, p. 41).

In context this statement refers to the work of the Bullionists and it reflects Marshall's habit, especially in later life, of neglecting the importance for his own thought of what he had derived from J. S. Mill. Mar-

---

60. *OP*, 365–420; *MCC*, pp. 193–8; *EEW*, 2, pp. 80–9, 94–111; *Memorials*, pp. 449–50. See also Whitaker, 1975, 2, pp. 89–94. On the controversy over Torrens's *The Budget* see Robbins, 1958, Chapter 7, and O'Brien, 1975, pp. 189–97.
61. *MCC*, pp. 213–17; *OP*, pp. 395–9, 408–12; *EEW*, 2, pp. 106–8; *Memorials*, pp. 258–65, 471–4; *IT*, pp. 760–2; 1917, pp. 330–45; 1904, pp. 94–8. See also 1903; McCready, 1955; Wood, 1982; and Whitaker, 1975, 2, pp. 89–91.
62. *EEW*, 2, pp. 63–89; *MCC*, pp. 219, 265; *OP*, pp. 389–90, 394, 399, 415–20; 1917, pp. 329–30, 341–5; 1904, p. 97.

shall's monetary thought was in fact derived very largely from Mill, though supplemented by other writers including Ricardo and (especially) Thornton. It represented a continuation of the Classical tradition, particularly in its special Millian version, incorporating elements of both Currency and Banking Schools in the literature which developed both before and after the Bank Charter Act of 1844.[63] Marshall also drew on the work of Giffen, particularly in relation to the bank deposit multiplier (*OP*, pp. 27, 37; *MCC*, p. 60n.; Eshag, 1963, pp. xiii, 16–18), but this does not alter the truth of the statement above because Giffen's work is essentially classical and, in any case, the deposit multiplier had been put forward much earlier by Torrens on the basis of work by Pennington.[64]

Marshall's main theoretical approach was thus via the quantity theory, but with a recognition of the variability of velocity of circulation, and of the importance of commercial confidence. Like Thornton, he recognised the existence of links between velocity and confidence. Thus, accepting that velocity could vary if commercial confidence altered or if paper currency was increased in amount and its status undermined, Marshall could not accept the full rigour of the Currency School position that the amount of paper currency could only be equal to the metallic currency it had displaced. Nonetheless his whole emphasis was, as in the classical writings, on currency rather than bank deposits. He regarded the latter as devices for increasing velocity rather than as money themselves.[65]

Approaching monetary theory from this direction, Marshall showed clear appreciation of the operation of precious metal flows and their interaction with the balance of payments, and of the concept of the equilibrium distribution of the precious metals.[66] His discussion of the transmission mechanism emphasised the "indirect" mechanism, just as Thornton's had done; it is ironic that textbooks should treat this, indisputably inherited by Keynes from Marshall,[67] as some kind of particularly Keynesian innovation.[68] An inflow of precious metals increased

63. On the Currency and Banking controversy background see O'Brien, 1975, pp. 153–9. Marshall's monetary theory is in *OP*, pp. 1–195, 263–326, and *MCC*, pp. 12–97, 225–72, 282–4; see also *EEW*, 1, pp. 164–77; 2, pp. 277–8.

64. On Torrens and Pennington see Robbins, 1958, pp. 109–11; Pennington, 1826–40, and O'Brien, 1984, pp. 15–16.

65. *OP*, pp. 5–6, 22, 24–7, 34–40, 118, 267–8; 1923, pp. 42–50, 81–8, 246–63, 282–4; Thornton, 1802, pp. 96–100, 197 n.

66. *OP*, pp. 65–7, 115–26, 144–7, 150, 170–4, 177–80, 188, 191–5, 293, 296–7; see also Keynes in *Memorials*, pp. 30–1; *MCC*, pp. 38–67. On the Classical background see O'Brien, 1975, Chapter 6.

67. On this Keynes, 1911, is instructive. On the more general question of Marshall and Keynes see Jensen, 1983; Birch, 1985; and Loasby, 1978.

68. The idea is also central to the work of Wicksell, 1898, and of Mises, 1912, and Keynes certainly knew of Wicksell's work. But it has roots that go back far beyond those writers and Marshall – see Angell, 1926, p. 120, and O'Brien, 1984, pp. 30–1.

banking reserves, leading to a lowering of the rate of interest below the marginal profitability of investment, producing an increased demand for loans. Price rises resulted. These were further enhanced by expectations of inflation following the inflow of gold. Rising price levels in turn increased the demand for working balances.[69]

Marshall used this analysis, and showed his appreciation of the issues involved, to very considerable advantage, in the debate over the metallic standard. His exposition is contained in his answers to enquiries on trade depression (1886), gold and silver (1887), and Indian currency (1899) (*OP*, pp. 1–16, 17–195, 265–326). He was able to show the irrelevance of bimetallic proposals both to the question of price level stability and to that of India's exports; and he put forward a plan, deriving from Ricardo's *Economical and Secure Currency* for "Symmetallism", proposing that paper could only be exchanged for metal on the basis of receiving two bars of two different metals (*OP*, pp. 14, 28, 30, 165; Ricardo, 1816, especially pp. 65–73). Gresham's Law would thus not be able to produce monometallism, because the gain from selling one of the metals would be mirrored by the loss on the other, while the latter could not be used as currency since currency requirements would be met by paper.[70]

The scheme was a neat one, but it involved no great jump from the proposals of the 1810s and 1820s. On the other hand, his enthusiasm for indexed contracts (a "tabular standard of value") did involve a significant advance beyond the classical position. Though index numbers have a very long history (Maunder, 1970), they played virtually no part in the classical literature. Even the great *History of Prices* by Tooke and Newmarch did not use them, although Arthur Young had done so (Young, 1812). Marshall's starting point was, unsurprisingly, Jevons.[71]

Acceptance of the classical macroeconomic apparatus did not, it should hardly now need emphasizing, involve an unwillingness to recognise problems of aggregate demand fluctuations. While Marshall accepted J. S. Mill's version of the Law of Markets as the long run proposition which Mill meant (that is, economic growth should not result in general overproduction because purchasing power would rise with output), Marshall also recognised (again like Mill) the possibility of excess

69. *OP*, pp. 10, 22–3, 38, 40–1, 51–2, 124, 126–8, 130–1, 158, 272–4; MCC, pp. 73–
     6, 255–8; *Memorials*, p. 190. See also Eshag, pp. 13 n. 55, 57 n. 51.
70. *OP*, pp. 14, 28–31, 101–4; *Memorials*, pp. 204–6 (see, however, ibid., pp. 476–7);
     MCC, pp. 64–7.
71. Marshall notes (*Memorials*, p. 197) also the work of Joseph Lowe and of Scrope.
     Marshall did work on index numbers himself (for example, *Memorials*, pp. 207–11);
     he is credited by Keynes (in ibid., p. 31) with developing the "chain" method of index
     numbers. See also Edgeworth, 1925, Vol. 1, p. 213, where Marshall is acknowledged
     as arriving independently at a formulation used by Edgeworth.

demand for money as a disequilibrium problem which could arise, in particular, if there were a loss of economic confidence.[72]

Marshall also borrowed from Overstone the theory of an *endogenous* cycle of commercial confidence which could (as Overstone himself had argued) be amplified by banking accommodation of entrepreneurial demands for loans in the upswing.[73] In the course of the cycle, profits varied while wages remained fairly rigid. The labour market adjusted through quantity variation and thus exhibited unemployment. Marshall's cautious discussion of the remedies for this – improved market knowledge, discouragement of fraud, of speculation, and of fashion changes, reduced trade secrecy, an increased fiduciary issue (this a Banking School element) and the use of a tabular standard of value[74] – would not, with the exception of the last, have seemed at all unusual to the Classical economists.

It is then undeniable that Marshall had a very substantial Classical inheritance, that he began his economics by working at the Classical writers, and that their influence persisted throughout his life as a writer on economics. But there is very much more to the picture than this, and to leave the story at this juncture would be to overstate greatly the degree of continuity between Marshall's thought and that of the Classical economists.

IV   The Nonclassical Material

It is important to examine closely the Nonclassical elements in Marshall's work because of his tendency to overstress the continuity of his own work with that of his predecessors. It might almost be said that his famous motto about continuity in economic phenomena (*natura non facit saltum*) extended to the subject matter of economics itself – *economica* as well as *natura*. When we look at Marshall's microeconomic work, however, both the extent of his departures from his predecessors and the degree of his own achievement become rather clearer.

72. *Principles*, pp. 709–11; *OP*, pp. 91–4; 1879*b*, p. 34; 1879*a*, pp. 154–5; *Memorials*, pp. 130, 192, 463; J. S. Mill, 1848–71, II, pp. 570–6.
73. 1879*a*, pp. 150–5; see also ibid., pp. 161–4; *Principles*, pp. 594–5, 709–11; *MCC*, p. 246. See also ibid., pp. 18–19, 75, 238–45, 249–53, 257; 1885*a*, p. 178; *Memorials*, pp. 190–4; *OP*, pp. 9–10. According to Eshag, 1963, p. 95, Marshall had a marked personal copy of Overstone, 1837–48.
74. *Principles*, pp. 555–6, 594–5, 687–8, 710–11; *Variorum*, p. 180; *OP*, pp. 9–11, 92–7; *Memorials*, pp. 191, 205 n. 2 (see also p. 206 n. 2); *MCC*, pp. 18, 244, 258–63; 1885*a*, pp. 174–9.

Markets

His development of partial equilibrium analysis, with *ceteris paribus* made explicit, was a significant development.[75] One has only to look at the use Marshall made of it compared with *any* of his predecessors, let alone the classical writers whose discussion of individual markets was of a much more generalised nature, to see the extent of Marshall's contribution. His detailed exploration of market clearing, and of stability, encompassing both quantity adjustment and price adjustment models, goes far beyond anything in the classical literature and thus altered the whole *balance* of the treatment, in its emphasis upon the detailed microeconomic underpinnings.[76]

Demand

Although demand curves predate Marshall – as a concept in Say, as a function in Cournot, and as a graphical device in Fleeming Jenkin – demand itself received very little analysis in the main body of classical literature (despite Marshall's startling claims noted earlier in this discussion) except for J. S. Mill's great discussion of *aggregate* demand in the context of international trade. Nor did classical analysis, with a few limited exceptions (Say, Longfield, and, to some extent, Senior) make much use of utility. Ricardo, despite Marshall's claims, satisfied himself that utility had no influence on price.[77] Marshall himself, however, used utility analysis extensively and the major source is clearly Jevons. Marshall's analysis makes utility the basis of consumption, with the individual demand curve derived from the premise of diminishing marginal utility.[78] This enabled Marshall to make sense of Say's dictum, rejected by Ricardo, that price measured utility (Say, 1803, p. 62). Price, in Marshall's analysis, measured the *marginal* utility for a *given* individual though, as Marshall repeatedly emphasized, a shilling had a different marginal utility for a rich man and a poor man. He extended the analysis to intertemporal maximisation and combined intertemporal and in-

---

75. See in particular *Principles*, pp. 366, 379–80, 460–1; *Variorum*, p. 49; *Memorials*, pp. 312, 314–15; 1898, p. 49 and *passim*.
76. *Principles*, pp. 330–6, 345, 348, 369–72, 378–80, 805–9; *Variorum*, pp. 361–3; 1879a, pp. vii, 158; *EEW*, 1, pp. 119–59, especially pp. 132, 143–4; Newman, 1960, pp. 587–93; Davies, 1963.
77. Ricardo, 1817–21, p. 281. The idea of a (functional) relationship between price and quantity goes back to long before Say. See Creedy, 1986.
78. *Principles*, pp. 64, 86–91, 93–4, 95–6. Marshall also seems to have drawn on Jevons's discussion of the King-Davenant law; see Creedy, 1986, pp. 195, 202.

tratemporal equilibrium.[79] Of course the analysis, with its additive utility function and quasi-constant marginal utility of money, has limitations which have been endlessly discussed since Marshall's time, but it clearly represents such a major departure from the classical literature that the gap between Marshall and later demand theory (Slutsky and Hicks) is incomparably smaller than the gap between Marshall and the classics, not only in the analysis itself but in the very choice of topic on which to concentrate. This is particularly apparent in the concentration of the analysis on the individual demand curve, making the transition to a market curve by a somewhat imprecisely defined process of aggregation. (*Principles*, pp. 98–9, 104–5; *Variorum*, p. 244).

Consumer Surplus

Linked with the demand analysis is the discussion of consumer surplus, a concept which could hardly have originated with classical economics, with its very limited treatment of demand. Marshall did have forerunners in the French engineering school, particularly Dupuit,[80] but his own analysis was probably developed independently of them.[81] In view of the insoluble aggregation problems and the partial equilibrium limitations, almost all well known to Marshall,[82] the classical economists may have had good sense in not pursuing this path. But the truth is that it was never on their agenda. Marshall, by contrast, was deeply concerned about this tool, and was very disappointed that its problems proved insoluble[83] – even though it was never really likely that a partial equilibrium tool could be used for general equilibrium problems of community welfare.[84] Yet his concern demonstrates how far his own analysis had gone beyond that of the classical economists, in both distance and direction. Even on the question

79. *Principles*, pp. 92–7, 100, 117–23, 230–4, 838–9, 841, 845–6; *Variorum*, pp. 236–45; 1879*a*, pp. 69–71. On the nature of Marshall's demand analysis see the excellent article by Loasby, 1978.
80. For references to Dupuit see Marshall, *Principles*, pp. 101 n., 476 n.; *Variorum*, p. 263 n. For general discussion see Hébert and Ekelund, 1984, pp. 55–60; Ekelund and Hébert, 1985.
81. *EEW*, 1, p. 39 (Marshall to Seligman, October 1896). Whitaker's view that Marshall did not know of Dupuit's work when developing consumer surplus seems indisputable, 1975, 2, p. 281.
82. Marshall discusses a number of these problems in *Principles*, pp. 124–37; see also ibid., pp. 96, 842; *Variorum*, p. 241; *Memorials*, p. 162. On Marshall's awareness of the problems with consumer surplus see also Dooley, 1983.
83. However, he continued to reproduce material dating from his original work on the concept, in successive editions of his *Principles*. See pp. 467–75, 489–93, 811; *EEW*, 2, pp. 72, 279–302. See also Bharadwaj, 1972. On his disappointment with the concept, see Guillebaud, 1971, p. 6.
84. See, however, Ekelund and Hébert, 1985, for a discussion of the reasons why the concept refuses to fade away.

of the precise nature of the marginal utility of money income, where not assumed constant, Marshall drew not on classical analysis (for which the problem had not arisen) but on the analysis of gambling by the eighteenth century mathematician Bernoulli (*Principles*, pp. 135, 842–3).

Supply and the Firm

When we come to the supply blade of Marshall's partial equilibrium "scissors" we find much the same picture. To Marshall economics owes the widespread use of the supply curve. It was, for him, a very much more complex concept than it has become: cost curves had a time dimension[85] (making them nonreversible) while rents lay below the supply curve as well as above because of differential cost advantages enjoyed by different firms ("particular expenses") (*Principles*, pp. 810–11 n.; see also *Variorum*, pp. 811–12). Knowledge of the supply response of an industry was obtained by examination of a Representative Firm (*Principles*, pp. 317–18, 342–3, 367–8, 377, 396, 459–61, 497, 805).

While the emphasis on a time dimension betrays classical roots, the whole emphasis on an industrial supply curve goes far beyond what is to be found in classical literature. Even where, in discussing the factor supplies which underlay cost curves, Marshall betrayed classical starting points most clearly, he still went beyond them. Despite ambiguities inherited from the classical analysis over increasing returns, diminishing returns, and decreasing returns to scale, he ultimately conceded the necessary distinctions, and generalised the concept of diminishing returns in the form of diminishing marginal product to all factors (*Principles*, pp. 150–9, 169–72, 319 n., 403–9).

To the analysis of the firm itself, Marshall made contributions of lasting influence. On the one hand he stressed entrepreneurship in a way that no one except Say (for rather special historical reasons) had done before him.[86] On the other, he placed the entrepreneur at the centre of the marginal adjustments leading to optimal factor combinations where relative factor prices and productivities were given – the "principle of substitution" (*Principles*, pp. xvi, 169–72, 341, 351–9, 404–6, 662–3, 665–6; see also pp. 418–21, 434–7). Despite Marshall's eccentric attempt in the first edition of the *Principles* to credit Ricardo with this, there is nothing like it in the classical literature.

Marshall's discussion of the firm itself has no parallels anywhere in the

85. *Principles*, pp. 455–7, 807–10; *IT*, pp. 187–8 n.; *Memorials*, pp. 439–41; *EEW*, 2, p. 193; see also Whitaker, 1975, 2, pp. 184–5; Newman, 1960, pp. 589–90.
86. See Hébert and Link, 1982, especially pp. 29–35; Koolman, 1971; James, 1977; Kaiser, 1980.

classical literature. Though Mill and Babbage had certainly discussed industrial organisation, Marshall's treatment is his own. Pricing is explored in terms of a (long run) marginal cost approach (though with a very different concept of marginal cost from that in modern textbooks since Marshall thought in terms of large finite changes and also recognised the problem of cost allocation in a multiproduct firm) and the firm is placed in the context of the industry via the Representative Firm.[87] We have the famous analogy of the trees of the forest, with demand changes affecting the relative rates of growth and decay of constituent firms in the industry.[88]

Within the industry, the discussion of competition – emphatically *not* perfect[89] – encompasses many of the issues present in later discussions of market power.[90] In particular, Marshall discussed product differentiation, advertising, barriers to entry, limit pricing, loss leaders, and tying clauses.[91] He also considered oligopolistic interdependence (including the question of the effect of high fixed costs – he led the profession into

87. *Principles*, pp. xvi, 361–2, 376, 394–402, 500–2; *Variorum*, p. 529; 1898, pp. 50–1; *IT*, pp. 181–96, 269–71, 424; see also 1879a, pp. 79–80. Cost "is to be estimated with regard to a whole process of production rather than a particular locomotive or a particular parcel of goods" – *Principles*, pp. 361–2. On the Mill–Marshall links on business organisation see also Phillips, 1979, and Rainelli, 1983.

88. *Principles*, pp. 285–6, 315–17, 323, 342–3, 378, 457–9; *Variorum*, pp. 69–70. See also Frisch, 1950, pp. 512–13. Cf. Levine, 1980, 1983, who believes that the biological elements in Marshall's work are irrelevant to the question of increasing returns and competition. But see Phillips, 1979.

89. *Principles*, pp. 5–12, 374, 458, 500–1, 540–1, 849–50; *Variorum*, pp. 411–12, 569, 573–4; *IT*, p. 182; see also Stigler, 1957, pp. 9–10; 1962, p. 282; Peterson, 1957, pp. 63, 65. On the question of the relation between increasing returns and competition see also Levine, 1980, 1983, and (especially) Loasby, 1978. See also Gee, 1983. Gee argues convincingly that Marshall saw only a limited use for statics and that he avoided a hard and fast distinction between the long run and the short run in the matter of fixed costs.

90. In particular he pointed the way towards "Monopolistic Competition". See *Principles*, pp. 341–2; *IT*, p. 397; see also Stykolt, 1956, citing *Principles*, p. 616 n. 3; Gerbier, 1976, p. 409, citing *Principles*, pp. 846–52; Peterson, 1957, pp. 73–4. Chamberlin has testified that his work was not part of the attacks on Marshall, and indeed that he obtained "marginal value product" from Note XIV of Marshall's Mathematical Appendix – 1961, pp. 516, 524, 532–43. The account by Blitch, stressing the Marshallian origins of the thought of Allyn Young, Chamberlin's supervisor, in this area, strengthens the connection between the later analysis and Marshall's work – see Blitch, 1985, p. 397. See, however, Loasby, 1978, pp. 6, 10–11, for a contrary view.

91. *IT*, pp. 234, 270–1, 300–2, 304–7, 396–8, 439, 524, 536–7, 597. The influence of American literature on Marshall's *IT* is important, but more important still was his study of the details of industrial organisation and practices. His *IT*, originally planned as (part of) Volume 2 of his *Principles* (see Whitaker, 1975, 1, p. 93, and *IT*, p. vi) reflects the continuation of his work beyond the *Principles* and it is unfortunate that its influence, despite good sales, was limited (Liebhafsky, 1955; Stykolt, 1956; Andreano, 1965).

adopting the accounting practice of distinguishing fixed and variable costs) and monopoly.[92]

It should hardly need emphasising that none of this has any parallel in the Classical literature which was concerned with macro distribution and growth, not the microeconomics of markets. Marshall's achievement was remarkable. On the one hand it is a small, and mathematically trivial, step from his analysis of monopoly to the marginal cost and marginal revenue analysis which apparently gave economists so much trouble in the 1930s[93] (Chamberlin himself used the *average* cost and revenue curves of Marshall for most of his analysis). On the other hand, Marshall not only explored price discrimination and the allocation of overheads according to elasticity, but at the same time emphasized something which tended to be forgotten in the 1930s literature – the *conditional* nature of monopoly, and the limitations on the maximising behaviour of monopolists.[94]

In all this discussion of the firm, there is very little indeed which is Classical. Marshall's concern about bureaucracy in large firms, and his belief in the need for small, innovative, firms, may bear some relation to Mill and even Babbage (Mill, 1848–71, Book 1, Chapter 9; Babbage, 1832; see note 87 above). But what Marshall has to say goes far beyond these authors, as does his path-breaking discussion of economies of scale under the headings of internal and external economies.[95]

92. *Principles*, pp. 285–7, 359–62, 373–5, 397, 415–17, 454, 458–9, 477–95, 497–8, 502, 805, 856–8; *IT*, pp. 397–9, 403–22; 425, 450 n., 515–20, 824–9, 835; see also Peterson, 1957, pp. 72, 76.

93. On the intellectual difficulties apparently posed at that time by the first derivative of the revenue function see Robinson, 1933, p. vi. Marshall's profit (π) maximisation condition is simply that average revenue (p) minus average cost (c), multiplied by output, is at a maximum, that is, $\pi = (p - c)q$ is maximised. The first order maximum condition obtained from this is, of course,

$$p + q\frac{dp}{dq} = c + q\frac{dc}{dq}$$

or marginal revenue equals marginal cost.

   In relation to note 90 above, if $p = c$ by *definition* (because only normal profits are being earned) then, trivially, the slope of the average revenue curve (dp/dq) and the slope of the average cost curve (dc/dq) will be equal at precisely the value at which average revenue equals average cost. As Schumpeter remarked, "the formal part of the marginal principle would be as familiar [to Marshall] as would be his breakfast bacon" (1954, p. 838). However, Marshall's economics are much more complicated than his mathematics, explicit or implied, and there are difficulties over his concept of marginal cost which cannot be explored here. They certainly helped to confuse his successors. But he himself clearly warned about the limitations of mathematics (*Principles*, p. 850).

94. *Principles*, pp. 493–5, 663, 693 (and see also pp. 486–9, 856–8); 1879a, p. 181; *IT*, pp. 395–672, especially pp. 397–8, 403–6, 414–22, 440–4, 449–50 n.

95. *Principles*, pp. 250–66, 278–90, 457–9, 500–1; *Variorum*, pp. 69, 521, 523–9; *IT*, pp. 214–49; *Memorials*, p. 407; *EEW*, 2, pp. 194–8.

Thus it is hardly surprising that his treatment of value, symmetrically placed after the discussion of the demand and supply "scissor blades" in Book V of the *Principles*, is significantly different in virtually every important respect from the classical cost of production theories, let alone the very special Ricardian theory. We do not have the classical emphasis (to the point of exclusion of other considerations) on cost of production, nor the particular approach of Menger and, to a lesser extent, Jevons, in which everything is viewed from the perspective of demand. Above all, Marshall emphasised, in obvious contrast to Mill's unfortunate dictum that value theory was settled, that "every plain and simple doctrine as to the relations between cost of production, demand and value is necessarily false."[96]

Thus, though Marshall started from J. S. Mill in value matters, he finished at a destination which was the other side of a watershed in the history of economics from Mill's work. He explored, in the context of different time periods of adjustment, the achievement of equilibrium through the interaction of the supply analysis that he had developed himself with the demand theory which he had made his own on the foundations of Cournot, Jenkin, and Jevons. The end result was a treatment of value which had such influence that it is difficult to imagine the history of economics without it.

Distribution

When we come to the matter of distribution, though the classical roots are more visible the end result would still have been unrecognisable to the Classical economists. Marshall started from the work of J. S. Mill, whose influence is particularly apparent in the *Economics of Industry,* but the source on which he ultimately drew more was von Thünen, developing a theory which treated the demand for factors in terms of marginal product.

It was marginal product equalised across different employments; and the marginal product was *net* (effectively *discounted*) marginal *revenue* product. Moreover the analysis was extended from the triad of land, labour, and capital to include entrepreneurship, the factor on which Marshall laid such stress.[97] Entrepreneurial earnings depended on demand for

---

96. *Principles*, p. 368. For Mill's unfortunate dictum see 1848–71, 2, p. 456. "Happily, there is nothing in the laws of Value which remains for the present or any future writer to clear up; the theory of the subject is complete". See also *Principles*, pp. 84–5, 90, 324–30, 348–9, 813–21; 1879a, pp. 91–3, 147–8, 165–7. On the distinction to be made in this context between Jevons and the Austrians see Black, 1981, p. 10.

97. *Principles*, pp. 409–10, 515–23, 536–40, 596–608, 620–4, 660–7, 846–52; *Variorum*, pp. 580–8, 670–5; 1879a, pp. 128–45 [Marshall explains (p. 133) that "net" marginal product takes account of implicit discounting]. Thünen's influence is stressed

the services of entrepreneurs which depended on their marginal productivity in different occupations, though equalisation of the rewards at the margin could be impeded by barriers to entry, and the rewards were higher if there was less routine management (allowing more scope for genuine entrepreneurship) as indicated by a relatively high ratio of circulating to fixed capital.[98]

Marshall's marginal productivity theory was not in as complete a form as that associated with Wicksteed and Euler's theorem[99] (Marshall never formally endorsed the latter), and the idea of product exhaustion is a little oblique in the *text* of the *Principles* though it *is* clear in a marginal note.[100]

It is true that when we look at Marshall's treatment of distribution as a whole, we see that the supply of factors was analysed very largely in Classical terms, with only a subsidiary emphasis on disutility in factor supply. The Classical elements noted in the previous section undoubtedly predominated. But by unifying these with the marginal-productivity factor-demand analysis, Marshall managed to provide a completeness of distribution theory which both his predecessors *and successors* (who neglected supply) lacked. In particular, he was able to draw on the classical analysis of capital supply through "abstinence", substituting McVane's term "waiting", and to combine this with his marginal productivity theory of demand for capital, thus using the most "modern" part of the classical analysis of factor supply and linking the two analytical streams further.[101]

This produced an analysis which his Classical predecessors would scarcely have recognised. The most advanced Classical analysis, that of

by H. M. Robertson, 1970, and by Marshall, who expressly denied any indebtedness to Walker. (Marshall to J. B. Clark, 2 July 1900, and 24 March 1908, in *Memorials*, pp. 412–13, 416–18). See also Marshall, 1898, p. 58. On Marshall's acknowledgement of priorities see Whitaker, 1975, 1, pp. 39, 69. Walker's distribution theory in his (1876) and even in his (1887) fell a good way short of Marshall, 1879*a*, both in analytical development and in clarity of exposition. See Walker, 1876, pp. 128–73 especially pp. 128–30 and 1887, *passim*, and cf. Marshall, 1887*b*. Essentially Walker made the Classical theory of rent the basis of his determination of rent and profit, leaving wages *as a residual*. See especially Walker, 1887, pp. 281–2, 287–8. See also Solow, 1987. Marshall's characteristically clear-headed reply (1887*b*) courteously identified a number of points at which Walker's analysis was inferior to that in Marshall, 1879*a*, notably in the treatment of the *supply* of entrepreneurship.

98. *Principles*, pp. 605–24; *Variorum*, pp. 661–2; 1879*a*, pp. 74–5, 135–45, 177–8; see also 1885*a*, p. 174; *EEW*, 1, pp. 206–12.

99. For a comprehensive discussion of this see Stigler, 1941, Chapter 12.

100. *Principles*, p. 536; see also ibid., p. 830, and Whitaker's comment, 1975, 2, p. 326.

101. The reference to McVane is in *Principles*, p. 233 n. On the return to capital more generally see *Principles*, pp. 21, 73–4, 81–2, 122, 220–36, 362, 377, 411–12, 419–20, 518–21, 533–4; *Variorum*, pp. 374, 461–92, 495; 1879*a*, pp. 41–2, 119–27, 146; *MCC*, pp. 285–94.

Cairnes, went no further than treating distribution as the result of the demand for each other's output by noncompeting groups (except within the groups themselves, where normal Classical analysis applied).[102]

Macroeconomics

The Classical inheritance is much more dominant outside the microeconomic core of Marshall's work. But this is hardly surprising. Of the three subjects, economic growth, international trade, and money, the last two are those in which developments and refinements of the classical analysis are still the basic part of modern theory. Marshall's Classical continuity was greatest in precisely those areas where modern continuity with the Classical analysis is greatest. Even with Marshall there are differences of emphasis. Apart from the differential equation approach to economic growth noted above, Marshall's work is also characterised by an emphasis on the role of entrepreneurship in economic growth (*Principles*, pp. 240–77, 291–313; *IT*, pp. 350–94) and by the idea that increased state activities would have to be financed by increased (and progressive) taxation of incomes.[103] The idea of progression in relation to income tax was anathema to the chief Classical writers on public finance, McCulloch and J. S. Mill (see O'Brien, 1975, pp. 245–6, 251–2, 255, for references). The departures from the Classical analysis in the treatment of economic growth are few, however, and they are even fewer in the trade material. Even Marshall's comparative advantage table (anticipated in any case, in superior form, by Edgeworth) was only working out the implications of what Senior and (unknown to Marshall) Longfield had been driving at (see O'Brien, 1975, pp. 180–1 for references).

In the field of monetary economics Marshall's treatment is distinct from what went before in only two respects. First, he spelt out what had to remain fixed in the "pound" of *ceteris paribus* for there to be a straightforward relationship between money and the price level (*OP*, pp. 5–6, 21–2, 24–7, 34–5, 37, 40, 267–9; *MCC*, pp. 42–8). Second and more important, his theory, in harmony with his individualistic and nonclassical emphasis on microeconomic underpinnings, laid stress on the demand for cash balances and interpreted this in a marginal, maximising, manner

102. Cairnes, 1874, pp. 149–294. According to Cairnes "wages and profits, regarded as relative phenomena, are governed by Cost of Production, where the producers are in effective competition with one another, and, where they are not, by Reciprocal Demand" (1874, p. 149).

103. *OP*, pp. 337, 362; 1909; 1916; 1917, pp. 317–22, 325–28. For consideration of the role of the State more generally see *Principles*, p. 304; 1879a, p. 113; *IT*, pp. 486, 494–7, 666–72; 1885a, p. 174; *Memorials*, p. 118; 1917, pp. 313–14, 345; 1891a; 1891b.

with the marginal utility of cash balances equated with the marginal utility of alternative uses of the funds. He was thus enabled to explore tentatively a variety of real balance effects.[104] Marshall provided a direct link between the classical analysis and the Keynesian treatment of liquidity preference (which, not surprisingly, has been linked by twentieth century writers with Thornton's work on which Marshall also drew).[105]

V Conclusion

Marshall was certainly not "just" a Classical economist. The whole history of economics would have been very different without Marshall's writings, which one cannot say, for instance, of such later nineteenth century economists as Fawcett or even Sidgwick. But neither can one say that his work would even have existed, let alone taken the form it did, without his Classical inheritance. The essential point is that Marshall, more aware than any of the leading economists of his time of the achievements of Classical economics, made the marginal revolution "work" by plugging it into the general circuit of the existing body of economic literature in England. This not only helped others to grasp the nature of the new forms of analysis and to see their potential, it also enabled the new forms of analysis to develop enormously, not least in Marshall's own hands, so that their achievements distracted attention from the Classical inheritance and ultimately produced a Gestalt switch for economists. Marginalism, once Marshall had shown its role, was recognised as (to use the terminology of the philosophy of science) much more than a progressive scientific research programme: and for this perception, the work of Marshall is to a very considerable extent responsible. Unfortunately, in the very process of "plugging in" the new forms of analysis, Marshall was led to make claims about the nature of classical analysis – notably in the Appendices to the *Principles* – which are difficult to interpret as anything other than an exaggerated "pietas" with rhetorical undertones. To many this is probably a great deal less objectionable than the posture adopted by any self-proclaimed intellectual revolutionary striving to attract public attention and caring little for elementary accuracy, let alone scholarship, in his references to his predecessors. Viewed from the perspective of a century later the effect is nonetheless unfortunate.

104. *MCC*, pp. 18, 256; *OP*, pp. 5–6, 22, 52. See, however, 1879a, pp. 155–6 where a possible real balance effect is ignored; see also Patinkin, 1965, pp. 186–8, 603–10.
105. *MCC*, pp. 38–9, 43–5; *OP*, pp. 177, 267–8 (and see also pp. 36, 44); *EEW*, 1, pp. 165–77; Whitaker, 1975, 1, pp. 164–5; Thornton, 1802, pp. 232–3; Hicks, 1967, pp. 174–88.

When Marshall had done his work, the change of focus thus produced so affected economists that they came to interpret Marshall himself in purely static, *post-Marshallian*, terms thus *mis*-interpreting and, not infrequently, maligning him. This in turn led other commentators to react by making unsustainable claims about the "Ricardian" nature of Marshall's analysis.[106]

The essential truth is clear enough: Marshall started economics by reading J. S. Mill, and, while still an able mathematician in the 1870s, followed a "research programme" of mathematising parts of Mill.[107] In the course of his research he read more extensively in classical literature and reacted strongly against the claims of those like Jevons who sought to neglect the classical inheritance. He was influenced by Jevons, however, by the Austrians, and by Walker, as well as by Cournot and Thünen, and he had the breadth of vision to appreciate the necessity of connecting their work with the classical apparatus in which his own beginnings as an economist lay. His life's work then involved reconciling these two streams, developing the more recent one in its own right, but always restraining it by appeals to factual information, economic history, and his own highly developed sense of economic reality. The result was a synthesis which, at least as far as English economics went, made the marginal revolution work. Without Marshall, the message of the bewildered Cairnes on reading Jevons might have become the theme of many economists of a later generation.

> So far as I can see, economic truths are not discoverable through the instrumentality of Mathematics. If this view be unsound, there is at hand an easy means of refutation – the production of an economic truth, not before known, which has been thus arrived at; but I am not aware that up to the present any such evidence has been furnished of the efficacy of the mathematical method.[108]

By the time Marshall died the younger generation were in no doubt, as a result of his powers of analysis, synthesis, and exposition, as to what

106. See note 30 above.
107. See also Hicks, 1976, p. 368. In correcting Keynes's account of the development of Marshall's ideas, Hicks wrote, "It is now quite clear that that is all wrong. Marshall began, as one would expect, from Mill. He does not stress the filiation to Mill, since he was conscious of moving on from Mill, and wished to call attention to his differences from Mill. Yet Mill is the basis from which he starts".
108. Cairnes, 1875, pp. vi–vii. Schabas, 1985, has pointed out that nonetheless Cairnes (and J. S. Mill) had more in common with the general methodological position of the post-1870 marginalists than with the Historical School; see also Black, 1960. But, as Schabas argued, a gulf existed between the Mill–Cairnes continuation of the Classical thinking and the post-1870 developments, concerning mathematical (and mathematically inspired) theorising. Marshall was effectively able, without ever overplaying the role of mathematics, to bridge that gulf.

these truths were. Economics as a subject looked very different from that which Cairnes knew.

References

Andreano, R. L. (1965). "Alfred Marshall's *Industry and Trade:* A Neglected Classic in Economic History". In Andreano (ed.), *New Views on American Economic Development.* Cambridge, Mass.: Shenkman.

Angell, J. W. (1926). *The Theory of International Prices.* Cambridge, Mass.: Harvard University Press.

Ashley, W. J. (1891). "The Rehabilitation of Ricardo", *Economic Journal* 1:474–89.

Babbage, C. (1832). *On the Economy of Machinery and Manufactures.* London: Knight.

Bharadwaj, K. (1972). "Marshall on Pigou's *Wealth and Welfare*", *Economica* N.S. 39:32–46.

Birch, T. D. (1985). "Marshall and Keynes Revisited", *Journal of Economic Issues* 19:194–200.

Black, R. D. C. (1960). "Jevons and Cairnes", *Economica* N.S. 27:214–32.
  (1981). "W. S. Jevons, 1835–82". In D. P. O'Brien and J. R. Presley (eds.), *Pioneers of Modern Economics in Britain.* London: Macmillan.

Blandy, R. (1967). "Marshall on Human Capital: A Note", *Journal of Political Economy* 75:874–5.

Blaug, M. (1958a). "The Classical Economists and the Factory Acts – A Reexamination". Reprinted in A. W. Coats (ed.), *The Classical Economists and Economic Policy.* London: Methuen, 1971.
  (1958b). *Ricardian Economics.* New Haven: Yale University Press.

Blitch, C. P. (1985). "The Genesis of Chamberlinian Monopolistic Competition Theory: Addendum", *History of Political Economy* 17:395–402.

Bowley, M. E. A. (1937). *Nassau Senior and Classical Economics.* London: Allen and Unwin.

Buchanan, D. H. (1929). "The Historical Approach to Rent and Price Theory", *Economica* 9:123–55.

Cairnes, J. E. (1874). *Some Leading Principles of Political Economy Newly Expounded.* London: Macmillan.
  (1875). *The Character and Logical Method of Political Economy.* London: Macmillan.

Chamberlin, E. H. (1961). "Origin and Early Development of Monopolistic Competition Theory", *Quarterly Journal of Economics* 75:515–43.

Chasse, J. D. (1984). "Marshall, the Human Agent and Economic Growth", *History of Political Economy* 16:381–404.

Chipman, J. S. (1965). "A Survey of the Theory of International Trade: Part 2, the Neo-Classical Theory", *Econometrica* 33:685–760.

Coase, R. H. (1984). "Alfred Marshall's Mother and Father", *History of Political Economy* 16:519–27.

Collard, D. (1968). Introduction and editorial material in J. E. Tozer, *Mathematical Investigation of the Effect of Machinery* (1838). Reprinted, New York: Kelley.

Creedy, J. (1986). "On the King-Davenant 'Law' of Demand", *Scottish Journal of Political Economy* 33:193–212.

Davies, D. G. (1963). "A Note on Marshallian versus Walrasian Stability Conditions", *Canadian Journal of Economics* 29:535–40.

Dooley, P. C. (1983). "Consumer's Surplus: Marshall and his Critics", *Canadian Journal of Economics* 16:26–38.

Edgeworth, F. Y. (1925). *Papers Relating to Political Economy*. 3 vols. London: Macmillan.

Ekelund, R. B., and Hébert R. F. (1985). "Consumer Surplus: the First Hundred Years", *History of Political Economy* 17:419–54.

Eshag, E. (1963). *From Marshall to Keynes*. Oxford: Blackwell.

Frisch, R. (1950). "Alfred Marshall's Theory of Value", *Quarterly Journal of Economics* 64:495–524.

Gårdlund, T. (1958). *The Life of Knut Wicksell*. Stockholm: Almqvist and Wiksell.

Gee, J. M. A. (1983). "Marshall's Views on 'Short Period' Value Formation", *History of Political Economy* 15:181–205.

Gerbier, G. (1976). *Alfred Marshall. Théoricien de l'Action Efficace et Critique Radical de l'Economie Pure*. Doctoral thesis, Grenoble.

Groenewegen, P. (nd). "Marshall on Ricardo" (mimeo).

Guillebaud, C. W. (1971). "Some Personal Reminiscences of Alfred Marshall", *History of Political Economy* 3:1–8.

Harrison, R. (1963). "Two Early Articles by Alfred Marshall", *Economic Journal* 73:422–30.

Hébert, R. F., and Link, A. N. (1982). *The Entrepreneur*. New York: Praeger.

Hébert, R. F., and Ekelund, R. B. (1984). "Welfare Economics". In J. Greedy and D. P. O'Brien (eds.), *Economic Analysis in Historical Perspective*. London: Butterworths.

Hicks, J. R. (1967). *Critical Essays in Monetary Theory*. Oxford: Clarendon.

(1976). Review of EEW. *Economic Journal* 86:367–9.

Hollander, S. (1979). *The Economics of David Ricardo*. Toronto: University of Toronto Press.

Hutchison, T. W. (1952). "Some Questions about Ricardo", *Economica* N.S. 19:415–32.

(1956). *A Review of Economic Doctrines 1870–1929*. Oxford: Clarendon.

(1978). *On Revolutions and Progress in Economic Knowledge*. Cambridge: Cambridge University Press.

James, M. (1977). "Pierre-Louis Roderer, Jean-Baptiste Say, and the Concept of Industrie", *History of Political Economy* 9:455–75.

Jensen, H. E. (1983). "J. M. Keynes as a Marshallian", *Journal of Economic Issues* 17:67–94.

(1985). "Marshall Revisited: A Reply", *Journal of Economic Issues* 19:967–74.

Jevons, W. S. (1879). *The Theory of Political Economy*. 2d ed. London: Macmillan. Reprinted, ed. R. D. C. Black. London: Penguin, 1970.

Kaiser, T. E. (1980). "Politics and Political Economy in the Thought of the Ideologues", *History of Political Economy* 12:141–60.

Keynes, J. M. (1911). Review of I. Fisher, *The Purchasing Power of Money*. *Economic Journal* 21:393–8.

Koolman, G. (1971). "Say's Conception of the Role of the Entrepreneur", *Economica* N.S. 38:269–86.

Levine, A. L. (1980). "Increasing Returns, the Competitive Model and the Enigma that was Alfred Marshall", *Scottish Journal of Political Economy* 27:260–75.

(1983). "Marshall's *Principles* and the 'Biological Viewpoint': A Reconsideration", *Manchester School* 51:276–93.

Liebhafsky, H. H. (1955). "A Curious Case of Neglect: Marshall's *Industry and Trade*", *Canadian Journal of Economics and Political Science* 21:339–53.

Loasby, B. J. (1978). "Whatever Happened to Marshall's Theory of Value?", *Scottish Journal of Political Economy* 25:1–12.

McCready, H. W. (1955). "Alfred Marshall and Tariff Reform, 1903. Some Unpublished Letters", *Journal of Political Economy* 63:259–67.

Marshall, A. (1874). See Harrison, R. (1963).

(1876). "Mr. Mill's Theory of Value", *Fortnightly Review*, April. Reprinted in *Memorials* 119–33.

(1879b). *The Pure Theory of (Domestic) Values*. Reprinted London: London School of Economics, 1930, 3d impression 1949. Also in *EEW*, 2, pp. 186–236.

(1883). Published as "Alfred Marshall's Lectures on Progress and Poverty", ed. G. J. Stigler and R. H. Coase, *Journal of Law and Economics* 12(1969):181–226.

(1884), "Where to House the London Poor", *Contemporary Review*, February: 224–331. Reprinted in *Memorials*, pp. 142–51.

(1885a). Contributions (pp. 76–9, 82, 173–99, 213–14, 505) to *Industrial Remuneration Conference. Report of the Proceedings and Papers . . . under the Presidency of Sir Charles W. Dilke*. London: Cassel.

(1885b). "Present Position of Political Economy", *The Times*, 2 June (11e).

(1886). "Political Economy and Outdoor Relief", *The Times*, 15 February (13b).

(1887a). Preface to L. L. F. R. Price, *Industrial Peace: Its Advantages, Methods and Difficulties*. London: Macmillan. Substantially reproduced in *Memorials: 212–26*.

(1887b). "The Theory of Business Profits", *Quarterly Journal of Economics* 1:477–81.

(1887c). "Is London Healthy?", *Pall Mall Gazette*, 13 April: 3.

(1891a). "The Post Office and Private Enterprise", *The Times*, 24 March (11e).

(1891b). "The Post Office and Private Enterprise", *The Times*, 6 April (13b–c).

(1892a). "The Poor Law in Relation to State-Aided Pensions", *Economic Journal* 2:186–91.

(1892*b*). "Poor-Law Reform", *Economic Journal* 2:371–9.

(1893). "On Rent", *Economic Journal* 3:74–90. Reprinted in *Variorum*, pp. 492–512.

(1898). "Distribution and Exchange", *Economic Journal* 8:37–59. Partly reprinted in *Memorials*, pp. 312–18; *Variorum*, pp. 62–75, 229–33.

(1903). Letter to F. Manners-Sutton, secretary of the Unionist Free Food League. Published in *The Times*, 23 November (10e).

(1904). "Discussion of Mr. Schuster's Paper", *Journal of the Institute of Bankers* 25:94–8.

(1905*a*). "Education and the Classics", *The Times*, 3 March (15a-b).

(1905*b*). "Education for Business Men", *The Times*, 23 November (4c).

(1905*c*). "Education for Business Men", *The Times*, 18 December (13d).

(1905*d*). "University Education for Business Men", *The Times*, 29 December (5d).

(1907). "The Social Possibilities of Economic Chivalry", *Economic Journal* 17:7–29. Reprinted, with alterations, in *Memorials*, pp. 323–46.

(1909). "Rates and Taxes on Land Values", *The Times*, 16 November (10c).

(1916). "The Need for More Taxation", *Economist*, 30 December: 1228.

(1917). "National Taxation after the War". In W. H. Dawson (ed.), *After-war Problems*. London: Allen and Unwin.

Marshall, A., and Marshall, M. P. (1879*a*). *The Economics of Industry*. London: Macmillan.

Marshall, M. P. (1947). *What I Remember*. Cambridge: Cambridge University Press.

Maunder, W. F. (1970). *Bibliography of Index Numbers*. London: Athlone Press.

Mill, J. S. (1848–71). *Principles of Political Economy*. 7 eds., 1848–71. Ed., J. M. Robson, 2 vols. Toronto: University of Toronto Press, 1965.

Mises, L. von (1912). *The Theory of Money and Credit*. Trans. H. E. Batson. London: Cape.

Newman, P. (1960). "The Erosion of Marshall's Theory of Value", *Quarterly Journal of Economics* 74:587–601.

O'Brien, D. P. (1970). *J. R. McCulloch. A Study in Classical Economics*. London: Allen and Unwin.

(1975). *The Classical Economists*. Oxford: Clarendon.

(1977). "Torrens, McCulloch and Disraeli", *Scottish Journal of Political Economy* 24:1–18.

(1984). "Monetary Economics". In J. Creedy and D. P. O'Brien (eds.), *Economic Analysis in Historical Perspective*. London: Butterworths.

Overstone, Lord (1837–48). *Tracts and Other Publications on Metallic and Paper Currency*. London: privately printed, 1857.

Parsons, T. (1931). "Wants and Activities in Marshall", *Quarterly Journal of Economics* 46:101–40.

(1932). "Economics and Sociology: Marshall in Relation to the Thought of his Time", *Quarterly Journal of Economics* 46:316–47.

Patinkin, D. (1965). *Money, Interest and Prices,* 2d ed. New York: Harper and Row.

Pennington, J. (1826–40). *Economic Writings.* Ed. R. S. Sayers. London: London School of Economics, 1968.

Peterson, S. (1957). "Antitrust and the Classic Model", *American Economic Review* 47:60–78.

Petridis, A. (1973). "Alfred Marshall's Attitudes to the Economic Analysis of Trade Unions: A Case of Anomalies in the Competitive System", *History of Political Economy* 5:165–98.

Phillips, J. D. (1979). "The Theory of Small Enterprise: Smith, Mill, Marshall, and Marx", *Explorations in Economic History* 16:331–40.

Rainelli, M. (1983). "Entrepreneur et Profits dans les 'Principes' de John Stuart Mill et d'Alfred Marshall", *Revue Economique* 34:794–810.

Ricardo, D. (1816). *Proposal for an Economical and Secure Currency.* In P. Sraffa (ed.), *Works and Correspondence of David Ricardo,* Vol. 4. Cambridge: Cambridge University Press, 1951.

(1817–21). *On the Principles of Political Economy and Taxation.* In P. Sraffa (ed.), *Works and Correspondence of David Ricardo,* Vol. 1. Cambridge: Cambridge University Press, 1951.

Robbins, L. (1930). "On a Certain Ambiguity in the Conception of Stationary Equilibrium", *Economic Journal* 40:194–214.

(1952). *The Theory of Economic Policy in English Classical Political Economy.* London: Macmillan.

(1958). *Robert Torrens and the Evolution of Classical Economics.* London: Macmillan.

Robertson, H. M. (1970). "Alfred Marshall's Aims and Methods Illustrated from his Treatment of Distribution", *History of Political Economy* 2:1–65.

Robinson, J. V. (1933). *The Economics of Imperfect Competition.* London: Macmillan.

Samuels, W. J. (1966). *The Classical Theory of Economic Policy.* Cleveland, Oh.: World Publishing.

Say, J. B. (1803). *A Treatise on Political Economy.* 4th ed., 1819. Trans. C. R. Prinsep. Reprinted New York: Kelley, 1971.

Schabas, M. (1985). "Some Reactions to Jevons' Mathematical Program: The Case of Mill and Cairnes", *History of Political Economy* 17:337–53.

Schumpeter, J. A. (1954). *History of Economic Analysis.* London: Allen and Unwin.

Senior, N. W. (1826). Appendix to Whately (1826).

Shove, G. F. (1942). "The Place of Marshall's *Principles* in the Development of Economic Theory", *Economic Journal* 52:294–329.

Smith, A. (1776). *An Inquiry into the Nature and Causes of the Wealth of Nations.* Ed. R. H. Campbell, A. S. Skinner, and W. B. Todd. 2 vols. Oxford: Clarendon.

Solow, R. M. (1987). "What Do We Know That Francis Amasa Walker Didn't?", *History of Political Economy* 19:183–9.

Spengler, J. J. (1955). "Marshall on the Population Question", *Population Studies* 8:264–87; 9: 56–66.

Stigler, G. J. (1941). *Production and Distribution Theories*. New York: Macmillan.

   (1955). "The Nature and Role of Originality in Scientific Progress". Reprinted in *Essays in the History of Economics*. Chicago: University of Chicago Press, 1965.

   (1957). "Perfect Competition Historically Contemplated", *Journal of Political Economy* 65:1–17.

   (1962). "Marshall's *Principles* after Guillebaud", *Journal of Political Economy* 70:282–6.

Stykolt, S. (1956). "A Curious Case of Neglect: Marshall on the Tangency Solution", *Canadian Journal of Economics and Political Science* 22:251.

Thornton, H. (1802). *An Enquiry into the Nature and Effects of the Paper Credit of Great Britain*. Reprint, ed. F. A. von Hayek. London: Allen and Unwin, 1939.

Walker, F. A. (1876). *The Wages Question*. London: Macmillan.

   (1887). "The Source of Business Profits", *Quarterly Journal of Economics* 1:265–88.

Walker, L. W. (1983). "A Comment on 'Marshall and the Classical Tradition' ", *Journal of Post Keynesian Economics* 5:664–6.

Wearne, B. C. (1981). "Talcott Parsons's Appraisal and Critique of Alfred Marshall", *Social Research* 48:816–51.

Whately, R. (1826). *Elements of Logic*. London: Mawman.

Whitaker, J. K. (1972). "Alfred Marshall: the Years 1877 to 1885", *History of Political Economy* 4:1–61.

   (1974). "The Marshallian System in 1881: Distribution and Growth", *Economic Journal* 84:1–17.

   (1975). Introductory and editorial material in *EEW*.

   (1977). "Some Neglected Aspects of Alfred Marshall's Economic and Social Thought", *History of Political Economy* 9:161–97.

Wicksell, K. (1898). *Interest and Prices*. Trans. R. F. Kahn. London: Macmillan, 1936.

Wood, J. C. (1982). "Alfred Marshall and the Origins of his 'Memorandum on the Fiscal Policy of International Trade', (1903): Some Unpublished Correspondence", *Australian Economic Papers* 21:261–9.

Worcester, D. A. (1946). "A Reconsideration of the Theory of Rent", *American Economic Review* 36:258–77.

Young, A. (1812). *An Enquiry into the Progressive Value of Money in England as Marked by the Price of Agricultural Products*. London: McMillan.

7

Cambridge after Marshall

DAVID A. COLLARD

I Introduction

The period to be covered by this essay, from the beginning of the Economics Tripos in Cambridge to the late 1920s, is not the most exciting in the
history of economics. It includes the long twilight of Marshall but falls
just short of the *Years of High Theory* (Shackle, 1967). The revealed
preference of historians of economics has been to search these doldrums
for anticipations of Keynes's *General Theory*. In this chapter Keynes falls
into place as just one of a number of distinguished Cambridge economists
of the period. Far from being a revolutionary period it qualifies as much
as any period in economics as one of "normal science" (Kuhn, 1962).

The first section sets out the main features of Marshall's "Organon".
In these post-Lakatosian days the term has quite a modern ring and may
be interpreted as a Marshallian "research programme". It is a particularly appropriate term in Marshall's case as it is elastic enough to include
a formal treatise as well as a method or system of thought. Further, the
Organon has to be seen as a device for the successful professionalisation
of Economics so the setting up of the Economics Tripos and the gradual
ascendancy of Cambridge Economists in the *Economic Journal* were to
be important to its success. Both the Tripos and the *Journal* are therefore
discussed. Much of the rest of the chapter is devoted to brief assessments
of the principal Cambridge economists of the period in relation to the

I am grateful to Elizabeth Leedham-Green, Colin Lawson, Donald Moggridge, and Austin
Robinson for comments or advice. Errors are, of course, the author's responsibility.

Organon. The original intention was to provide assessments for all the economists in Figure 7.1 but as space did not permit this those subsequent to Guillebaud are excluded. R. G. Hawtrey is not included though often referred to as a Cambridge economist.

II The Organon, the Tripos, and the Journal

The Organon

The main features of the Marshallian Organon or "instrument of thought" are its core theory, its motivation and style, its professional orientation, its ability to discover "concrete truth" and, finally, its method of propagation. At the risk of great simplification the Marshallian view on each of these is set out.

Core Theory. The core theory is to be found in the *Principles* and to a lesser extent in *Industry and Trade* and *Money Credit and Commerce*. Marshall's analysis of the cycle and of short term movements in prices was seriously incomplete and its systematisation and elaboration were left for other members of his School to flesh out. The theoretical core of the *Principles* was, however, broadly accepted as fairly complete (see the discussion of Lavington, below, for a striking case of this), including key technical concepts such as elasticity, the principle of substitution, consumers' surplus, period analysis, increasing and diminishing returns, jointness, the representative firm, etc. But behind these concepts lay a rather fuzzy dynamics which seemed to be evolutionary rather than mechanical. As it turned out the Cambridge School made some use of Marshall's tools, though rather less than one might have hoped, and by the end of our period some of them were actually being rejected.

Motivation and Style. The economist's calling for Marshall and Pigou was "a high and responsible one, worthy to fill a man's life" (Pigou, *Memorials*, p. 89). People have their own motivations and good science can come from bad motives. Marshall would not have denied this but he would have insisted that some reminder (like the face of his "patron saint") was needed to draw the theorist back from idle speculation. Motivation is important for scope if not for method. Style is also closely connected with motivation and purpose. Marshall was fearful of committing anything to print until he was sure that he had got it absolutely right. This led to unreasonably long publication delays. Keynes took the opposite view, that ideas should be floated for others to criticise and improve. To take decades over the preparation of a treatise suggests that its statements are intended to be final. Another aspect of style is the flaunting of

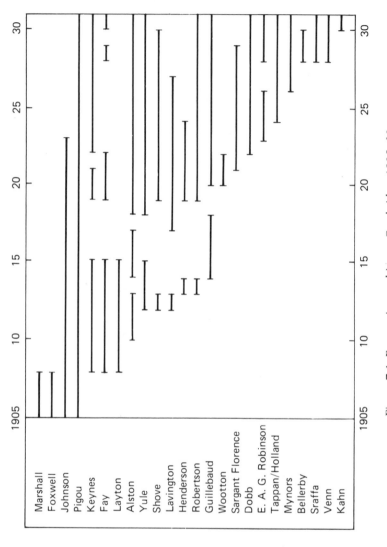

Figure 7.1. Economics teaching at Cambridge, 1905–30.

mathematics, a habit Marshall deplored. The kindest thing to say is that the Cambridge School followed Marshall's advice. Most of the mathematical contributions to the *Journal* were from economists outside of Cambridge: Edgeworth, Bickerdike, and Bowley.

Controversy. Marshall's general view about controversy was that the economist must distance himself from it in order to maintain professional detachment. This view was shared by some of his successors (for instance, Pigou, Shove, and Lavington) though not by others (Keynes, for instance, and Henderson). Marshall breached his own rule over bimetallism and free trade, however, and he might have found controversy irresistible had he been a young economist in the more tumultuous 1920s.

Truth. The Organon was to be a machine for the discovery of concrete truth. Keynes remarks (*Memorials*, p. 36) that Marshall was not good at the discovery of concrete truth. Beatrice Webb noticed (Koot, 1987, p. 180), after staying with Marshall, that he had an extraordinary penchant for making "an astounding observation with no basis in fact". If one uses the *Economic Journal* as a guide there is no lack of "facts" in the work of the Cambridge School but the facts are, as it were, low level facts. Except in monetary economics and in the work of Pigou there is little creative confrontation between fact and theory. There was no Bowley in Cambridge; that is why the loss of Layton (see below) was so unfortunate.

If the Organon was to survive and grow, two "institutions" were desperately important to it, the Tripos and the *Economic Journal* (referred to here as the *Journal*). Marshall fought very hard for both of these. They ensured that Marshallian economics would not go the way of Jevonian economics. The Tripos was indeed a great success. Ironically the *Journal* remained rather dull up to the point at which it became a vehicle for "revolutionary" economics.

The Tripos

The establishment of the Tripos in 1903 was a tremendous achievement for Marshall even though by that time he had long been, according to Cunningham, "the acknowledged head of the new School" (Kadish, 1982, p. 230). As early as 1888 Foxwell had remarked (*Memorials*, p. 59) that "half the economic chairs in the United Kingdom are occupied by his pupils, and the share taken by them in general economic instruction in England is even larger than this".

Marshall fought for 18 years for the Tripos, was increasingly fearful of the competition from Birmingham and London, and was pessimistic about its chances right up to 1902 (Coats, 1967). The establishment of the Tripos was certainly a milestone on the road to what Maloney (1985) has called the professionalisation of economics and both Marshall and his successor Pigou had high hopes for it. Writing to Walter Layton in 1907 (Hubback, 1985), Marshall referred to his "brilliant compact group of eminent men, full of the highest promise for the future" (p. 22). He wrote in similar terms to Keynes at about the same time. The overt Cambridge purpose, later stressed by Pigou, was "to increase the number of those whom Cambridge . . . sends out into the world with cool heads but warm hearts" (*Memorials*, p. 89).

One of the most striking things about the enterprise is its small scale, even in later years when the number of undergraduates had increased substantially. It was a compact group, consisting of A. C. Pigou, W. E. Johnson, Lowes Dickinson, John Clapham, C. R. Fay, H. O. Meredith, John Maynard Keynes, Walter Layton (who joined it at the same time as Keynes), and Leonard Alston. In terms of ability the list is an impressive one but only Pigou, Keynes, and Layton were to be serious economists. Clapham, Fay, and Meredith were primarily economic historians. Dickinson was a political philosopher. Johnson made one brilliant contribution to economics but his main interest was in logic. Alston lectured only to "the poll men – undergraduates reading for a pass degree" (Skidelsky, 1983, p. 209). The numbers continued to be small. Dobb (1978) notes that when he was appointed to a lectureship in 1924 the Faculty was small and understaffed. Even as late as 1930–31 Austin Robinson (1977) tells us that apart from the Professor (Pigou) and the Reader (Robertson) there were only seven economists: Claude Guillebaud, Gerald Shove, Maurice Dobb, Austin Robinson, Humphrey Mynors, Piero Sraffa, and Marjorie Hollond (nee Tappan). The durable Alston, though still teaching the pass degree, took no part in research. For the greater part of our period there were only two University posts (apart from the Chair) specific to economics. These were the Girdlers Lectureship and the University Lectureship and were held as shown below.

Girdlers	University
Keynes 1911–20	Layton 1911–19
Lavington 1920–28	Henderson 1919–23
Robertson 1928–30	Shove 1923–29

Figure 7.1 indicates the main lecturing responsibilities in economics at Cambridge for the whole period 1905–30. In general economic historians, even the great Clapham, have been left out though the lesser Fay is included because he contributed to some of the economics teaching and thought of himself as a Marshallian. Also omitted are economists who taught for only a short time or who taught only pass degree students or peripheral subjects. This still leaves quite an extensive list. A casual inspection of Figure 7.1 reveals that very substantial contributions were made,

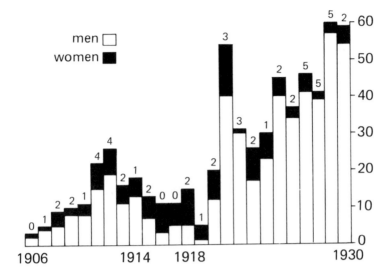

Figure 7.2. Number of economics Tripos graduates, 1906–30. The column head numerals indicate number of firsts.

taking the period as a whole, by Pigou, Keynes, Shove, Lavington, and Guillebaud among the serious economists, and by Fay, Johnson, Yule the statistician, and Alston. No attempt has been made to indicate differences in loads. For example, as will be seen, Keynes carried a very heavy load in the years up to the First World War but very light loads thereafter when he had no University post. Those teaching only the pass degree students also carried heavy loads (Alston, for example) but were presumably not expected to do much research.

Figure 7.2 shows the number of students graduating in the Tripos (that is, those taking and passing Part II of the examination). The initial figures were low for the new Tripos still had a reputation to win. It must be remembered that academic activity was something of a minority interest at the time. At Trinity, for example, 36 percent of the men were reading for honours, 32 percent for a pass degree and the rest for nothing at all. The trend rose steadily up to 1912 but fell off a little even before the devastation of the War hit Cambridge. The *University Reporter* for 1914 carried the following footnote: "Mr. Fay, Mr. Keynes, Mr. Layton and Mr. Sproxton being absent on duties arising out of the War, the lectures originally announced under their names for the Lent and Easter terms cannot be delivered". (Sproxton was an economic geographer.) The absence of a generation of eighteen-year-olds at the Front meant that

Table 7.1. The Production of Cambridge Economists by Means of
Cambridge Economists, 1906–30

Economist	Tripos	Tripos Year	Tripos Class
W. T. Layton	Trinity	1907	I
F. Lavington	Emmanuel	1911	I
G. F. Shove	Kings	1911	I (dist.)
W. S. Thatcher	Non Collegiate	1911	II (i)
H. D. Henderson	Emmanuel	1912	I
D. H. Robertson	Trinity	1912	I
C. W. Guillebaud	St. Johns	1913	I
P. Sargant Florence	Caius	1914	I (dist.)
R. W. Stanners	Caius	1915	II (i)
B. F. Wootton	Girton	1919	I (sp. dist.)
M. H. Dobb	Pembroke	1922	I
E. A. G. Robinson	Christs	1922	I (dist.)
J. V. Maurice (Joan Robinson)	Girton	1925	II (i)
H. G. B. Mynors	Corpus	1925	I
R. F. Kahn	Kings	1928	I (dist.)
R. L. Cohen	Newnham	1929	I

women dominated in the years 1915 to 1920. The most triumphant among them was Barbara Wootton, awarded a First with Distinction in 1919. The position of women was still not an easy one at Cambridge; they were not permitted to take their degrees until 1926. Marshall had voted against their admission. In the case of Keynes it is difficult to dissociate his declared attitude from his own sexuality. "I seem to hate every movement of their minds", he told Duncan Grant (Skidelsky, 1983, p. 212). This attitude seems not to have affected his practical judgements, as witness Lynda Grier, who gave some of his lectures in 1915. As the great post-War bulge worked its way through the system the proportion, and even the absolute numbers, of women declined. By the late 1920s, when the Tripos comprised very respectable numbers, the proportion of women was lower than it had been at its start.

If the Tripos was designed as a machine for producing Cambridge economists, how did it fare? Not at all badly. Table 7.1, The Production of Cambridge Economists by Means of Cambridge Economists, lists those economists produced by the Tripos who in turn took teaching appointments at Cambridge. It therefore does not include a number of distinguished economists who went to other institutions. The list does, however, indicate a strong, successful, Cambridge professionalisation. The Organon had, it seems, found a way of perpetuating itself.

A comparison of the lecture lists for 1905 and 1924–5 indicates the increasingly modern nature of the Tripos. In the earlier year Marshall was still giving a course on advanced economics for second and third year students. Cunningham and Foxwell (rivals respectively for the Chairs of Marshall and Pigou), primarily economic historians, also taught economics, Cunningham political economy, and Foxwell industry, currency and banking. Macgregor, who taught only until 1907 but was later to help edit the *Economic Journal,* taught both economic history and industrial combination. Johnson gave a course for second and third year students on the diagrammatic treatment of pure economic theory. Green, who taught elementary political economy to the first years, left in 1907. Pigou's responsibility was the main economics course for the first and second years. The *Reporter* drew attention to the fact that "Professor Marshall will be at home to students at 6, Madingley Road from 4 to 6 P.M. on Thursdays". These were the famous Thursday afternoons: "to his pupils he was and remained, a true sage and master, outside criticism, one who was their father in the spirit" (*Memorials,* p. 57). In the previous year (1904) he had been lecturing on the topics that were to be the subject matter of his two long delayed books.

Up to about 1908 and the accession of Pigou, the Tripos carried with it a considerable amount of non-Marshallian baggage left over from the Moral Sciences days. The appointments of Layton and Keynes gave Marshall and Pigou the opportunity to complete their palace revolution. Maloney quotes Fay to the effect that the Tripos in the years before 1914 consisted of "potted Marshall and sugared sticks of Hartley-Withers" (1985, p. 232). Robertson "recalled an atmosphere of calm that now seems somewhat forced and unnatural as well as characteristically British in its insularity and complacency" (Coats, 1967, p. 708). This rather complacent mood characterised both the *Journal* and the Tripos. By 1925 Cambridge, though still insular, was much less vulnerable to jibes such as Fay's. Marshall's *Principles* was still the Bible, but a number of relatively recent Cambridge books were on the reading lists: Henderson's *Supply and Demand,* Robertson's *Money,* Pigou's *The Political Economy of War,* Lavington's *The English Capital Market,* and other relatively modern books including two by Bowley.

Among those lecturing in 1924–5 were Pigou, Yule, Sargant Florence, Robertson, Guillebaud, Lavington, Shove, Austin Robinson, Keynes, and Dobb. The over-all list, as a list of professional economists, was beginning to be an impressive one. The home-produced generation of Table 7.1 was beginning to take command.

The Journal

At the time of the establishment of the Tripos Edgeworth was still editing the *Economic Journal*. It might be expected that under Keynes, who took over as editor in 1911 (and astonishingly continued as editor until 1946), the *Journal* would become more exciting. But it was very slow to develop and remained what must seem to modern eyes a dull and second-rate quarterly. This was partly due to the relatively nontechnical nature of the subject at that time. It was also because the *Journal* was felt to be *the* professional journal in economics in an age lacking the ready access to the sophisticated and immediate flow of economic comment we take for granted today. Thus there were detailed comments on industrial disputes of the day and on official papers related to economics. Far-flung parts of the Empire contributed regular economic intelligence. Its role as the leading academic journal in the subject became clear only in the late 1920s.

Marshallian economics for the years 1890 to 1915, as it unfolded in the pages of the *Journal,* has fortunately been analysed with painstaking scholarship by Jha (1973). Jha discusses four topics: international trade, the labour question, the economics of poverty and welfare, and public finance. On the whole he is very positive about the Marshallian influence.

> The influence of Marshallian economics with its emphasis on a realistic and scientific analysis of economic phenomena on the one hand, and on the urgency of reform on the other, pervades most of the writings. (p. 200)

> The influence of Marshallian economics seems to have been all pervasive. (p. 14)

But,

> [T]o some extent Marshall seems to have discouraged progress on econometric lines and the achievements of British economists in this respect before the 30s perhaps for that reason do not seem to add up to anything significant. (p. 21)

> [T]he articles in the Journal are, more often than not, in the nature of essays in applied economics. They are the non-theoretical half of what Marshallians or the neo-Classical economists had to offer to their generation. (p. 14)

The nature of the material in the *Journal* did not change a great deal over the period we are considering. Taken as marker years are 1908 and

1924 the first because it was the year of Pigou's accession to Marshall's chair and the second because it just predates the next, more exciting, phase. The articles are divided here by topic.

Scope and Method. As it happens, each of the two years contained a piece on the teaching of economics, one by T. N. Carver in 1908 on the importance of numerical examples, and an interesting one by A. L. G. Mackay and H. Heaton on teaching by means of experiments in 1924. W. J. Ashley's 1908 plea for business economics, "The Enlargement of Economics," is relevant to present day discussions about the relationship between economics and business studies. An anthropological article on interest-bearing money appeared in 1924. That year also saw Robertson's contribution to the mini-Methodenstreit started by the famous Clapham-Pigou exchange of 1922, "On Empty Economic Boxes". (Perhaps Robertson at his worst?) Pigou's reply in this barbed little exchange appeared in the same volume.

Foreign Reports. In each year the *Journal* carried several contributions on the economic problems of other countries. The 1908 volume carried reports on labour exchanges and railway nationalisation in Italy, the cutlery trade of Solingen, and the American crisis of 1907. The 1924 volume carried reports on Australia, New Zealand, France, and India. Many of these reports were written at a low level of analysis but it is noteworthy that in 1924 D. B. Copland and A. H. Tocker were making use in their reports of, respectively, business cycle data and the monetary analysis of open economies. Tocker's piece is quite technical and very well done.

Economic Policy. By 1924 the emphasis in articles on policy had changed from rather low level pieces on applied microeconomics to grander monetary issues. In the year 1908 there were three articles on railway ownership or reform, three on rates or land values, and one on factory legislation. None of these carried any references to the literature, except for official publications. One does not get the impression of a powerful and well oiled Organon being wheeled into play. In contrast, the 1924 treatments of the *Dawes Report* by C. W. Guillebaud and of family allowances by J. H. Richardson made good use of theory and data. There were orthodox pieces by J. R. Bellerby and by E. Cannan on a return to gold, a reply by Keynes, and a discussion on monetary reform which included Cannan, Hawtrey, and Keynes, this last important as part of the continuous reassessment of monetary theory during the 1920s. Less important were what amounted to a review by J. A. Venn and a prescription for real wage adjustment by H. Clay.

Theory. Aside from the analysis of monetary policy, however, the 1908 volume contained more economic theory than that of 1924. S. J. Chapman put forward an interesting notion of "consumption of the second order" which seems to have included what we now know as public goods. Edgeworth contributed two articles in a series on "Appreciations of Mathematical Theories." There were slight pieces by E. C. K. Gonner on saving and by D. H. Macgregor on surpluses. The most distinguished theoretical article was Pigou's "Equilibrium Under Bilateral Monopoly" which acknowledged help from J. M. Keynes. Most of these articles, unlike those on the more applied topics, made substantial reference to the literature.

There were only three articles which one could classify under theory in 1924. One was W. Ashley's "Presidential Address to Section F on Free Trade." It is interesting that Ashley makes no reference to the Cambridge School except for Lavington. T. N. Carver had a very Marshallian article on the incidence of costs. Much more interesting was C. F. Bickerdike's article "Individual and Social Interests in Relation to Saving", at the very frontier of the subject, on the relationship between interest and growth rates.

There were more articles in 1924 than in 1908 (21 compared to 16). In addition to those discussed above, there were three historical articles as well as Keynes's classic appreciation of Marshall. There were two statistical articles, a characteristic one by A. L. Bowley on demography and one by J. W. F. Rowe on the cotton industry which made use of some data from Bowley. The 1924 *Journal* was a little unusual in that about a third of the articles were contributed by Cambridge economists, that is, economists teaching in Cambridge at or about that time. There had been an increasing trend of Cambridge participation rising to about 16 percent by 1908, though it is not true that the *Journal* had become a Cambridge house journal. By the end of the 1920s Cambridge participation was well below 20 percent.

The *Journal* was certainly part of the Organon of orthodox British economics but the regular presence of, for example, Bickerdike on theory and Bowley on statistics indicated that it was not primarily a journal of Cambridge economics or even of Marshallian economics.

III Johnson, Layton, Fay, Alston

Keynes, Pigou, and Robertson are dealt with jointly in Section V below. In the meantime let us look briefly at some of the economists and others associated with Pigou up to about 1912.

W. E. Johnson

Though Johnson was practically the only theorist (apart from Pigou) teaching in the period immediately following Marshall's retirement he was not an economist but was Sidgwick Lecturer in Moral Sciences. He gave a course on theory (described under Marshall as Diagrammatic Treatment of Pure Economic Theory) from 1905 to 1922. A Fellow of Kings, he lectured on logic, philosophical psychology, and mathematical economics. According to Braithwaite (1931) he is best known to philosophers for a three-volume book on logic and "his treatment of probability, as the field of rational but not certain belief, was similar to that of John Maynard Keynes, who, in his *Treatise on Probability* (1921) acknowledged his debt to Johnson", who had been one of his fellowship dissertation examiners. This connection is especially interesting in view of recent work on Keynes's early excursions into probability from 1904 (Carabelli, 1988). Johnson is well known to economists (though little read) for his *Journal* article "The Pure Theory of Utility Curves" (1913, pp. 483–513). This remarkable article clearly anticipates much later work. Using geometry and the calculus and basing himself firmly on Edgeworth rather than Marshall, Johnson presents indifference curves, the income consumption curve, the decomposition of price effects into what we now call income and substitution effects, inferior goods, Giffen goods, substitutability and complementarity and (for good measure) optimisation of product value given the production function and input prices. One wonders how this sort of stuff went down with the "potted Marshall and sugared sticks of Hartley-Withers".

Walter Layton

Though Layton lectured only from 1908 to 1914 and wrote only one article (in 1905) for the *Journal* (and that while a first-year undergraduate) his and Keynes's arrival brought an important infusion of new blood. Layton's statistical talents and his great interest in pratical affairs were such that his departure left a great gap where Cambridge was at its weakest.

While Walter Layton was still at University College, London, studying history and economics he helped C. P. Sanger with statistical work for the Board of Trade. He then went to Trinity, a bright scholarship boy, and associated not with the Apostles but with "another group drawn from both Oxford and Cambridge, many of whose members later reached influential positions in practical affairs" (Hubback, 1985, p. 12).

He went to all of Marshall's lectures and (unlike Keynes) found them very clear and well worth attending. Though he ignored Marshall's advice to restrict his outside activities, he got his First in 1907 as well as the Cobden Prize. In the same year he carried out a prodigious amount of statistical work on railway wage rates with Bowley and twenty assistants. It was at this stage that Pigou personally financed a lectureship for him. Layton's start in academic life could hardly have been more promising. He lectured a little on theory but his main teaching concerned various aspects of industry and labour. In a short space of time he produced two books, *An Introduction to the Study of Prices* (1912) and *The Relations of Labour and Capital* (1913). It is on the *Study of Prices* (a later edition was co-authored with G. Crowther) that Layton's claim to academic distinction rests. It was reviewed very favourably in the *Journal* by L. L. Price (1912, pp. 270–4) who concentrated on Layton's advocacy (like Marshall but unlike Jevons) of falling prices. Unlike anything else being done at Cambridge, the book contained a vast apparatus of economic statistics carefully analysed. With his practical judgement and capacity for hard work he could, had he stayed on after the War, have provided Cambridge with much needed strength in applied economics.

Moving to Whitehall in 1914, Layton was tremendously successful, finishing the War a Companion of Honour. Both Keynes and Marshall urged him to return to Cambridge. Marshall wrote that by returning to Cambridge Layton could "do more towards fashioning the life of Britain in the second and third quarters of this century than anybody else" (Hubback, 1985, p. 51).

Layton, however, went instead to the Iron and Steel Federation for a few months, then to the League secretariat, to *The Economist* (as editor), and to the chairmanship of the *News Chronicle* in 1930. Yet Layton did not completely sever his connection with Cambridge economics. As director and mainspring of the Liberal Summer Schools from 1922 he worked closely with Keynes, Henderson, and Robertson. He was the driving force behind the research leading to the Liberal Yellow Book. Like Henderson he drew back from supporting Keynesian economic policies in the 1930s. Unlike Maynard Keynes he was very widely trusted.

C. R. Fay

As an economist Fay is of only minor importance. He is relevant here as one of Marshall's "earnest men," a Cambridge figure who remained steadfastly Marshallian. Fay was a Scholar of Kings and a close friend of Keynes. After a First in History he went as a research student to the LSE and became a Fellow of Christs and College Lecturer in History and Economics in

1908. He lectured principally on English nineteenth-century economic history and, to a lesser degree, on Canada and the United States and on agriculture. Over the years 1912 to 1930 he wrote half a dozen articles for the *Journal*. Most of these were on historical subjects but he also took a contemporary interest in copartnership or cooperatives. Over our period he wrote several books on British economic history, mainly since 1700, and an internationally flavoured book on cooperatives. During the First World War he was a lieutenant in the Buffs and served with distinction in France, being mentioned in despatches. In 1919 he was appointed Gilbey Lecturer in the History and Economics of Agriculture. He remained at Cambridge for only a short time, however, resigning in 1921 to become a professor at Toronto. The rest of our period finds him dividing his time between Cambridge and Canada.

His *Times* obituaries (November 21, 23, 1961) paint him as an attractive Cambridge character but by no means a major scholar. For Fay history was story telling rather than scientific investigation. In terms of methodology, technique, and interest he was not within the Organon. His was not the sort of history that Marshall wanted done and quite the opposite of that being done by Clapham.

Leonard Alston

Alston was definitely below the salt and made no significant contribution of his own, yet he deserves mention here for the sheer volume of his teaching. Most of his teaching was at "pass degree" level. Austin Robinson recalls (in conversation) from the end of our period that "no responsible tutor would let Alston anywhere near a good Tripos man". Alston taught every year but two right through from 1911 to 1930, almost entirely for the Special Examination or for the Ordinary Degree. His topics included industrial, monetary, and labour economics as well as economic principles. He was born and educated in Australia and took the History Tripos while at Christ's Cambridge. Following an earlier career as a schoolmaster he was appointed Director of Non-Collegiate Students in Economics and in History. His publications, written mainly between 1905 and 1910, ranged from early Christianity to Indian taxation. He also produced a brief flurry of work in the early 1930s, a nonmemorable article on money in the *Journal* (1932, pp. 225–36) and a book, a collection of three lectures, in 1932. Cannan, writing a derisory review of the book, *The Functions of Money*, for the *Journal* in 1933 (pp. 273–8) refers to poor Alston as a "University Lecturer" (in inverted commas). This brief resumé of Alston's career demonstrates that the teaching of advanced economics at pre-War Cambridge was essentially in the hands of three people, Pigou, Layton, and Keynes.

IV   Yule, Shove, Lavington, Henderson, Guillebaud

George Yule

The departure of Layton may have deprived Cambridge of a unique combination of statistics and applied economics but the presence of Yule ensured a steady input of theoretical and applied statistics from a first rate statistician. Except for the War years Yule lectured from 1912 to 1930 on statistical theory and on various applied topics of particular interest to economists – index numbers, the cost of living, the census, vital statistics, etc. Yule had been Newmarch Lecturer at University College, London, from 1902 and was a friend of the great statistician Karl Pearson. His *Introduction to the Theory of Statistics* of 1911 (subsequently Yule and Kendall) was very successful, running through eleven editions. He moved to Cambridge to a lectureship in statistics in 1912. During the War he served as a government statistician. Yule's familiarity with official statistics made him a valuable asset to the Tripos, fortunate in being able to draw upon the services of so eminent a statistician. He made no significant contribution to the development of economics, however.

Gerald Shove

Shove got a First with distinction in 1911 but, although he submitted a Fellowship dissertation (on the rating system) to King's, Keynes obtained a Fellowship for him only in 1926. He and Keynes were extremely close (see Skidelsky, 1983, pp. 195, 265) as Shove was both an Apostle and a member of the Bloomsbury Group.

Shove initially lectured on the economic functions of government. He did not lecture between 1913 and 1919, when he ran a pacifist monthly called *Face the Facts* and, having married a niece of Virginia Woolf, became one of Lady Ottoline Morrell's "honorary gardeners" at Garsington. When he began lecturing again in 1919 his topics were labour, distribution, and social welfare. As well as teaching second and third year Tripos students, he also taught extensively for the Ordinary Degree, for the qualifying examination, and for first year students.

Shove published very little. It is a little surprising to find him in Blaug (1986). He published for the first time in the late 1920s, producing two papers, one on the theory of the firm and the other on the theory of the industry. The latter was commissioned by Keynes as a contribution to the 1930 Symposium on Increasing Returns. Neither paper made a lasting contribution to economics. The 1928 paper is essentially a restatement of Allyn Young's criticism of Pigou's construction of Marshall's treatment of increasing and decreasing returns. In this paper Shove displays a good grasp of the relevant economic theory. The 1930 paper was straightforwardly Marshallian in spirit, Shove arguing that Pigou's and Robertson's attempts to rehabilitate the representative firm were unnecessary, stressing (at Austin Robinson's suggestion) the importance of time and rates of growth. Shove claimed that, in this, he was being faithful to Marshall. It is interesting that a portion of the article is taken straight from an "unpublished study of the relations between cost and output on which I have been engaged for several years" (p. 94).

Evidently there was something in Shove's bottom drawer but neither the articles discussed above nor his later publications persuade one that it amounted to anything innovative.

Shove emerges as a substantial local Cambridge figure but, at the end of the day, as only a minor contributor to the rethinking of Marshall's theory of the industry.

Francis Lavington

Lavington took a First in the Tripos of 1911 and lectured in 1912 on the market for capital (analytically treated). He contributed three articles on monetary topics to the *Journal* in the consecutive years, 1911, 1912, 1913. The most important and most often cited of these was his remarkable "Uncertainty in Relation to the Rate of Interest" (*Journal*, 1912, pp. 398–409) which firmly established him as a central figure in the Cambridge monetary tradition. An illness associated with the pancreas kept him out of the War. After a period in the Board of Trade he returned to Emmanuel College in 1918 and in 1920 was appointed Girdler's Lecturer, following Keynes's resignation. His lectures were initially concerned with matters of finance and capital, but from 1920 he was also lecturing regularly on the structure and problems of industry. He published two articles in the *Journal*, in 1925 and 1926, on "Business Risks."

Unfortunately Lavington did not live to complete any substantial work on industrial economics. He died in 1927 at the early age of 46. His reputation rests on his 1912 article, on *The English Capital Market* (1921), and (to a lesser degree) on *The Trade Cycle* (1922). *The English Capital Market* was not quite what City financiers might have expected being, in concept, a theoretical book. It gives a good account of the "speculative" demand for money and contains a succinct statement of the "three-margins" doctrine:

> The quantity of resources which he holds in the form of money will be such that the unit of resources which is just and only just worth

holding in this form yields him a return of convenience and security equal to the yield of satisfaction derived from the marginal unit spent on consumables, and equal to the net rate of interest.   (p. 30)

Though he clearly made original contributions to monetary theory (Bridel, 1987) Lavington had a reputation for extreme orthodoxy. H. Wright, in his *Journal* obituary (1927) comments.

> Lavington was the most orthodox of Cambridge economists. The whole Cambridge School is supposed, by some people, to be dominated by the teaching of Marshall, and it is true that Marshall's analysis is broadly accepted as the background of economic thought. But Lavington went much further than this. He seemed almost to believe in the literal inspiration of Marshall's *Principles*. His own work on the Capital Market was designed to fill in the details of one corner of Marshall's broad picture, but he held that the work of economic analysis had been practically completed, once and for all, by Marshall and that only the application of that analysis to practical problems remained to be done. "It's all in Marshall" was one of his favourite dicta.   (p. 504)

His *Trade Cycle* was essentially a textbook. Though he acknowledges in the preface the influence of Robertson, Wesley Mitchell, and A. Aftalion, his cycle is mainly driven by business confidence so the influences of Marshall and Pigou were again dominant.

Lavington must surely be the very model of a Marshallian economist though it is perhaps doubtful that even Marshall would have desired such devoted orthodoxy.

Hubert Henderson

After getting a First in the Tripos of 1912 Henderson, later Sir Hubert Henderson, took over Shove's course on the economic functions of government. He taught only a year before the outbreak of war, when poor eyesight kept him out of active service and he went to the Board of Trade under Walter Layton. He contributed two pieces to the *Journal*, in 1914 and 1915, on the effects of the War on employment and unemployment. After the War he taught briefly on the structure and problems of modern industry and then swapped with Lavington for a course on money, interest, and prices. According to Clay (1955) he was a lucid and successful teacher. His two publications in the *Journal* at this time (1919) were very much concerned with practical problems of industrial policy though they were analytical, not merely industrial reporting.

Henderson's minor classic, *Supply and Demand* (1922), was the first in the Cambridge Economic Handbook series of which he was editor. Keynes initially placed this series solidly within the Marshallian tradition and Henderson was certainly a Marshallian though not a slavish one. The book was openly critical of Marshall's rehabilitation of Ricardo and its discussions of joint and composite production and of risk in relation to marginal utility contained original contributions. But if he was a critic, Henderson was an immanent critic working from well within the tradition.

Henderson's new interests were to take him right outside of academic life, at least for the time being. At the instigation of Keynes, its new chairman, he became editor of the *Nation* in 1923. Thereafter he was active in the Liberal Summer Schools with Keynes and Layton and also in the Liberal Industrial Inquiry. He and Keynes wrote the famous pamphlet *Can Lloyd George Do It?* (1929) which fell just short of a proper working out of the multiplier. In spite of his campaigning efforts in the 1920s he remained very much a moderate, distancing himself from Keynesian policies in the 1930s. Henderson became joint secretary of the important Economic Advisory Council in 1930, a Fellow of All Souls and, eventually, Drummond Professor at Oxford. In this last capacity he initiated the pioneering Oxford 1930s surveys of businessmen.

The parallels with Layton are obvious. Both got Firsts in the still fairly new Tripos. Both were drawn into government by the War. Both withdrew from Cambridge during the post-War period. Both went into journalism. Both maintained an interest in applied economics. One cannot help but feel that Cambridge would have been strengthened in this, its weakest area, had these two men of the world seen fit to retain, in the manner of Keynes, some sort of link with the Tripos.

Claude Guillebaud

Guillebaud, a nephew of Marshall, was an orthodox Marshallian. (He produced the Variorum edition of the *Principles* in 1961.) He obtained a First in the Tripos in 1913 while at St. John's (Marshall's old college), became a tutor at his own College, and began lecturing in 1915. Apart from a break in 1919–20 when he served on the staff of the Supreme Economic Council in Paris he lectured from 1915 to the end of our period, though for much of the time not to final year students. He covered a wide range of subjects coming to specialise in trade, finance, and industry. Guillebaud had the reputation of being an excellent College member, serving variously as faculty chairman and editor of the Cambridge Economic Handbook series.

He was a sound but not ambitious or great economist and had a realistic sense of his own limitations (*Times* obituary, August 23, 1971). Guillebaud was involved in various sorts of public service, for example, on wages boards where he was regarded as a sympathetic chairman. In spite of his unexceptionable pedigree and his orthodoxy as to theory, he could be something of a maverick – the *Guillebaud Report* on the finances of the National Health Service of 1956 did not produce the expected condemnation of NHS costs and he began to be seen as rather more sympathetic to labour in industrial disputes than an orthodox economist ought to be. Earlier he had rather blotted his copybook by an overly admiring attitude towards Nazi Germany. He published very little in the *Journal*. He wrote a piece on "The Economics of the Dawes Report" (1924, pp. 540–55) and his book *The Works Council* (1928) was a very thorough piece of work. In short Guillebaud was a good professional economist who kept the Organon in working order, as it were, without significantly adding to or changing it.

V Pigou, Keynes, Robertson

Much has been written about Pigou, Keynes, and Robertson and there is little advantage in going over old ground again. There are a few points in relation to the Organon, however, which are worth discussing.

Teaching and the Tripos

Robertson (Tripos 1912) was taught by Pigou and Keynes, who had been taught by Pigou and Marshall. Pigou was already teaching when the Tripos was introduced. Keynes began teaching in 1908 and Robertson in 1913 (effectively 1919).

Over our period Pigou made by far the greatest contribution to Tripos teaching of any member of the Cambridge School. (However, he played little or no part in administration, which he loathed.) He taught the main principles course to second and third year students from 1909 to 1930 except for three years just before the War when it was taught by Keynes. During the War he was engaged in often dangerous ambulance work as well as dealing with considerable teaching. He usually taught a second final year course on the structure and problems of modern industry, distribution and labour or public finance, depending on his interests at the time and on who else was available. He also gave one-off lecture courses on subjects which interested him and on which he happened to be writing, for example, *The Political Economy of War* (1921). The *Cambridge University Reporter* has Pigou down for some 60 courses over the period 1905 to 1930. Like Keynes he had a brilliant lecturing style in his early years, which he seems to have lost later on.

Though Keynes had not been trained as an economist (he was Twelfth wrangler in Mathematics in 1912) he had attended lectures by Marshall and Pigou in preparation for his Civil Service exam. Pigou suggested to Marshall that Keynes might be persuaded to return to Cambridge after service in the India Office and, as in Layton's case, Keynes was offered a lectureship at £100 a year financed by Pigou.

The years leading up to the War were, in a sense, the golden age of Keynes's active day-to-day involvement in Cambridge economics, for he was making major contributions to the Tripos, the *Journal*, and the Faculty. Keynes's lectures on various aspects of money (the Stock Exchange, the money markets, currency and banking) were an enormous success. Once appointed Girdler's Lecturer in 1911 he was also given the principles course to teach. J. N. Keynes clearly felt that Maynard's load was unreasonably heavy.

> [Pigou] disliked lecturing and examining, at least before the First World War, and in 1911 Keynes "had to give him rather a pi-jaw which he took rather well. He said that he was quite unaware that he was giving the impression of avoiding duties". . . . Keynes's pique with Pigou may have been due to the fact that he had to take over Pigou's main lecture course on Economic Principles in 1910–11, why it is not clear. At any rate his father wrote in his diary on 8th October 1911 that "in many ways he [Maynard] seems to be taking Pigou's place as Professor of Political Economy".
>
> (Skidelsky, 1983, p. 211)

Actually there is no great mystery here. The tradition that the Professor should give the main principles course was not yet well established (Pigou chose at that time to lecture on industry, trade, and distribution instead) and it would not be surprising if Pigou wanted to cut back a little while preparing *Wealth and Welfare*. Having said this, there is no doubt that Keynes was working very hard. He had an unusually heavy teaching load; he ran the Political Economy Club for bright undergraduates he had started in 1909; he was heavily involved as a member of the Indian Royal Commission; in 1911, at the age of 28, he succeeded Edgeworth as editor of the *Journal*; he was secretary to the Faculty Board.

When War came Keynes went to the Treasury where his fluency and cleverness soon brought him respect. Under his editorship the *Journal* was much affected by the War. In 1915, for example, the articles were divided into two sections. The first section, on the War, contained 21 articles ranging from "Clothing the Allies' Armies" to "The Law Relating to

Trade with the Enemy". Unlike Layton, Keynes did not move entirely into public affairs after the War. He had, through the *Journal,* maintained his links with academic economics. In addition, he had strong personal, family, and social links with Cambridge – and the regular flow of young men must have been an attraction. By this time, too, Keynes had ample private means and was able to strike a mutually advantageous bargain. He continued to edit the *Journal* (with Edgeworth helping out until 1925) and reduced his lecturing to one hour a week per term on a topic of his own choosing. He had no University appointment but was a supernumerary Fellow of King's.

Keynes's post-War lectures were usually based on material for the next book: eventually he was reduced to reading out from the proofs. Thus the earlier ones were on the Treaty; then on the sort of practical problems dealt with in the *Tract on Monetary Reform* (1923); then increasingly on the subject matter of the *Treatise on Money* (1930).

Robertson's period as an undergraduate coincided almost exactly with the rather brief period when Keynes was carrying so much of the lecturing load. Thus he was taught by Pigou on industry and by Keynes on money but not by Marshall, who ceased to lecture after 1908. Robertson's Fellowship dissertation for Trinity, *A Study of Industrial Fluctuation,* was published in 1915. He did some general teaching before and immediately after returning from War service. By 1926 he was lecturing to Part II students on the theory of money, later money, credit and prices, subjects in which he had come to specialise. After the death of Lavington he became Girdler's Lecturer in 1928, and a Readership was established for him in 1930. After Pigou's retirement, he earned a great reputation for his principles course.

Research

The present writer has commented elsewhere (Collard, 1981) that Pigou was caught between the shadow of Marshall and the pyrotechnics of Keynes. There can now be little doubt of his stature as a great economist and he certainly dominates the period being considered here.

Pigou's contributions to the *Journal* were numerous, many of them written at an accessible level to clarify discussion of the issues. He contributed some twenty-two articles (not counting reviews, comments, etc.) over our period. His major books up to 1930 were *Wealth and Welfare* (1912) and subsequent editions of *The Economics of Welfare* (from 1920), *Industrial Fluctuations* (1927), and *A Study in Public Finance* (1928). Each was a major treatise. Pigou produced books as his way of getting to grips with problems (Robinson, 1977, p. 30). Perhaps he had been warned, by Marshall's example, of the dangers of delay.

Pigou's central theoretical contribution was to turn Marshall's *Principles* into an engine for the analysis of economic policy. Thus he made the simplifying assumption that changes in welfare could be proxied by changes in the size, distribution, and variability of the Social Dividend. As it turned out this was a somewhat heroic assumption but it did enable Pigou to begin to carry out empirical work within a rigourous theoretical framework. Hutchison was surely too severe in describing the *Economics of Welfare* as "a vast loose-leaf review of different measures of economic policy" held together by "an amalgam of Benthamite concepts, Comteist social enthusiasm, Marshallian moral uplift and G. E. Moore definitions" (Hutchison, 1953, p. 289). Pigou was surely right in arguing for a mapping between economic welfare and the actual size and distribution of income. The approach enabled him to ask of any proposed policy, from price or wage regulation to an output subsidy, how it would affect the size and distribution of income and hence economic welfare.

In assessing policies in this way Pigou relied on Marshall's technical apparatus, though he adapted it in various ways not all of which were to Marshall's liking. This was true even in such a simple case as elasticity where Marshall had neglected finite changes (on the demand side) and was reluctant to agree to Pigou's use of the elasticity concept on the supply side. Thus, when Pigou made use of the concept in *Principles and Practice of Industrial Peace* (1905), he noted that it was not yet a term sanctioned for use by Marshall. On Marshall's reservations about what he regarded as Pigou's too mechanical approach to supply, see also Bharadwaj (1978).

Pigou's other major modification of Marshall was his recognition that taxes or subsidies might be necessary even in conditions of competition. His general recommendation (in *Wealth and Welfare*) of subsidies for increasing returns industries brought criticism following Allyn Young's review (1913). Pigou's difficulties over the supply side were hardly surprising in view of the *Journal* debates on increasing returns in the late 1920s. He remains, however, the leading British theorist of the period and his subsequent performance amply justifies Marshall's choice of him as his successor.

Keynes had been a tremendous success at the India Office and was regarded as an expert by both outsiders and insiders. He played a prominent part in the proceedings of the Royal Commission on Indian Finance and Currency of which he was a (very young) member. Of his Annexe to its Report, Marshall wrote: "verily we old men will have to hang ourselves, if young people can cut their way so straight and with such apparent ease through such great difficulties" (Keynes, 1971, p. 268). Keynes had also lectured on Indian finance for the Tripos in 1910 and 1912.

Despite his minimal formal training Keynes seems to have shone as an orthodox and particularly clever Marshallian economist. His other significant work of this period was the *Treatise on Probability* (1921), written as a Fellowship dissertation in 1908 but not published until 1921. This contained Keynes's own distinctive version of "subjective" probability theory which was consistent with his later treatment of investment but cannot be said to have made an impact upon the profession.

Keynes was very active in the affairs of the *Journal*, to which he contributed some 15 major articles and a host of reports, reviews, etc., over our period. Nor can we forget his place in the famous "oral tradition". Bridel sees Keynes as involved with Lavington, Pigou, Hawtrey, and Robertson in "a progressive attempt to integrate monetary and trade cycle theory with Marshall's long run analysis" (Bridel, 1987, p. 3). It is not easy to unravel Keynes's unique contribution here. Dimand (1988) strongly argues for the originality of Keynes's contributions particularly in respect of the nominal interest rate differential. Eshag (1963), however, takes the extreme view that the evolution of traditional monetary theory was pretty well continuous from Bagehot right through to the *Treatise* and that the really important breakthrough was Keynes's principle of effective demand which came after the end of our period. Explicit statements of the Cambridge equation in the *Tract*, had been anticipated by Pigou (1917). So it is actually quite hard to identify Keynes's own contribution within the oral tradition.

One's impression of Robertson is that he took rather a time to get into the swing of things after the War. His contributions to the *Journal* over this period were neither numerous nor distinguished so he must essentially be judged by his books.

A Study of Industrial Fluctuation was not a particularly original book. In stressing the role of technology Robertson was preceded by Tugan-Baranowski (with whom he disagreed), by Schumpeter (whom he had not yet read), by M. Labordère (whom he did not sufficiently acknowledge), by A. Aftalion, and by Wesley Mitchell. The works of these men were virtually unknown in England so, in introducing them to Cambridge, Robertson did an excellent job in the international transmission of ideas. Robertson's was a "real" theory based on the gestation period of capital goods and innovation. In spite of Robertson the Cambridge tradition (embodied in Marshall, Pigou, and Lavington) continued to emphasise psychological factors and Robertson's own interests (on the surface at least) appeared to move towards monetary aspects of the cycle.

He continued to believe, however, that real factors were much more important than monetary ones. Thus *Money* starts with the proposition that

> "money is not such a vital topic as is sometimes supposed" and the preface to the 4th edition states that "money is, after all, a subject of secondary importance." In much of his monetary work of the 1920s he was trying "to re-integrate the theory of money into that of the trade cycle".
>
> (Dennison, 1968)

Robertson not only followed but did much to propagate the oral tradition at that time and later. His central contribution in *Money* was the sketch of a theory of forced saving filled out more carefully in *Banking Policy and the Price Level*. The latter, essential to the *Treatise*, was the high water mark of collaboration between Robertson and Keynes. The first part of the book merely reworked chapters 10 to 16 of *Industrial Fluctuation*, by then out of print. The collaboration took place over chapters 5 and 6 which instigated Robertson's oft-quoted remark that "neither of us knows how much of the ideas contained therein are his and how much is mine" (p. 5). Robertson's terminology in these chapters is extremely (almost wilfully) awkward: Long, Short and Unproductive Lacking (Robertson's word for abstinence), Dis-lacking, Automatic Stinting, Automatic Splashing, and so on. But behind this obscurity lay a perfectly good research programme, his dynamic or "step by step" analysis which, as he complains in the 1949 preface (p. xi), never got under Keynes's skin.

As a public figure in economics Robertson gained importance far beyond the period being considered here and he was to become a successful expositor of economic principles to generations of Cambridge students. His important creative work, however, was done in our period and on that it is difficult to put him in the top rank. The pity is that he involved himself in the long imbroglio with Keynes rather than pursuing his own original research programme.

Quantitative Economics

Marshall encouraged Bowley to use statistics as an aid in discovering "concrete truth." A recurring complaint of this chapter has been the lack of good empirical work in Cambridge and both the departure of Layton and the early demise of Lavington have already been bemoaned.

Taking Pigou's output as a whole the proportion of serious quantitative work is rather small, but he made great use of statistical time series by Bowley and others in *Industrial Fluctuations* and some use of them in articles for the *Journal* (for example, in "Prices and Wages from 1896–

1914," 1913, pp. 163–71). That marriage between theory and observation which is the hallmark of great science was achieved only in his *Journal* note on "A Method of Determining the Numerical Value of Elasticities of Demand" (1910, pp. 636–40). According to Deaton (1975, p. 9) Pigou's pioneering effort is "still one of the best examples of indirect measurement by use of theory to be found outside of the physical and biological sciences."

Pigou returned to this theme in 1930 and 1936 but neither he nor his colleagues had pursued it further in the interim. Apart from Keynes there was probably no one at Cambridge at that time who understood the significance of what Pigou was trying to do. The blame for the absence of good empirical work at Cambridge can hardly be laid at Pigou's door.

Robertson made use of statistical series in *Industrial Fluctuation* but he did little empirical work thereafter. Keynes commonly made use of statistics but mainly to corroborate his views rather than as a device for getting at the truth. In this regard his dispute with the statistician Pearson on drunkenness (Skidelsky, 1983, pp. 221–7) is revealing (of Marshall as well as of Keynes).

Both Keynes and Robertson (and initially Henderson) were active in the 1920s in producing the Bulletins of the London and Cambridge Economic Service. The London members of its executive committee were Bowley and Beveridge. Keynes, later with the assistance of J. W. F. Rowe, wrote a series of papers for the Service titled "Stocks of Staple Commodities" (see Robinson, 1978).

Motivation, Style, Controversy

Pigou is rightly regarded as very much a Marshallian economist. He disliked being involved in public life, much less in controversy. Though he served on three bodies, the Cunliffe Committee (1919), the Royal Commission on the Income Tax (1920), and the Chamberlain Committee (1925), he acknowledged that he was ill suited to such activities. Writing much later (Pigou, 1937) about experience and a feel for character he noted (in a characteristically barbed disclaimer) that "these the present writer, like most academic persons, does not possess and, unlike some academic persons, he is aware that he does not possess them" (p. 137). Pigou did not entirely agree with Marshall on the use of mathematics. "Might it not be better [for people] not to understand and know that they do not, rather than roll about, self-satisfied and complaisant, in a sea of mental cotton-wool?" (1953, p. 7). He doubts whether Marshall could have disapproved of Ramsey. Pigou used mathematics quite widely though not much in *The Economics of Welfare* and usually in footnotes. He seldom used diagrams.

Compared with Marshall and Pigou, the good humoured and self-deprecating Robertson gives the impression of being what the present generation would call "laid back" about economics and economic policy. It is not clear how far he considered that economics could "do good" and, unlike Keynes, he did not go into battle. He obviously took economic policy seriously, however. He worked with Keynes and others in connection with the Liberal Summer Schools; outside of our period he served on several important public bodies (Presley, 1981).

Partly because of his classical background Robertson had a reputation for great literary style (Dennison, 1968), a reputation perhaps also derived from his successful Cambridge Economic Handbooks (*The Control of Industry*, 1923; *Money*, 1922), from his well received lectures, and from his habit of quoting from "Alice". He could be arch, whimsical, and obscure. Even Pigou found his ambitious *Banking Policy and the Price Level* (1926) difficult: "with pain and grief I have, as I believe, succeeded in opening the oyster" (Pigou, 1926, p. 215). Samuelson (1963), in a rather uncharitable obituary, found the book almost unreadable. Luckily many of Robertson's ideas were later embodied in his straightforward and readable *Money*. He made little (and sometimes muddled) use of mathematics and later on made rather a virtue of being the "plain man" in respect of new tools.

In terms of style and earnestness of purpose Keynes adopted a very un-Marshallian approach. He was attracted to economics because it enabled clever men to work out solutions to practical problems. If the solutions were obstructed by stupidity it was necessary to employ ridicule. Economics was not only important, it was also fun. Very early Keynes had written to Lytton Strachey:

> I find economics increasingly satisfactory, and I think I am rather good at it. I want to manage a railway or organise a Trust or at least swindle the investing public. It is so easy and fascinating to master the principle of these things. (Skidelsky, 1983, p. 65)

The moral earnestness of Marshall or Pigou was entirely absent. Nor did Keynes believe that an economist should sit down to write a magnum opus:

> Economists must leave to Adam Smith alone the glory of the Quarto, must pluck the day, fling pamphlets into the wind, write always *sub specie temporis*, and achieve immortality by accident, if at all.
> (*Memorials*, p. 36; italics in original)

Keynes had to pay for this attitude. Distinguished articles in the *Journal* were not enough to offset the sin of brilliant journalism and Keynes came to understand that if he wished to influence professional opinion he must turn to the formal structure of a treatise.

For almost the whole of our period, then, this distinguished trio of economists was working very well together within a common acceptance of the Marshallian framework (stretched, however, to near breaking point). The greatest of them (over this period at least) was unquestionably Pigou.

VI Conclusion

The period from the beginning of the present century to the late 1920s in Cambridge was certainly one of "normal" science. For much of the time the contents of the *Journal* were rather dull and not all the economists concerned were first rate. But some first rate work was being done by Pigou, Robertson, Keynes, Layton, Lavington, and Henderson, and a new generation, produced by the Tripos, of Dobb, Kahn, and the Robinsons was coming along. The years were not simply a doldrums waiting for (the real) Keynes to happen.

References

Alston, L. (1932). *The Functions of Money.* London: Macmillan.

Bharadwaj, K. (1972). "Marshall on Pigou's Wealth and Welfare", *Economica* 39:32–46.

Blaug, M. (1986). *Who's Who in Economics.* Brighton: Wheatsheaf.

Braithwaite, R. B. (1931). "W. E. Johnson 1858–1931". In L. G. Wickham Legg (ed.), *Dictionary of National Biography 1931–1940.* London: Oxford University Press.

Bridel, P. (1987). *Cambridge Monetary Thought.* London: Macmillan.

Carabelli, A. M. (1988). *On Keynes's Method.* London: Macmillan.

Clay, H. (1955). "Introduction". In Henderson (1955).

Coats, A. W. (1967). "Sociological Aspects of British Economic Thought", *Journal of Political Economy* 75:706–29.

Collard, D. A. (1981). "A. C. Pigou 1877–1959". In D. P. O'Brien and J. R. Presley (eds.), *Pioneers of Modern Economics in Britain.* London: Macmillan.

Deaton, A. (1975). *Models and Projections of Demand in Post-War Britain.* London: Chapman and Hall.

Dennison, S. R. (1968). "Dennis Holme Robertson". In D. Sills (ed.), *International Encyclopaedia of the Social Sciences*, Vol. 13. New York: Free Press.

Dimand, W. (1988). *The Origins of the Keynesian Revolution*. Aldershot: Elgar.

Dobb, M. H. (1978). "Random Biographical Notes," *Cambridge Journal of Economics* 2:115–20.

Eshag, E. (1963). *From Marshall to Keynes*. Oxford: Blackwell.

Guillebaud, C. W. (1928). *The Works Council: a German Experiment in Industrial Democracy*. Oxford: Oxford University Press.

Henderson, H. D. (1922). *Supply and Demand*. London: Nisbet.

(1955). *The Inter-War Years and Other Papers*. Oxford: Clarendon.

Henderson, H. D., and Keynes, J. M. (1929). *Can Lloyd George Do It?* Reproduced in *Essays in Persuasion*, Vol. 9 of *The Collected Writings of John Maynard Keynes*. London: Macmillan, 1972.

Hubback, D. (1985). *No Ordinary Press Baron: A Life of Walter Layton*. London: Weidenfeld and Nicholson.

Hutchison, T. W. (1953). *A Review of Economic Doctrines 1870–1929*. Oxford: Clarendon.

Jha, N. (1973). *The Age of Marshall: Aspects of British Economic Thought 1890–1915*. London: Cass.

Kadish, A. (1982). *The Oxford Economists in the Late Nineteenth Century*. Oxford: Clarendon.

Keynes, J. M. (1913). *Indian Currency and Finance*. London: Macmillan.

(1921). *Treatise on Probability*. London: Macmillan.

(1923). *A Tract on Monetary Reform*. London: Macmillan.

(1930). *A Treatise on Money*. London: Macmillan.

(1971). *Activities 1906–1914*. Vol. 15 of *The Collected Writings of John Maynard Keynes*. London: Macmillan.

Koot, G. M. (1987). *English Historical Economics 1870–1926*. Cambridge: Cambridge University Press.

Kuhn, T. S. (1962). *The Structure of Scientific Revolutions*. Chicago: University of Chicago Press, 2d ed., 1970.

Lavington, F. (1925). "An Approach to the Theory of Business Risks", *Economic Journal* 35:186–99; 36:192–204.

(1921). *The English Capital Market*. London: Methuen.

(1922). *The Trade Cycle*. London: King.

Layton, W. T. (1913). *The Relations of Labour and Capital*. London: Macmillan.

(1912). *An Introduction to the Study of Prices*. London: Macmillan. Revised 1935, G. Crowther, co-author.

Maloney, J. (1985). *Marshall, Orthodoxy and the Professionalisation of Economics*. Cambridge: Cambridge University Press.

Pigou, A. C. (1905). *Principles and Practice of Industrial Peace*. London: Macmillan.

(1912). *Wealth and Welfare*. London: Macmillan. Revised as *Economics of Welfare* 1920, 1924, 1929, 1932.

(1917). "The Value of Money," *Quarterly Journal of Economics* 31:38–65.

(1921). *The Political Economy of War*. London: Macmillan.

(1927). *Industrial Fluctuations*. London: Macmillan.

(1928). *A Study in Public Finance*. London: Macmillan.

(1937). *Socialism versus Capitalism*. London: Macmillan.

(1953). *Alfred Marshall and Current Thought*. London: Macmillan.

Presley, J. R. (1981). "D. H. Robertson 1890–1963". In D. P. O'Brien and J. R. Presley (eds.), *Pioneers of Modern Economics in Britain*. London: Macmillan.

Robertson, D. H. (1915). *A Study of Industrial Fluctuation*. London: King.

(1922). *Money*. London: Nisbet.

(1923). *The Control of Industry*. London: Nisbet.

(1926). *Banking Policy and the Price Level*. London: King. Reprinted 1949, with a new preface.

Robinson, E. A. G. (1977). "Keynes and his Cambridge Colleagues". In D. Patinkin and J. C. Leith (eds.), *Keynes, Cambridge and The General Theory*. London: Macmillan.

(1978). "London and Cambridge Economic Service". Kraus Bibliographical Bulletin No. 26, June.

Samuelson, P. A. (1963). Obituary notice of D. H. Robertson, *Quarterly Journal of Economics* 77:517–36.

Shackle, G. L. S. (1968). *The Years of High Theory*. Cambridge: Cambridge University Press.

Shove, G. (1928). "Varying Costs and Marginal Net Products", *Economic Journal* 38:258–66.

(1930). Contribution (pp. 79–116) to "Increasing Returns and the Representative Firm: A Symposium", *Economic Journal* 40:39–116.

Skidelsky, R. (1983). *John Maynard Keynes*. Vol. 1. *Hopes Betrayed*. London: Macmillan.

Young, A. A. (1913). "Wealth and Welfare," *Quarterly Journal of Economics* 27:672–86.

Yule, G. (1911). *Introduction to the Theory of Statistics*. London: Griffin.

The location of most of the *Economic Journal* articles is clear from the text. No references are given for the comparative analysis of 1908 and 1924 as all the articles referred to may be found in the *Journal* for those two years.

8

What Happened to the Second Volume of the Principles? The Thorny Path to Marshall's Last Books

JOHN K. WHITAKER

In April 1887, when he was aged 44, Alfred Marshall wrote to the publishers Macmillan and Company offering "the central work of my life", a work on "Economics" to be published in two volumes "of which the first will, I hope, appear this autumn and the second about two years later".[1] The first volume finally appeared to wide acclaim in July 1890 as *Principles of Economics, Vol. 1*. The second volume never materialised. In the event, there was an extraordinary lapse of *twenty-nine* years before Marshall's next major work, *Industry and Trade*, appeared in 1919, to be followed in 1923 by *Money Credit and Commerce*. The latter promised a "companion volume on the quality of progress in work and life, and the economic conditions favourable to it" (p. 191) but no real advance had been made with this when Marshall died in July 1924 at the age of 81.

My intention here is to reconstruct, as far as the available evidence will allow, the thorny path by which Marshall's literary ambitions and plans advanced after 1890. The story, told as far as possible in Marshall's own words, is a sad, perhaps cautionary, one. It throws considerable light on the intentions and aspirations underlying his last volumes, their relation to each other and to the main corpus of his earlier work. To grasp the true

Manuscript material is reproduced by the permission of the following, which permission is gratefully acknowledged: the Master and Fellows of Balliol College, Oxford; the Keeper of Manuscripts of Cambridge University Library; and the Librarian of the Marshall Library, Cambridge. Unless otherwise indicated, manuscript material is from the collections held in the Marshall Library. Letters are identified by the Library's classification number. A general description of the Library's Marshall papers is given by McWilliams [-Tullberg] (1969).

1. See Guillebaud (1965, p. 519), *EEW*, 1, pp. 88–9.

character of *Industry and Trade* and *Money Credit and Commerce*, they must be seen as the imperfect products of Marshall's thirty-year struggle to reduce to finite compass his prodigious knowledge and subtly intertwined views on all aspects of economic and social life and history.[2]

The period from 1890 to 1924 falls into four broad phases. The first is 1890 to 1903 when Marshall was still actively working on Volume 2 of his *Principles*. In the second, 1903 to 1910, under the impetus of the tariff controversy, he diverted his efforts to the production of a *pièce d'occasion* dealing with *National Industries and International Trade*. During this period, he abandoned all hope of completing his *Principles* on the original plan, a decision reached by 1907 and finalised in 1910, when "Volume I" was removed from the title page. The next period, 1910 to 1920, saw the belated completion of the first volume of a multi-volume work on *Industry and Trade*, the direct descendant of the attempted *pièce d'occasion*, but by then Marshall's chief obsession. The last phase, 1920–24, ending with Marshall's death, saw the publication of earlier material as *Money Credit and Commerce* and desultory efforts to edit some of his earlier essays. By then further constructive work was beyond his powers.

In an unused manuscript fragment written for the preface of *Industry and Trade*, Marshall gave "some account of, and a serious apology for" his failure "to complete the general treatise on economics to which I had proposed to devote my life." He continued

> The first volume of my *Principles* was published in 1890. During the next thirteen years I gave what time I could to preparing material for continuing it. But even then I worked slowly; and meanwhile my official duties, especially those which were indirect, increased in weight. Considerable time was also occupied in partly rearranging and rewriting several editions of my *Principles* Vol. I; and in arranging a compressed edition of it under the title of *Elements of Economics* Vol. I. My attendance on and work for the Labour Commission 1891 to 1894 was the best possible employment for my own education; for it gave me an insight into the thought, feeling and action of employers and employed many times as great as I could have got by spending the time in any other way: but it delayed my writing and widened the spread of my projects. Similar results on a smaller scale followed in regard to less helpful work in several other directions; and in 1903 a very rough draft for the continuation of my *Principles* extended to more than a thousand pages; and it was becoming obvious that I could not hope to finish the work on the scale to which I

2. The story is recounted briefly in J. M. Keynes's (1924) memoir on Marshall, *Memorials*, pp. 1–65, especially pp. 59–65. See also *EEW*, 1, p. 93. The checklist of Marshall's publications, *Memorials*, pp. 500–8, provides a useful backdrop to the account given here.

was then working. The particular direction taken by the inevitable change was governed by what seemed at the time to be a trifling incident.

In July 1903 I received a request from the Chancellor of the Exchequer for my opinions on some questions connected with the incidence of import duties, and with the manner in which the economic changes of the preceding sixty years had affected the basis of England's fiscal policy. A part of the M.SS. of the answer which I wrote as a *Memorandum on the Fiscal Policy of International Trade* was lost in the post: I was advised that it would be recovered; I waited till the end of the year for it. By that time the Chancellorship had fallen into other hands; the particular phases of the discussion to which the *Memorandum* was addressed had passed away; I decided to develop it quickly into a small somewhat extended occasional piece. I proposed to write it quickly.[3]

Detailed evidence will be shown to corroborate this explanation. It also demonstrates that the path from the proposed work of 1903 to the last two books was no less thorny than that leading to the abandonment of the second volume of *Principles*.

I The Period 1890 to 1903

The scope initially proposed for Volume 2 of the *Principles* was indicated in a manuscript note of October 1887:[4]

Book VII	Foreign Trade
Book VIII	Money and Banking
Book IX	Trade Fluctuations
Book X	Taxation
Book XI	Collectivism
Book XII	Aims for the Future
	Mathematical Appendix

With the eventual appearance of Volume 1 in July 1890,[5] the way became open for serious work on Volume 2, but progress was slow. Within a few months of the appearance of Volume 1 Marshall embarked on a substantial revision for a new edition. J. N. Keynes noted in his diary for January 15 1891, "He [Marshall] is making very extensive alterations in the 2nd

3. Written when *Industry and Trade* was planned as two volumes, probably around 1916, and slightly edited. The continuation (if one existed) has not been traced.
4. See *EEW*, 1, p. 89. At the time, Volume 1 of *Principles*, which had seven Books when it appeared in 1890, was planned to have only six Books, a plan reverted to in subsequent editions.
5. See *EEW*, 1, pp. 89–92 for an account of the completion of Volume 1 of *Principles*.

editn. of his Book. I agree with Mrs. Marshall in thinking that it would have been wiser not to attempt any rewriting at present."[6]

In a letter of March 18, 1891, Marshall explained to Keynes

> I am putting my Book VI back again into the place to wh. it origi-
> nally belonged, viz. the middle of Book V. This makes great hash of
> the details. Berry has promised to look at the proofs from the point
> of view of my main aim in the change wh. is to make more clear what
> I mean by true or long period normal supply price, (& negatively
> inclined supply curves).[7]

As soon as the second edition of Volume 1 was out of the way (the preface is dated June 1891) Marshall commenced the condensation that was to replace the earlier *Economics of Industry,* written with his wife, Mary Paley Marshall, which had gone through several minor revisions since its first appearance in 1879.[8] He told Macmillan, "I propose to go to press with that at the beginning of July & hope to work it off rapidly".[9] But the chapter on trades unions specially prepared for this book was not completed until January 1892, and it was mid-1892 before the final product (Marshall 1892) appeared under the title *Elements of Economics of Industry, Being the First Volume of Elements of Economics.*[10]

The chapter on unions, which drew heavily on the treatment of the subject in the earlier *Economics of Industry,* was included because "the practical convenience of discussing them in close connection with the main theory of distribution seemed to outweigh the disadvantages of treating them prematurely and in some measure incompletely".[11] Marshall expected to reuse some of this material when discussing unions in Volume 2 of *Principles.*[12] But by deferring his full treatment to that volume he hoped to be able to explain more adequately how the influence of unions "depends much on the course of foreign trade and on commer-

---

6. Cambridge University Library, Add Mss 7827–67. John Neville Keynes, Marshall's student and colleague, was the father of John Maynard Keynes.
7. Keynes 1(101). Arthur Berry was a young Cambridge mathematician with an interest in economics. For a fuller account of the changes made in successive editions of the *Principles* see *Variorum,* pp. 15–26, and Guillebaud (1942).
8. For further details of Marshall and Marshall (1879) see *EEW,* 1, pp. 67–82.
9. Letter of June 12, 1891, Marshall 4(3). Marshall's correspondence with Macmillan and Company from this time on was predominantly with Frederick, later Sir Frederick, Macmillan. For simplicity the generic name Macmillan will be used. Originals of the Marshall–Macmillan correspondence are in the British Library (Add Ms 55174) and the Marshall Library (Marshall 2(·)). The latter also has copies of most items in the former (Marshall 4(·)). This correspondence is drawn on heavily below.
10. This work is referred to hereafter as *Elements.* There were new editions in 1896 and 1899. The projected second volume never appeared but the title remained unaltered.
11. *Elements,* p. v. He expected ultimately to remove this chapter to the second volume of the *Elements.* Letter to Macmillan, March 19, 1896, Marshall 4(11).
12. Letter to Macmillan of March 4, 1892, Marshall 4(7).

cial fluctuations" (*Elements*, p. v). He also hoped to analyse the entire question of "industrial groups and employer–employé questions" in terms of the offer curves he had developed to express the theory of international trade, and which were to be presented in the first of the Books planned for *Principles*, Volume 2.[13]

Marshall was forced to inform Macmillan in October 1891 that "I am getting on very slowly with Principles Vol. II".[14] In that same month he commenced his onerous duties as a member of the Royal Commission on Labour which continued until the Commission issued its Final Report in 1894.[15] Mrs. Marshall wrote to Benjamin Jowett, "Alfred's Labour Commission work begins next week. He finds it very interesting, but it will hinder Vol. II w^h. has now been entered upon. But as that volume is to deal with Trade Combinations I daresay the Commission experience will fit in".[16]

Progress on the new book was further delayed by the need to respond to various criticisms of Volume 1 – those of William Cunningham being particularly nettling.[17] Still, in May 1893 Marshall was "immersed in 'Money' & 'Foreign Trade' ",[18] and Jowett was glad in August "to hear that the 'Opus Magnum' is getting on", adding "Now that people are in a

13. See letters to F. Y. Edgeworth of March and April 1891 reproduced in *Variorum*, pp. 792–8. Also see *EEW*, 2, pp. 117–28, for the text of Marshall's early statement of the parallel.
14. Letter to Macmillan of October 3, 1891, British Library.
15. According to Mrs. Marshall "A great part of the Labour Commission Report was his, especially T.Us, Minimum Wage, Irregularity of Employment". She reported that Gerald Balfour, another member of the Commission, said of Marshall "he held us in the hollow of his hand" (Manuscript notes: see also *Memorials*, p. 52). Marshall was a member of Committee B on Transport and Agriculture. The minutes of evidence show him taking a substantial, but not dominant, part in cross examination. A conspectus of the Commission's voluminous output is given by Spyers (1894). Although it was time consuming, Marshall much later claimed that by service on the Commission "I received from working men and other witnesses, and from the members of the Commission, the most valuable education of my life" (*IT*, p. vii).
16. Letter of October 29, 1891, Balliol College Library. In a letter of November 6 she added "Alfred is in London at the Labour Commission. Each of its three groups meets now once in three weeks for four days at a time. . . . In connection with the Labour questions we have been reading some books about Australia where they are kind enough to be making experiments in most of the directions towards wh. we are only glancing in England".
17. See the checklist, *Memorials*, pp. 500–8, for details of Marshall's published rejoinders. In this period he was also concerned with Poor Law reform, giving extensive evidence before the Royal Commission on the Aged Poor in 1893. The full text is given in *OP*.
18. Letter to E. Cannan of May 5, 1893, British Library of Political and Economic Science, Cannan Collection 1020(18–19). On September 30, 1893, Marshall proposed to devote his advanced lectures to (i) Foreign Trade and Economic Functions of Government, (ii) Money, Banking and Modern Markets for Goods and Labour, treating each topic in alternate years (Letter to J. N. Keynes, Keynes 1(112)).

troubled state of mind about the currency is the time for its appearance". He hoped that Alfred was not getting into "a quagmire of bimetallism".[19]

In 1894, according to Mrs. Marshall, Alfred changed his plans and "began a historical treatment which he called later on a White Elephant because it was on such a large scale that it would have taken many volumes to complete. . . . For a long time he intended to make it a continuation of *Principles* but in the end determined against this plan".[20]

Marshall looked to the summers, spent away from the vexations of Cambridge, to make real progress with his writing. The summer of 1895 was, however, largely consumed by the preparation of the third edition of Volume 1 so that Volume 2 became "moribund".[21]

Writing to President Eliot in September 1895 to decline an invitation to visit Harvard, Marshall explained

> I got out the first volume of my book five years ago: it is a poor truncated affair, the jagged edges of wh. I then hoped I shd. have joined up with the second volume ere this. But I found one thing after another to tempt me aside; I said to myself – this is really rather exceptional, I will just do *this* & then I will stick to my second volume. In particular I accepted an invitation to join the Commission on Labour. I thought the experience wd. be instructive, & not take much time. It was instructive : but it took the better part of my time for three years. Last spring I set to work to remedy some of the more grievous obscurities of my first volume; allowing two months for the task. It has taken me seven, & it is only today that I have sent off copy for the last page. In short I have made such progress with my second volume, that, if I kept it up steadily, the volume would be out in about 30 years time! So I have vowed a vow, that no temptation however biting shall induce me to do anything whatever that I am free to decline, until I have either finished the volume or at all events made solid progress with it.[22]

There followed a period of some years in which other commitments were quite light. But the enormous scale of the task Marshall had embarked upon was becoming increasingly and dauntingly clear. This

19. Letter to Mrs. Marshall of August 7, 1893, Marshall 1(139).
20. Manuscript notes; see also *Memorials*, p. 52. Mrs. Marshall claimed that portions of the White Elephant were later embodied in *Industry and Trade*. A letter of November 1897 to Lord Acton, quoted below, suggests that the White Elephant was primarily concerned with the "history of foreign trade".
21. Letter to E. Cannan of September 9, 1895, British Library of Political and Economic Science, Cannan Collection 1020(46–53).
22. Letter to C. W. Eliot of September 3, 1895, Marshall 3(87). Marshall, always something of a valetudinarian, added that he was perfectly well if he rested for an hour after meals, but that this seriously curtailed his working time. "If I had a good digestion &c, my Vol. II wd. be well on its way".

realisation was accompanied by a growing ambivalence about the purpose and style of Volume 2. The sheer difficulty of organizing coherently such a mass of material was becoming evident. In 1907, he was to claim that about 1895 "I began to despair of completing my scheme in two volumes" and that he then decided to eliminate consideration of the economic functions of government.[23] There is, however, no contemporary indication of such a definite change in plan.

In April 1897, Marshall confessed to H. S. Foxwell, "I know I do not focus my work enough. . . . I think I might focus more, if I could give time to it. But I want to get my difficulties solved before I die. I know I can't do that: but every day I give to form keeps me back from that & that is the only thing I really care for."[24] The growing uncertainty about the book's organisation was conveyed in a letter to Foxwell of the same month: "I have consumed nearly a ream of paper on myriad drafts of the table of contents of my book."[25] In November of the same year Marshall wrote to Lord Acton to decline an invitation to contribute to the *Cambridge Modern History,* explaining

> My book makes no progress. The work for it wh. I feel I must do before finishing it grows: there is more of it ahead than there was when I had finished my first volume. The history of foreign trade seduced me: I thought it exceptionally instructive for modern times: & I spent an incredible time in laboriously producing several chapters about it. And yet, after all, I find they wd. make the main argument hang so, that I am forced to fall back on the awkward expedient of putting them into an appendix, & making frequent references to them in illustration of my argument. I made the resolve sadly; but at the same time I resolved to read as little history as possible till I had finished my main work. I find that the illustrations wh. I want to take from recent events alone will occupy more time than I can spare, & will fill more paper than people will have patience to read. I must leave economic history to others.[26]

23. From the preface to the fifth edition of *Principles:* see *Variorum,* p. 45. An ampler quotation is given below.
24. Letter of April 14, 1897, Marshall 3(32).
25. Letter of April 26, 1897, Marshall 3(55). As the result of "a portentous number of experiments in classification" Marshall had concluded that "Markets in general belong to the broad outlines of value; but that Markets in particular with realistic details should come just before Commercial Fluctuations & just after a general description of the Money Market".
26. Letter of November 13, 1897. Cambridge University Library, Add Mss 6443(205). Marshall added "my own chapters are not properly histories, that is, ordered records of facts. I read history to distil from it the leading ideas suitable for my main problems".

In 1898 a new edition of Volume 1 of the *Principles* was called for, the fourth. Some consideration was given to relegating the early historical chapters to appendices as suggested by a young American "who had been to a good many German universities", but in the event the change was not made and the original plan of the book was stoutly defended in the *Economic Journal* article on "Distribution and Exchange".[27] The nature of the changes actually made was indicated in a letter of April 1898 to the Dutch economist N. G. Pierson.

> I am preparing a new Edition of my Vol. I: a large one, so that I may not have to turn aside soon for another. I am adding nothing, but trying to simplify some things. I am trying to collect into one place all that I have to say about Rents & Quasi-rents in relation to cost. I had hoped to make myself clear: but the fact that so eloquent an economist as Nicholson has failed to discover what it is all about disheartens me.[28]

Other activities occupied the years from 1899 to 1903. In 1899 there was the evidence for the Indian Currency Commission and the Royal Commission on Local Taxation.[29] After this, rising to a successful crescendo in 1903, came Marshall's carefully orchestrated campaign for a separate Faculty and Tripos in economics and politics at Cambridge to free his subject from the incubus of the Moral Sciences Tripos under which it had long laboured. Marshall's efforts here were strenuous.[30]

Occasional glimpses of Volume 2 can be discerned through this flurry of activity. Marshall told Bishop Westcott in October 1899 that "I am just now working at the good and evil of Stock Exchange fluctuations. Like everything else which I touch in my second Volume, which will be more concrete than my first, I find it grows in difficulty in my hands. Thence I am to pass to speculation in goods" (*Memorials,* p. 385). A letter of May 1900 to E. R. A. Seligman lamented "I am lost in a mass of material relating to Trade, Money, etc. which I cannot get into order. I can't recollect what I have said in one chapter, and am constantly saying

---

27. Marshall (1898): see *Variorum*, pp. 62–3. The quotation is from a letter to J. N. Keynes of October 17, 1897, where Marshall added "I saw Foxwell just now, & told him [about the suggestion]. Foxwell says Vol. I is too big; & for that & other reasons (particularly I thought *other* reasons) he wd. like those chapters taken out of Vol. I & worked up elsewhere. I told him that there was no chance of my being able to do that for many years" (Keynes 1(114)). The identity of the American is unclear. H. R. Seager seems the likeliest.
28. Letter of April 30, 1898, Marshall 3(95). On J. S. Nicholson's views see *Variorum*, p. 433.
29. See *OP* for the full texts.
30. Much of the correspondence preserved in the Marshall Library concerns these questions. Marshall also published several lengthy statements, especially his "Plea" (reproduced in *Variorum*, pp. 161–81). See *Memorials*, pp. 55–7, 596.

the same thing twice, and wasting time".[31] In August 1902 he told Edgeworth that the notion that Trusts are stabilizing "is being developed in my vol. II" (*Memorials*, p. 436). While in December 1902 Marshall informed Macmillan that "I am giving myself up to my Second Volume with ever increasing resoluteness, so far as I am free. But I have not much freedom, & my progress is not fast".[32]

By 1903, however, a turning point had been reached. No further progress was to be made along the lines he had been following, although the hope of sometime, somehow completing the *Principles* lingered for several years. In a later manuscript note Marshall recorded (*EEW*, 1, p. 93) that

> The order proposed for the continuation of my *Principles* changed many times: but I left it in 1903 fairly settled as follows:–
>
> 1. Currency (first stage)
> 2. International Trade (first stage)
> 3. Credit and its markets
> 4. Produce markets
> 5. Business combinations and Monopolies, Transport Problems
> 6. Association and Combination in relation to Employment
> 7. Credit Fluctuations (including second stages of Currency and International Trade)
> 8. The Distribution of the National Income (concluded on the basis of Book VI of my first volume)
> 9. Public Finance

Hardly anything remains of the thousand-page rough draft of this material and many portions of it must have been cannibalized for the later books. Miscellaneous rough notes bearing on the contents of Volume 2 have survived from the period 1890–1903,[33] but only one finished fragment can be ascribed definitely to this 1903 draft. Headed "From PXI III [that is, *Principles* Book XI, Ch. 3] To be replaced 2.9.05" it discusses bilateral monopoly. Written no earlier than 1898 (it refers to the fourth edition of that year) the gist was added as a new Section 9 to Book V, Chapter 14, "The Theory of Monopolies", in the fifth edition (1907) of *Principles*.

Speculation as to the detailed contents and overall state of completion of the lost manuscript can have little basis. It is likely that much of the

31. See Dorfman (1941, p. 410).
32. Letter of December 13, 1902, Marshall 4(17).
33. For example, there are about 50 pages of notes on "Foreign Exchange Dissimilar Currency" dated 1897 and a package headed "Retail Prices a few fragments from Vol II *Principles*". But this material is too rough and incomplete to be of much interest.

material did eventually come to light in the last books, but much of interest, especially from a theoretical viewpoint, must have been irretrievably lost. By 1906 Marshall's interest, and even competence, in economic theory had dwindled. As he explained to the Austrian economist Richard Lieben, "I practically never use any diagrams at all in lectures now, & have forgotten much that is in my own *Principles*".[34] It thus seems likely that some theoretical developments originally intended for Volume 2 found no place in the last books, and even those that did were emasculated and enfeebled compared to what Marshall might have produced at the height of his powers in the 1890s.

The failure to complete Volume 2 of the *Principles* did not seriously embarrass Volume 1, whose allusions to the companion volume were never conspicuous and usually vague. As the closing sentences of Volume 1 observed, "in real life nearly every economic issue depends, more or less directly, on some complex actions and reactions of credit, of foreign trade, and of modern developments of combination and monopoly. But the ground which we have traversed . . . is, in some respects, the most difficult of the whole province of economics; and it commands, and gives access to, the remainder".[35] Volume 1 could thus stand as an independent introduction to the subject. In one important respect, however, the advantage of this commanding ground was never exploited due to the failure to complete Volume 2.

One of the best known analytical features of the *Principles* is the time analysis, with its familiar distinction between long-period and short-period normal values. Although the distinction is carefully made, little use is in fact made of the short-period concepts. The explanation is that the short-period analysis was intended to be an important tool for the second volume, so that "when at a later stage we come to consider the quickly moving oscillations of trade and commerce, the short-period normal . . . will claim more of our attention".[36] As Marshall had told A. W. Flux in 1898, "The supplementary cost question can . . . only be touched in Vol. I. It will give a chief motive to a great part of Vol. II, especially as to Fluctuations of credit and prices" (*Memorials,* p. 407). Unfortunately, this aspect of Marshall's thought was to remain largely unexpressed.

---

34. Letter of June 19, 1906, Marshall 1(27).
35. *Principles*, p. 722. So since 1898.
36. *Variorum*, p. 395, deleted in 1907. Similarly, short-period and market equilibria were to "come into prominence when we discuss, in a later volume, fluctuations of prices and wages arising from quickly passing changes in the state of commercial credit, and other causes; together with the allied problems of trade unions and combinations of employers" (*Variorum*, p. 396, added in 1907, deleted in 1916).

II   The Period 1903 to 1910

It was in 1903 that the tariff controversy erupted in Britain, following Joseph Chamberlain's attack on established free-trade policies. Marshall was drawn in as a signatory – afterwards a rueful one – of the infamous "Professors' Manifesto".[37] His more important involvement, however, came when he was asked to write a private memorandum on the issues for the use of the then Chancellor of the Exchequer, David Ritchie, a confirmed free trader. In agreeing, Marshall observed that "the rather long time wh. I have given to International Trade has not resulted in much print as yet. The problems now in the air occupy a large space in that part of my Vol. II which is nearly ready for press".[38] The memorandum was composed in the summer of 1903. Marshall observed "I had at first intended to make it short. But the course of the discussion in England & especially the Tracts, which are being issued by the million under Chamberlain's auspices from Birmingham – have induced me to make it long and to publish its substance ere long".[39] The first draft Marshall felt to be "horribly confused & out of proportion" but unfortunately the only copy of his revisions was lost in the post. He thought that he *might* "rewrite it about Christmas", although fearing that he could not be sufficiently "crude and unscientific" to counter Chamberlain's agitations effectively.[40] As events transpired, however, the memorandum did not see the light until June 1908, when Lloyd George, then Chancellor, came across it in the files and referred to it in the House of Commons. Marshall was persuaded to have a revised version published in November 1908 as a Parliamentary paper with an explanatory preface.[41]

Although the memorandum itself was not developed further, its composition turned Marshall's thoughts to the production of a tract for the

37.   For details see McCready (1955), Coats (1968). As early as June 1902, Marshall had been "a good deal tempted . . . to write about the Zollverein principle" (*Memorials*, p. 432).
38.   Copy of letter of August 14, 1903, to T. Llewellyn Davies (Ritchie's private secretary and one of Marshall's former students). Marshall Library. Unclassified. Reproduced in Wood (1982). The allusion to material "nearly ready for the press" seems to rest on wishful thinking, and the later statement (*IT*, p. vi) that in 1904 some of Volume 2 had been set up in type appears baseless.
39.   Letter of August 20, 1903, to Lujo Brentano, reproduced in McCready (1955, pp. 262–3).
40.   Letter to Brentano of September 29, 1903. McCready (1955, pp. 266–7). Meanwhile Ritchie had resigned.
41.   *Memorandum on the Fiscal Policy of International Trade*, House of Commons No. 321, November 11, 1908, reproduced in *OP*, pp. 365–420. For further details see Wood (1980, 1982).

times on the tariff issue. The scheme was first broached to Macmillan in December 1903.

> I am thinking of bringing out a book of 200–300 pp. on *National industries & international trade*. It is to be an economic monograph adapted for the general reader, supplemented by some detailed statements & some rather difficult reasonings for the serious student . . . to be printed as appendices. They will for the greater part be taken out of the M.SS. of Vol II of my *Principles*.[42]

Macmillan was accommodating but, as always, the scheme grew rapidly in Marshall's hands. He described the character of the emerging work in a letter of March 19, 1904, to A. W. Flux, whose considerable help in this early stage was particularly acknowledged subsequently (*IT*, p. ix).

> The first half, which is only half written, is on the causes and nature of Industrial Leadership treated historically as well as analytically. The second is on International Trade; while at the end is to come an application of the basis thus provided to current issues.

In the third part, Marshall proposed "to give a little freedom to my *sentiment*, as distinguished from my reason; and to speak as a citizen rather than specially as an economist" (*Memorials*, pp. 407–8). By May, although 150 pages were already in type or at the printers, it had become clear that the target proposed to Macmillan of completion by June could not be met: "it is certain that the book will not be out till the autumn and probably not till later . . . the further I go the slower I go. Just at present I am getting out of the industrial problems of Germany into those of U.S.A. That will bring my Part I to 200 pp. or more" (Letter to Flux of May 26, 1904, *Memorials*, pp. 408–9). Fortunately, the urgency of rapid completion seemed to have diminished, as

> Several books have appeared setting out the principles of international trade with reference to current issues; Also it is now clear that Mr. Chamberlain has not captured any considerable section of the working classes; & that the critical fight over his "programme" if ever there is one at all, will not take place during 1904.

Marshall now perceived "a growing demand for a careful study on rather broader lines – And as time does not press, I proposed to try to write one". He now projected a length of four to five hundred pages.[43]

In November 1904 he had to confess that his new book made "slow progress", adding

42. Letter of December 12, 1903, Marshall 4(23).
43. Letter to Macmillan of May 25, 1904, Marshall 4(24). See also letters of April and June 1904 to Henry Cunynghame (*Memorials*, pp. 448–52).

Events move fast. The more obvious things are being repeated in periodical literature so frequently that much, which would have seemed fresh a year ago, would be stale now. Thus delay causes delay; for it makes me inclined to lay more and more stress on industrial conditions which underlie the fiscal issue of the day.

Thus I am giving a couple of months or so more than I had intended to do to the question "How far is it true that large industrial aggregations (Trusts, Cartels &c) in a country are a source of strength to her and of menace to her neighbours?"[44]

A year later, in November 1905, the plan of the book was changing still further.

I am giving every fraction of free time & strength to *National Industries & International Trade*. But I do not work fast; & the work direct & indirect demanded by the new Tripos is very heavy.

Also the book is changing its form a little. Its general notion is that the courses of trade are controlled by the contours of industry, as watercourses are controlled by those of the hills. And therefore I had always intended to treat the issues of International Trade as subordinate to those of National industries. But as I go on I incline to carry the subordination even further than I originally proposed.[45]

More than half of the book was to deal with "National Industries", and he now projected "five or six hundred pages of text together with rather more than a hundred of Appendices", fearing that the book could not appear until 1907. He lamented the delay partly "because it keeps me away from Vol II of my *Principles*". By June 1906 the projected length had grown to eight hundred pages and the possibility of two volumes was being broached.[46] In January 1907 he looked forward to publication by September 1908. But the moment of truth had arrived. At last he gave up hope of ever completing his *Principles* on the original plan.

When that [publication of *National Industries and International Trade*] is over I shall have to consider what part of my original project can be accomplished in my life time, supposing that to be fairly long. After a year's consideration, I shall probably recast Vol I as an independent treatise, keeping *National Industries & Trade* as another & aiming at perhaps two more before I cease. Meanwhile I may perhaps try to finish my *Elements* as a complete textbook. I fear

---

44. Letter to Macmillan of November 16, 1904, Marshall 4(25).
45. Letter to Macmillan of November 20, 1905, Marshall 4(26). See *IT*, p. 4, for a repetition of the simile.
46. Letter to Macmillan of June 9, 1906, Marshall 4(27).

it is impossible to complete my *Principles* on the scale – so vastly
enlarged during the present generation – required for it.[47]

As an interim step he immediately began revising *Principles*, Volume 1,
for a fifth edition which was completed in August 1907. Although there
was substantial recasting (this was the edition in which the early historical material was relegated to appendices) the appellation Volume 1 was
still retained. He described the nature of the revisions to Macmillan as
follows:

> In the last ten years there has been a great deal of controversial
> writing, chiefly in U.S.A. as to the fundamentals of economics: & not
> a little of this has been specially concerned with my *Principles*. Much
> of it is not very solid, & some of it is apparently written rather for the
> love of striking effects. But I have thought it necessary to read a good
> deal of it lately; & without changing the substance in any way, I am
> modifying the form of about a hundred pages. Also I am writing a
> little new matter.[48]

The "new matter" included some discussion of the effects of trades
unions, probably added in an attempt to make the volume more self
contained, as had been the case in 1892 for the *Elements*.[49]

In the preface to the fifth edition, Marshall confided in his readers and
offered

> some explanation of my failure to fulfil the implicit promise, made
> seventeen years ago, that a second volume completing the treatise
> would appear within a reasonable time. I had laid my plan on too
> large a scale. . . . About twelve years ago I began to despair of com-
> pleting my scheme in two volumes. Accordingly I set aside the eco-
> nomic functions of government (*Wirtschafts-politik*) for a third vol-
> ume; and rearranged, in ampler space, the materials which I had got
> together on the modern conditions of industry and trade; of credit
> and employment . . . But gradually it became clear that the enlarged
> space was still too small, and that four thick volumes would be
> needed for the task. This called a halt: for life is short. . . . Accord-
> ingly I now propose to bring out as soon as possible an almost
> independent volume, part of which is already in print, on *National
> Industry and Trade*. . . . This may be followed at no very long inter-
> val by a companion volume on *Money, Credit, and Employment*.
> And finally it may be possible to compress these two volumes, to-
> gether with some discussion of the functions of government, into a

47. Letter to Macmillan of January 31, 1907, Marshall 4(29).
48. Letter to Macmillan of April 9, 1907, Marshall 4(31).
49. The material on unions was added to Book V, Chapter 13.

single volume; which may supplement the present volume, and form a consecutive treatise of moderate length.

The contents of the forthcoming volume were described as follows:

> About one half of it is occupied with the evolution of the present forms and conditions of national leadership in industry, with special reference to the recent changes in the character and functions of giant businesses and of combinations: the second half applies the conclusions of the first half to the modern problems of international trade.   (*Variorum*, pp. 45–6)

In 1908, at age 65, Marshall resigned his professorship to free more time for his writing.[50] He planned to rely less on working away from Cambridge for

> the ever more realistic tendencies of my work make it increasingly wasteful of time & effort to be compelled to put off looking up authentic statements of facts wh. I am using for *illustrative* purposes – I don't much believe in the possibility of direct induction – till I have come home & got out of the stratum of thought for wh. I wanted the reference.[51]

In the autumn of 1908 he had just spent "some months wading through the detestable mud of international trade statistics".[52] At this time, too, the 1903 Memorandum on Fiscal Policy was published as a Parliamentary paper. Marshall observed, "At first I was annoyed at having to prepare it for press: but now I am rather glad. For it makes me more free to keep the controversial element in *National Industry & Trade* very low". He added that " 'Protection and Free Trade' are in view during a part of [the book's] course; but they do not dominate it. It is in the main a study of industry in relation to trade".[53]

The deficiencies of the *Memorandum* were explained in its preface. "It offends against my rule to avoid controversial matters; and, instead of endeavouring to probe to the causes of causes, as a student's work should, it is concerned mainly with proximate causes and their effects" (*OP*, p. 368).

50. As early as 1901 he had told J. N. Keynes "I should retire if I could afford it. But I cannot. If I did I should have an income of only about £150 a year exclusive of the rental equivalent of my house, & sundry checks from Macmillan". Letter of January 8, 1901, Keynes 1(122).
51. Letter to J. N. Keynes of September 27, 1908, Keynes 1(135).
52. Letter to William Bateson of October 26, 1908, Marshall 3(2). "They have little interest for me because I know that everything in them that is of much importance can be got by massive observation and conjecture . . . so I have to waste time on analysing statistics for other people's benefit".
53. Letter to Macmillan of November 17, 1908, Marshall 4(38).

The book was to be "a solid structure encompassing the ground covered by the Memorandum" and was to deal with "the causes of those causes which are changing the methods & the courses of industry & trade".[54]

In November 1908 Marshall told Macmillan "I am now making relatively fast progress" and promised to "live as a recluse" until the book appeared, although fearing that this would not be until 1910.[55] At the end of the following year he lamented that "my slow progress at National Industries & Trade, my waning strength, & my chagrin at the recrudescence of stupid fallacies even in the speeches of an alert man like Lord Milner make me care about little else than that book".[56]

Early in 1910 he completed the revisions for the sixth edition of the *Principles*. It was in this edition that "Volume I" was dropped and the title became *Principles of Economics: An Introductory Volume*. The consequential changes were slight, however, and the text little altered.[57] Marshall seems to have abandoned by now his ambition of January 1907 to recast the *Principles* as an independent treatise and finish the *Elements* as a complete textbook. No substantial changes were made in either work after 1907.

In the preface to the new edition, dated March 1910, Marshall announced a modification of his plans for the continuation of his work beyond *National Industry and Trade*.[58]

> This may be followed by a companion volume on *Money, Credit, and Employment:* and perhaps by a third, which will treat of the ideal and the practicable in social and economic structure, with some account of taxation and administration.   (*Variorum*, p. 56)

He explained to Macmillan that in the preface

> I speak with even less confidence about the future than in the corresponding passage of the last edition. I have a great deal of material which seems nearly ready. But the realistic part needs to be largely

---

54. Letter to Macmillan of November 22, 1908, Marshall 4(39). Letter (draft) to S. Armitage-Smith of June 27, 1908. Marshall Library. Unclassified.
55. Letter of November 17, 1908, Marshall 4(38).
56. Letter to Macmillan of December 30, 1909, Marshall 4(44).
57. See *Variorum*, pp. 390, 396, for references to "a later volume" deleted from the seventh edition. However, at least one such reference, and even one to "the second volume", survived in the eighth edition (*Principles*, pp. 805, 849).
58. "It must be 'National Industry & Trade' please (not 'Trade & Industry'): for a chief note of the book is that Industry masters Trade" (April 7, 1910). "The change from 'Industries' to Industry [first made in the 1907 preface but not consistently adhered to] means that I have been forced to abandon the original notion of treating particular industries in some detail" (September 9, 1910). Letters to Macmillan, Marshall 4(46, 48).

rewritten once in a decade; & the analytical part is as difficult to my
mental muscles as is a steep mountain slope to my feet, though as a
young man I could climb it without conscious effort.

Of the forthcoming book he added

I think the book may run to about 1000 pages. Later on I will give
you a closer estimate & ask you whether it should appear as one
volume or two. I do not like to prophecy. But I hope – in spite of the
sluggishness of my weary old brain – to begin to print again before
the end of this year & to publish before the end of the next. I have
tried your patience sorely.

He expected that "about a third or quarter" of the book would consist of
Appendices containing pieces of "complex analysis or hard reasoning",
relegated so as to "get the book read by practical men, without spoiling it
from the rigidly scientific point of view".[59]

III   The Period 1910 to 1920

There were now few outside interruptions and Marshall devoted himself
to his book. John Bates Clark, who visited Marshall in the summer of
1910, reported that "Professor Marshall is in much better health than I
expected to find him in and is working vigorously on a book, which he
hopes will appear in two years. It will not be the entire Part II of his work,
but will deal with International Values, Protection, and I know not what
other subjects".[60] Matters must have been well advanced by May 1913
when Macmillan wrote envisioning that the new work would extend to
three volumes: "I understand that your present scheme is to go to press
with Volumes I and II of "National Industry and Trade" in the Autumn of
this year leaving Volume III to follow as soon as may be".[61]

Unfortunately, this was not to be, and the outbreak of war in 1914
greatly increased the uncertainties and difficulties surrounding the project. In a letter to Macmillan of April 1916 Marshall reported

I make very slow progress with my new book. I have now got nearly
the whole of the first volume into slips: but if the thing is ever
finished, it will run to three volumes, each about three fourths as
long as my *Principles*.

59. Letter of March 5, 1910, Marshall 4(45). Some typewritten fragments on interna-
    tional trade from the draft of this period have been preserved, but are not of great
    interest. See McWilliams [-Tullberg] (1969) for details.
60. Letter to Seligman of October 26, 1910, reproduced in Dorfman (1941), p. 411.
61. Letter of May 14, 1913, Marshall 2(14).

I am dropping "National" and calling it "Industry & Trade".
Vol I consists of:—

Book I   Origins of the present problems of industry
           and trade (a historical introduction)
Book II   The organization & administration of busi-
           ness (very realistic)
Book III   Tendencies to monopolistic aggregation.

Vol II is to be on International Trade & some monetary problems.
Most of it is typewritten. Vol III exists only in fragments & old
material. It is designed to cover social & governmental applications
of the other two etc.

About three years ago I found myself unable to do much work. I
found that diseased gums had brought on blood pressure. I fell into
able hands, & am in relatively good health, though I cannot work
much. But I find that what I wrote before I knew I was ill is not
satisfactory: & I cannot expect to bring out Vol II, without much rewriting.

I had therefore proposed to suggest that Vol I should come out as
soon as ready. But in view of the war my own inclination is now
distinctly to wait & bring out Vols I and II together.

If I do not finish Vol III (I am now in my 74th year), I propose to
arrange that it should be converted in large measure into a collection
of essays &c. already published, & selected with a view to the main
purpose, which I propose for the Volume, if I should be able to
complete it.[62]

This, for the first time, comes close to describing what became the final
outcome. The change in title to *Industry and Trade* was explained as
"caused by the slowness of my progress, which convinced me that I
cannot hope to bring out any considerable work after this: & therefore I
am changing the scope of this, & giving it a more elastic title. My work
has been interrupted, chiefly by causes connected with the war: but I am
now proceeding with it".[63] The preface to the seventh edition of the
Principles, dated June 1916, announced

I am now engaged in writing an independent work, which is to extend
to more than one volume, on *Industry and Trade.* It is designed to
cover a considerable part of the ground over which I had hoped to
travel: but it will be directed mainly to a study of the causes which
have brought about the present methods and organization of business:
to the influences which they exert on the quality of life: and to the ever-
widening problems to which they give rise.   (*Variorum,* p. 61)

62. Letter of April 5, 1916, Marshall 4(52).
63. Letter to Macmillan of November 3, 1916, Marshall 4(54).

Macmillan had agreed that it would be best to bring out Volumes 1 and 2 together, adding "I expect this only means postponing the publication until the war is over, and the discussion of the matters with which you deal will be very apropos".[64] Marshall was soon reporting, however, that "The last few chapters of Volume I are taking much more work than I had expected: & I have been unable to refuse to contribute to a sort of manifesto in support of a resolute, but moderate, policy after the war.[65] Also my power of work rapidly diminishes". He added

> As things are I do not expect that my new Vol I will be ready much before the end of the war. If any notice of it is published – as to the advisability of wh. I have no opinion – it may perhaps be described as concerned with "Origins and problems of the present industrial structure, with special reference to its monopolistic tendencies".
>
> I should have liked to publish the somewhat elaborate discussion of the fiscal policy of international trade, which is to occupy a considerable part of Vol II, before the country settled down to post-bellum conditions: but I now find that that is impossible. The matter however is very old; & it will always be new.[66]

A few months later, he reiterated "I have found the plan of bringing out my two volumes of *Industry & Trade* together impracticable. Vol I will, I hope, be ready so far as I am concerned about Easter [1917]: you must decide when it is to be published. I now work so slowly, & propose to put so much matter into Vol II, wh had originally been relegated to Vol III, that it is not likely to be ready for two or three years".[67] In August 1917 it was settled that Volume 2 was to be "put off for an indefinite time". Although more than half typewritten it needed "a good deal of rewriting". In consequence of this postponement, Marshall was "shifting to Appendices nearly all matter [in Volume 1] relating to the development of the policies of international trade" (on this see *IT*, p. 12).

> I must wrap myself in the white sheet, & hold the candle of the penitent [wrote Marshall] when I pass to speak of my new work. For I know I have run up a huge printers bill on it. . . . I will not narrate the history of my vacillations as to scope and arrangement of the work. They have been caused partly by external events; partly by my

64. Letter of April 17, 1916, Marshall 2(16).
65. This appeared as "National Taxation After the War" in Dawson (1917). In reluctantly agreeing to participate, Marshall told Dawson "so much of my half-done work will in any case have to be scrapped when I depart this life, that no honorarium however great wd. have led me even to consider a suggestion for any work wh. I could not represent to myself at all events as 'doing my bit' ". Letter of June 5, 1916, Marshall 3(4).
66. Letter to Macmillan of July 20, 1916, Marshall 4(53).
67. Letter to Macmillan of November 7, 1916, Marshall 4(55).

tardy recognition of the magnitude of the task proposed: but chiefly
by the mental inertia caused by "blood pressure" before I knew that
such a malady existed, & by the extreme slowness of work which I
am told is the only condition under which I can hope to work at all.
So long as I obey orders, I am in excellent health.[68]

At this point Marshall had settled on what was to be the final title:
"Industry and Trade: A study of industrial technique and of business
organization, and of their influences on the conditions of various classes
and nations". By June 1918 he was able to inform Macmillan that "my
Industry and Trade Vol I is now so far advanced that I think I may get it
out in the early Autumn". He added:

> I have postponed as long as possible the suggestion that it should go
> to Press; because the far-reaching changes in public opinion & in the
> activities of Whitehall, which were notable before 1914, are now
> moving at an unprecedented pace. This is one reason for the great
> changes which I have made since the first proofs of the book were set
> up long ago: though the chief reason is to be found in my failure to
> anticipate the extent to which my task would grow on my hands.
> Also things changed in perspective, as time went on; very much as
> the apparent contour of the Alps does when one travels past. Some of
> the things that I have still retained are less appropriate to actual
> conditions than when I wrote them: but a good deal of the book
> happens to bear directly on large issues, which have risen above the
> horizon very recently.[69]

By this time all was written except the last chapter, "which may become
two" and which was to deal with "monopolistic tendencies in Britain in
relation to 'Industrial Reconstruction' ". On this, he was waiting for the
clouds that obscured the implications of the Whitley Report to clear.[70] In
October 1918 he had finalised the last chapter but one "after in effect
rewriting it about four times". He explained that

> The Board of Trade & the Ministry of Reconstruction are at work on
> the same lines as those of that & the last chapters. Blue books, one
> after another are coming out wh. give new information & alter
> relative proportions of the matters I am thinking about: there never
> has been in the whole history of the past so much official & impor-
> tant new work on a particular class of problems. This *embarras des
> richesses* causes delays: but it is lucky that my book was not printed

---

68. Letter to Macmillan of August 25, 1917, Marshall 4(57). Marshall told Dawson, in a
    letter of February 2, 1916, "I have for some years not been allowed to work for more
    than an hour at a time; & the output of an hour diminishes without cease" (Marshall
    3(3)).
69. Letter of June 8, 1918, Marshall 4(60).
70. Letter to Macmillan of June 11, 1918, Marshall 4(59).

off a little while before the flood came. It tends to make some parts of the book rather opportune.[71]

Marshall was somewhat chagrined to discover that Macmillan – once bitten twice shy – was planning to omit "Volume I" from the title of the new book. He feared that purchasers might be disappointed. "For Vol I does not get very far into the study of 'the conditions of various classes,' & does not touch directly on those of various nations".[72] But he was soon persuaded.

> I think you are right about dropping the words "Volume I". There is enough matter in semi-final form for my second volume to be printed, even if I should be unable to do anything more at it. I propose to speak of it in my Preface to this volume as a companion volume: and perhaps to indicate, more or less precisely, that its title will probably be *"Industry and Trade,* a study of the organization of employment, of international trade, and of other influences on the conditions of various classes and nations." I cannot think of any other fitting titles on the backs than "Industry and Trade" in both cases. The companion volume might have ** on its back: & perhaps this might have a single asterisk.[73]

Macmillan agreed to the asterisk but it did not in fact appear on the spine of *Industry and Trade.*[74]

In June 1919 the last corrections had been sent off and Marshall was confessing that "almost every day's newspaper gives me some additional reason for regretting that the book is not already out: but I know that the blame for the delay rests wholly on me".[75] As with all his books, Marshall was anxious that the price be lower than Macmillan proposed "even if it were necessary to forgo all profit *to myself".*[76] He observed

---

71. Draft of letter to Macmillan of October 12, 1918, Marshall 2(21). The final version (same date: Marshall 4(62)) is more subdued. It appears that the eventual final chapter on "The Decline of Exclusive Class Advantages in Industry" formed two chapters at this time.
72. Letter to Macmillan of October 12, 1918, Marshall 4(62). This alludes to the subtitle of *Industry and Trade.*
73. Letter to Macmillan, no date, Marshall 4(72).
74. Letter from Macmillan of October 24, 1918, Marshall 2(22). A corrected copy of the first edition of *Industry and Trade* in the Marshall Library has an asterisk inked on the spine. Marshall did not give up easily!
75. Letter to Macmillan of June 26, 1919, Marshall 4(63).
76. Letter to Macmillan of July 2, 1919, Marshall 4(66). See also Marshall 4(69) of August 26, 1919, where Marshall adds "I know that a higher price might probably have yielded larger net profits; while the benefit, which an author derives from bringing his notions to the attention of an enlarged circle of readers, is not shared equally with his publisher".

I have put so much more work into it than I put into my *Principles,*
that I think it may run to a second edition – though being more
largely concerned with details that change from decade to decade, it
may become superannuated ere long more completely than is likely
to be the case with discussions of general "principles". But I think
that a very high price might militate against its getting such a hold, as
would make its life tolerably long.[77]

Industry and Trade finally appeared in the bookstores in August 1919,
to achieve a considerable success with the public. The preface, dated June
1919, explained that

The present volume is a study of industry and trade: with special
reference to the technical evolution of industry, and its influences on
the conditions of man's life and work. It is designed to be followed
by a companion volume, which is to be occupied with influences on
those conditions exerted by the resources available for employment;
by money and credit; by international trade; and by social endeavour.

(*IT*, p. v)

The relation between the two books was further clarified in Book I,
Chapter 1, paragraph 3:

The present volume as a whole may be regarded as concerned first
with the origins of modern industrial technique and business organization; secondly with the parts played by particular nations in developing them; and thirdly with the problems rising out of that development. [The book progresses increasingly] towards consideration of
the harmonies and discords of interest among the several sections of
a nation, and between each of these sections and the nation as a
whole. . . . In the second Volume these harmonies and discords are to
be studied more closely, in connection with the harmonies and discords of interest among different nations.[78]

A second edition of *Industry and Trade* was already under preparation
in October and appeared in December 1919, only four months after the
first. In April 1920, Marshall was pleased that "the rather rapid sales –
for so stodgy a book – indicated that it was being read by business men",
resolving that "the little strength, which is left to me, must be given to a
forlorn attempt to get its companion volume ready".[79]

77. Letter to Macmillan of May 31, 1919, Marshall 4(65).
78. *IT,* pp. 8–9. He added, "Changes in the purchasing power of money, though not as
    important as appears at first sight, put difficulties in the way of agreements between
    different sections. . . . Therefore it is proposed that the second volume shall include a
    short study of money and credit in relation to industry and trade". For other refer-
    ences to the promised companion volume see *IT,* pp. 7, 12, 13, 381, 393 n.
79. Letter to Macmillan of April 7, 1920, Marshall 4(76).

IV   The Period 1920 to 1924

Marshall reported in October 1919 that "I have already made a little progress with the semi-final draft of the companion Volume".[80] By now, however, his ability to work was sadly diminished. Mrs. Marshall records that

> After I & T came out his health began to give way. He suffered from acidity & nausea (wh. I believe was the beginning of his final illness) & his memory began to fail, tho. he did not know it. On this account I did all I could to hasten the appearance of MOCC especially as Dr. Brown told me in 1921 that his working life was over, & that he was incapable of constructive work.[81]

The eighth edition of the *Principles* appeared in 1920, essentially a reprint of the seventh. The preface, dated October 1920, stated

> *Industry and Trade,* published in 1919, is in effect a continuation of the present volume. A third (on Trade, Finance and the Industrial Future) is far advanced. The three volumes are designed to deal with all the chief problems of economics, so far as the writer's power extends.   (p. xii)

Some manuscript draft title pages of about this period suggest alternative possible titles being considered for the final volume, among them:

1   Industry and Trade Volume II. A study of the organization of modern commerce and finance. And of their influences on the conditions of various classes and nations; with special reference to the economic possibilities of the future.

2   Commerce and Finance: The Economic Future. A companion volume to Industry and Trade.

3   Money, Commerce and Finance: The Economic Future. A study of organization, national and international.

The writing of new material on the scale these titles implied was beyond his power, however. In December 1921 he wrote to Macmillan:

---

80.   Letter to Macmillan of October 20, 1919, Marshall 4(73).
81.   Manuscript note. In 1919 Marshall had written "my strength fails fast; and I have much half-ready material, belonging to my special province, which will need to be cremated on my funeral pyre". Also, "My health is good but my power of work decreases, chiefly because my memory is vanishing. I can't recollect, when I get halfway through a page, what I had meant to drive at". See *Memorials*, p. 377; Scott (1924–5, p. 457). Also see *Memorials*, pp. 64–5, for J. M. Keynes's account of these last years.

I am now in my eightieth year: & I have a huge mass of M.S.S. in
various stages of preparation for printing. They fall in the main
under two heads:—

A   Currency, the Money Market and International Trade
B   Functions of government and Possibilities of Social ad-
    vance

A is practically ready to go to press, & will consist mainly of matter
that has not yet appeared in print.

B will consist mainly of reprints: & while A is passing through the
press, I propose to make arrangements for B's being printed – after
my departure if necessary.[82]

The material under A was now prepared for publication with a speed that
seems remarkable after the long history of delay. By December 1922
Marshall was able to report that "*Money Credit & Commerce* is now out
of my hands", that being the title finally settled on, and the book itself
appeared early in 1923.[83] Much of it must have been written in the period
1903–16, although some portions were of considerably earlier origin.[84]
The preface, dated August 1922, referred to the companion volume promised in the preface to *Industry and Trade,* adding:

But that task is heavy, and achievement has been slow; therefore it
has seemed best to publish without further delay the present volume,
which aims at accomplishing one-half of the task. A little progress
has been made in regard to the second half: and, although old age
presses on me, I am not without hopes that some of the notions,
which I have formed as to the possibilities of social advance, may yet
be published.[85]

His thoughts had been turning to a last volume on economic progress.[86]
Some rough manuscript notes, dating from the early 1920s, suggest the
tenor of his thinking. One gives the following rough outline for the
volume.

---

82. Letter of December 28, 1921, Marshall 4(85).
83. Letter to Macmillan of December 1, 1922, Marshall 4(86). The prefatory note to the
     third edition of *Industry and Trade* (p. ix), dated March 1923, gave the title *Money,
     Trade and Commerce!*
84. For example, portions of Appendix J were written in the 1870s. See *MCC*, p. 330 n.;
     EEW, 2, pp. 114–15. Also, much of Book IV on Fluctuations was a pastiche of
     material written in the 1880s and '90s.
85. *MCC*, p. vi. See also pp. 191, 210, 224, 234, 245, for allusions to a projected further
     volume.
86. J. M. Keynes gives the title *Progress: its Economic Conditions* (*Memorials*, p. 65) but
     the warrant for this is unclear.

Book I   The Nature of E[conomic] P[rogress]

   I   Introductory conditions of E.P.
   II   Various tendencies of E.P.
   III   Interactions among the tendencies of E.P. Note on diagrams in lower type
   IV   Sectional interests in E.P.

Book II   Functions & Resources of Government in regard to E.P.

   Intrody.
   Currency
   Stability of Credit
   Taxes
   I[nternationa] T[rade] competition
   Commercial policy

Book III   The Economic Future

   Influences of E.P. on the quality of life
   Retrospect & prospect
   Ideal & attainable. Poverty.

In another note, Book I was to cover "I the study of economic tendencies, II influences of character on economic progress, III sectional interests in national economic progress". A note of August 1922 shows his thought returning to the kind of issue discussed in his 1907 address on "The Social Possibilities of Economic Chivalry". No further constructive writing was possible, however, and his efforts turned at last towards editing for publication his previously published occasional pieces. In December 1922 he announced "I have no intention of writing anything new: but I am lazily collecting various selected essays, &c. for publication after my death if not before".[87]

Among the titles considered for the collection were, if rough manuscript notes are to be believed,

Economic Progress: Its methods and its possible future. Essays by Alfred Marshall

Essays on Economic Progress and other matters, by Alfred Marshall

A draft for the preface reads

Nearly all the substance of the present essays has been before the public for a good many years. But most of them are to be found only in the Official Reports of Royal Commissions of Inquiry; or else in

87.   Letter to Macmillan of December 1, 1922, Marshall 4(86).

back numbers of the *Economic Journal* or some other periodical. They are collected here in a form that is less difficult of access than their original sources: care being taken to indicate the few substantial differences that exist between the present reissues and their originals.

Before this scheme could be completed Marshall died on July 13, 1924, at age 81. But the posthumous publication of *Memorials of Alfred Marshall* in 1925 and *Official Papers of Alfred Marshall* in 1926 effectively fulfilled his last intentions.[88]

V   Concluding Reflections

What assessment should be made of this tangled history of thwarted aspirations and failed intentions? Clearly the plan initially formulated in 1887 to complete both volumes by 1889 was absurdly optimistic. Volume 1 had already been under way since the early 1880s and took three more years to complete. Given Marshall's careful habits of thought and writing, the earliest date at which Volume 2 could reasonably have been looked for was the mid-1890s. However, little or no progress had been made by 1895.

In retrospect it seems a great pity that these critical years were allowed to slip by with Volume 2 moribund. The Labour Commission was perhaps an unavoidable public-service obligation for the acknowledged leader of British economics, although the education there received was expensive in forgone opportunities. The first two revisions of Volume 1 certainly improved it, but the postponement of substantial revision until Volume 2 had appeared would surely have been the wiser choice.[89]

Marshall's creative powers were probably at their peak in the early 1890s, but Volume 1 had set a standard that it would be difficult to sustain. Volume 2 would inevitably have been somewhat disjointed, as was characteristic of the comprehensive two-volume treatises of the era.[90] Each of the projected Books of Volume 2 would have comprised a semi-independent essay, with only limited interconnections. But this was Marshall's forte. He was at his most engaging and direct in the short focussed treatment of a limited topic, where the baffling subtlety of his thought could be contained and prevented from paralysing him and bewildering the reader with insuperable expositional difficulties. To write a one-

---

88. See particularly the Editor's Preface to *Memorials*.
89. Guillebaud's view is that the third (1895) edition of *Principles* was the best and that the further tinkering tended to spoil it. See *Variorum*, p. 18.
90. For example those of J. S. Nicholson, N. G. Pierson and F. W. Taussig. Indeed, a complete synthesis over the whole range of Marshall's territory is still elusive.

hundred- to one-hundred-fifty-page interim essay on each of the six broad topics initially proposed for Volume 2 would have left Marshall dissatisfied. But his overscrupulousness in the years up to 1900 or so, when he might reasonably have accomplished such a task, resulted in the topics being either never treated systematically or dealt with, often feebly, at a time of waning powers.

Unfortunately, the longer the delay in producing Volume 2 and the greater the expectations Marshall felt compelled to satisfy, the more unacceptable any practicable scheme of completion must have seemed. His ambitions had become virtually self-defeating and drastic reassessment was called for. The necessary catalyst was the writing of the Memorandum on Fiscal Policy in 1903.

The decision to write a tract for the times on the fiscal issue was a reasonable one and Marshall seems for a time to have envisaged this as the first in a series of restricted monographs.[91] But the incubus of the incomplete Volume 2 doomed it, his ambitions becoming, if anything, more not less unmanageable. As *National Industries and Trade* developed, it aspired to present much of the material from the abandoned Volume 2, now intertwined with a realistic discussion of the trends and policy questions affecting the industrial structure and international trade of Britain and other advanced economies. How much easier the latter discussion would have been if only Volume 2 had been completed, even imperfectly, by 1903.

Marshall struggled valiantly with the Hydra into which his new book soon turned. But for the war he might just have succeeded in bringing it out in two or three volumes. The outbreak of war in 1914 was singularly unfortunate for the 72-year-old author. Apart from book-production difficulties, and the distraction of potential readers, the very basis of the discussion of current economic problems was suddenly made obsolete. Much had to be painfully reworked with an eye on post-war reconstruction and the new order to follow. As the nightmare of the war dragged on, and its toll became ever more unthinkable, the uncertainties ramified. In the face of such discouragements and the burdens of age and ill health, Marshall's persistence and selfless concern for his country's future became almost heroic. When *Industry and Trade* at last appeared in 1919 it was a noble book, full of ripened wisdom and deep thought. It was an unsatisfactory book, however, in terms of overall coherence and organisation.[92] An obvious reason for this, made doubly clear by the detailed

---

91. See the letter to Macmillan of April 9, 1907, and the preface to the fifth edition (1907) of *Principles,* both quoted above.
92. See J. M. Keynes's discussion of this, *Memorials,* p. 62.

history, was the book's genesis as only one fragment of an intended larger work.

Money Credit and Commerce was not in any real sense a continuation of *Industry and Trade*. The latter's treatment of monopolistic tendencies in class and sectoral relations was to have been extended to the international level: to the connections between *national* industry and *international* trade and to the conflicts between cosmopolitanism and national or sectional interest. None of these was treated more than tenuously in Marshall's last book, which turned away from the closely woven historical and institutional approach of its immediate predecessor, and reverted to the kind of exposition of general principles that had characterised the *Principles*. If anything, *Money Credit and Commerce* is better seen as a last ditch attempt to rescue material hoarded over many years and offer some kind of continuation, however inadequate, to the *Principles*. That the 80-year-old author should have produced the book at all was a remarkable achievement, but it is a disappointing work and shows the unmistakable signs of sadly waning powers. Little of it had not been said better in earlier essays and evidence, and none of it could not have been written better and more forcefully in a few months in the 1890s. It is a pale ghost of the Volume 2 of the *Principles* outlined in 1887 and promised for 1889.

Of the six books originally proposed for Volume 2 of the *Principles*, Books VII (Foreign Trade) and VIII (Money and Banking) were covered fairly fully in *Money Credit and Commerce,* while Book IX (Trade Fluctuations) was touched upon, but only marginally and inadequately. Books X, XI, XII (Taxation, Collectivism, Aims for the Future) were never treated comprehensively, being addressed only in occasional essays and evidence. The projected last work on *Economic Progress* that was to cover those topics must be dismissed as largely a fiction. A trace of George Eliot's Casaubon clings to Marshall.

Ill luck and poor judgement undoubtedly contributed to Marshall's undue delays,[93] and one must not underestimate the sheer pressure of events on an author dubious about the value of unadorned theory and anxious to adapt his thinking to an ever-changing reality. The "trust" question and the related problems of labour combination, both central issues of *Industry and Trade,* probably gave him the greatest trouble. Monetary questions, international issues, and the growing welfare state also involved important institutional changes. But there was more to it than this. Without indulging too far in popular psychology, one can suspect in his self-defeating propensity to elaboration an unreasonable

93. See *Memorials,* pp. 33–8, for J. M. Keynes's assessment of the sources of these delays. See also Cannan (1924, pp. 260–1).

perfectionism bordering on the pathological. The result was those "growing inhibitions" and consequent, almost insuperable, difficulties of "bringing him to the point of delivering up his mind's possessions" that were remarked by J. M. Keynes (*Memorials,* pp. 53–6). Give Marshall a deadline and he would produce a short vigourous piece, which he would then proceed to grumble at and denigrate (as with the *Memorandum on Fiscal Policy*), but allow him to operate without limitation on time or space and incessant fruitless recasting would inhibit his progress, leading often to a virtual paralysis. As a publisher, Macmillan was remarkably permissive and tolerant, perhaps too much so for Marshall's own good. A less accommodating attitude might well have benefited both parties. As it was, Marshall seems to have had carte blanche to take manuscript to the University Printer in Cambridge and have it set up into "slips" at Macmillan's expense without any oversight from the latter.[94] With no editorial oversight, Marshall was effectively in sole control during the thirty-five or more years after 1887. The story of those years is lamentable in many ways. It was not given to Marshall to realise his great ambition of completing his magnum opus. Nevertheless, by absolute standards there was still great achievement, and this remains so even if one leaves *Principles,* Volume 1, out of account. Few economists can aspire to as much as Marshall achieved after 1890. Only by reference to what might have been can a judgement of failure be rendered.

References

Cannan, E. (1924). "Alfred Marshall 1842–1924", *Economica* 4:257–61.

Coats, A. W. (1968). "Political Economy and the Tariff Reform Campaign of 1903", *Journal of Law and Economics* 11:181–229.

Dawson, W. H., ed. (1917). *After-War Problems.* London: Allen and Unwin; New York: Macmillan.

Dorfman, J. (1941). "The Seligman Correspondence", *Political Science Quarterly* 56:107–240, 270–86, 392–419, 573–99.

Guillebaud, C. W. (1942). "The Evolution of Marshall's *Principles of Economics*", *Economic Journal* 52:330–49.

(1965). "The Marshall–Macmillan Correspondence over the Net Book System," *Economic Journal* 75:518–38.

Keynes, J. M. (1924). "Alfred Marshall 1842–1924", *Economic Journal* 34:311–

---

94. Prior to 1907 Marshall had these slips set up from a single hand-written manuscript in order to have duplicate copies to revise and circulate for comment. This must have been common practice in the days of inexpensive printing and before the typewriter became common. After 1907 he had his manuscript typed and went to the printer at a later stage.

72. Reprinted in *Memorials* (1–65) and in the various editions of Keynes's *Essays in Biography*. Page references are to the *Memorials* version.

McCready, H. W. (1955). "Alfred Marshall and Tariff Reform, 1903: Some Unpublished Letters", *Journal of Political Economy* 63:259–67.

McWilliams [-Tullberg], R. (1969). "The Papers of Alfred Marshall", *History of Economic Thought Newsletter*, No. 3: 9–19. Reprinted in J. C. Wood (ed.), *Alfred Marshall: Critical Assessments*. London: Croom Helm. Vol. 4.

Marshall, A. (1892). *Elements of Economics of Industry, Being the First Volume of Elements of Economics*. London: Macmillan.

  (1898). "Distribution and Exchange", *Economic Journal* 8:37–59. Partly reprinted in *Memorials*, pp. 312–18, *Variorum*, pp. 62–75, 229–33.

  (1907). "The Social Possibilities of Economic Chivalry", *Economic Journal* 17:7–29. Reprinted in *Memorials*, pp. 323–46.

Marshall, A., and Marshall, M. P. (1879). *The Economics of Industry*. London: Macmillan.

Scott, W. R. (1924–5). "Alfred Marshall 1842–1924", *Proceedings of the British Academy* 11:446–57.

Spyers, T. G. (1894). *The Labour Question: An Epitome of the Evidence and the Report of the Royal Commission on Labour*. London: Swann Sonnenschein; New York: Scribner.

Wood, J. C. (1980). "Alfred Marshall and the Tariff-Reform Campaign of 1903", *Journal of Law and Economics* 23:481–95.

  (1982). "Alfred Marshall and the Origins of his 'Memorandum on the Fiscal Policy of International Trade' (1903): Some Unpublished Correspondence", *Australian Economic Papers* 21:261–9.

9

Alfred Marshall and the Theory of Capital

CHRISTOPHER BLISS

I Marshall as a Capital Theorist

When assessing Alfred Marshall's writings on the theory of capital it is important to bear in mind the time in which they originated. Most of us have on our bookshelves the eighth edition of *Principles of Economics,* dated 1920.[1] It is thus easy to imagine this familiar work as contemporaneous with the writings of Irving Fisher and Knut Wicksell.[2]

Guillebaud (1942) makes clear, however, and Keynes (1975) and Whitaker (1975) confirm, that Marshall had completed his development of the theory of interest and profit in all its essentials well in advance of the publication of the first edition of the *Principles* in 1890. The changes in subsequent editions involve no new insight or fundamental change of view. Shove asserts "He began his work in 1867–8 before Jevons' treatise or Menger's had appeared" (1942, pp. 402).

Is it fair to Marshall's capital theory, therefore, to compare it, perhaps unfavourably in certain respects, with the contributions of Jevons and the Austrians, let alone Fisher or Wicksell? This question is not best answered by a forensic analysis of intellectual priorities and influences. Publication dates can be misleading. For example, the *Principles,* the

---

1. All references to Marshall's *Principles of Economics* will be to the 8th edition, to be referred to as *Principles.*
2. The original Swedish edition of Wicksell (1951) dates from 1911. Fisher (1961) was first published in 1930, but it is a rewrite of *The Rate of Interest,* published in 1907, a work with which Marshall was certainly familiar.

outcome of a long rumination, as Shove reminds us, would be counted by the Chinese, who measure age from the time of conception, as having attained much more than the one hundred years allowed it by the Western standard.

In addition, unless a writer leaves a clue by way of citation, influences are uncertain and even citation can be indecisive. How deeply, for example, had Marshall studied the positive contribution of Böhm-Bawerk (excluding the latter's criticisms of earlier writers)? Marshall's text does not answer this question. From Gårdlund's account (1958) of the meeting between Marshall and Wicksell it seems that Marshall had not devoted much time to Böhm-Bawerk's theory.[3]

There are three levels of originality. The analysis of sources and influences establishes what Schumpeter calls *subjective originality*.[4] In Schumpeter's classification those who make the break-through show *objective originality*. Perhaps we should reserve subjective originality for those who unknowingly repeat another's finding. That leaves us with a third type, *unnecessary originality* or "re-inventing the wheel" in popular parlance. An important sub-species of the last is Myrdal's *unnecessary Anglo-Saxon originality*. Myrdal's barbed terminology was aimed at Keynes, but a similar charge can sometimes be directed at Marshall.

Marshall's work on capital can legitimately be compared with the contributions of the great writers who were his predecessors and his contemporaries, especially Böhm-Bawerk, Jevons, and Walras, whose work he knew, to a certain extent at least. Such comparisons can, however, be difficult and can include some extreme positions, such as that of Keynes: "As a scientist he was, within his own field, the greatest in the world for one hundred years" (1975, pp. 173). Moreover they raise the serious issue of whether Marshall was sufficiently generous in his acknowledgements to others.

One difficulty is that capital theory in this period and for many neoclassical writers was not accorded the leading role we might now believe appropriate. Marshall's capital theory, in particular, is embedded in his overall model of the economic system.[5] Though similar in many respects to models proposed by other neoclassical writers, Marshall's model is unique in approach and style. For he, more than others, viewed the economic system from the perspective of its component parts, looking at

---

3. Even so, the end of the footnote to p. 583 of the *Principles* makes the valid point that Böhm-Bawerk's concentration on roundabout methods is somewhat misplaced.
4. Schumpeter (1954, p. 838).
5. In comparing Marshall on capital and interest with Böhm-Bawerk and Fisher on the same subject bear in mind that Marshall's *Principles* was a general treatise on economics, while Böhm-Bawerk and Fisher published treatises on capital and interest.

the economy from inside the firm or the household, rather than from above. This was his partial method.

Marshall well understood that the analyses of the behaviour of component parts his partial method revealed must be welded together to form a system of equations describing the whole economy. As a trained physicist he could not fail to notice this. Yet the components of the economy, especially the individual firm, continued to interest him more than the whole. This, as much as his vanity, may well explain why he was grudging in his acknowledgement of writers whose interests were the reverse of his own.

The method with which Marshall approached economic theory, while superbly adapted to illuminating certain questions, was not well designed to deal with some of the persistent and difficult issues characteristic of capital theory. These issues involve precisely the question of how the mutual equilibrium of many capital-providing and capital-using units works itself out, and what happens when it is disturbed. This is the "general equilibrium" question par excellence, and its neglect is one reason why Schumpeter, in his great *History of Economic Analysis*, criticises Marshall sharply.

Schumpeter (1954) on Marshall is extremely interesting, and all that he wrote should be noted if his view is to be taken as more than simply a negative evaluation. Schumpeter's admiration for Marshall's vision of the capitalist system and for his deep understanding of how the modern business functions is clear. Note also the uninhibited praise when Marshall's work is said to "point the way forward" (1954, p. 840). The admiration is tempered with disapproval, however, perhaps because Marshall relegated the general equilibrium problem, for Schumpeter the central insight of modern economic theory, to a meanly housed note (Note XXI) at the back of the *Principles,* immediately following a disparaging discussion of the use of the mathematical method in economics. That alone would have been enough to annoy Schumpeter, but there was more. Marshall's "unbelievably insular" (1954, p. 835) discussion of the history of economics could not fail to irritate the unfailingly broad-minded Schumpeter.

It is important to view Marshall's contribution from an undistorted perspective. Some of Schumpeter's negative evaluation may be a reaction, perhaps an over-reaction, to a tendency of his disciples and of the man himself to oversell his undoubted achievements. The following passage belittling Marshall's originality reads like a prosecution lawyer making the best he can of a less than commanding case:

> A man such as Marshall, who was trained in mathematics and physics and to whom the concept of limits and hence the formal part of

the marginal principle would be as familiar as would be his breakfast bacon, need only have allowed his mind to play on Mill's loose statements and to work out their exact model (system of equations) in order to arrive at a point where the purely theoretical parts of the *Principles* came in sight.   (1954, p. 838)

If, from a modern perspective, Marshall's capital theory appears to be incomplete and excessively informal, perhaps it is an area in which his method is at its least effective. Why did Marshall not do better in this area? Certainly not because he lacked the ability or the background. Marshall demonstrated clearly he could undertake the examination of a simple but formal general equilibrium model. His failure to follow through can only be explained, therefore, by a positive distaste for the exercise.

In a view that became a tradition, Marshall felt that the simple formal models left too much out to be of interest. It was not that a finished, but simple, capital model would have been finished that put him off; it was its simplicity he would have hated. There is at times an almost neurotic fastidiousness about Marshall's attitude to theory:

> Further all these mutual influences take time to work themselves out, and, as a rule, no two influences move at equal pace. In this world therefore every plain and simple doctrine as to the relations between cost of production, demand and value is necessarily false: and the greater the appearance of lucidity which is given to it by skilful exposition, the more mischievous it is. A man is likely to be a better economist if he trusts to his common sense, and practical instincts, than if he professes to study the theory of value and is resolved to find it easy.   (*Principles*, p. 368)

This voice was faithfully echoed by some who thought they had "renounced allegiance"[6] to Marshall, notably John Maynard Keynes and Joan Robinson.

The history of economic thought, like the history of other battles, is written by the winners, and Marshall's allegiance was not to the victorious side. Nor did it deserve to be. Though a sense of the subtlety and complexity of reality, and of the modern business, is one of the glories of the *Principles*, what Marshall achieved with his partial method can be completely encapsulated in simple models. Why should the same not be true of answers to the great issues of general equilibrium capital theory?

Marshall's claim for the superior efficacy of a treatment of economic reality uncompromised by crude simplification is somewhat bogus, first, because the master was unable to practise the rule. For example, the

6. Schumpeter (1954, p. 833).

theory of the short and the long period, one of the strong points of Marshall's theory, can stand up very well without the assistance of Marshall's undoubtedly rich and subtle view of the firm. Second, and more important, his purist approach to economic theory, far from always cutting deeper, as one might tend to suppose, sometimes resulted in a rather superficial treatment of a deep problem. Nowhere is this more clearly demonstrated than with Marshall's capital theory, as a comparison with Böhm-Bawerk's work with its inferior technique, makes abundantly clear.

II   What Was Marshall's Theory of Capital?

Our question should allow of a concise answer, supported by page references to the *Principles*. That it does not is typical of Marshall. His gems are seldom left lying around. The reader interested in a precise understanding has to do some digging. For the capital theory he has to dig deeply and even then without complete success.

How deeply Marshall expected his readers to dig is unclear. Reading the *Principles* can resemble nothing so much as hearing a great romantic symphony for the first time. One emerges humming some unforgettable tunes, pleasantly unencumbered with the weight of a musicological reduction of the work. Marshall, who hoped that ordinary readers would enjoy the *Principles,* might even have liked to be considered a Brahms of economics. However, where capital theory is concerned his symphonic contribution is strong on good melodies and loose and incomplete with regard to structure.

In other regions of the analysis there are a toughness and a rigour which can be discerned even after the flow and ease of the text have skillfully disguised it. This is what Schumpeter had in mind when he referred to the "analytic skeleton under the smooth skin and all the flesh" (1954, p. 836). However, the analytic skeleton of Marshall's capital theory is immature, at the least, if it is not malformed.

It is in Chapter 3 of Book V that we first encounter an analytic view of capital. The discussion is concerned with the supply price of a good, and it is explained that this price has to be paid "in order to call forth an adequate supply of the *efforts and waitings* [my italics] that are required for making it" (*Principles*, p. 339). The theme of efforts and waitings recurs several times. This model, according to which capital is waiting, and interest is the reward of waiting, is fairly familiar. We find versions of it in Smith, Ricardo, and Mill. Whether it is called an *abstinence* theory or an *impatience* theory or a *waiting* theory is unimportant. Moreover, in the case of Mill we find the waiting of the capitalist combined with the disutility of the worker's effort, exactly as in Marshall's account. The source of the idea is plain.

This theory tarnished its reputation by being seen in the company of ideologues for capitalism, but it is quite a good way of viewing the process of capital investment, an opinion I shall defend below. By itself, however, it is incomplete. In particular, it fails to explain the following points:

1 Why does a positive market valuation attach to "waiting"?

2 What is the relationship between waiting, which implies more lengthy processes, and capital deepening, in the form of more resources or effort applied to a process of given length?

3 How can waiting as a force acting on the rate of interest be reconciled with other forces acting on the same, notably the productivity of investment?

On many of these points Marshall's thoughts can be discerned from passages that follow later, but the matter is disposed of in an unorganized and piecemeal fashion that fails to make the grand structure clear. This is a pity, because Marshall, using only the equipment he displays elsewhere in the *Principles*, could have shown the whole field in a clear light.

Consider the illustration of Book V, Chapter 4: "the case of a man who builds a house for himself on land, and of materials, which nature supplies gratis; and who makes his implements as he goes, the labour of making them being counted as part of the labour of building the house" (*Principles*, p. 351).

What a neat model to examine, and how perfectly chosen for Marshall's method for here the individual agent confronts nature on his own, and his equilibrium will be the general equilibrium. The model is thus ill suited to demonstrate the solution to the general capital theoretic problem, but that is not my objection to Marshall's treatment. Even this elegant little model is not fully and correctly worked out. Two lines of differential calculus would have done it; but the one-time Second Wrangler[7] eschews even a diagrammatic treatment, and the words that he offers his readers do not equate with what a formal analysis of the model shows.

To continue the quotation:

> He would have to estimate the efforts required for building on any proposed plan; and to allow almost instinctively an amount increas-

---

7. For an explanation of the apparent paradox that Marshall, ranked second below the future Lord Rayleigh in the Cambridge Mathematical Tripos, showed a lack of real flair for mathematics, see Whitaker (1975), p. 5.

ing in geometrical proportion (a sort of compound interest) for the period that would elapse between each effort and the time when the house would be ready for his use. The utility of the house to him when finished would have to compensate him not only for the efforts, but for the waitings.

When this illustration is translated to a formal model the result can be quite complicated. The words seem to imply that each effort is like a withdrawal from a loan account, subsequently increased by compound interest until the house is ready. Marshall directs the reader to Note XIII of the Mathematical Appendix, where the problem receives a more formal treatment, and the expressions, although not complicated, do involve integrals of discounted disutilities of effort and of the benefits of the house. Marshall makes nothing of these expressions, although a modern student would start looking for maximum conditions at once. It appears that Marshall chanced upon a formulation he considered too elaborate to be worth developing.

Let us assume that the utility depends only on the total effort expended on the house's construction, denoted X, and that this utility is discounted at an exponential rate v for the total time that elapses until the house is ready, denoted T. We thus effectively ignore the influence of the timing of effort on final utility, a simpler formulation than that of Note XIII, but not obviously wrong.[8] Then if the house builder maximizes the difference between his discounted utility and the cost of his efforts, assumed linear in the effort, the problem becomes:

$$\text{Max} \quad U(X,T)e^{-vT} - X \tag{9.1}$$

Utility increases with both X and T, as more effort and more time both produce a better house.

Maximizing (9.1) by choice of X and T yields two conditions:

$$X: \quad U_X e^{-vT} - 1 = 0 \tag{9.2}$$

$$T: \quad -vU(X,T) + U_T = 0 \tag{9.3}$$

where subscripts denote partial derivatives. Rearranging these conditions yields:

$$v = \log(U_X)/T \tag{9.4}$$

$$v = U_T/U(X,T) \tag{9.5}$$

where log denotes logarithms with base e.

8. Why should the disutility of fitting an awkward lock to the front door be less if the job is done as the final act of completing the house?

In this simple formulation v, the house builder's rate of impatience, has been treated as a constant. More complex expressions result if it varies with T, as Marshall's verbal presentation sometimes suggests, but the basic principles are the same. Both conditions give values which must be equated to v. The second of the two conditions is the more familiar, for it is essentially Wicksell's "tree-cutting" rule (Wicksell, 1951, Vol. 1, pp. 172–84). The first condition looks mysterious, but it follows directly from (9.2) and has a plain meaning, for (9.2) says that the discounted value of the additional utility from extra effort should equal the present cost of that effort, which is 1 in this simple model.

Two interesting points emerge from this little exercise. First, we see some of the cost of Marshall's excessive informality. His example is excellent and characteristically comprises more than he makes available to the reader. The second point is less immediate but more important. The two equilibrium conditions show how the rate of interest may be equated simultaneously with the marginal productivity of capital (X in this case) and with the marginal productivity of waiting (T in this case). There is no conflict between the two versions of capital theory (the standard neoclassical and the Austrian).

Note that we have not derived a "the-rate-of-interest-is-equal-to-the-marginal-product-of-capital" condition, but rather a cost-benefit evaluation of the laying down of a little more capital. However, this last is the fundamental insight. When T is zero and U_X is a perpetual flow with present value U_X/v, then (9.2) reduces to $U_X = v$, and the familiar condition is seen to be a special case of (9.2).

Central to Marshall's theory of the rate of interest, in the sense of his explanation for the tendency of the rate of interest to be positive, is an impatience theory. Put simply, this says that the rate of interest tends to be positive because wealth holders value present consumptions more highly than future consumptions, *ceteris paribus*, so that were the rate of interest ever to reach zero, wealth would be consumed. Marshall's formulation of the impatience theory of interest is not so crude as my formulation suggests, and goes further than the house-builder model. Repeated reference to the *principle of substitution*, the description of how the "alert business man" (1920, p. 359) plans his investment project, and the idea of the general accumulation of costs and the discounting of benefits (1920, p. 353) all point the way to a richer general equilibrium model of capital, investment, and saving. Yet we never discover that model in the *Principles*; it is hinted at but is always just out of reach.

The style of Marshall's approach to capital theory is extraordinary. It is as if the more he entered a complex and difficult corner of economic theory, the more he felt the need to explain that he was only laying out what everyone already knew. A single page of the *Principles*, p. 581, typifies this style. The page heading is ECONOMIC DOCTRINE INTERPRETS COM-MON EXPERIENCE.There is repeated reference to what "everyone" knows or is aware of. One of the things that everyone knows is

> that few, even among the Anglo-Saxon and other steadfast and self-disciplined races, care to save a large part of their incomes; and that many openings have been made for the use of capital in recent times by the progress of discovery and the opening up of new countries: and thus everyone understands generally the causes which have kept the supply of accumulated wealth so small relatively to the demand for its use, that use is on the balance a source of gain, and can therefore require a payment when loaned. Everyone is aware that the accumulation of wealth is held in check, and the rate of interest so far sustained, by the preference which the great mass of humanity have for present over deferred gratifications, or, in other words by their unwillingness to "wait".

The footnote to the page reads

> That the supply of capital is held back by the *prospectiveness* of its uses, and men's unreadiness to look forward, while the demand for it comes from its *productiveness*, in the broadest sense of the term, is indicated in II.iv.

In view of the footnote, of extensive passages elsewhere, and because the text cited in the first quotation runs on to stress the need for econom-ics to "make an organic whole" out of familiar truths, and then to sketch a picture of a different world in which people would weight the future more heavily, it is not entirely correct to characterize Marshall's theory as simply an "impatience" theory. What the reader is invited to take away is a view of two blades of a pair of scissors cutting, impatience on one side and productivity on the other.

Perhaps so, but the borrowing of Marshall's blades-of-the-scissors anal-ogy is deliberate. In fact Marshall used that analogy, not in connection with capital theory, but in the context of the determination of price when cost and demand might both be influential. Its context is a claim that, in the long run, cost of production is the determining influence on price. The scissors analogy allows a formal concession to simultaneity for a model which has in fact been decomposed into a one-equation system. When Marshall's readers are told that two blades cut the paper they are also reminded which blade to focus on. While they are clearly told that two forces act on the rate of interest, they are also repeatedly invited to focus on the impatience blade.

The blades of the scissors are supply and demand curves intersecting in a plane figure on which a point is a combination of a value of the price variable and a value of the quantity variable. For the capital model one might imagine a similar figure with the rate of interest on one axis and "waiting" on the other. That Marshall does not go that way, which would be more in the spirit of Böhm-Bawerk or Fisher, is a good indication of how he took more than one view of the capital problem, without, however, reconciling his different approaches.

Marshall does have a supply and demand figure in mind, with the rate of interest on the vertical axis. We meet it on page 534 of the *Principles*, a model of long-run equilibrium.[9] It measures neither effort nor waiting on the horizontal axis, however, but a quantity of capital. What is a quantity of capital a quantity of? For some, his failure to elucidate this point is the vital lacuna of Marshall's capital theory, but although Marshall's treatment is unfinished, unclear, and even inconsistent, this is the area to which he contributed what may be judged, where capital theory is concerned, his best single idea. I refer to the concept of free, or floating, capital.

III   Free or Floating Capital

> That which is rightly regarded as interest on "free" or "floating" capital, or on new investments of capital, is more properly treated as a sort of rent – a *Quasi-rent* – on old investments of capital.
> (*Principles*, p. viii, repeated p. 412)

Contrary to what has been asserted, everything is not "in Marshall". However, there is more than may be apparent. There are some wonderful ideas that are never clearly and fully developed and it would be difficult to find a better instance of this than Marshall's concept of what we shall call, for convenience, floating capital. The distinction between floating capital and specific collections of capital goods, central to the modern theory of capital, has often emerged in controversies about the measurement of capital.

We have seen above that Marshall took for granted some unspecified natural aggregation of capitals. He was not even uncomfortable with the idea. We always know when Marshall feels uncertain of his position: a flood of qualifications and footnotes results. However, in the case of an unexplained quantity of capital, Marshall gives no indication that he is embarrassed. He puts the point simply and straightforwardly:

9.   The marginal note reads: "The rate of interest is determined in the long run by the two sets of forces of supply and demand respectively".

> But if we are considering the whole world, or even the whole of a large country as one market for capital, we cannot regard the aggregate supply of it as altered quickly and to a considerable extent by a change in the rate of interest. For the general fund of capital is the product of labour and waiting; and the extra work, and the extra waiting, to which a rise in the rate of interest would act as an incentive, would not quickly amount to much as compared with the work and waiting of which the total existing stock of capital is the result.   (*Principles*, p. 534)

Therefore, we are told, an extensive increase in the demand for capital will be met for a time not by an increase in supply but by a rise in the rate of interest. This can be dismissed not unreasonably as so much nonsense. Businessmen whose demand for capital has increased want more of specific machines and working capital. They would not know what to do with Marshall's "extra work and extra waiting." Moreover, insofar as a demand–supply equilibrium must emerge for what exists at the moment when the – presumably unanticipated – shift in demand takes place, the natural price variables to accommodate that are the prices of various capital goods, not the rate of interest, although both may play a part. Marshall has concluded otherwise, first, because he has identified a shift in the demand for capital with an increased demand for his own elusive work and waiting, and second, because he sees the rate of interest as the price of capital.

The long-run character of the model may partially justify this but how is left unexplained. Imagine, for example, that the increase in the demand for capital is quite transitory. A war is about to be fought. Victory will soon result but there is a huge increase in the demand for capital goods of all kinds to produce that outcome.[10] After the war, demand will return to its previous levels.

Insofar as the demand and supply of capital goods are arranged through the price system, we can discuss the impact on prices. It is not immediately obvious why there should be any effect on the rate of interest. It is too late to borrow funds to build new capital goods for the war. However, the prices of the services of individual capital goods must shoot up just for the short period. How can this happen? The argument must take us beyond Marshall and into a somewhat technical discussion of the kind that he disliked. As it may have interest in its own right, however, we consider it briefly.

10. We are not talking of money or nominal prices and a fixed stock of money. This is a real model. Hence we assume that this war, unlike real wars, is highly capital intensive. The shock it entails involves a short-run shift of demand away from labour towards various capital goods.

The basic point is quite simple. The demand and supply for capital goods are a demand for and a supply of their services. Therefore the shock of the war must imply an upward jump in the rentals of various capital goods. The post-shock structure of rentals need not concern us. It depends on the detail of the model, on possibilities for substitution in demand, and so forth. Generally speaking, however, rentals must jump up and later return to their previous values. Take a single capital good for the sake of simplicity. Even then we cannot work out what must happen by concentrating on the market for the services of that good by itself.

We can, however, solve our problem by combining an additional simplifying assumption with the basic consideration of how a perfectly foreseen price has to behave. Let the outbreak of the war be entirely unforeseen, on the one hand, and its end be perfectly foreseen on the other. Also let the war be short enough, and cheap enough in terms of capital destroyed, to leave the demand and supply of capital goods in the future largely unchanged. Assume that the effect on the real rate of interest during the war may be neglected. Then the price of the capital good must carry all the burden of war-time adjustment.[11]

It must do more than that. The price of a capital good has to conform to three conditions:

1   The price must equal the marginal cost of producing an extra unit.

2   The price must be a continuous function of time.

3   The price and the time rate of change of that price must be such that the yield on the good, taking account of the flow of rent to a unit, will be equal to the rate of interest.

The reason for the first condition is plain. It has no considerable implication for our example, as the supply price of the capital good will increase sharply in the short run when production is boosted. We can imagine the factories roaring through the night during the war to make more of the capital good and slightly augmenting the stock as a result. The second condition is a necessary requirement of foreseen, because calculable, price movements. Were the price of the capital good to jump up or down, selling it and repurchasing it a moment later, or buying just before the jump would be profitable.[12]

The third condition gives us a differential equation in the price of the

11.   We are not claiming that this is exactly what will happen. It is just an illustrative possibility.
12.   We are ignoring transactions costs. Also, our assumption of a constant rate of interest rules out an unbounded blip in its value.

capital good. To examine it, denote the price by p, the flow of rent to the good by q and the rate of interest by r. The rate of interest is constant throughout; q leaps up when the war commences and returns to its steady state, or lower, value when the war ends. Denote the steady-state value of q by q^- and the war-time value by q^+.

The third condition may now be applied to the steady state, the pre-war status to which the economy will return after the war. In general we must have:

$$r = (q + dp/dt)/p \qquad (9.6)$$

However, in the original steady state $dp/dt = 0$ and $q = q^-$; so (9.6) becomes:

$$0 = rp - q^- \qquad \text{or} \qquad p = q^-/r \qquad (9.7)$$

When war breaks out a new differential equation in p takes over:

$$dp/dt = rp - q^+ \qquad (9.8)$$

The new relation will hold throughout the war at the end of which p must have arrived at its steady-state value of q^-/r.

The solution to (9.8) is

$$p = q^+/r + C_0 e^{rt} \qquad (9.9)$$

where C_0 is a constant. Let the war last for a time T. Then to satisfy the end condition according to which p will return to its long-run value when time T has elapsed, we must have:

$$q^+/r + C_0 e^{rT} = q^-/r \qquad (9.10)$$

which gives an expression for C_0 which may be substituted back into (9.9) to obtain the solution of the time path of p:

$$p = \{q^+(1 - e^{-r(T-t)}) + q^- e^{-r(T-t)}\}/r \qquad (9.11)$$

a solution which applies for values of t from 0 to T. As $e^{-r(T-t)}$ lies between 0 and 1, (9.11) indicates the price of the capital good is a convex combination of the pre-war and post-war steady-state value q^-/r and the value that would obtain in a steady state with permanent war-time demand, that is q^+/r. The weighting factor of the convex combination is $e^{-r(T-t)}$ and it ranges from e^{-rT} initially up to 1.

When $t = 0$, that is at the moment the war is announced, p must jump to $\{q^+(1 - e^{-rT}) + q^- e^{-rT}\}/r$. Then it falls through time as the weight attaching to the lower value q^-/r rises with time until eventually all the weight is on the long-run steady-state value. The price subsequently remains at q^-/r until such time as the system receives another shock. Substituting the solution for p back into (9.8), we see that the time rate of change of the price is given by

$$dp/dt = rp - q^+ = q^- e^{-r(T-t)} - q^+ e^{-r(T-t)} \qquad (9.12)$$

which is equal to $q^- - q^+$ when $t = T$. It follows that the time derivative of the price is negative at (strictly just before) the end of the war and must become zero after the war. Thus there is a discontinuity of the time rate of change of the price – it stops falling abruptly – although, after its initial leap, the price itself is a continuous function of time.

In his discussion of the effect of an increased demand for capital, Marshall has in mind a longer period than our example of a quick war, but not long enough for large changes in the stock of capital. It is similar to his short period. Our analysis above is far from Marshall in content. By assuming r to be constant we are, it is true, doing something like partial analysis. However, an explicit dynamic model is not the sort of tool that Marshall reached out for. Even so, although the model corrects a flaw in Marshall's argument, by pointing out that prices of capital goods ration capital, and not just the rate of interest, it is thoroughly Marshallian in spirit.

During the war period the capital good earns a surplus over its normal return, equal to $q^+ - q^-$. The expectation of a flow of q^- was sufficient to bring the good into existence. The surplus $q^+ - q^-$ is a *quasi-rent*. As Marshall puts it.

> So long as capital is "free", and the sum of money or general purchasing power over which it gives command is known, the net money income, expected to be derived from it, can be represented at once as bearing a given ratio (four or five or ten per cent) to that sum. But when the free capital has been invested in a particular thing, its money value cannot as a rule be ascertained except by capitalizing the net income which it will yield: and therefore the causes which govern it are likely to be akin in a greater or less degree to those which govern rents.
>
> (*Principles*, p. 412)

The reader who has understood this passage already comprehends what the model of capital price adjustment has to teach. Thus Marshall, despite the informality of his approach, reached far. Important questions, however, not only remain unanswered, but are not even posed. Among them is an issue that has continued to dog capital theory in modern times. If old investments of capital are a collection of capital goods earning scarcity rents, like various grades of land, what precisely is the "floating capital" – so far uncommitted – which will earn the general rate of interest, and how is its quantity measured? One of the most important things to understand about Marshall's approach to capital theory is that he simply did not see how important and difficult this question might be.

IV   The "Reward for Waiting"

> And similarly if a person expects, not to use his wealth himself, but to let it out on interest, the higher the rate of interest the higher his reward for saving. If the rate of interest on sound investments is 4 per cent., and he gives up £100 worth of enjoyment now, he may expect an annuity of £4 worth of enjoyment; but he can expect only £3 worth, if the rate is 3 per cent.   (*Principles*, p. 234)

The running head of the chapter from which the above quotation is taken reads GROWTH OF WEALTH THE REWARD OF WAITING. That there is something unmistakably nauseating in the suggestion that the rich be "rewarded" for postponing their consumption was recognized by Marshall. Despite that recognition, he insisted on the importance of waiting as a concept, indicating the importance he attached to it as an analytical tool.

In Marshall's usage the term "reward" is a code word. It indicates compensation for something onerous and also indicates the character of what is being paid for. When the two sides of a capital market meet they can conveniently be seen as trading the same service. It is as if, in a dramatization of the transactions, the chorus of the sellers (lenders) of capital were to chant: "It hurts us to postpone; it is a costly thing to do; and we look for a compensation in the interest that we can earn."

This is clear, as is the manner in which its ideological overtones are suspect. It is interesting to note, however, that if lenders are selling waiting, then borrowers are buying it. From this idea comes straight economic analysis of the most illuminating kind. If the borrowers are buying time, then time is money in the specific sense that the fact of being allowed more time is something with a positive real product.

This last insight can too readily be commandeered by an Austrian perspective, and more time identified with a longer period of production. To allow that, however, is to permit the vital and general insight to slip away. The true lesson is that the rate of interest is the reward for waiting because *it is the relative price of earlier and later delivery*. It is the reward for waiting in precisely the same sense that a premium for high protein wheat is a reward for high protein.

There can be little doubt that Marshall understood a large part of this. There can be even less doubt that Irving Fisher understood it, and his way of looking at capital, in terms of the various consumption streams that are possible, best shows the rate of interest in its base relative price aspect. Finally, Solow understood the same idea arguing, in his well known (1963) De Vries lecture, that the rate of return to saving was an illuminating way of looking at capital theory and a possible way round the quagmires of capital measurement.

In Bliss (1975, Chapter 10) I criticised Solow's way of formulating his idea, but in a sense it was his timidity to which I was objecting. In pointing out that equality of a single rate of return with the rate of interest was the wrong objective, I argued that there may be many waitings for different periods, and many relative prices that will support these waitings. (This came from the discrete linear production models which were receiving a great deal of attention at the time.) The conclusion that relative prices of presents and futures (the plurals are required here) are what matter was perfectly robust even to models with paradoxical properties.

V Beyond Marshall

To look at Marshall's contribution to economics from the point of view of the theory of capital is akin to judging the British people from a gastronomic point of view. Capital theory, which to Marshall meant the theory of interest and profits, may not show him at his best. Much original and penetrating thought awaits the reader of the *Principles*. Two items in particular deserve our attention here, since Marshall might have made more use of their implications for capital theory, as later writers did. I refer to the famous theory of long- and short-period analysis of Book V, Chapter 5, and to the concept of a steady state equilibrium growth path, which, while not explicit in Marshall's treatment of equilibrium, is outlined on pages 368 to 369 of the *Principles*.

Generally speaking, Marshall's influence on Hicks was relatively weak, especially for an English economist of the time.[13] However, Hicks applied the period analysis to what is in effect capital theory, and the acknowledgement of Marshall's influence is explicit (Hicks, 1939, pp. 119–23). The notion of a *temporary equilibrium* powerfully evokes Marshall's analysis. Yet we see something different – indeed more Walrasian – than we find in Marshall. Marshall's short-period equilibrium has an imperfectly adjusted capital stock. Hicks's temporary equilibrium lacks access to the ideal forward markets that would make it a full intertemporal equilibrium.

---

13. For a brief discussion of the reasons why, see Bliss (1987).

To remove the constraint that makes Marshall's short-period equilibrium short is to allow it to return any item of its capital stock to the shop and obtain a full refund in terms of floating capital. The result is a balanced equilibrium, although if there is to be capital deepening, for instance, it may not have a stationary future. To remove the constraint that makes Hicks's temporary equilibrium temporary is to allow it to open up futures markets that will at once make possible an intertemporal general equilibrium, which, however, may not be stationary over time.

The notion of a steady state equilibrium growth path is not unique to Marshall (the name of Marx springs to mind). It is difficult, however, to find another writer at such an early date who is as explicit as Marshall in the identification of a growing economy and long-run equilibrium. Because Marshall's discussion is so distinctive, its influence in Robinson (1956, p. 99) is unmistakable. Marshall's long-run growing equilibrium is Joan Robinson's *Golden Age*.

Though Joan Robinson was deeply influenced by Marshall, she did not like to be reminded of the fact, and tried to show that the capital theory she learned from Marshall was fatally flawed. One of the chief problems for the anti-Neoclassical school that eventually arose at Cambridge is that it consisted of two wings, not easily reconcilable. One, inspired by Joan Robinson, fought the Marshallians, to a great extent with their own weapons. Another, inspired by Piero Sraffa, fought various neoclassical writers with weapons designed by Marx.

Joan Robinson reacted equally against Marx and Marshall. Her *Essay on Marxian Economics* (1966), first published in 1942, records her response to Marxism, which is one of sympathy moderated by distaste and incomprehension, and though the title indicates this work is about Marx, as much space and energy are allocated to dissecting orthodoxy and developing the position she argued for, and continued to develop, for the rest of her life. Joan Robinson's chief objection to Marshall is that his system is not "closed". Thus she argued in her (1966) essay, and thus she continued to argue in later work. In her *Economic Heresies* she says of the growth model which she recognizes as implicit in the *Principles* "there is nothing in the story to say what determines the normal rate of profit" (1971, pp. 13–14).

Is this fair to Marshall? In a way it is wildly unfair, yet it is an unfairness that Marshall seemed to court. Probably no answer that an apologist for Marshall could offer would have satisfied Joan Robinson, for it seemed to be a simple and unique explanatory factor to fix the rate of profit that she found to be missing. Marshall's plain message is that the rate-of-profit paper is cut by scissors that are at least double bladed. It was a bad habit of the Classical writers to look for the single cause of a thing and Marshall's vision had reached beyond that.

Was it his overwhelming wish to be read by ordinary men, or was it a residue of a Classical view, that led Marshall so frequently to compromise his essential vision? One can cite a dozen passages and footnotes that unquestionably show Marshall's understanding of simultaneous determination. Yet there are nearly as many passages in which he "waves his hands" in the direction of a one-blade view. The simple model that tempted Marshall was a crude impatience model. It could never satisfy his refined analytical sense, but it may have had an irresistible appeal to his ever assertive moralism.

Where it concerned saving and investing, Marshall's moralism is more than just sanctimoniousness. There is an analytical core to it, and a real, if exaggerated, understanding of how the fortunes of businessmen and their heirs worked themselves out in an age when capitalism was more of a Snakes and Ladders game than it is today. When Marshall wrote the following:

> It used commonly to be said in England that the families of a rich man and his coachman would probably change places within three generations. It is true that this was partly due to the wild extravagance common among young heirs at that time, and partly to the difficulty of finding secure investments for their capital. The stability of the wealthy classes of England has been promoted almost as much by the spread of sobriety and education as by the growth of methods of investment,   (*Principles*, p. 621 n.)

he may have been simply passing an accurate judgment on the Victorian Age.

References

Bliss, C. (1975). *Capital Theory and the Distribution of Income*. Amsterdam: North-Holland.

   (1987). "J. R. Hicks". In J. Eatwell, M. Milgate, and P. Newman (eds.), *The New Palgrave: A Dictionary of Economics*. London: Macmillan.

Fisher, I. (1961). *The Theory of Interest*. Reprinted, New York: Kelley. (First published 1930.)

Gårdlund, T. W. (1958). *The Life of Knut Wicksell*. Translated from the Swedish by Nancy Adler. Stockholm: Almqvist and Wiksell.

Guillebaud, C. W. (1942). "The Evolution of Marshall's *Principles of Economics*", *Economic Journal* 52:330–49.

Hicks, J. R. (1939). *Value and Capital*. Oxford: Clarendon.

Keynes, J. M. (1972). "Alfred Marshall", Chapter 14 of *Essays in Biography,* Volume 10 of *The Collected Writings of John Maynard Keynes.* London: Macmillan. First published 1924. Also in *Memorials,* 1–65.

Robinson, J. V. (1956). *The Accumulation of Capital.* London: Macmillan.

(1966). *An Essay in Marxian Economics,* 2d edition. London: Macmillan.

(1971). *Economic Heresies: Some Old-Fashioned Questions in Economic Theory.* New York: Basic Books.

Schumpeter, J. A. (1954). *History of Economic Analysis.* New York: Oxford University Press.

Shove, G. F. (1942). "The Place of Marshall's *Principles* in the Development of Economic Theory", *Economic Journal* 52:294–329.

Solow, R. M. (1963). *Capital Theory and the Rate of Return.* De Vries Lecture. Amsterdam: North-Holland.

Whitaker, J. K. (1975). Introduction to *EEW.*

Wicksell, K. (1951). *Lectures on Political Economy.* Vol. 1: *The General Theory;* Vol. 2: *Money.* Trans. E. Classen, ed. L. Robbins. London: Routledge and Kegan Paul.

10

An Aspect of Marshall's Period Analysis

I Market Price, Natural Price, Equilibrium Price

The idea that the observed price of a commodity – the price as it actually obtains in the market – is a temporary occurrence, that it fluctuates around, or gravitates toward a "norm", is at least as old as Adam Smith's *Wealth of Nations*. Smith draws a distinction between "market price" and what he calls the "natural price". Natural price is a norm, the price which just compensates for the costs incurred in the process of production and marketing of a commodity. The market price, on the other hand, is the price at which a commodity is "commonly" bought and sold in the market.

Adam Smith does not tell us at what price precisely the market is cleared, given the supply. There is no analysis of demand, no clear concept of a demand schedule, in his treatment of price. Nor, I believe, would he much care for it. Smith's primary concern was with natural price – a level of price at which the market tends ultimately to settle down. He adopts this price for deriving a measure of value – the labour command measure.

What, then, is the "cost" to which the natural price of commodities is supposed to correspond? The classical concept of cost is less simple than it looks. Adam Smith defines cost as the sum of prices of factors that the

I received helpful comments on this chapter at its draft stage from Amartya Sen and Partha Dasgupta. My thanks are due to them. Thanks are also due to the editor of the volume for his helpful intervention in regard to one or two matters discussed in the paper.

242

producers have to employ for the production of a commodity. One may call it the factor-price approach and it seems to stand to ordinary intuition. As we shall see later, it is just the approach one must take in considering, as Smith often does, the market for a single commodity where factor prices are given from outside.

It leads to an anomaly, however, as one considers the cost of commodities in general, when one must take account of the fact that prices of commodities and prices of factors are interrelated. For industry as a whole it is as true to say that prices of factors are determined by commodity prices as it is to say that prices of commodities are determined by factor prices. Smith's attempt to solve the problem by making his theory of factor prices independent of commodity prices involved him in an error; it allowed the value of output to change with changes in its distribution – an awkward admission. The approach thus is untenable. The passage from *an* industry to industry *as a whole* is not so smooth.[1]

Adam Smith's theory of value is deficient. His theory of market price is slovenly, while his concept of cost is not firm enough to sustain the theory of natural price, when considered in relation to industry as a whole. Yet with all this, here is an early recognition, albeit in a rudimentary form, of the significance of the element of time in the theory of value. Adam Smith proposes a two-fold division of time. His market price relates to a period which is so short that the supply is absolutely fixed, while his natural price relates to a period which is so long that supply is fully flexible. There is no intermediate territory; Smith does not entertain fixed capital in his analytical system.

David Ricardo took note of it, though incidentally. His chapter, "On Machinery", is designed to exhibit a possible contrast between the short-period effect of the introduction of machinery and its long-period effect. His thrust unquestionably was on the long period. Ricardo avoided Smith's error concerning the definition of cost by adopting a factor-quantity approach. But, as one knows, this led him to the controversial one-factor model, the labour theory of value.

With the advent of marginalist economics (Neo-classical, as it is often misleadingly called), all this vanishes. There is no time sequence in the marginalist theory of value. The marginalist system proceeds on the assumption that the supply of resources and their division among the people being given, each economic subject endeavours to make the best of the situation he faces – the consumer to maximise utility and the producer to maximise profit. Their activities, given perfect competition in the market, result in the establishment of a set of relationships be-

1. On this see Dasgupta, 1985, Chapter 4, pp. 48–9.

tween commodities and factors of production, such that no individual –
consumer or producer – can improve his position by altering the relationships without injuring others. These are equilibrium prices for commodities and factors. Commodity prices and factor prices are simultaneously determined in their respective markets and if they are to be in
equilibrium, then under conditions of perfect competition relative prices
are to be equal to relative costs.

The process through which these equilibrium prices are established in
the market is, to use the language of grammar, "understood". W. S.
Jevons suppresses it by invoking what he calls the "Law of Indifference",
urging that in an "open market" the price of different units of the same
commodity must be the same, which must also be the equilibrium price.
L. Walras puts up a kind of auctioneer who would "cry prices", the
parties then hitting upon the price that would just clear the market. F. Y.
Edgeworth's rule permitting "recontract" serves the same purpose. That
purpose is to ensure that negotiations through which the parties to exchange are to acquire knowledge about the demand and supply data take
place *aside,* that actual buying and selling take place at no other price
than the equilibrium price. In marginalist economics the actual price of a
commodity in the market *is* equilibrium price.

The marginalists were aware of a problem here, the problem that John
Hicks (1973, pp. 81–2) has taught us to call the "traverse". They knew
that the parties gather knowledge about the actual condition of the
market – the condition of demand and supply – as they proceed along
the traverse. They also knew that the problem was tricky, that any error
in price fixing along the traverse might disturb the entire demand-supply
configuration, thus rendering the system indeterminate. Jevons, for example, recognises this complication explicitly. "Theoretically speaking", he
observes, "it would not usually be possible to buy two portions of the
same commodity *successively* at the same ratio of exchange, because no
sooner would the first portion have been bought than the conditions of
utility would be altered" (1911, p. 92; italics in original). He disregards
this complication, however, and concentrates on what he calls "the final
rate of exchange." For, as he says, "it is far more easy to lay down the
conditions under which trade is completed and exchange ceases, than to
attempt to ascertain at what rate trade will go on when equilibrium is not
attained" (1911, p. 94). This is precisely the procedure the later marginalists adopted. Marginalist economics thus became an analysis of the
equilibrium condition of the system of prices in the commodity and factor
markets. Jevons's law of indifference, Walras's crying of prices, and Edgeworth's recontract are alternative ways of bypassing the problem of the
traverse.

II   The Method of Marshall

It is just this "traverse" which interested Alfred Marshall. Marshall is a marginalist, one of the early discoverers of the marginalist principle, but he takes over the method of analysis – the role of time – from the classics, from Smith and Ricardo, giving it a form all his own. Whereas the classics were essentially interested in what they called the natural price, the ultimate price of a commodity at which the market settles, and referred to the market price only incidentally, Marshall pays quite a lot of attention to the market price and builds up a structure linking market prices to the natural price, or "long period normal price" as he calls it.

Marshall provides an integrated system, in which market price is linked to the long-period normal price via a system of short-period normal prices. Thus in his system the passage from the market price to normal price is explicitly worked out. In the market for a very short period – a "day", let us call it – the stock is fixed. As the period is extended, it tends to vary. The degree of variability, however, depends on the intervening length of time.

A long period is long enough for supply to be fully adjusted to demand. In the long period all capital is variable; there is thus no "fixed" cost associated with the process of production. In the short period there are some kinds of capital, and hence costs, which are fixed. Price is linked only to the variable cost; the cost due to the use of fixed capital is irrelevant. What these fixed costs are depends on the period allowed in between a "day" and the long period. One thus contemplates a succession of short periods linking the day at one end and the long period at the other.

Marshall confines his value analysis to the market for a single commodity. Why does he do it? It is not that he was not acquainted with the general-equilibrium system of Walras or Edgeworth. Indeed, he himself worked out a similar system, but he relegated it to the Mathematical Appendix.[2] The typical Marshallian theory of value is confined to the market for a single commodity; the equilibrium is "partial".

Clearly this is to be explained in terms of his recognition of the importance of knowledge in value theory. Full equilibrium implies knowledge

2.   See *Principles,* Mathematical Appendix, Note XXI, pp. 855–6. Having worked out a general equilibrium system, he says, as Walras would, "however complex the problem may become, we can see that it is theoretically determinate, because the number of unknowns is always exactly equal to the number of the equations which we obtain". Marshall here points to a theoretical possibility. In the text (Book V, Chapter 6) to which the Note is appended, Marshall only gives an account of the various types of relationships which obtain in the market for commodities and factors, showing how complex the relationships are.

of the condition of the market. Acquisition of knowledge, however, is a process through time. Walras and Edgeworth eliminated time by assuming that no transactions take place until buyers and sellers acquire full knowledge about the condition of the market. The objective apparently is to exhibit the condition of a possible equilibrium, to see, as it were, what the economy would look like in equilibrium if knowledge of the conditions of the market were given to buyers and sellers. Marshall assumes ignorance to start with. Thus in his system actual transactions take place at what Hicks calls "false prices". Once this possibility is allowed, one does not know where precisely the economy will rest. The final relationship between commodities ceases to be independent of the path; equilibrium becomes indeterminate. Walras and Edgeworth avoid this complication by ignoring the path. Marshall faces the problem, but he does it by limiting his analysis to one single market where the path is supposed not to have an appreciable effect on the final point of equilibrium.

In the market for a single commodity, transactions take place between the commodity on the one hand and money on the other. Sellers hold a commodity and buyers hold money. Since money stands for all commodities outside this particular market, small variations in the price of the commodity have but little effect on its marginal utility. The "income effect", as Hicks would call it, is spread thin over the area and can be neglected. For his partial equilibrium analysis Marshall thus assumes the marginal utility of money to remain constant. The assumption could not be sustained in the context of the Walrasian general market.[3] Marshall's buyers and sellers start transactions without full knowledge of the condition of the market. They acquire knowledge in the course of buying and selling. Transactions take place initially at prices other than the equilibrium price. A path is thus traced on which false prices prevail. Will the market have a tendency, as knowledge is gathered, towards an equilibrium that is unique and determinate? Marshall's concentration on the market for a single commodity, with its corollary that the marginal utility of money against which it is exchanged remains constant throughout the process of exchange, is meant to answer this question. Let us see how he does it.

---

3. Hicks, however, proposes an extension of the condition of zero-income effect to his general equilibrium system, on the assumption that the income effects of buyers and sellers cancel one another. It is true that the income effects of buyers and sellers due to any given variation in price run in opposite directions – buyers gain while sellers lose as the price falls, and vice versa. But they cancel one another only when the parties are similar in respect of the pattern of their expenditure, too delicate an assumption to be relied on. See on this, Hicks, 1939, note to Chapter 9, pp. 127–9.

Marshall's "Market Price"

Unlike the Classical economists, Marshall takes the theory of the market price seriously. His analysis of the market for a day is intended to provide a clue to the entire theory of value with which he is concerned. The extension of time to the short period or the long period is but a way of exhibiting how variations in supply react on the price of a commodity. On a day the stock of a commodity in the market is fixed; there is no role of production. As the period is extended production is allowed to take place, though under different degrees of constraint. In the short period (or periods, for there may be several short periods for the market for a commodity) some sorts of capital employed in the process of production are fixed, while others are variable. In the long period all capital is variable. As the period is extended, the supply curve in the market for the commodity becomes more and more elastic – that is all; the demand curve is supposed to remain constant.

The property of a day is that over it the stock of a commodity remains absolutely fixed; it cannot be increased however high the price may be, nor can it be decreased without loss, for if it is to be an "economic" good, its price must in any case remain positive.

How is the price of a commodity determined in the market for a day? Sellers hold a fixed stock of the commodity – corn, to take Marshall's example – and buyers hold money. Since our commodity is corn, a day obviously covers the entire sowing and harvesting season – in a closed economy the stock of our commodity remains fixed for the entire season. For analytical purposes, however, one may take, as Marshall does, a specific period and a specific place, "a corn-market in a country town"; the essential point is that the stock is given and fixed.

How do the parties proceed when, as one assumes, they start with less than full knowledge about the condition of the market? The market begins with false prices, a little too high or a little two low, depending on the relative bargaining power of the two parties. In the end, however, the parties are supposed inevitably to hit upon what Marshall calls the "true" equilibrium price. While the marginal utility of the commodity – corn in the example – is allowed to vary with the transfer of successive units from the sellers to the buyers, the marginal utility of money, by hypothesis, remains constant whatever the amount transferred from the buyers to the sellers. If indeed the marginal utility of money is held constant for both buyers and sellers and only the marginal utility of the commodity is allowed to vary, then, as exchange proceeds, there must come a point, a definite and determinate point, where the marginal utility of the commodity for both will bear the same proportion to the given marginal utility of money.

Marshall uses a numerical example, a table instead of a diagram, to explain the process. I reproduce it verbatim below.[4]

At the price	Holders will be willing to sell	Buyers will be willing to buy
37s	1000 quarters	600 quarters
36s	700　　"	700　　"
35s	600　　"	900　　"

The table describes the demand and supply schedules of corn. Sellers hold corn and buyers hold money. The parties have but imperfect knowledge of the condition of the market.[5] Nor do they acquire knowledge of each other's bargaining positions through "crying of prices" or "recontracting". Unlike Walras and Edgeworth, Marshall allows actual transactions to take place at prices other than the equilibrium price. The market may begin at 37s per quarter, or it may begin at 35s per quarter, depending on the relative bargaining strength of the two parties at the initial stage. Yet, as the table shows, it will inevitably settle at 36s per quarter, at which 700 quarters of corn will be bought and sold. There will be no further exchange, for any movement either way would be unacceptable to one or the other of the parties. For the 700th quarter of corn, the demand price will be just equal to the supply price, no matter whether the market starts at 37s per quarter or at 35s per quarter. The marginal utility of money remaining constant, price variations will be solely due to variations in the marginal utility of corn.

There is thus equilibrium where 700 quarters of corn are bought and

4. Apparently Marshall attached special importance to the illustration. Originally the table was put in a footnote. It remained as a footnote until the 4th edition of the *Principles*. In the 5th edition it was elevated to form a part of the text, and there it has remained since.

　　It is interesting that Marshall, who was so fond of diagrams, should have deviated from his general practice and used a table in this case. His own explanation is that his "market price" – the price on a day – relates to a "stock" and is to be distinguished from the concept of a "flow" which is relevant to the problems of "normal price". See Marshall, 1898, p. 46; also his letter to F. Y. Edgeworth, *Memorials*, p. 435.

5. Note that the dealers are not completely ignorant of the condition of the market; they do not start altogether with a clean slate, for they have their past experiences. In the corn market example deviation from the equilibrium price either way is shown to be less than 3 per cent. In any case the range of deviation postulated is narrow, for otherwise the assumption of constant marginal utility of money would not be valid.

sold and where the price is 36s per quarter. This equilibrium is determinate; it is independent of the price at which the market starts and of the path it traverses. Note, however, that while the amount of corn, as also the price at which it is bought and sold, is determinate, the amount of money that passes from the buyers to the sellers remains indeterminate. The sellers find themselves richer or poorer according as the market starts with 37s per quarter or with 35s per quarter. Marshall's partial equilibrium looks further attenuated; it fails to cover money.

Contrast this with a situation in which the marginal utility of money also varies as the parties are left with more or less of it. This happens when the market is taken to cover a wide range of commodities (even a single commodity, if it is one on which the consumers spend a large part of their income), in the limit, the entire range of exchangeable commodities. Marshall considers this general case in an Appendix (*Principles*, Appendix F, pp. 791–3). There he gives an example, again a numerical example, of an exchange between apples and nuts, showing how the ultimate rate of exchange at which the market for the two commodities settles depends on the initial rate and the intermediate rates along the traverse.

A is supposed to hold 20 apples and *B* to hold 100 nuts. *A*, let us say, has superior bargaining power and succeeds in exchanging 4 apples for 40 nuts at the rate 1:10. *B* now has 4 apples and is left with only 60 nuts. He will be unwilling to offer more nuts except at a less unfavourable rate. Suppose the rate comes down to 1:8.5, at which 2 more apples are exchanged for 17 nuts. *B* now has 6 apples, and can be persuaded to accept one more apple only against 8 nuts. The rate thus comes down to 8 nuts for an apple. Here the market closes, for *B* will not be willing to accept an additional apple except at a rate yet more favourable to him. On the other hand, *A*, having parted with 7 apples already and having been in possession of as many as 65 nuts, will not part with another apple even for 8 nuts; he will ask for more. There will thus be no further exchange; the market will be in equilibrium. But it will be just one possible equilibrium, not *the* equilibrium. Turning the table in favour of *B*, one gets a different result. Marshall provides an alternative example, with *B* as the superior bargainer, where the market begins with 2.5 nuts for one apple, and via a series of transactions, settles at 5 nuts for one apple. One can construct a variety of tables, with different initial rates and different sets of intermediate rates, which would yield different equilibrium rates, even though the initial data remained the same.

How perfect, one may ask, is Marshall's perfectly competitive market? A full answer to the question must wait till we come to the long-period market. In the context of the corn market for a day, Marshall chooses to remain vague. Buyers are enough in number for competition to be perfect; they hold money which happens to be in many hands. One is not so sure about sellers. Marshall does not tell us how many sellers constitute his corn market and what degree of competition they face. In the barter case the basic example is that of one apple holder dealing with one nut holder, but this is only a preliminary exercise. He hastens to tell us that the situation would remain essentially the same if the market were extended to cover 100 apple holders and 100 nut holders.

The important point these exercises are designed to demonstrate is that competition cannot be perfect unless buyers and sellers have perfect knowledge about the condition of the market. Walras and Edgeworth allow buyers and sellers to acquire full knowledge of the condition of the market before they start actual transactions. Thus in their systems perfect competition implies that the number of buyers and sellers is such that each knows that he cannot by himself influence the price in the market. Marshall assumes imperfect knowledge, to begin with, and permits actual transactions to take place at false prices; no wonder that the number of dealers in his example receives less attention.

A Digression

On a day the stock of a commodity is fixed. What is one to say about supply? This apparently is a simple question: one would surely say that the part of the stock the holders would give away to buyers, which is what "supply" is supposed to be, depended upon price. This is Marshall's answer also. In the corn market example, the stock is assumed to be 1000 quarters. The supply, however, is allowed to vary with the price. If in equilibrium the amount sold comes to 700 quarters, as in Marshall's example, the sellers retain 300 quarters. What do they do with this unsold stock? Marshall's answer, one imagines, would be simple. The sellers, he would say, retain it for future sale. "The amount which each farmer or other seller offers for sale at any price is governed by his own need for money in hand, and by his calculation of the present and future conditions of the market with which he is concerned" (*Principles*, p. 332). Clearly supply is here seen as distinct from stock; while the stock is fixed, supply is not.

This apparently simple proposition caused some misgivings in Cambridge after Marshall. John Hicks announces that in Cambridge, after Marshall, they replaced corn by fish in their analysis of the market for a day. Hicks endorses the procedure. "It is a curious corn market", he observes, "in that corn is rather oddly assumed to be non-storable; for this reason it became common, in later Cambridge tradition, to replace 'corn' by 'fish' ".[6] If D. H. Robertson can be taken to represent this later Cambridge tradition, it appears that Marshall's "day" came to be interpreted there in a somewhat distorted manner. Robertson in his lectures in Cambridge illustrated his "market for a moment" (Marshall's "day") by reference to the "fish-market on Saturday night". The object apparently was to emphasise that the supply, not just the stock, is given and fixed, that the sellers are required to sell off the entire stock within the period.

This is definitely not Marshall's concept of a day. Marshall's day permits supply to vary, even though the stock remains fixed. In his corn example the amount bought and sold is shown to vary with price. In equilibrium the supply happens to be 700 quarters while the stock initially held by the sellers is 1000 quarters; the sellers thus keep back 300 quarters. The stock is fixed, it follows from the definition of a "day"; but what portion of it the sellers are disposed to part with depends on price. The sellers have a supply schedule and this schedule depends, Marshall is careful to note, on the price, as it is expected to be beyond the day. Curiously, in spite of his choice of fish on Saturday night, Robertson does not rule out the possibility of the sellers withholding a part of the stock "even at the moment". As he hastens to say, "unless the thing is very perishable, the seller, too, can choose whether to hold back stocks or to press them on the market, – the quantity 'available' is not the same thing as the quantity in existence". In a right Marshallian way Robertson allows a part of the stock to be held back![7]

Marshall's choice of corn for the analysis of price determination in the market for a day is not just casual. It is not that he did not care for fish; fish figures as an example in his analysis of longer period markets where the stock itself is variable, where therefore the choice of fish is innocuous.

I would argue that Marshall's choice of corn in the context in which he uses it is deliberate. To take fish as one's example would amount to putting the sellers at a relative disadvantage as bargainers, insofar as they would not have a reservation price. Clearly Marshall would much rather have the parties evenly matched; the sellers could choose not to sell the entire stock, even as the buyers had the option not to buy the entire stock. More important, in Marshall's system there is a link between the market for a day and the longer period markets. Contrary to Hicks's assertion, Marshall's period is not self-contained. His day is linked to his short period, even as his short period is linked to his long period. To this I now turn.

6. See Hicks, 1969, pp. 53–4. It is interesting to note that in his earlier book, Hicks referred to the "fish market" while discussing Marshall's "temporary equilibrium" as if it were Marshall's own example. See Hicks, 1939, note to Chapter 9, p. 129.
7. On all this see Robertson, 1957, p. 94.

Beyond the Day

What happens when the time horizon is extended beyond the day? A new variable is introduced, "output". A day is too short for production to take place; on a day the stock is fixed. The present stock is the result of past activity and cannot be altered. As the period is extended one recognises the scope for variation in output. The determinant of price thus acquires a new dimension. Besides demand (demand schedule, that is), which is taken as given, one must reckon with cost. As time is extended beyond the day, output becomes flexible; it is allowed to react to price. The extent of this reaction, however, depends on the length of the period one sets one's sights on. Marshall's division of time into short and long periods is designed to bring out the nature of this reaction.

In the long period the output is fully flexible. Since Marshall adopts a one-commodity model, resources are allowed to be transferred from, or to, the rest of the economy with perfect ease. The cost per unit of the commodity thus remains the same whatever the output.[8] This cost governs price under competitive conditions; output is determined by the condition of demand. With a horizontal supply curve and a downward sloping demand curve one gets an equilibrium of price and output which is unique and determinate. This equilibrium would be attained, Marshall contends, provided enough time were allowed for the buyers and sellers to acquire full knowledge about the condition of the market and to adjust the productive apparatus accordingly.

Reference here is clearly to a tendency, not necessarily to a fact. The tendency operates, provided other things remain the same. The conditions under which long-period equilibrium could be realised, Marshall warns us, are hard to obtain. "A theoretically perfect long period", he states, "must give time enough to enable not only the factors of production of the commodity to be adjusted to demand, but also the factors of production of those factors of production and so on" (*Principles,* p. 379 n.). Carried to its logical conclusion, it thus leads to a stationary state, clearly an imaginary state, yet useful as showing the direction of a tendency.

Marshall pays a lot of attention to the short period. In the short period, as Marshall defines it, production is constrained because, unlike the long-period case, some resources, like machinery or specialised skills, are fixed. In the corn case, for example, while the supply of seeds might be flexible, the supply of tractors is not. Production of corn thus encounters

8. Marshall does not rule out the possibility of diminishing costs in an industry even under conditions of competitive equilibrium. See *Principles,* Appendix H, pp. 805–12. Admission of diminishing costs reinforces the central argument proposed later on, that the process towards equilibrium, as Marshall views it, is irreversible.

resistance from tractors; producers must make do with the existing stock of tractors, though they can vary the employment of seeds. Moreover, since in reality there are different kinds of fixed capital, some having a longer service tenure than others, or requiring longer time for construction, production encounters declining resistance as time is extended. There are thus several intervening short periods as the industry moves from a day towards the long period; in the long period all capital is liquid.

Short periods play a crucial role in Marshall's price theory. The typical Marshallian concepts – quasi-rent, supplementary cost, and prime cost – belong to the short period. On a day costs are just "bygones" (as Jevons would say) and hence irrelevant to the determination of price. As the period is extended and time is allowed for production to be varied, costs come in as an element to reckon with.

Producers begin with imperfect knowledge about the condition of the market. They may thus begin with too much investment in fixed capital or with too little. Given time, they acquire knowledge and make adjustments of their apparatus to the condition of demand, but there are resistances to overcome in the process. If in the initial state the stock of capital is found to be too short relative to demand, more capital goods will be produced. In the opposite case where the initial stock of fixed capital is too large, it will be allowed gradually to shrink. In the former case the proceeds from fixed capital – quasi-rent, as Marshall calls them – will be abnormally high, higher than the normal rate of interest. In the latter case the quasi-rent will be abnormally low.

This latter case raises a question of special importance for Marshall's economics. Assume that there is over-investment to start with. The potential supply of goods is too large when considered in relation to the given demand. There is thus need for restriction of output below the full capacity of the existing stock of fixed capital. How intensively will it be used? What will determine the level of price in the short period?

It is in the answer to these questions that one comes across the typically Marshallian concepts – prime cost on the one hand and supplementary cost and quasi-rent on the other. These concepts belong to the short period. Prime costs vary with variations in output; thus the price in the short period will not be allowed to fall below the level of prime cost. The producers will employ less of variable factors and reduce output if the price shows a tendency to fall below prime cost. Will the price be allowed to touch the prime cost of production? Marshall's answer to the question is significant. The producers, he says, will adjust production in such a way that the price covers not only the prime cost but also a part of the supplementary cost, that the short-period price will in any event carry some quasi-rent, be it ever so small.[9] The sellers, Marshall urges, are afraid of "spoiling the market". In Marshall's system an individual producer (or seller) is not altogether passive; he is allowed to have some control over the price. The number of sellers operating in his corn market is not infinite in relation to demand. Nor are the parties to have perfect knowledge of the condition of the market, except at the point of long-period equilibrium, a point the market tends to reach, but never does. Marshall's perfect competition is not that perfect after all.[10]

In Marshall's system the path along which the industry moves is important. Long-period equilibrium is a state towards which the industry tends to move, given the condition of demand. As Marshall describes the full implications of the long-period equilibrium he clearly suggests that he does not count on its realisation in practice. Marshall's period analysis is designed to show that there is a gradation of short periods intervening as the market proceeds from the day to the long period. The day merges into a short period, even as the short periods tend to merge into the long period.[11] On the other hand, the day carries a legacy of the past; it does not begin with a clean slate. If our day leaves a legacy of 300 quarters of corn for the future, as in Marshall's example, it must have had a similar legacy from its predecessor. Economic operations have continuity; the present is tied to the past, as also to the future. *Natura non facit saltum* – this is Marshall's motto for his *Principles of Economics*.

Marshall's division of the time horizon into a day or a short period is apparently an expository device, not to be taken too literally. The so-called "equilibrium" on a day is disequilibrium in relation to the short period, as a short-period "equilibrium" is disequilibrium in relation to the long period. Each period leaves a trail linking it to its successor; the process is continuous and irreversible. If the process is seen as leading to a

---

9. "Supplementary costs must generally be covered by the selling price to some considerable extent in the short period" (*Principles*, p. 360).

10. It is as well that Marshall keeps the definition of perfect competition a bit loose. The Walrasian assumption of perfect competition, apparently involving an "infinitely" large number of buyers and sellers having full knowledge of the condition of the market, is difficult for any market to swallow; the situation seems inevitably to lead to combination. When the sellers, for example, know that they will make only "zero profit" working individually, they are likely to combine, at any rate marginally, as will the buyers, when they know that by combining they can prevent the sellers from exploiting them. One here recalls what Frank Knight wrote nearly seven decades ago: "There does seem to be a certain Hegelian self-contradiction in the idea of theoretically perfect competition after all" (1921, Ch. 6, p. 193).

11. For a diagrammatic treatment of the process of adjustment of output to demand over time, see Dasgupta, 1985, p. 110. The diagram exhibits the process under alternative assumptions with respect to the position from which it starts. The process of adjustment, it will be seen, is continuous, as indeed Marshall would have it.

stationary state, it is because one element in the system is held constant – the condition of demand.

One is tempted to compare Marshall's theory of long-period equilibrium with that of Ricardo. Ricardo, it will be remembered, considers in his corn model the end-point of a process of adjustment of population (labour, shall we say?) to a given quantity of land. The supply of labour (and capital, used in a fixed proportion) is assumed to be perfectly elastic at a given real wage rate and is allowed to press on the fixed stock of land, this latter being assumed to be "specific" to the production of corn. There is thus diminishing return from the employment of labour. Production is a continuous process, leading up to a point where the marginal return is just equal to the given wage rate. The economy – the corn economy – thus tends to attain a stationary state. The same sort of situation arises in Marshall's system. The same "corn" figures in it, though the definition of corn is less comprehensive. Corn here is assumed to form a small part of the total economy and its supply is assumed to be perfectly elastic. What is given and fixed is the condition of demand – the demand curve, assumed to be downward-sloping. Thus here, too, the process of production also leads up to a stationary state.

Both cases represent a process, and both lead up to a stationary state because, in both, one of the elements constituting the system is held constant – land in Ricardo, and demand in Marshall. The process in both is irreversible and hence, as I would judge, "dynamic".[12]

III   Concluding Note

I have argued that Marshall's period analysis shows how an industry moves from an original position where buyers and sellers associated with it have but imperfect knowledge about the condition of the market, that the passage from the "day" to the "long period" is one along which the parties acquire this knowledge. The condition of demand is assumed to be given; demand is allowed to adjust itself sharply to price. The adjustment of supply, however, is tardy, for it faces technical resistance. The passage from the day to the long period, as viewed by Marshall, is thus one marked by a process of adjustment of supply to a given condition of demand. It is a continuous process; the periods "shade into one another

12. It is intriguing that Roy Harrod, who has done so much towards the clarification of the concept of dynamics, calls Marshall's system static while describing Ricardo's as a dynamic system. See Harrod, 1948, Lecture One, p. 15. John Hicks, on the other hand, is consistent: according to him both the systems are static, the "periods" involved in both being defined as "self contained". See Hicks, 1985, pp. 35–51. If I argue otherwise, it is because I see movement and continuity in both.

gradually", Marshall would say. The industry is supposed to grow or decline over time in response to the given demand.

I do not believe Marshall would ever go in for an over-all growth theory. Substitution between goods and factors which, like his marginalist contemporaries, he recognised as basic in economic theory, would present a formidable obstacle to process analysis in the context of the economy as a whole. As it is, Marshall assumes stationariness for the whole economy, as he does for his chosen commodity; a single commodity could obviously not be in stationary equilibrium unless the rest of the economy which feeds it remained stationary also. Award a positive value to the rate of growth for the rest of the economy and assume a unitary income elasticity of demand for your chosen commodity, and you have the spectacle of a "uniformly progressive economy", as Marshall called it. The distinctive features of a stationary state, he tells us, "may be exhibited in a place where population and wealth are both growing, provided they are growing at almost the same rate, and there is no scarcity of land: and provided also the methods of production and the conditions of trade change but little; and above all, where the character of man himself is a constant quantity" (*Principles,* Book V, Chapter 5, p. 368). This, I imagine, is as far as Marshall would allow himself to go.[13] Clearly it is a bench mark, as much of a bench mark as the stationary state and to be treated likewise.

It is of interest to note that in his short (and solitary) excursion into trade cycle theory Marshall describes depression as deviation from a norm, a deviation characterised by a cumulative running down of prices and output, arising from a loss of confidence on the part of traders and producers. With a revival of confidence, he argues, the economy tends to return to the original state. "Confidence by growing would cause itself to grow; credit would give increased means of purchase and thus prices would recover". This is how Marshall views the process as he winds up his account of the trade cycle (*Principles,* pp. 710–12). Clearly the state to which he thinks the economy would tend to return is the old stationary state.

Many of the major contemporary growth theories have grown largely

13. Harrod wonders if what he would recognise as dynamic theory was reserved by Marshall for his proposed "fourth volume, which he never completed". This, as it turns out, is a delusion. The manuscripts Marshall left behind have since been published, presenting fragmentary notes on growth models he had contemplated (see *EEW,* 2, pp. 305–16). He did not push his models for publication, even as Appendices, to his *Principles* or to *Industry and Trade.* Apparently, as Whitaker suggests, he soon got "discouraged" (*EEW,* 2, p. 309). On the other hand, there is an informal discourse on the factors of economic development in Book IV of the *Principles* which, though little read, is not inconsequential.

along the Marshallian one-commodity line. Harrod's growth model, which set the pattern of modern growth theory, is based on the assumption that relative prices remain constant along the growth path. This is also the assumption of his contemporaries, Joan Robinson and Nicholas Kaldor. These latter went to the length of repudiating the theory of value altogether, insofar as it interfered with their approach to the theory of growth.[14] Marshall would not have it. He was too much involved in the theory of value, too much wedded to the principle of substitution to have acquiesced in an approach which involved the assumption of constant prices over time. He would much rather confine himself to his one-commodity world where he could enunciate propositions which were free of ambiguity.

References

Dasgupta, A. K. (1985). *Epochs of Economic Theory*. Oxford: Blackwell.

Harrod, R. F. (1948). *Towards a Dynamic Economics*. London: Macmillan.

Hicks, J. R. (1939). *Value and Capital*. Oxford: Clarendon.

    (1965). *Capital and Growth*. Oxford: Clarendon.

    (1973). *Capital and Time*. Oxford: Clarendon.

    (1985). *Methods of Dynamic Economics*. Oxford: Clarendon.

Jevons, W. S. (1911). *The Theory of Political Economy*, 4th ed. London: Macmillan.

Kaldor, N. (1972). "The Irrelevance of Equilibrium Economics", *Economic Journal* 82:1237–55.

Knight, F. H. (1921). *Risk, Uncertainty and Profit*. Boston and New York: Houghton Mifflin. LSE reprint 1931.

Marshall, A. (1898). "Distribution and Exchange", *Economic Journal* 8:37–59.

Robertson, D. H. (1957). *Lectures on Economic Principles*, Vol. 1. London: Staples.

Robinson, J. V. (1956). *The Accumulation of Capital*. London: Macmillan.

14. "Economic theory, serving for two centuries to win our understanding of the Nature and Causes of the Wealth of Nations, has been fobbed off with another bride – the Theory of Value", complains Joan Robinson, opening the preface to her *Accumulation of Capital* (1956). See also Kaldor, 1972.

11

The Great Barter Controversy

PETER NEWMAN

Early in 1891 Marshall and Edgeworth had a passage of arms over the treatment of barter in the first edition of the *Principles*. A misleading representation of this controversy is well known but what the fight was really about has seldom been discussed and certainly not in recent years. With the modern increase in appreciation of Edgeworth's theory of contract this omission seems curious, for although it may not have seemed so at the time it was essentially that theory that was at issue. Edgeworth's defeat at the hands of Marshall and Berry may well have been decisive in his subsequent turning away from the deeply original beginnings of contract theory in *Mathematical Psychics,* to work instead on such more traditional (and hence safer) economic theories as those of distribution, monopoly, and taxation. There his contributions were substantial, but almost of necessity they lacked the originality of his earlier work.

I Prologue

Just as the publication of the *Principles* made 1890 a momentous year for Marshall, so for Edgeworth the years 1889 to 1891 were a time of "soaring", to use a word he once applied to Irving Fisher (Fisher, 1956, p. 69). At last, at the age of 44 and after years spent in the minor leagues of academia, he gained in rapid succession a series of important posts that signalled his general recognition as a major figure in British economics.

They began in 1889 with his presidency of Section F (Economic Science and Statistics) of the British Association for the Advancement of Science, in which he was followed a year later by Marshall. In 1890 he moved from a simple professorship in political economy at King's College, London, to its more prestigious Tooke Professorship of Economic Science and Statistics, and in autumn of the same year he became sole editor of the *Economic Journal*, published by the newly formed British Economic Association (subsequently, the Royal Economic Society). His rapid ascent reached its apogee early in 1891 with election to the Drummond Professorship at Oxford, succeeding Thorold Rogers, who had died after a tenure of only two years; Edgeworth was to hold the Chair for the next 31 years.

It seems unlikely that this progress could have occurred without Marshall's support and encouragement, for which there is indirect evidence in the latter's fervent congratulations on the Drummond election (Creedy, 1986, p. 10). J. N. Keynes was always Marshall's first preference for such posts, however, even as early as 1887 when the editorship of the proposed *Economic Journal* was first mooted, and again in 1888 when the Drummond Professorship was vacant before Rogers's appointment (Maloney, 1985, Chapter 3). Unlike Keynes, Edgeworth was not a Cambridge man and moreover, Marshall considered him "extreme" in his devotion to the "scientific and analytical" treatment of economics (ibid., p. 46).

These three years also saw a sharp change in Edgeworth's scientific interests, from statistical theory towards economic theory. After the rather cool reception by Jevons and Marshall of *Mathematical Psychics* in 1881 he had moved rapidly and decisively into probability and statistics. An unpublished and incomplete bibliography compiled under Harry Johnson's direction records 44 publications by Edgeworth during the period 1882 to 1888, of which all but five were on probability, statistics, or index numbers. Two of these five appeared in 1882, the first on Leslie Stephen and the other a pedagogical note on rent theory; two of the remainder applied probability theory to banking, and the last was a brief comment in 1884 on exchange theory, discussed below.

Thus until 1889 Edgeworth's only significant publication in pure economics was *Mathematical Psychics*. Its influence is clearly present in his presidential address (1889*b*), his only other substantial work in economic theory appearing before Marshall's *Principles*. For example, the address's remarkable note (*e*), which is less than a page sets out modern general equilibrium conditions for an exchange economy with "*m* dealers and *n* articles", is clearly in direct descent from pages 41 and 42 of *Mathematical Psychics*.

II The Theory of Contract

That his contract theory still dominated Edgeworth's conception of economics can be seen in an important passage towards the close of his address, where in drawing an analogy with the fundamental role played by the theory of errors (that is, the central limit theorem) in probability, he argued that "It may be said that in pure economics there is [also] only one fundamental theorem, but that is a very difficult one: the theory of bargain in a wide sense" (1889*b*, p. 500). It is useful, therefore, to recall the essentials of that theory, which was his main weapon in the battle over barter. All the quotations in the following account are from (1881, pp. 16–20), and with one indicated exception all the italics in them are his.

"[E]very agent is actuated only by self-interest". *Competition* takes the form of engaging with others in either *contract* or *war*. By definition, in contract the agent acts with "the consent of others affected by his actions", whereas in war the opposite is true. *Recontract* occurs when, for example, an auctioneer accepts a higher bid or a landlord, on the expiration of one lease, signs a new one with another tenant; thus recontracting is usually an act of war. The *field* of competition "consists of all the individuals who are willing and able to recontract about the articles under consideration", and "free communication throughout a *normal* competitive field " is presupposed.

"A *settlement* is a contract which cannot be varied with the consent of *all* [italics added] the parties to it." Reflecting on these definitions, we see that a settlement is what is now called a Pareto-optimal allocation. Contrast "A *final settlement* [which] is a settlement which cannot be varied by recontract within the field of competition". The set of *final* settlements is thus that subset of settlements (Pareto-optima) which is now called the *core* of the exchange economy.

For Edgeworth, "Contract is *indeterminate* when there are an indefinite [that is, infinite] number of *final settlements*" (Stephen Stigler has noted that an annotation in Edgeworth's own copy replaced "are" by "may be"). His fundamental theorem on indeterminacy of contract states that "(α) Contract without competition is indeterminate, (β) Contract with *perfect* competition is perfectly determinate, (γ) Contract with more or less perfect competition is less or m re indeterminate".

This theorem obviously requires that perfect competition be carefully defined, and in this respect Edgeworth has seldom been surpassed. "The conditions of a *perfect* field are four:

I. Any individual is free to *recontract* with any out of an indefinite number . . .

II. Any individual is free to *contract* (at the same time) with an indefinite number . . . [which] appears to involve the indefinite divisibility of each *article* of contract . . .

III. Any individual is free to *recontract* with another independently of, *without the consent* being required of, any third party . . .

IV. Any individual is free to *contract* with another independently of a third party . . .

The failure of the first [condition] involves the failure of the second, but not *vice versâ;* and the third and fourth are similarly related."

Purely as tools to prove this theorem, Edgeworth invented such standard concepts as the general utility function, indifference curves and surfaces, and convexity of preferences. Most important for our purposes, he introduced the pure *contract-curve,* the locus of final settlements. He proved two basic results: that recontract plus convexity of preferences together imply that the contract-curve shrinks as more competitors are introduced; and that all the contracts resulting from a perfectly competitive market are on the contract-curve.

He also conjectured but did not prove (it is not easy) that as the number of competitors increases without limit the contract-curve shrinks to precisely the set of competitive equilibria. This set he usually regarded as a singleton, "very generally *unique*" (1881, p. 46), but he recognised that there could be a finite multiplicity of equilibria, a possibility discovered earlier (and independently of each other) by Walras and Marshall.

Although he realised that indeterminateness could arise solely from indivisibility of the articles (that is, a failure of condition II), Edgeworth placed almost exclusive emphasis on the role of large numbers of competitors in securing determinacy of contract. Without large numbers there is no assurance of determinate allocations, nor even of uniformity of price. The latter was the main point of "The Rationale of Exchange" (1884), and it was emphasised strongly again in (1891*a*) which, since each paper refers to the other, was obviously written at the same time as his comment (1891*b*) on Marshall's *Note on Barter.* The long footnote in (1891*a*) in which this reference occurs is so illuminating that it warrants extensive quotation here (the translation is mine; with one indicated exception, so are all the other translations in this chapter).

The idea that equilibrium is attained when an exchange-ratio is reached at which no buyer wants to demand more, nor any seller supply more, is not, I believe, very appropriate in the case when there is a *small* number of traders, on either both sides or just one. In this case, there is no need to presume a uniform rate of exchange for everyone. Suppose for example that A^1 and A^2 negotiate with B^1, B^2, B^3 and B^4. A^1 proposes a certain deal to B^1 and B^2, they supplying a certain *quid pro quo*, and A^2 deals similarly with B^3 and B^4. It is not a necessary postulate that in the final equilibrium *a/b*, the *quid* given divided by the *pro quo* received, should be the same for the 2 As. The only condition that must hold at equilibrium is that A^1 cannot improve his position by offering B^3 and B^4 more advantageous conditions than they are already provisionally receiving in their contract with A^2.

All abstract reasoning on price determination between two traders in the absence of competition . . . would be greatly facilitated, we believe, by leaving aside the condition that there is a unique price, which can only be applied when a market has, on one side at least, a large number of competitors. Compare the *Note on Barter* in the *Principles of Economics* of Professor Marshall and my observations on this note in the *Giornale degli Economisti* of January [actually, March] 1891.   (1891*a*, p. 16 n.)

Designate by $\mathscr{A}$ the type of question of the form: How does the core of the economy behave as its agents increase in number? Such $\mathscr{A}$ questions must be distinguished sharply from questions of a quite different type $\mathscr{B}$, namely: Given the number of agents, how does the economy move from a noncore allocation to one that is in the core? When this given number of agents is large, the relevant $\mathscr{B}$-type question takes the more traditional form: How does a market, or system of markets, which is out of equilibrium converge to an equilibrium allocation and price, or vector of prices?

Edgeworth had a clear-cut position on $\mathscr{B}$-type questions: "[A]s Jevons points out, the equations of exchange are of a statical, not a dynamical, character. They define a position of equilibrium, but they afford no information as to the path by which that point is reached" (1889*a*, p. 435). Bortkiewicz, defending Walras against Edgeworth's review of the second edition of the *Eléments*, asserted that Walrasian *tâtonnement* actually corresponds to "the real process, effectively employed on the market" (1890, p. 85). In rebuttal, Edgeworth roundly declared that "I maintain that the game of all this higgling by which market prices are determined, the direction which the system follows in order to arrive at the position of equilibrium, does not belong to the sphere of science" (1891*a*, p. 12).

Here Edgeworth was simply echoing Marshall in *The Pure Theory of Foreign Trade* (1879), where he asserted that "even if we knew exactly the shapes which the curves assumed in any particular problem, we should not have the data on which to base a calculation of the precise path which the exchange point would describe" (*EEW*, 2, pp. 162, 152n.). Edgeworth was also making clear, what was later misunderstood (for instance, by Uzawa, 1962, and Newman, 1965, pp. 68–9), that for him recontracting was to be used only for $\mathcal{A}$ questions, never for those of type $\mathcal{B}$.

III Marshall's *Principles* Appears

Edgeworth's joy at the publication of the *Principles* compelled him to write two quite separate reviews (1890*a*, *b*) having in common only their high (though not entirely unqualified) praise for this brilliant new "light of dawn" (1890*b*, p. 166). Still, it must have shocked Edgeworth to discover Marshall's scant recognition of his own work. There were just two footnotes, on pages 151 and 152 of the *Principles,* citing only the utilitarian calculus of (1881) and (1877), respectively, in support of typical Marshallian bromides on intertemporal and interpersonal comparisons of utility.

The structure of the *Principles,* spreading as it did backwards and forwards from the detailed partial equilibrium supply and demand analysis of the industry contained in Book V, was scarcely conducive to a detailed appreciation of the theory of pure exchange. When Marshall did touch on the subject, however, in the famous *Note on Barter* placed at the end of Chapter 2, Book V, on *Temporary Equilibrium of Demand and Supply* (pp. 390–7), there was not even an implicit acknowledgement of Edgeworth's work on contract. Even worse was his curt dismissive comment that "the theory of . . . [barter] . . . is curious rather than important" (*Principles,* p. 394). This must have seemed a splash of cold water on Edgeworth's treasured "one fundamental theorem" of pure economics, "the theory of bargain in a wide sense". Nor could Edgeworth comfort himself with the thought that Marshall was simply ignorant of the content of *Mathematical Psychics,* for had he not in June 1881 given it a full and rather patronising review in *The Academy*? Reprinted in *EEW*, 2, pages 265 to 268, this was the second and last of Marshall's book reviews.

Edgeworth was "modest and self-effacing" (Keynes, 1933, p. 287), but even the most self-effacing person might have felt frustrated by Marshall's almost ostentatious neglect of the "Economical Calculus" of *Mathematical Psychics.* Remembering that Edgeworth was also "proud, and touchy" (ibid., p. 290) goes far to explain why he soon felt sufficiently provoked to pick a rash fight with Marshall, which he lost. As we shall see, over 30 years later he was still smarting from the unhealed wounds of that defeat.

IV   Temporary Equilibrium

Chapter 2, Book V, of the first edition of the *Principles* deals with an economy in which agents exchange their fixed endowments of two commodities, corn and money. Implicitly, these traders are presumed to be sufficiently numerous to ensure competitive behaviour, while 'money' is understood as shorthand for the stock of all other goods, deflated by a suitable price index. How this deflator changes when attention is switched to the market for a commodity other than corn is left unanalysed, and it seems best for present purposes to regard this money simply as the numéraire good.

The "true equilibrium price" of corn in terms of money in this market is that obtained by intersecting the buyers' demand and sellers' supply schedules for corn; in Marshall's example (which carries all the argument) this price is 36s per quarter. Its designation as the *true* equilibrium price is justified by the argument that "if it were fixed on at the beginning, and adhered to throughout . . . [trading] would exactly equate demand and supply" (p. 392). Marshall is chiefly concerned to establish that even if actual trades take place at prices differing from 36s, "the market will probably close on a price of 36s" (ibid.).

Thus, in contrast to his position in *The Pure Theory of Foreign Trade*, Marshall is here worried about a type $\mathcal{B}$ question. Traders have imperfect knowledge of each other's demand schedules, and – to use Hicks's useful phrase – "false" trades do occur, out of equilibrium. The temporal sequence of the false prices at which these trades take place, however, is convergent, and the limiting price to which it converges is precisely the competitive "true equilibrium price."

Marshall claimed that these remarkable results followed from his assumption that each trader has a constant marginal utility of money. He further argued that this assumption was empirically well justified, the exceptions being "rare and unimportant in markets for commodities", although "in markets for labour they are frequent and important" (p. 394). So strong was Marshall's professed belief in the truth of this assumption for markets in commodities that he actually used it to *define* barter: "The real distinction then between the theory of buying and selling and that of barter is that in the former it generally is, and in the latter it generally is not, right to assume that the marginal utility of one of the things dealt with is practically constant" (p. 397).

V Convergence to Equilibrium

Marshall did not publish a formal proof that convergence of false prices to the "true equilibrium price" follows from universal constant marginal utility of money, but his informal arguments for the proposition appeared persuasive to his contemporaries. Though some might query the assumption's empirical truth, none questioned the theorem's logic. The present proof is included only to clarify the structure involved; a graphical proof may be found in Walker (1969).

To fix ideas (a favourite Edgeworthian phrase, usually ascribed to "the mathematicians"), consider first a simple exchange economy with two persons A and B and two goods x and y. The utility functions u of A and v of B are $u(x_a, y_a) = \ln x_a + 0.5 y_a$ and $v(x_b, y_b) = 0.5 \ln x_b + y_b$, and the endowment vectors (x_a^0, y_a^0), (x_b^0, y_b^0) are $(3,1)$, $(2,4)$, respectively; each person's marginal utility of y is a constant. The unique competitive equilibrium allocation of this economy is easily seen to be $(x_a^*, y_a^*) = (4, 1/2)$ and $(x_b^*, y_b^*) = (1, 9/2)$, while the unique equilibrium price p^* of x in terms of the numéraire y is $1/2$.

Now reverse the individual endowments of y from $(y_a^0, y_b^0) = (1, 4)$ to $(y_a^{00}, y_b^{00}) = (4, 1)$ but leave the individual endowments of x unchanged. Solving for the new competitive equilibrium shows that while the y's change to $(y_a^{**}, y_b^{**}) = (7/2, 3/2)$, all the other variables remain as they were, that is, $p^{**} = 1/2$, $x_a^{**} = 4$, and $x_b^{**} = 1$. This invariance of (p^*, x_a^*, x_b^*) to changes in (y_a^0, y_b^0) follows from the implied assumption that each person's marginal rate of substitution of x for y at any bundle is independent of the amount of y in that bundle. Constancy of each marginal utility of y suffices for this property, but the property itself in no way depends upon the measurability of utility. To see this, change u to the utility function U by the strictly monotonic increasing transformation $U = e^u$, and/or change v to $V = e^v$. The marginal utility of y is then no longer constant, but neither is there any change in the previous results.

Now move on from this example to the general case of an exchange economy with m agents and $n + 1$ goods (x, η), where x is now a vector of n goods x_i and η is the proposed numéraire. Constancy and positivity of the marginal utility of η for each agent h is then equivalent to assuming that each utility function u_h may be written

$$u_h(x_h, \eta_h) = f_h(x_h) + k_h \eta_h \qquad h = 1, 2, \ldots, m \qquad (11.1)$$

where k_h is a positive constant. Among other things, this implies that η always has a positive price and is thus an appropriate numéraire.

Since such problems are largely irrelevant here, assume for simplicity that the data of this exchange economy $\mathscr{E}\{(x_h^0, \eta_h^0), u_h\}$ are "nice" enough both to rule out any problems of existence, uniqueness, or non-interiority of solutions, and to permit the valid application of the usual Lagrangean techniques with equality constraints. Denoting by p_i the price of good x_i in terms of η, a competitive equilibrium $\{(x_h^*, \eta_h^*), p^*\}$ of this economy is then defined as a set of $m + 1$ positive vectors which satisfy the following three conditions:

(A) For all h, $u_h(x_h, \eta_h) > u_h(x_h^*, \eta_h^*) \Rightarrow \langle x_h, p^* \rangle + \eta_h$
$$> \langle x_h^0, p^* \rangle + \eta_h^0$$

where $\langle .,. \rangle$ denotes inner product (*utility maximisation*).

(B) For all h, $\langle x_h^*, p^* \rangle + \eta_h^* = \langle x_h^0, p^* \rangle + \eta_h^0$
$$(budget\ constraints)$$

(C) $x^* = x^0$ and $\eta^* = \eta^0$

   where $x^* = x_1^* + x_2^* + \ldots + x_m^*$

and similarly for x^0, η^* and η^0 (*market-clearing equations*).

To solve this system, derive the first-order conditions for utility maximisation (A) and note from (11.1), that for each h these may be written in terms of the $n + 1$ variables $x_{h1}, x_{h2}, \ldots, x_{hn}, \eta_h$ as

$$\partial f_h(x_h)/\partial x_{hi} = \lambda_h p_i \qquad\qquad i = 1, 2, \ldots, n$$
$$k_h = \lambda_h$$

where λ_h is the Lagrange multiplier in the hth budget constraint (B). Thus,

$$\partial f_h(x_h)/\partial x_{hi} = k_h p_i \qquad\qquad i = 1, 2, \ldots, n \quad (11.2)$$

Equations (11.2) are nm in number, and adding the n market-clearing equations $x^* = x^0$ from (C) yields a self-contained subsystem of equations, say $\mathscr{S}$, which, barring accidents, should suffice to provide unique positive solutions for all the $n(m + 1)$ unknowns (x_{hi}^*, p_i^*). But $\mathscr{S}$ does not require as data any of the m numbers η_h^0, the individual endowments of the numéraire. The latter are used only in the budget equations (B) where, together with the already obtained solution values of $\mathscr{S}$, they yield unique positive solutions for the m equilibrium η_h^*.

The structure revealed here contrasts with that where utility functions are not separable in this way. That case usually requires knowledge of all the data of the economy $\mathscr{E}\{(x_h^0, \eta_h^0), u_h\}$ in order to solve for any of the x_{hi}^*, η_h^*, or p_i^*.

This completes the first stage of the proof. The second stage returns to

Marshall's simple corn market. Hicks pointed out that any change in price during false trading "has the same sort of effect as a redistribution of wealth" (1939, p. 128). A purchase of x of corn at any false price p can thus always be decomposed as the sum of two transactions, a purchase of x at the equilibrium price p^*, plus a transfer of $x(p - p^*)$ units of numéraire from buyer to seller if $p > p^*$, or from seller to buyer otherwise. From the first part of the proof, if the numéraire has constant marginal utility for everyone then such transfers cannot affect anyone's behaviour. Put another way, in this simple market false trading can "only give rise to income effects" (ibid., p. 129), and with universal constant marginal utility of money all these income effects are zero. The theorem is proved.

VI The Note on Barter

The *Note on Barter* is little more than two pages long. Its actors are two persons A and B each equipped with a basket, one full of apples, the other full of nuts. It is implicit that their respective marginal rates of substitution of nuts for apples differ, so that trade is possible. Marshall argues that even in the assumed absence of a market there is still a true equilibrium exchange ratio (in his example, six nuts for one apple), based on the agents' utility functions and endowments. But because of the definitional nonconstancy of all marginal utilities in barter, "there is no reason to suppose that it [the true ratio] will be reached in practice" (p. 395). He gives numerical examples of two quite different paths of false trading and shows that each is likely to have its terminus in a position where, in effect, the marginal rate of substitution of nuts for apples that is common to A and B differs not only from that at the other terminus, but also – and this is the main point – from the "true" equilibrium exchange ratio.

He claims that this difference will not be significantly narrowed by adding more competitors, as long as all marginal utilities continue to be variable. Suppose that 100 people have baskets of apples, and 100 have baskets of nuts. Then "whether there was free communication throughout the market or not, the *mean* of the bargains would not be so likely to differ very widely from the rate of six nuts for an apple as in the case of barter between two people. But yet there would be no such strong probability of its adhering very closely to that rate as we saw was the case in the corn market" (p. 396; italics added).

Edgeworth begins his criticism (1891*b*) of the *Note on Barter* with many compliments to Marshall, expressed in the impossibly flowery language he uses for such things: "the recent and already classic work of Alfred Marshall", "soaring over the others like an eagle", and so on. But, he warns, "like the little bird in the fable, I am going to risk a little flight of my own".

The first beating of his wings is a demonstration of how easily Marshall's two paths of false trading can be fitted into the geometric framework of contract theory, with a resulting gain in perspicuity. In a letter to Edgeworth probably written in March 1891 before he had fully studied (1891*b*), Marshall thought this diagram "so neat in itself" (*Variorum*, p. 793) that he proposed to include it in the imminent second edition of the *Principles*. The result was the quite new and slightly schizophrenic Appendix Note XII*bis* (pp. 755–6), whose acid last paragraph reflects Marshall's further brooding on the paper. His letter did not say why he, the only living reviewer of *Mathematical Psychics* and thus the one person who might be expected to be quite familiar with contract theory, had not himself thought of such a simple application. Perhaps a complaint in his review of Edgeworth (1881), to the effect that its "reasonings . . . are rather hard to follow", in part because of "the frequent use of unexplained metaphor" (*EEW*, 2, p. 267), seriously understated Marshall's analytical difficulties with contract theory. The sad fact is that, for whatever reason, this theory was ignored by almost everyone except Edgeworth himself, not only in his own time but also well into ours, until its rehabilitation by Martin Shubik in 1959.

Edgeworth then goes on to observe that, whereas Marshall lays primary blame for the indeterminacy of bilateral barter on the variability of all marginal utilities, he himself believes the main culprit to be fewness of numbers: "[I]f the market mechanism could be made more perfect in . . . [these] . . . respects, this circumstance [the nonconstancy of marginal utilities] would not be a cause of difficulty" (1891*b*, p. 239). Edgeworth is careful to say that "I do not object to any of Marshall's conclusions" (p. 239), but instead offers a lame and vague objection to "certain formulations which, receiving his [Marshall's] authority, could result in detriment to the science".

Since he could manage only such pale protest, why had he written the article at all? He could hardly write, what was probably his real rationale, "Please notice that I have worked much more deeply on these matters than has Marshall". But he does the next best thing, devoting most of his article to a rather clear outline of the contract theory of *Mathematical Psychics*, to which he refers his readers "for a more minute and exact exposition" (ibid., p. 236 n.). There is no analytical advance from this earlier work, however, apart from a more extensive discussion of bargains between employers and employees. This subsidiary aspect of the controversy was analysed at length by Hicks (1930) in his first theoretical article, and will not be discussed here.

One formulation of "detriment to the science" was Marshall's mistaken discussion of barter with 100 competitors on each side. This completely overlooked contract theory's main result, that the addition of competitors necessarily shrinks the core. Edgeworth pointed this out (pp. 239ff), but was too polite to say that it was an oversight on Marshall's part.

VII Edgeworth's Error

Denoting apples by x and nuts by y, Edgeworth (1891b, pp. 235–6) shows that constant marginal utilities of y imply that the contract curve is a line parallel to the y axis. He also asserts without proof (it follows from the subsystem $\mathscr{S}$ of Section V) that the common slopes of the indifference curves of the two agents are then identical ($=\Theta$, say) everywhere along this contract curve. Edgeworth thought that a gain for him and a loss for Marshall, since even with Marshall's own assumption there remain an indefinite number of final settlements. Thus the outcome of the barter is still, in Edgeworth's sense, indeterminate.

Uncharacteristically unsubtle, perhaps ensnared by the *hubris* of his own "little flight", Edgeworth then disastrously fails to notice some further implications of this analysis, implications which reverse that gain and loss. For if the marginal utilities of y are constant then the terminus on the contract curve of every false trading path will yield the same terminal exchange ratio Θ and the same individual holdings x_a and x_b; from the analysis in Section V these will be the exchange ratio and individual x holdings of the competitive equilibrium. The terminal individual y holdings, on the other hand, depend on which false path has been followed into the core, so they are not necessarily those of the competitive equilibrium; to that extent, there is indeed indeterminacy of contract in Edgeworth's sense. But the competitive equilibrium quantities ($p^* = \Theta$, x_a^*, x_b^*) are all fully determinate.

Edgeworth was mildly but firmly admonished by Arthur Berry for not realising these further implications. "It may seem presumptuous for a dilettante in economics to suggest that the Professor at Oxford has misunderstood his colleague at Cambridge, but I am going to take that risk" (1891, p. 550). In a letter sent to Edgeworth on April Fools' Day (*Variorum*, pp. 793–5), which includes most of the substantive points in his brief note published in June, Berry pointed out that Marshall "works throughout with two unknowns, amount of commodity and price, and when he speaks of determinateness or indeterminateness he refers to these two things only. Amount of money hardly occurs explicitly but it is implicitly stated (pp. 391,2) that this is indeterminate".

This was quite right and just, save in one particular. Marshall never "speaks of determinateness or indeterminateness" in either the text of Chapter 2 or the *Note on Barter,* but only of *equilibrium,* contrasting "*the* [or "the true"] equilibrium price" with "*an* equilibrium price". By the former price, Marshall means in the case of the corn market that which is determined by the static demand and supply schedules, and in the case of barter that which is determined by (as we would now say) preferences and endowments. By the latter price, he means in the corn market case that which is reached at the close of the trading day by any false path and which still differs from *the* price; and in the case of barter, that which is reached when trade is no longer mutually beneficial, and which still differs from *the* price.

There is no place in these Marshallian concepts for Edgeworth's idea of indeterminacy of contract. Let us call an exchange economy *determinate in Edgeworth's sense* if it has just one final settlement (here fudging the possibility of finitely many such contracts), and *determinate in Marshall's sense* if every trading sequence converges to (1) the same set of individual holdings of all but the numéraire good η and (2) the same vector of prices expressed in terms of η. Then the following logical implications obtain, and only those:

Agents h are sufficiently numerous $\Rightarrow$ Determinate in Edgeworth's sense
    For all h, $\partial u_h(.)/\partial \eta_h = k_h > 0$ $\Rightarrow$ Determinate in Marshall's sense

VIII   Marshall's Reaction

Edgeworth could have defended himself against Berry by arguing that Marshall had never actually spoken of "determinateness and indeterminateness", everything being left implicit and so with room for natural and forgivable misunderstanding. Alternatively, he could have gone on to attack, arguing that Marshall's concept of determinacy is not useful and constant marginal utility is not sensible, either empirically or as a peg on which to hang the distinction between markets and barter.

Admittedly, his admired authors Auspitz and Lieben (1889) had also assumed constant marginal utility of the numéraire, but their debate with Walras had made it clear that for them it was an explicit simplifying device, adopted to obtain sharp results from a general equilibrium system (see Walras, 1890; Auspitz and Lieben, 1890; Jaffé, 1965, 2, pp. 421–3). For Marshall, in contrast, the assumption appeared to be both that and something more, an empirical truth distilled from his priestly knowledge of the arcana of the transcendental world of business. "It is now nearly twenty years since I decided that the plan which you [Edgeworth] and Auspitz follow would, probably if not necessarily, lead to hopeless unreality and unpracticality" (*Variorum*, p. 797).

Instead, Edgeworth neither defended himself nor attacked Marshall but meekly surrendered, pleading *mea culpa* (1891c, p. 316). He "confessed frankly" that he had indeed confused Marshall's meaning of determinateness with his own, and that "I had attributed to him a proposition which he did not have in mind." Presumably, this was the proposition that bilateral barter with universal constant marginal utilities of one particular good is determinate in Edgeworth's sense.

Why Edgeworth folded so completely remained an unsolved puzzle for seventy years, until the publication of *Variorum* in 1961 provided material (pp. 790–8) from which a possible answer can be constructed. Being sure of neither his mathematics nor his Italian, Marshall had asked young Arthur Berry (age 29) to read Edgeworth's article and to write a reply, a manoeuvre which amusingly parallels the impressment of the young Ladislaus von Bortkiewicz (age 21) into Walras's own controversy with Edgeworth. Bortkiewicz's article (1890), while purporting to be a review of the second edition of the *Éléments,* had in fact been commissioned by Walras to rebut Edgeworth's offending review of the same work (1889a); Jaffé (1965, 2, pp. 363ff) presents the epistolary evidence.

Whereas Bortkiewicz attacked Edgeworth with vigour enough to satisfy even Walras's exacting standards in such matters, Berry proved a gentle hit-man, finding Edgeworth's "argument as to recontracts which would disturb temporary equilibria, . . . very interesting and it seems to me quite true" (*Variorum*, p. 794). However, "I hardly think it bears directly on Marshall's chapter, where recontracts are tacitly excluded". (So much is "tacit" or "implicit" in Marshall that it is not surprising that Cambridge, according to Leontief (1937), was the home of "implicit theorizing".)

At the end of his letter to Edgeworth of April 1st, Berry said that "Prof. Marshall is anxious to print off the note on barter as soon as possible, and he would be glad if you would be kind enough to send any answer you may care to make to these criticisms to me under cover to him". For all the speed of the postal services of late-Victorian England, any such reply by Edgeworth to Berry's polite sandbagging could hardly have completed the round-trip to Cambridge in only three days. Yet even that was too long a wait for the anxious Marshall, who was abnormally sensitive to criticism. On April 4th he fired off to Edgeworth a long shrill letter, full of a self-centredness and petulance remarkable even for academia; no mere extract can capture its full unlovely flavour.

Having seen Berry's incontrovertible proof that Edgeworth had quite misunderstood the *Note on Barter,* Marshall must have realised that he was victorious and Edgeworth beaten and that the world would know it soon enough (Victorian academic publishing, like its mails, was faster than ours). The defeat was so severe that both humanity and humility called for magnanimity on the victor's part, the first because they were friends, the second because Marshall must have recognised, if he had read (1891*b*) that far, the force of Edgeworth's criticism of his own analysis of 100-a-side barter. In a similar situation the forthright Jevons, who had not held back from criticising his friend Edgeworth – "an uncouth and even clumsy piece of literary work" (1881, p. 583) – would probably have written to the effect: "Your criticism was a silly mistake, please don't let it happen again; and, please, no more of those fulsome, hollow, compliments". That, in brief, was the actual substance of Marshall's complaint; but his long tirade lacked all charity.

Three samples indicate the hectoring tone: "What I want to say is that I do not think you at all appreciate the deadly and enduring injury that *A* does to *B,* if he reads rapidly a piece of hard argument on which *B* has spent an immense deal of work; and then believing that argument to be wrong, writes an article full of the most polite phrases, in which a caricature of that argument is held up to the most refined, but deadly scorn" (p. 796). "You did not even take the trouble to find out that I had proved explicitly every single thing that you had proved with the only problem which I had formulated, or had any desire to discuss at that particular place. You thus got easily the credit of saying something new, whereas it was not new" (p. 797). "You supplement my discussion by some of your own on extraneous topics [that is, contract theory]. They may be important. . . . Very likely they may be really more important than all I have said on that and all other subjects" (p. 797).

When Marshall sat to Will Rothenstein for his retirement portrait, the painter was taken aback to discover that "In talking with Marshall one had need to be circumspect. For everything one said he took literally and met with the full weight of his pedantry the most casual remarks. I tried to speak cautiously, to be conciliatory, to be thoroughly non-committal, but in vain; no gleam of humour lightened his talk. Fortunately, he also took sitting seriously, for he was vain, and vain men make the best sitters" (1932, p. 130).

The colloquial phrase "lighten up" was surely coined with Marshall in mind.

IX Consequences for Edgeworth

Concluding (1891c) with a discussion of Berry's views on bargaining, Edgeworth's last sentence was: "But I make this defence with all modesty, as one who has already burnt his fingers and fears the fire of controversy" (Guillebaud's translation, *Variorum*, p. 798). His readers must have been puzzled at this description of Berry's temperate criticism and perhaps put it down to the rich exuberance of Edgeworth's prose style. But of course it was Marshall's wild outburst and not Berry's restrained comment that required appeasement; anything for a quiet life.

It is tempting to speculate on the long-term consequences for Edgeworth of this defeat. The assertion that after *Mathematical Psychics* he "never again returned to the theory of contract" (Newman, 1987, p. 96) is at best misleadingly phrased, but it is true that he never advanced contract theory beyond the point reached there. Editorship of the *Economic Journal* took up much of his time; the rest he spent on statistics and on topics more in the mainstream of theoretical and applied economics.

One omission in his later work was the theory of consumer's demand. *Mathematical Psychics* and even the earlier *New and Old Methods of Ethics* showed Edgeworth already in full control of all the necessary mathematical tools, such as Lagrange multipliers, and the later book had invented most of the necessary economic tools, such as convex preferences. Yet the theory of demand had to wait for Fisher, Pareto, Johnson, and Slutsky. Perhaps a curious devotion to Marshall's assumption played an inhibiting role, for even as late as 1915 Edgeworth still held that "with reference to internal trade at least, the marginal utility of money may be treated as constant" (1925, 2, p. 465).

X Epilogue

The passage between Marshall and Edgeworth over barter hardly merits Hicks's description of it as "the great controversy with Marshall" (1930, p. 217), for neither showed greatness in battle and each was petty in victory or defeat. Its strangest aspect was left until a generation later, when in the year after Marshall's death *Papers Relating to Political Economy* was published at the behest of the Royal Economic Society (Keynes, 1933, pp. 287–8). Editing this collection gave Edgeworth an unexpected chance to get his own back on barter, a chance he seized upon in his own eccentric way.

For consider: (α) He changed the title of his "translation" (1925, 2, pp. 313–19) of (1891*b*), from the long original "Observations on the mathematical theory of political economy with special reference to the *Principles of Economics* of Alfred Marshall", to the more compact "On the Determinateness of Equilibrium", thus omitting all reference to Marshall and putting the emphasis squarely on the problem he felt to be at issue.

(β) He thoroughly filleted his "translation", leaving out "several long passages which purported to be restatements of theories more accurately enunciated in [*Mathematical Psychics*]" (1925, 2, p. 314), and without saying so also omitting several other relevant passages, some complimentary to Marshall and others not. These various cuts were so large in total (the 13 pages of original being reduced to four pages of "translation"), that a reader of the *Papers* alone can scarcely have any idea of what the fight was about, or even that there was one. That may well be just the effect intended.

(γ) Strangest of all, Edgeworth told a bare-faced lie when he claimed that "The inquiry [1891*b*] takes its start from a passage in the then recently published second edition of Marshall's *Principles,* where he adduces from the present writer's essay on *Mathematical Psychics* a construction there largely employed in the investigation of economic equilibrium, the *contract-curve*" (1925, 2, p. 313).

The evidence is that Edgeworth had seen no relevant part or draft of the second edition of the *Principles* before he wrote (1891*b*). All its quotations from the *Principles* are from the first edition; n. 2 on page 234 even quotes a passage (from p. 418) that was deleted from the second and all subsequent editions! Moreover, a footnote at the end of (1891*b*) by the editors of the *Giornale* (de Viti de Marco, Mazzola, Pantaleoni and Zorli) states that: "It will probably not be possible to publish the other parts of this article by the distinguished Prof. Edgeworth in the April issue, because a new edition of Marshall's work, with corrections and additions, is already announced for the end of March and Prof. Edgeworth wishes to compare the last parts of his article with this new edition" (1891*b*, p. 245, n. 1). Apparently, these "other parts" never were published, either that April or at any later time.

Even without this internal evidence from (1891*b*), however, the respective dates make Edgeworth's claim (γ) incredible. His article was published in March 1891 while the Preface to *Principles* (2d ed.) is dated June 1891, the book itself appearing sometime later that year. The new Appendix, Note XII *bis* of that edition refers not only to *Mathematical Psychics* (as Edgeworth says) but also to (1891*b*), incidentally getting its month of publication wrong in the process.

There are at least three questions to ask about (γ). First, why did

Edgeworth do it? Second, how could he have expected to get away with it? Third, did he get away with it?

We can only guess as to the first question. A charitable answer is that as old age overtook Edgeworth the true sequence of events became hazy in his mind. The cunning displayed in (α) and (β) argues against that, however, as does such a brilliant late work as (1922). Less generously, it is possible that (α) through (γ) were deliberately designed to interact together so as to direct the reader's attention away from his mistaken criticism of Marshall.

As to the second question, Edgeworth knew that statistically speaking his life was rapidly nearing its close (he died in February, 1926), so perhaps he just did not care whether, later, he was found out; after all, he had no descendants. On the other hand, knowing the scholarly habits of his fellow economists, maybe Edgeworth did not expect that any of them would actually check on the truth of (γ). This expectation was rational, for no one does seem ever to have doubted the truth of his claim, at least in print; on the contrary, it has been trustingly and quite naturally repeated more than once by later economists.

The answer to the third question must therefore be an unequivocal "yes", which illustrates once again the perennial truth of Schumpeter's well known dictum "the majority of economists *do not read*" (1954, p. 1045 n. 48, italics his).

References

Auspitz, R., and Lieben, R. (1889). *Untersuchungen über die Theorie des Preises.* Leipzig: Duncker and Humblot.

(1890). "Correspondance", *Revue d'Economie Politique* 4:599–605.

Berry, A. (1891). "Alcune Brevi Parole Sulla Teoria del Baratto di A. Marshall", *Giornale degli Economisti*, Second Series 2:550–3.

Bortkiewicz [Bortkévitch], L. von (1890). Review of Léon Walras, *Eléments d'Economie Politique . . . Deuxième Edition. Revue d'Economie Politique* 4:80–6.

Creedy, J. (1986). *Edgeworth and the Development of Neoclassical Economics.* Oxford: Blackwell.

Edgeworth, F. Y. (1877). *New and Old Methods of Ethics.* Oxford: Parker.

(1881). *Mathematical Psychics.* London: Kegan Paul.

(1884). "The Rationale of Exchange", *Journal of the [Royal] Statistical Society* 47:164–6; not in Edgeworth (1925).

(1889a). Review of Léon Walras, *Eléments d'Economie Politique Pure. Nature* 40, September 5:434–6. Not in Edgeworth (1925), although parts may be found in the afterword (1925:2, 310–12) to the reprint of (1889b).

(1889*b*). "Opening Address to Section F of the British Association", *Nature* 40 (September 19):496–508. Also in: *Journal of the [Royal] Statistical Society* 42 (December 1889):538–76; *British Association Report for 1889* (London: John Murray, 1890): 671–96; and Edgeworth (1925, 2).

(1890*a*). Review of Alfred Marshall *Principles of Economics*. *Nature* 42, August 14:362–4; not in Edgeworth (1925).

(1890*b*). Review of Alfred Marshall *Principles of Economics*. *The Academy* 38 (August 30):165–6; not in Edgeworth (1925).

(1891*a*). "La Théorie Mathématique de l'Offre et de la Demande et la Coût de Production", *Revue d'Économie Politique* 5:10–28; not in Edgeworth (1925).

(1891*b*). "Osservazioni Sulla Teoria Matematica dell' Economia Politica con Riguardo Speciale ai *Principi di Economia Politica* di Alfredo Marshall", *Giornale degli Economisti*, Second Series 2:233–45; greatly abridged "translation" in Edgeworth (1925, 2).

(1891*c*). "Ancora a Proposito della Teoria del Baratto", *Giornale degli Economisti*, Second Series 3:316–18; a part is in Edgeworth (1925, 2).

(1922). "The Mathematical Economics of Professor Amoroso", *Economic Journal* 32:400–7; not in Edgeworth (1925).

(1925). *Papers Relating to Political Economy*. 3 vols. London: Macmillan, for the Royal Economic Society.

Fisher, I. N. (1956). *My Father, Irving Fisher*. New York: Comet.

Hicks, J. R. (1930). "Edgeworth, Marshall and the Indeterminateness of Wages", *Economic Journal* 40:215–31.

(1939). *Value and Capital*. Oxford: Oxford University Press.

Jaffé, W. (ed.) (1965). *Correspondence of Léon Walras and Related Papers,* Three Volumes. Amsterdam: North-Holland.

Jevons, W. S. (1881). Review of F. Y. Edgeworth, *Mathematical Psychics*. *Mind* 6:581–3.

Keynes, J. M. (1933). *Essays in Biography*. London: Macmillan.

Leontief, W. W. (1937). "Implicit Theorizing: A Methodological Criticism of the Neo-Cambridge School", *Quarterly Journal of Economics* 51:337–51.

Maloney, J. (1985). *Marshall, Orthodoxy and the Professionalisation of Economics*. Cambridge: Cambridge University Press.

Newman, P. (1965). *The Theory of Exchange*. Englewood Cliffs, N.J.: Prentice-Hall.

(1987). "Edgeworth, Francis Ysidro". In J. Eatwell, M. Milgate, and P. Newman (eds.), *The New Palgrave: A Dictionary of Economics*. London: Macmillan.

Rothenstein, W. (1932). *Men and Memories, 2*. New York: Coward-McCann.

Schumpeter, J. A. (1954). *History of Economic Analysis*. New York: Oxford University Press.

Shubik, M. (1959). "Edgeworth Market Games". In A. W. Tucker and R. D. Luce (eds.), *Contributions to the Theory of Games, 4*. Princeton, N.J.: Princeton University Press.

Uzawa, H. (1962). "On the Stability of Edgeworth's Barter Process", *International Economic Review* 3:218–32.

Walker, D. A. (1969). "Marshall's Theory of Competitive Exchange", *Canadian Journal of Economics* 2:590–8.

Walras, L. (1890). "Observations sur le Principe de la Théorie du Prix de MM. Auspitz et Lieben", *Revue d'Économie Politique* 4:320–3.

12

Marshall's Consumer's Surplus in Modern Perspective

JOHN S. CHIPMAN

In 1941 Hicks observed (p. 108): "When Marshall's *Principles* was first published in 1890, his theory of Consumers' Surplus was immediately recognised as the most striking novelty in the book". There is no question that, whether or not Marshall discovered the idea himself or learnt it from Dupuit (1844),[1] he was the first to incorporate it into economic theory as the basic tool of analysis of welfare problems. It was fundamental to his theory of public finance and his theory of monopoly.

Since the validity of the concept rests on approximations, as Marshall readily acknowledged, it has been controversial from the start. The skeptics, notably Walras (1890), Pareto (1892–3), Nicholson (1893, 1894), and Samuelson (1942, 1947), form as distinguished a group as the protagonists Edgeworth (1891, 1894*a*, 1894*b*, 1897), Barone (1894*a*, 1894*b*, 1894*c*, 1894*d*), Pigou (1910), Lerner (1934), Hotelling (1938), and Hicks (1941, 1942, 1943, 1945). What are the issues that have continued to separate these groups into strongly antagonistic camps?

In this chapter I will try to sort out the main issues that have continued to be debated, and form an evaluation of both the historical importance and practical usefulness of the concept. Among the questions to be addressed (which are by no means unrelated) are the following: Is consum-

Work supported by NSF grant 7924816.

1. Apparently we will never know (see the discussion in *EEW*), but one factor in support of the hypothesis of Marshall's originality is his disregard of Dupuit's formula expressing the consumer's loss from an excise tax as proportional to the square of the tax, a formula emphasised by Hotelling (1938) and (implicitly) by Hicks (1941).

er's surplus best suited to first-best or second-best problems in welfare economics? Is its status as a cardinal measure of welfare change an essential or incidental feature? How robust are the conclusions drawn from this analysis against departures from assumptions that would make it an exact analysis? And finally, is it more practical, easier to implement, than exact methods?

I A Tool for First-Best or Second-Best Analysis?

If we examine the uses to which Marshall put the concept, it seems clear that he was primarily interested in "first-best" analysis. He used the tool to conclude that excise taxes were inferior to income taxes, in a context in which one could treat the latter as lump-sum taxes that did not involve a departure from an optimum. He characteristically cautioned the reader that the formal analysis had to be subjected to many qualifications; nevertheless his formal analysis compared an optimal with a suboptimal situation. His proposal that industries subject to decreasing returns should be taxed to subsidise industries subject to increasing returns, while as usual subject to many practical qualifications, was a proposal for an optimal system of taxation.[2] Finally, the same can be said for his analysis of monopoly, followed up by those of Edgeworth (1894) and Lerner (1934), whose purpose was to show that the monetary gains of the monopolist did not offset the losses to consumers.

The whole power of the tool of consumer's surplus consists in its ability to compare a monetary quantity, whether tax revenues or monopoly profits, with a nonmonetary one. This has constituted its great appeal from the beginning. Prior to the development of this tool, public officials tended to ignore nonmonetary beneficial or adverse effects of government policies, simply because there was no way to quantify them. To this day, cost accountants ignore nonpecuniary effects of measures undertaken in businesses such as hospitals, schools, and universities that produce outputs hard to quantify and measure.[3] There can therefore be no question of the enormous advance in economic science made possible by the development of this tool.

That being said, however, one must meet the fundamental objection raised by Samuelson (1947, p. 197):

2. Hicks (1941, p. 115) interpreted this proposal as an example of second-best welfare economics. So it is, from the partial-equilibrium point of view, but not from that of general-equilibrium analysis.
3. A good example is the concept of "indirect costs" used by universities to tax research grants, without taking into account any indirect benefits gained by the research.

If one were to begin afresh to give answers to the following problems, in no one of them would consumer's surplus be necessary or
desirable: Should Robinson Crusoe, a Socialist state, or a capitalist
economy build a particular bridge? Should indirect taxes be pre-
ferred to direct taxes? Should discriminatory prices be allowed if a
uniform price will not keep an activity in business? ... Should a
particular small industry be expanded or contracted by means of tax
or subsidy? etc. etc. Aside from their extraneous inter-personal aspects, all of these questions can more conveniently (and more hon-
estly!) be answered in terms of the consumer's ordinal preference
field.

One of the strongest protagonists of the concept of consumer's surplus
essentially concurred. According to Hicks (1941, p. 112):

The first task of welfare economics is the formal study of the conditions of optimum organisation [i.e., of Pareto optimality] ... The
second task of welfare economics is the study of deviations from this
optimum, and it is here that consumers' surplus has its part to play.
The idea of consumers' surplus enables us to study in detail the
effects of deviations from the optimum in a particular market. It is
not merely a convenient way of showing when there will be a deviation (consumers' surplus is not necessary for that purpose, since the
basic optimum conditions ... show us at once when there will be a
deviation); it also offers us a way of measuring the size of the deviation. This, if we are right in our general viewpoint, is a most important service.

Hicks went on to extend the analysis in Marshall's diagram (*Principles*, p.
811 n.) to the case in which a distortion (by monopoly output) was
followed by a further distortion (a tax), and came to the conclusion (p.
114): "When output has already been contracted below the optimum, a
further contraction is very damaging."

The implication of Hicks's statement, as I understand it, is that an
increase in an excise tax from t monetary units to $2t$ of these units is
worse (in fact much worse) than the initial increase from 0 to t. This
implies the possibility of a *quaternary ordering* of alternatives, that is, the
possibility of comparing the change in utility in going from 0 to t with the
change in utility in going from t to $2t$; as is well known, this is the basic
requisite for "cardinal utility". It is possible that such a comparison could
be made operational. For example, we might be able to say that an excise
tax on commodity 1 is just as bad as one on commodity 2; and that,
starting from an excise tax on commodity 1 but none on commodity 2, an
equal excise tax on commodity 2 would be preferable to a doubling of the
excise tax on commodity 1. Or more generally, any movement away from

uniformity of excise taxes is deleterious. But for such an argument to be made rigourous one would need the kind of analysis that could deal with two or more industries simultaneously, not just one. Nevertheless the suggestion is most intriguing, especially coming from the century's leading proponent of the nonmeasurability of utility.

Hicks's position may be characterised as the "second line of defense" of the concept of consumer's surplus. What about the first line of defense? What is not brought out by Samuelson's statement quoted above is that (1) at the time Marshall wrote, there were no alternative convincing proofs of what is now known as the "fundamental theorem of welfare economics"; and (2) the method of proof of this theorem now currently taught to all graduate students of economics owes its origin to Marshall's treatment of this proposition in the *Principles*. At the outset it should be recalled that the concept of "Pareto optimality"[4] was first formulated by Marshall (*Principles*, pp. 470–1). True, it was presented somewhat diffidently as "one interpretation of the doctrine according to which every position of equilibrium of demand and supply may fairly be regarded as a position of maximum satisfaction". It was formulated quite clearly, however, as the doctrine that "when equilibrium has been reached, . . . no terms can be arranged which will be acceptable to the buyer, and will not involve a loss to the seller." It is well documented that Pareto was closely acquainted with the *Principles*, and there can be no question that it was the most important stimulus to his approach to welfare economics – much aided by the prodding of Pantaleoni and Barone. In the middle of his 1894 paper on the optimality of free competition (which he had first tried to establish by means of what Marshall had called "maximum aggregate satisfaction in the full sense of the term" involving interpersonal comparison of utilities) he stated that under the influence of Pantaleoni and Barone he had decided to present an independent proof based on the possibility of pecuniary compensation among the parties.[5] Barone (1894c) had reacted positively to Marshall's concept of consumer's surplus, Pareto (1892) negatively, because of his skepticism of a method based on approximate constancy of the marginal utility of income. We may assume that Pareto considered it a challenge to establish Marshall's propositions concerning what we would

4. The term is due to Little (1950).
5. The first half of this paper, as well as Pareto's main 1892–3 result on the implications of constant marginal utility of income and Barone's (1894c, 1894d) papers on consumer's surplus, was summarised by Sanger (1895), but unfortunately not the second. Marshall (*Principles*, p. 132 n.) cited Sanger's paper by way of calling upon Barone's authority as backing for his thesis that when expenditure on a commodity formed a small proportion of a consumer's income, variations in the marginal utility of income would be of "the second order of small quantities". He did not refer to Pareto's opposing result.

now call the Pareto optimality of competitive equilibrium without having to resort to Marshall's approximative assumptions. Pareto's subsequent (1902) attempt to arrive at a rigourous proof that an economy with a monopolist and a price-taker was not Pareto optimal may be regarded as rising to the challenge of providing an exact rigourous proof to replace Marshall's much simpler and more intuitive reasoning based on the assumption of a constant marginal utility of income.

The methods of analysis derived by Barone and Pareto, only subsequently rendered completely explicit and transparent by Arrow (1951) as well as by McKenzie (1957) and Hurwicz and Uzawa (1971), involved the duality between maximisation of utility subject to a budget constraint and minimisation of expenditure subject to a utility constraint. How this tool could be used to prove the fundamental theorem of welfare economics was beautifully shown by Koopmans (1957). In substituting an income-compensation function or expenditure function for the concept of consumer's surplus, these methods were able to transcend Marshall's by dispensing with any approximations. However, Marshall's role in formulating the problem to begin with and providing a very simple and appealing, though approximative and sometimes treacherous, tool of analysis should not be forgotten. The modern approach is entirely in the spirit of Marshall's, perhaps more so than that of those who insist on clinging to the old tools of analysis with their approximative assumptions.

That consumer's surplus can be a treacherous tool cannot be questioned. For example, after analysing the effect of an excise tax on agricultural produce (*Principles*, p. 473 n.) Marshall concluded (p. 475):

> it is commonly argued that an equal *ad valorem* tax levied on all economic commodities (material and immaterial), or which is the same thing a tax on expenditure, is *primâ facie* the best tax; because it does not divert the expenditure of individuals out of its natural channels: we have now seen that this argument is invalid.

Here, Marshall proceeded – without recognizing the need for justification – from an analysis of a single industry to a conclusion concerning the whole economy. As it happens he was mistaken. The same error was committed by Hotelling (1938), as pointed out by Frisch (1939) and conceded by Hotelling (1939).[6] On the other hand, Marshall with his tools was able to enunciate a fascinating and very original proposition: that optimality would require taxation of industries operating under decreasing returns and subsidisation of industries operating under increasing returns. This proposition was treated with scorn by Samuelson (1947, p.

6.   For a detailed discussion of the argument see Chipman (1987).

196);[7] on the other hand the present writer has shown that under certain admittedly restrictive but definite assumptions the proposition, as well as Marshall's arguments in its support, is rigourously correct.[8] Thus, the concept of consumer's surplus has given rise both to false propositions that have been believed and true propositions that have not been believed; it has also given rise to better methods that can yield exact and incontrovertible results.

II Constancy of the Marginal Utility of Income

Marshall's argument was stated as follows (*Principles*, p. 842):

> It should be noted that, in the discussion of consumers' surplus, we assume that the marginal utility of money to the individual purchaser is the same throughout. Strictly speaking we ought to take account of the fact that if he spent less on tea, the marginal utility of money to him would be less than it is, and he would get an element of consumers' surplus from buying other things at prices which now yield him no such rent. But these changes of consumers' rent (being of the second order of smallness) may be neglected, on the assumption, which underlies our whole reasoning, that his expenditure on any one thing, as, for instance, tea, is only a small part of his whole expenditure.

While the basic idea was in Auspitz and Lieben (1889), Edgeworth (1891a) was the first to provide an exact interpretation of Marshall's assumption of constancy of the marginal utility of income. In the two-commodity case, a utility function of the form $U(x_1,x_2) = x_1 + W(x_2)$ would yield income-consumption paths that are parallel to the x_1-axis, thus yielding zero income elasticity of demand for commodity 2. Interpreting commodity 1 as an "instrumental good" or "ideal money" in Barone's terminology, it would have a constant marginal utility. The implications for the pure theory of exchange were explored by Berry

---

7. In his words:
> Historically the important propositions concerning increasing and decreasing cost industries, which are attributed to Marshall's consumer's surplus notions, may be said at best to have been incomplete derivations, and at worse may be said to be absolutely incorrect statements which, by a pun or play on words, seem to resemble the Pigouvian doctrine concerning industries with external economies and diseconomies. In its earlier form the Pigouvian doctrine is close to that of Marshall, but from the writings of Knight and Pigou himself we know that earlier form to be quite wrong.

8. Cf. Chipman (1970) where it is assumed that consumers have Mill–Cobb–Douglas preferences and that there is a single factor of production.

(1891) and Edgeworth (1891*b*) as well as by Marshall (*Principles*, pp. 844–5). Using (implicitly) the concept of an indirect utility function introduced by Allen (1933), Samuelson (1942) showed that constancy of the marginal (indirect) utility of income when the price of commodity 1 is fixed (i.e., its independence of other prices and income) implies that preferences have the Edgeworth "parallel" form (to use the convenient terminology introduced by Boulding, 1945).

Pareto (1892–3) explored the implications of constancy of the marginal utility of income when income itself is fixed (i.e., its independence of prices) and in the case of additively separable utility obtained the condition that the utility function would have the Mill–Cobb–Douglas or loglinear (Bernoullian) form. Samuelson (1942) obtained the more general condition that income elasticity of demand would be unitary, a result implying that preferences would be homothetic.

An integrated treatment of these two cases was presented in Chipman and Moore (1976), who showed that with the respective assumptions of (1) a fixed price of commodity 1 and (2) fixed income, a necessary and sufficient condition for the consumer's surplus integral to be independent of path and to represent preferences is that these preferences be respectively (1) parallel and (2) homothetic. Typical applications of problems involving excise taxes in particular industries require use of the first assumption to be exact, while application of Marshall's tax-and-bounty scheme for increasing- and decreasing-return industries requires the second. Thus it is interesting to note that different applications of this tool involve different approximative assumptions about preferences that are obviously incompatible with one another. In place of the assumption of a fixed price of commodity 1 or fixed income, one can more generally impose a restriction on a linear combination of prices and income (or a somewhat more general nonlinear restriction); Chipman and Moore (1990) show that this yields, in order for consumer's surplus analysis to be exact, the requirement that preferences follow a particular subset of the Gorman (1961) "polar form" corresponding to the assumed restrictions.

Hicks proposed in place of Marshall's consumer's surplus integral the concept of *compensating variation,* which is equivalent to applying the method of consumer's surplus to compensated as opposed to Marshallian demand functions. In line with Hicks's dictum that the proper role of consumer's surplus is in analysing and measuring deviations from optima, one ought to be able to say that if the compensating variation in going from situation 0 to situation 2 is greater than that in going from situation 0 to situation 1, then it should be possible to conclude that situation 2 is superior to situation 1. Comparisons similar to those of Hicks have been proposed by Harberger (1964). However, Chipman and Moore (1980) show that in terms of this generalized form of compensating variation, exactly the same conditions on preferences are implied by the requirement that the analysis be exact as hold for the case of consumer's surplus.

The major problem in evaluating consumer's surplus as a practical tool of cost-benefit analysis is the definition of "approximation". Exactly what is meant by saying that the analysis is "approximately correct"? One approach would be to say that in certain applications preferences are "approximately parallel" and another that they are "approximately homothetic". We still lack information, however, as to how close the approximation of preferences must be in order for the results of a cost-benefit analysis to be good approximations of results of an exact analysis.[9] Samuelson (1947, p. 194) pointed out that the Marshallian reasoning in terms of "second order of smallness" was technically incorrect. In his classic argument with Nicholson (1893), the best Edgeworth (1894) could come up with was an analogy to the theory of the piston in physics, for which there is presumably a precise definition of the approximation process.

As far as I know, there is no theorem available in the literature stating that if the proportion of income spent on a particular commodity is less than some prescribed small number $\epsilon > 0$, the qualitative conclusions drawn from consumer's surplus analysis concerning the effect of an excise tax on welfare will be correct, no matter what the shape of the consumer's preferences may be. Nor do I know of an example showing that for some preferences and arbitrarily small ϵ, the classic conclusions of consumer's surplus analysis will be reversed. Thus, while Marshall's argument concerning "second orders of smalls" is suspect, his conclusions may still be correct. In the next section I go through a detailed examination of a particular case. The results may be suggestive of future directions of research.

---

9. Some headway in this direction has been made by Willig (1976). However, much of Willig's concern is to determine how well the consumer's surplus approximates the compensating variation. As suggested above, when the former is an inadequate measure of welfare gain or loss, so is the latter, so there is hardly any point in trying to approximate the former by the latter. When both are exact measures, in the case of parallel preferences one is a linear function of the other, whereas in the case of homothetic preferences the consumer's surplus is the logarithm of a linear function of the compensating variation (cf. Chipman and Moore, 1980, p. 945), hence the approximation result amounts to saying that in a certain neighbourhood a positive-valued function can be well approximated by its logarithm. Willig also considered approximation to the Hicksian equivalent variation, which is a genuine indirect utility function, but this still raises the question as to why the criterion of approximation should be closeness to a *particular* numerical utility function.

III The Welfare Effects of an Excise Tax –
A Detailed Example

Let us examine Marshall's argument quoted above with reference to a simple example, derived from one in Chipman and Moore (1976, pp. 90–1).

Let us suppose that an economy consists of a single individual who consumes two commodities, and a costless government which imposes an excise tax on one of the commodities and returns the proceeds to this individual. We wish to prove that the individual's welfare will be reduced. In order to provide our example with a general-equilibrium interpretation, we may suppose that the country produces fixed amounts $\bar{y}_1$ and $\bar{y}_2$ of the two commodities and trades with the rest of the world at fixed world prices $p_1(0)$, $p_2(0)$ of these two commodities. Thus our individual's income (equal to national income) is initially $Y(0) = p_1(0)\bar{y}_1 + p_2(0)\bar{y}_2$. Let the individual's demand function be defined by $x = (x_1,x_2) =$

$$h(p_1,p_2,Y) = \begin{cases} \left(\dfrac{Y}{p_1} - \gamma \dfrac{p_1}{p_2} , \gamma \left(\dfrac{p_1}{p_2}\right)^2 \right) & \text{for } Y > \gamma \dfrac{(p_1)^2}{p_2} \\[4mm] (0, \dfrac{Y}{p_2}) & \text{for } Y \le \gamma \dfrac{(p_1)^2}{p_2} \end{cases} \tag{12.1}$$

where γ is a positive parameter. This is generated by the utility function

$$U(x_1,x_2) = x_1 + 2\sqrt{\gamma x_2} \tag{12.2}$$

Thus, preferences are "parallel" with respect to commodity 1, since for any price ratios satisfying the first inequality in (12.1), the Engel curves are straight lines parallel to the axis of commodity 1 (cf. Chipman and Moore, 1976, p. 91). The corresponding indirect utility function is readily seen to be

$$V(p_1,p_2,Y) = \begin{cases} \dfrac{Y}{p_1} + \gamma \dfrac{p_1}{p_2} & \text{for } Y > \gamma \dfrac{(p_1)^2}{p_2} \\[4mm] 2\gamma \dfrac{p_1}{p_2} & \text{for } Y \le \gamma \dfrac{(p_1)^2}{p_2} \end{cases} \tag{12.3}$$

We note that as long as both commodities are consumed (so that the individual remains in the "parallel" subset of the indifference map) the marginal utility of income is $\partial V/\partial Y = 1/p_1$ which is constant so long as the price of commodity 1 does not vary.

Let us first consider the case in which an excise tax (specific rather than *ad valorem*) of t_2 is imposed per unit of commodity 2 consumed, so that the new price of commodity 2 faced by the individual is $p_2(1) = p_2(0) + t_2$. The revenue collected by the government is

$$R(t_2) = t_2 h_2(p_1(1), p_2(1), Y) = t_2 \gamma \left[\frac{p_1(0)}{p_2(0) + t_2} \right]^2 \qquad (12.4)$$

and the individual's new income level is $Y(1) = Y(0) + R(t_2)$.

A direct welfare analysis yields after a few steps

$$V[p_1(0), p_2(0) + t_2, Y(0) + R(t_2)] - V[p_1(0), p_2(0), Y(0)]$$
$$= \frac{-\gamma p_1(0) t_2^2}{p_2(0)[p_2(0) + t_2]^2} < 0 \qquad (12.5)$$

showing that the individual suffers a welfare loss.

The same situation may be analysed with Marshall's consumer's surplus. Consider the path

$$p_1(\xi) = p_1(0), \ p_2(\xi) = p_2(0) + t_2 \xi, \ Y(\xi) = Y(0) + R(t_2)\xi \ (0 \le \xi \le 1)$$

The consumer's surplus over this path is given by the line integral

$$S(t_2) = - \int_0^1 h_2[p_1(0), p_2(\xi), Y(\xi)] dp_2(\xi) + Y(1) - Y(0)$$
$$= - \int_0^1 \gamma \frac{p_1(0)^2}{[p_2(0) + t_2 \xi]^2} t_2 d\xi + R(t_2)$$

Introducing the change of variable $\zeta = p_2(0) + t_2 \xi$ this integral becomes, using (12.4), $-L(t_2) \equiv$

$$- \int_{p_2(0)}^{p_2(0)+t_2} \frac{\gamma p_1(0)^2}{\zeta^2} d\zeta + R(t_2) = \frac{-\gamma p_1(0)^2 t_2^2}{p_2(0)[p_2(0) + t_2]^2} < 0 \quad (12.6)$$

which defines the "deadweight loss" $L(t_2) = -S(t_2)$ from the tax; it differs from (12.5) only by the factor $p_1(0)$ (the reciprocal of the constant marginal utility of income). We have as $t_2 \to 0$

$$L(t_2) = \gamma \frac{p_1(0)^2}{p_2(0)^3} O(t_2^2)$$

that is, the loss varies approximately as the square of the tax.

This result is correct since the income elasticity of demand for commodity 2 is zero, preferences being parallel with respect to commodity 1. With p_1 fixed, the consumer's surplus correctly represents the welfare change.

Now consider the case in which it is commodity 1 that is taxed, at a rate of t_1 per unit of output. The revenue is then

$$R(t_1) = t_1 h_1(p_1(1), p_2(1), Y) = t_1 \left[\frac{Y(0) + R(t_1)}{p_1(0) + t_1} - \gamma \frac{p_1(0) + t_1}{p_2(0)} \right]$$

Solving this equation for $R(t_1)$ we obtain

$$R(t_1) = \frac{Y(0)p_2(0) - \gamma[p_1(0) + t_1]^2}{p_1(0)p_2(0)} t_1 \tag{12.7}$$

We may first carry out a direct welfare analysis. The change in direct utility resulting from the tax is easily found to be

$$V[(p_1(0) + t_1, p_2(0), Y(0) + R(t_1)] - V[p_1(0), p_2(0), Y(0)]$$

$$= \frac{-\gamma t_1^2}{p_1(0)p_2(0)} < 0 \tag{12.8}$$

yielding a welfare loss once again.

Let us see how Marshall's method fares in this case. Along the path

$$
\begin{array}{ll}
p_1(\xi) = p_1(0) + 2t_1\xi & \text{for } 0 \le \xi \le \tfrac{1}{2} \\
\quad\;\; = p_1(0) + t_1 & \text{for } \tfrac{1}{2} \le \xi \le 1 \\
p_2(\xi) = p_2(0) & \text{for } 0 \le \xi \le 1 \\
Y(\xi) = Y(0) & \text{for } 0 \le \xi \le \tfrac{1}{2} \\
\quad\;\; = Y(0) + (2\xi - 1)R(t_1) & \text{for } \tfrac{1}{2} \le \xi \le 1
\end{array}
$$

the consumer's surplus is given by the line integral

$$S(t_1) = - \int_0^{1/2} \left[\frac{Y(\xi)}{p_1(\xi)} - \gamma \frac{p_1(\xi)}{p_2(0)} \right] dp_1(\xi) + Y(1) - Y(0) =$$

$$- \int_0^{1/2} \frac{2t_1 Y(0)}{p_1(0) + 2t_1\xi} d\xi + \frac{\gamma t_1 p_1(0)}{p_2(0)} + \frac{\gamma t_1^2}{2p_2(0) + R(t_1)}$$

Introducing the change of variable $\zeta = p_1(0) + 2t_1\xi$ the integral in this last expression becomes

$$- \int_{p_1(0)}^{p_1(0)+t_1} \frac{2t_1 Y(0)}{\zeta} \frac{1}{2t_1} d\zeta = -Y(0)\{\log[p_1(0) + t_1] - \log p_1(0)\}$$

so that the consumer's surplus becomes, using (12.7), $S(t_1) =$

$$- Y(0) \log \left(1 + \frac{t_1}{p_1(0)} \right) + \frac{2Y(0)p_2(0)t_1 - 3\gamma p_1(0)t_1^2 - 2\gamma t_1^3}{2p_1(0)p_2(0)} \tag{12.9}$$

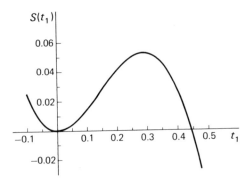

Figure 12.1. Marshall's consumer's surplus, $S(t_1)$, as a function of the excise tax rate, t_1, on commodity 1, for parameter values given by footnote 10.

This is obviously very different from formula (12.8). It is zero at $t_1 = 0$ and negative for sufficiently large t_1; however, it may be positive for small positive t_1. For, its first derivative

$$S'(t_1) = \frac{Y(0)}{p_1(0) + t_1} + \frac{2Y(0)p_2(0) - 6\gamma p_1(0)t_1 - 6\gamma t_1^2}{2p_1(0)p_2(0)}$$

vanishes at $t_1 = 0$ and its second derivative evaluated at $t_1 = 0$ is

$$S''(0) = \frac{Y(0)}{p_1(0)^2} - \frac{3\gamma}{p_2(0)}$$

This can certainly be made positive by suitable choice of initial conditions (see Figure 12.1).[10] Hence the Marshallian consumer's surplus can be made positive for sufficiently small positive t_1; but the tax, as shown in (12.8) above, must reduce welfare, so this gives an erroneous result.

We may verify, however, that the above initial conditions required for this result are inconsistent with the hypothesis that the individual initially devotes an arbitrarily small proportion of income to commodity 1. The above condition that the consumer's surplus be increased by the tax requires that

$$Y(0) > \frac{3\gamma p_1(0)^2}{p_2(0)} > \frac{\gamma p_1(0)^2}{p_2(0)} > 0 \qquad (12.10)$$

10. Figure 12.1 plots the function (12.9) for the case $p_1(0) = p_2(0) = 1$, $\gamma = 2$, and $Y(0) = 10$. These values satisfy inequality (12.10) below.

which implies the first inequality of (12.1). Now denoting by θ_1 the proportion of income spent on commodity 1 we have from (12.1) and (12.10)

$$\theta_1 = 1 - \frac{\gamma p_1(0)^2}{Y(0)p_2(0)} > \frac{2}{3}.$$

For this class of preferences, in the two-commodity case, we have seen that the classic qualitative conclusions of consumer's surplus analysis can be reversed, but only by violating Marshall's condition that the proportion of income spent on the taxed commodity be small. It is doubtful if the types of cardinal comparisons proposed by Hicks would fare nearly so well. It is remarkable that after 100 years, this whole question remains so far from being settled.

References

Allen, R. G. D. (1933). "On the Marginal Utility of Money and Its Application", *Economica* 13:186–209.

Arrow, K. J. (1951). "An Extension of the Basic Theorems of Classical Welfare Economics". In J. Neyman (ed.), *Proceedings of the Second Berkeley Symposium on Mathematical Statistics and Probability*. Berkeley and Los Angeles: University of California Press.

Auspitz, R., and Lieben, R. (1889). *Untersuchungen über die Theorie des Preises*. Leipzig: Duncker and Humblot.

Barone, E. (1894*a*). "Di Alcuni Teoremi Fondamentali per la Teoria Matematica dell'Imposta", *Giornale degli Economisti*, Second Series 8:201–10.

(1894*b*). "A Proposito delle Indagini del Fisher", *Giornale degli Economisti*, Second Series 8:413–39.

(1894*c*). "Sulla 'Consumer's Rent' ", *Giornale degli Economisti*, Second Series 9:211–24.

(1894*d*). "Sul Trattamento di Quistioni Dinamiche", *Giornale degli Economisti*, Second Series 9:407–35.

Berry, A. (1891). "Alcune Brevi Parole Sulla Teoria del Baratto di A. Marshall", *Giornale degli Economisti*, Second Series 2:549–53.

Boudling, K. E. (1945). "The Concept of Economic Surplus", *American Economic Review* 35:851–69.

Chipman, J. S. (1970). "External Economies of Scale and Competitive Equilibrium", *Quarterly Journal of Economics* 84:347–85.

(1987). "Compensation Principle". In J. Eatwell, M. Milgate and P. Newman (eds.), *The New Palgrave: A Dictionary of Economics*. London: Macmillan.

Chipman, J. S., and Moore, J. C. (1976). "The Scope of Consumer's Surplus

Arguments". In A. M. Tang, F. M. Westfield, and J. S. Worley (eds.), *Evolution, Welfare and Time in Economics: Essays in Honor of Nicholas Georgescu-Roegen*. Lexington, Mass.: Heath.

(1980). "Compensating Variation, Consumer's Surplus, and Welfare", *American Economic Review* 70:933–49.

(1990). "Acceptable Indicators of Welfare Change, Consumer's Surplus Analysis, and the Gorman Polar Form". In J. S. Chipman, D. McFadden, and M. K. Richter (eds.), *Preferences, Uncertainty, and Optimality*. Boulder, Colo.: Westview Press.

Dupuit, J. (1844). "De la Mesure de l'Utilité des Travaux Publics", *Annales des Ponts et Chaussées, Memoires et documents relatifs à l'art des constructions et au service de l'ingénieur*, Second Series 8 (2ᵉ semestre):332–75, Pl. 75.

Edgeworth, F. Y. (1891a). "Osservazioni sulla Teoria Matematica dell' Economia Politica con Riguardo Speciale ai Principi di Economia di Alfredo Marshall", *Giornale degli Economisti*, Second Series 2:233–45.

(1891b). "Ancora a Proposito della Teoria del Baratto", *Giornale degli Economisti*, Second Series 3:316–18.

(1894). "Professor J. S. Nicholson on 'Consumer's Rent' ", *Economic Journal* 4:151–8.

(1897). "La Teoria Pura del Monopolio", *Giornale degli Economisti*, Second Series 15:13–31, 307–20, 405–14. English translation in Edgeworth (1925), 1:111–42.

(1925). *Papers Relating to Political Economy*, 3 vols. London: Macmillan.

Frisch, R. (1939). "The Dupuit Taxation Theorem", *Econometrica* 7:145–50. "A Further Note on the Dupuit Taxation Theorem", ibid.:156–7.

Gorman, W. M. (1961). "On a Class of Preference Fields", *Metroeconomica* 13:53–6.

Harberger, A. C. (1964). "The Measurement of Waste", *American Economic Review Papers and Proceedings* 54:58–76.

Hicks, J. R. (1941). "The Rehabilitation of Consumers' Surplus", *Review of Economic Studies* 8:108–16.

(1942). "Consumer's Surplus and Index-Numbers", *Review of Economic Studies* 9:126–37.

(1943). "The Four Consumer's Surpluses", *Review of Economic Studies* 11:31–41.

(1945). "The Generalized Theory of Consumer's Surplus", *Review of Economic Studies* 13:68–74.

Hotelling, H. (1938). "The General Welfare in Relation to Problems of Taxation and of Railway and Utility Rates", *Econometrica* 6:242–69.

(1939). "The Relation of Prices to Marginal Costs in an Optimum System", *Econometrica* 7:151–5. "A Final Note", ibid.:158–9.

Hurwicz, L., and Uzawa, H. (1971). "On the Integrability of Demand Functions". In J. S. Chipman, L. Hurwicz, M. K. Richter, and H. F. Sonnenschein (eds.), *Preferences, Utility, and Demand*. New York: Harcourt Brace Jovanovich.

Koopmans, T. C. (1957). *Three Essays on the State of Economic Science.* New York: McGraw-Hill.

Lerner, A. P. (1934). "The Concept of Monopoly and the Measurement of Monopoly Power", *Review of Economic Studies* 1:157–75.

Little, I. M. D. (1950). *A Critique of Welfare Economics.* Oxford: Clarendon Press.

McKenzie, L. W. (1957). "Demand Theory without a Utility Index", *Review of Economic Studies* 24:185–9.

Nicholson, J. S. (1893). *Principles of Political Economy,* Vol. 1. London: Adam and Charles Black.

(1894). "The Measurement of Utility by Money", *Economic Journal* 4:342–8.

Pareto, V. (1892–3). "Considerazioni sui Principi Fondamentali dell' Economia Politica Pura", *Giornale degli Economisti,* Second Series 4:389–420, 485–512; 5:119-57; 6:1–37; 7:279-321. (May, June, August 1892, January, October 1893, respectively.)

(1894). "Il Massimo di Utilità dato dalla Libera Concorrenza", *Giornale degli Economisti,* Second Series 9:48–66.

(1902). "Di un Nuovo Errore Nello Interpretare le Teorie dell'Economia Matematica", *Giornale degli Economisti,* Second Series 25:401–33.

Pigou, A. C. (1910). "Producers' and Consumers' Surplus", *Economic Journal* 20:358–70.

Samuelson, P. A. (1942). "Constancy of the Marginal Utility of Income". In O. Lange, F. McIntyre, and T. O. Yntema (eds.), *Studies in Mathematical Economics and Econometrics, In Memory of Henry Schultz.* Chicago: University of Chicago Press.

(1947). *Foundations of Economic Analysis.* Cambridge, Mass.: Harvard University Press.

Sanger, C. P. (1895). "Recent Contributions to Mathematical Economics", *Economic Journal* 5:113–28.

Walras, L. (1890), "Observations sur le Principe de la Theorie du Prix de MM. Auspitz et Lieben", *Revue d'Economie Politique* 4:320–3.

Willig, R. D. (1976). "Consumer's Surplus without Apology", *American Economic Review* 66:589–97.

Index